S. Moreton Thomas
from T. J. Dyke. —

AN ESSAY

ON THE

WELSH SAINTS

OR THE

PRIMITIVE CHRISTIANS

USUALLY CONSIDERED TO HAVE BEEN THE

FOUNDERS OF CHURCHES

IN

WALES.

BY

THE REV. RICE REES, M. A.

FELLOW OF JESUS COLLEGE, OXFORD, AND PROFESSOR OF WELSH AT
ST. DAVID'S COLLEGE, LAMPETER.

LONDON:

LONGMAN, REES, ORME, BROWN, GREEN, AND LONGMAN,
REES, LLANDOVERY; AND BIRD, CARDIFF.

MDCCCXXXVI

WILLIAM REES, PRINTER, LOWER STREET, LLANDOVERY.

TO THE MOST HONOURABLE

THE MARQUESS OF BUTE,

PRESIDENT,

AND OTHERS, THE COMMITTEE,

OF THE

GWENT AND DYFED ROYAL EISTEDDFOD,

HELD AT CARDIFF AUG. 20, 21, & 22, 1834;

THE FOLLOWING ESSAY,

HONOURED WITH THEIR PATRONAGE UPON THAT OCCASION,

IS MOST RESPECTFULLY INSCRIBED

BY THEIR HUMBLE SERVANT,

THE AUTHOR.

"THE EXISTENCE OF A BRITISH CHURCH BEFORE THE ARRIVAL OF AUGUSTIN IN THE YEAR 597 IS A FACT CLEARLY ESTABLISHED. ITS INDE-PENDENT ORIGIN IS SUFFICIENTLY ATTESTED BY THE SUBJECTS OF CONTROVERSY BETWEEN THE ANGLO-ROMAN AND BRITISH CHRISTIANS. —THE BRITONS HAD CHURCHES OF THEIR OWN, BUILT AFTER A FASHION OF THEIR OWN; THEIR OWN SAINTS; THEIR OWN HIERARCHY."

BLUNT'S REFORMATION IN ENGLAND, CHAP. I.

PREFACE.

As an apology for presenting these pages to the public, it is perhaps necessary to inform the reader that they were originally written with a view to competition for a premium, offered by the Committee of the Gwent and Dyfed Royal Eisteddfod, for the best dissertation on the following subject:—

"The Notices of the Primitive Christians, by whom the Welsh Churches were founded, and to whom dedicated."

Out of several compositions transmitted for the approbation of the Society, the Essay, now printed in an enlarged form, was adjudged to be successful, accompanied with a recommendation that it should be published; and though some time has elapsed since the occasion which called it into existence, it is hoped that the interest naturally attached to its subject will ensure it a favourable reception.

Historians have laboured to trace the origin of the Britons, a profusion of learning has been expended in the endeavour to unravel the mysteries of Druidism, and the antiquarian, who finds any vestiges of the occupation of this island by the Romans, carefully records the discovery;—so long as the inhabitants of Britain feel an interest in the history of their forefathers, disquisitions upon those subjects must demand attention, though the materials of information are exceedingly scanty. Every author, therefore, who treats of the affairs of this country, prior to the departure of the Romans, has been

diligently consulted, and his expressions construed into every
variety of meaning so as to obtain a new illustration of the
points of enquiry. The present researches, however, relate to
a period comparatively neglected ; their object being to trace
the ecclesiastical history of the Britons, from the introduction
of Christianity, or more especially from the termination of the
Roman power in Britain, to the end of the seventh century.
From the close of this period, the annals of Wales have been
minutely detailed by several chroniclers whose labours are
extant ; before its commencement, the history of Britain may
be collected from the scattered notices to be found in classical
writers ; and if those notices are not so numerous as can be
wished, they are authentic, and are as many as may be expected when the distance of the island from the capital of the
Roman empire is considered. The interval between these
points is a historical blank ; for it must be confessed that the
Welsh, though possessed of a variety of records relating to
that time, have not preserved a regular and connected history
of their ancestors who rose into power upon the departure of
the Romans, and who, notwithstanding their dissensions, maintained a longer and more arduous struggle against the Saxons,
than the continental parts of the empire did upon the irruption
of the Goths and Vandals. In the middle ages, those records,
to which was added a large store of tradition, attracted the
attention of the romance-writers, who gradually invested
them with a cloud of fable, which at last, when arranged and
regularly digested, was suffered to usurp the place of history.
This remark is applied particularly to the Armorican chronicle
usually attributed to Geoffrey of Monmouth. It should, however, be allowed in justice to that person, that he was not its
inventor, for a Welsh version of the original is preserved,
which shows that he merely made a free translation, inserting
occasionally interpolations of his own. When the chronicle

alluded to was brought from Brittany to Wales by Walter de
Mapes in the twelfth century, its contents were found to be so
flattering to national vanity, that it was soon received as an
authentic record of facts, to the disadvantage of other records
of a less pretending nature. For a long time implicit faith
was given to the story of Trojan-British kings, and the super-
human actions of Arthur and his valorous knights commanded
the admiration of Europe, few caring to question the truth of
tales which suited the taste of the age and filled their readers
with delight. The criticism of later years has however determined the race of Trojan-British kings to be a pure fabrication, and most writers are contented to commence the history
of Britain with the invasion of Julius Cæsar, following the
Latin authorities until the termination of the Roman power in
the island, when, for want of more satisfactory information,
they are obliged to have recourse to records which they know
not where to trust, or leaving the affairs of the Britons in that
darkness which they could not dispel, they have confined
their researches to the Saxons.

It is but right to state, that the substance of several of the
fables in the Armorican chronicle was known in Wales before
the time of Walter de Mapes, a fair specimen of which may
be seen in the works of Nennius; but the Welsh were also
possessed of records of another and a different kind; these
were a collection of poems, triads, and genealogies, preserved
by the bards and written in the national tongue. The information to be derived respecting the Britons of the fifth and
two following centuries may, therefore, be divided into the
bardic and the legendary. The latter kind, which was preserved by the monks or clergy, was written principally in
Latin, and consists of the History of Nennius and the lives of
several Welsh saints. The genuineness and authenticity of
the works attributed to Gildas are questionable, and yet as

b

they are undoubtedly ancient they are deserving of some
attention. But it is remarkable that in all the records of the
Britons, both in Welsh and Latin, before the twelfth century,
historical allusions abound, which are at variance with the
narrative of the Armorican chronicle; even the most extravagant tales in Nennius are more limited than those of the
later fabulist; and the various ways in which the same tales
are related by the former, prove that in his time they had not
reached the consistency of history, whereas in the latter there
is no hesitation, but every story is told as positively as if the
writer were an eye-witness.

The amount of information, or rather tradition, preserved by
the Welsh relative to the Britons before the invasion of Cæsar
and during the sojourn of the Romans, is small, and that little
is intimately blended with bardic mythology. But it may be
asked, whether it is possible, discarding entirely the Armorican chronicle and its followers, to construct, out of the before-
mentioned older materials, a history, which shall supply the
hiatus between the departure of the Romans and the beginning
of the eighth century, where the authentic chronicles commence.—The present is the first attempt, upon such a system,
to supply the deficiency. The attempt, however, is but a
partial one; for as the purpose of this Essay was to treat of
the Welsh saints or founders of churches, national affairs are
only noticed incidentally. Whatever success therefore may
attend the present undertaking, it is hoped that if the idea be
approved, a more extended research may employ some maturer
judgment and an abler pen. The result of an accumulation
of the most authentic notices that can be collected, would be
the production of a history, displaying indeed many of
those moral features which distinguished the Welsh at a later
time, but bearing a very slight resemblance to its representation in the pages of Geoffrey.

In groping through this period of darkness, some glimmerings of light may be borrowed from Bede, the contemporary writers of Gaul, and perhaps from the Irish historians; and in compiling such a history, where authorities of the legendary kind must be consulted, a simple rule may be observed, which, if does not always elicit the truth, will produce the nearest approximation to it, namely to take the story of the oldest writer, which also is generally found to be the most limited. The character of fable is progressive, and a story, which originally was true, is in most cases repeated with additions. This rule has been established with great clearness by the author of "Europe in the Middle Ages," (in Lardner's Cyclopædia, vol. iv. p. 67:) observing the manner in which Nennius has been amplified by Geoffrey, he adds :—" There is no greater difference between Geoffrey of Monmouth and Nennius, than between Nennius and Gildas. This fact is very instructive; it may enable the judicious investigator into the antiquities of ancient Britain, and of Britain even in the Anglo-Saxon period, to steer his way through the darkest path ever traversed by historian."

The learned writer, whose words are quoted, regrets that he had not access to the ancient relics subsisting in the Welsh language, which he supposed must contain stores of information but little known to the public. Those relics, so far as they have been printed, form the principal materials of the following dissertation; and meagre as they may seem, they strongly confirm the presumption of their antiquity by the circumstance, that they are frequently at variance with the legendary authorities; and wherever they appear to agree, their statements are more circumscribed than those of the latter, presenting as it were the germs out of which subsequent fables have sprung. An examination of the bardic records, therefore, if it will not discover authentic materials of history, will

at least be of service in tracing the origin of romance, and in
this respect may tend to elucidate a large portion of the
literature of Europe.

Leaving the task of demonstrating the progress of fable to
the general writer, the business of the antiquary, whose object
is the history of his country, is to search after the oldest
authorities that can be procured, and afterwards to consider
them by themselves, divested of the misconceptions and exaggerations of later ages. By this mode of proceeding, many
statements which receive current belief, will be found to rest
on a slight foundation; and much of the remainder, being
placed in a new light, will assume a different character. The
operation of this rule is the cause why many assertions, which
have hitherto been credited, are rejected in the following
pages; but wherever such cases occur, the particular reason is
added, and the reader must decide according to his own
judgment upon its validity. It will be observed that even the
Welsh records are not allowed to pass without a scrutiny; many
of their positions, which are shown to be untenable, are surrendered; and that mistakes should have been committed, can
by no means be surprising, when the remoteness of the times
to which they refer is considered, as well as the neglect under
which they have been suffered to remain.

The documents, for the possession of which Wales has long
been celebrated, and to which of late years little attention has
been paid, are its genealogies. Of these a large store is preserved in manuscript, and though from their minuteness of
detail they must necessarily contain inaccuracies, yet, as the
pedigrees are numerous, they may be rectified upon comparison with each other. An attempt is now made to render them
available for the purpose of history, by arranging them so as
to construct an artificial chronology. In endeavouring to
connect the Roman period with the eighth century, such a

plan was absolutely necessary, for in the lapse of three hundred years very few dates occur upon which any reliance may
be placed; and without attention to this arrangement, the
events reported present only a mass of confusion. It is however satisfactory to learn, that the few dates that have been
ascertained, agree undesignedly with the arrangement of the
pedigrees, and so far confirm their correctness. The dates,
collected by Archbishop Usher in his " Britannicarum Eccles-
arum Primordia," and which he perpetually shows to be confused and contradictory, belong to chroniclers of the Armorican
school, and are of little value: the work of the Archbishop
however contains, amidst much irrelevant matter, a fund of
valuable information, for which the present writer is greatly
indebted. The reason why the pedigrees have been neglected
is their intricacy, and at first sight they are certainly un-
promising, but as they are interspersed with historical notices
they are deserving of attention ; and it should not be forgotten
that for many ages the only historians whom the Welsh possessed were their genealogists.

Localities are a very powerful auxiliary in forming a con-
structive history. In this respect the Armorican chronicle is
exceedingly deficient; for the few localities mentioned in it·
are certain towns and places which were well known and
flourishing at a late period, proving, not only that the record
was recent, but also that it was compiled in a distant country.
The scene of the fable is laid down in Britain, but the places
introduced are such as were of sufficient celebrity to be known
abroad. The events of history do not always occur at distinguished towns, and it might be expected that places, which
were celebrated in past ages, had afterwards become obscure.
National traditions often refer to a spot, it may be the summit
of a hill or a pass between mountains, which, but for those
traditions, might have possessed nothing remarkable. The

Welsh traditions and records abound in localities, the notices of which are generally precise; among these the situations of churches are not the least distinguished. A vast number of churches are called after the names of native saints, and therefore may be considered as so many undoubted monuments of existence of those persons; but Welsh tradition proceeds further and asserts, that the churches were so called, not so much because they were dedicated to the saints, as because they were founded by them.

If the assertion be true, it follows that many churches exist in the Principality, the origin of which must be dated from the fifth and sixth centuries, for in those ages most of the saints alluded to flourished. That churches, though frequently rebuilt, should continue uninterruptedly in the same situations from such high antiquity, will not be deemed extraordinary, when it can be proved by authentic testimony that the ground, on which the church of St. Martin at Canterbury stands, has been the site of a church, bearing the same name, from a date prior to the departure of the Romans. The cathedral in that city is another instance of equal antiquity, which also shows that wherever, from war or other causes, a sacred edifice had been demolished or had been for some time in ruins, such was the veneration attached to a spot once consecrated, that a new edifice was erected in the same situation; and it should be remembered that the Christianity of Wales did not, like that of Kent, suffer an eclipse from the intervention of paganism.

In the first three sections of this Essay it is shown by principles of induction that the churches, presumed to have been founded by the saints whose names they bear, are more ancient than those which are dedicated to the Apostles and the saints of the Romish Calendar; and therefore that the current opinion of their foundation is confirmed by existing circumstances. They were founded at a time when the Britons were not in communion with the Church of Rome, and before the practice of dedicating to saints according to the usual mode had become customary. From the testimony of Bede, it appears that the mode of consecration, practised by the Primitive Christians of this island, was peculiar.—Wherever a church was intended to be erected, a person of reputed sanctity was chosen to reside on the spot, where he continued forty days in the performance of prayer, fasting, and other religious exercises; at the expiration of the time, the ground was held sacred, and a church was erected accordingly.—It would naturally follow that the church should be called after the name of the person by whom the ground was consecrated, and in this sense the word "founder," as applied to the subject under consideration, must be understood. It remained for subsequent generations to regard the founder in the character of patron saint.

Popular opinion seems to maintain that all churches, which are named after Welshmen, were founded by them. An exception, however, should be made with respect to such as are, or may be proved to have been, chapels, which, for reasons that shall appear, cannot claim so early an origin; and with respect to parent churches the proposition may not indeed be true in every instance, but is assumed as a general fact, there being no criterion by which its exceptions may be distinguished. Edifices as they now exist, being purely an architectural question, constitute no part of the enquiry. The original churches of the Britons were all of them built of wood and covered with thatch, and it is singular that this circumstance was made a ground of objection to them by the Catholics.

So numerous are the Welsh saints, that their history is in a manner the ecclesiastical history of their time; but it must be confessed that nothing further is known of many of them than their genealogy and their churches.   The question of the celebration of Easter, and other points, on which the Primitive Christians of Britain differed from the Romanists, have been ably discussed in other publications; the object of this treatise is, if possible, to add to the stock of information from materials which have been but partially investigated.   To his predecessors, whose works have facilitated these researches, among whom may be named the authors of " Horæ Britannicæ" and " Hanes Crefydd yn Nghymru," the writer acknowledges his obligations; and though he has sometimes differed from their conclusions, he has done so with diffidence, and is aware that the same fate will in turn befal the present undertaking. Knowledge is the accumulation of past experience, and all that the best informed writer can expect to accomplish, is to contribute but a trifle to the general heap, leaving its amount to be estimated by his successor.

St. David's College,
Nov. 24, 1836.

AN ESSAY, ETC.

ANALYSIS OF CONTENTS.

SECTION I.

THE COMPARATIVE ANTIQUITY OF THE FOUNDATION OF CHURCHES AND CHAPELS IN WALES, ASCERTAINED FROM THE NATURE OF THEIR ENDOWMENTS.

Churches at first few, and their parishes extensive . 11
Subdivision of ancient parishes; Chapelries . . 12
Origin of vicarages 13
Instances of Churches of the earliest Foundation . 15
Churches of later Foundation . . . 15
Vested rights of Churches respected by the Welsh Princes 16
Parochial Chapels, and Chapels of Ease . . 18
Cells, Oratories, and Hermitages . . . 19
Use of the words "Llan, Capel, and Bettws" . . 20
The establishment of parishes gradual . . 21
Effects of the Law of Gavelkind . . 21
Parent Churches not converted into Chapels . . 23
Subordination of Churches and Chapels proved from the
    Charters of Monasteries . . . 24

SECTION II.

THE SUBORDINATION OF CHURCHES AND CHAPELS CONSIDERED WITH REFERENCE TO THE SAINTS TO WHOM THEY ARE DEDICATED.

Churches dedicated to St. Mary . . . 27
Their late origin proved from their situations historically
    considered 32
And from Domesday Book . . . 35
Churches dedicated to St. Michael . . . 36
More ancient than those dedicated to St. Mary; but . 40
Not so ancient as those ascribed to Welsh Saints . 42
Churches ascribed or dedicated to St. David . . 43
Their antiquity 45

Testimony of Gwynfardd Brycheiniog about A. D. 1200   48
Amended list of Churches of St. David, of which the   .   52
Parent Churches were probably founded by him, but the   54
Chapels and Subordinate Churches were erected after his
     decease   55
Their situations not arbitrarily chosen   .   .   56

SECTION III.

GENERAL OBSERVATIONS ON THE WELSH SAINTS AS DISTINGUISHED FROM THOSE OF THE ROMAN CATHOLIC CHURCH.

Dedication to Saints, not the practice of the ancient Britons   57
Separation of the Britons from the Church of Rome   .   58
Architecture of the British Churches   .   .   59
Mode of Consecration practised by the Primitive Christ-
     ians of Scotland   .   .   .   60
The same mode used apparently by the Primitive
     Christians of Wales; its effects .   .   61
Invocation of Angels   .   .   .   61
The homage paid to St. Mary, of late introduction   62
The Welsh Saints, the Founders of most Churches which
     bear their names   .   .   .   64
Second Class of Foundations   .   .   64
The Welsh brought into communion with the Church of
     Rome in the Eighth Century   .   .   65
Romish Computation of Easter introduced by Elbodius,
     Archbishop of Bangor   .   .   66
First notice of a Church dedicated to St. Michael, A. D. 717   67
Third Class of Foundations   .   .   69
Chapels named after Welsh Saints   .   .   69
Churches consecrated a second time .   .   70
Catholic Saints of Britain .   .   .   71
Welsh Authorities; "Bonedd neu Achau Saint Ynys
     Prydain"   .   .   .   ,   .   73
Triads   75

SECTION IV.

THE WELSH SAINTS FROM THE INTRODUCTION OF CHRISTIANITY TO THE END OF THE SECOND CENTURY.

Account of the Introduction of Christianity into Britain
     by Bran ab Llyr   .   .   .   77
Its authenticity questioned   .   .   78
Account of Bran in the Mabinogion .   .   80

Companions and Descendants of Bran . . 81
Lleurwg or Lucius 82
His History uncertain . . . 83
Dyfan, Ffagan, Medwy, and Elfan . . . 84
Lucius possibly the founder of a Church at Llandaff, said
    to have been the first in Britain . . 85
Memorials of his Contemporaries . . . 86

SECTION V.

AN EXAMINATION OF THE EARLY WELSH PEDIGREES, WITH A VIEW TO
ASCERTAIN THE PERIOD ABOUT WHICH THE COMMENCEMENT
OF THEIR AUTHENTICITY MAY BE DATED.

Deficiency of Welsh tradition from Lucius to Maximus
    A. D. 383 88
Descendants of Bran ab Llyr . . . 89
Inconsistencies in the Pedigree . . 90
Descendants of Beli Mawr 91
Fabrication of Pedigrees which relate to the Roman-
    British Period 92
Cadfrawd, a Saint and Bishop . . . 92
Mistakes, in the presumed Lineage of Bran ab Llyr,
    explained 93
Age of Cadfrawd, Coel Godebog, and Cynan Meiriadog . 94
The Authenticity of Welsh Pedigrees commences in the
    fourth century 94

SECTION VI.

THE WELSH SAINTS FROM A. D. 300 TO A. D. 400.

Alban, Amphibalus, Aaron, and Julius . . 96
Constantine the Great, not a native of Britain . . 97
Helen, not a British Saint . . . 98
British Bishops at the Council of Arles A. D. 314 . 100
Councils of Sardica and Ariminum . . 101
Descendants of Coel Godebog . . . 103
Settlement of Cynan Meiriadog in Armorica . . 104
St. Ursula and the eleven thousand Virgins . . 105
Pelagius 105

SECTION VII.

THE WELSH SAINTS FROM A. D. 400 TO A. D. 433.

Emancipation of Britain from the Romans A.D. 408 or 409 106
Owain ab Macsen Wledig, Chief Sovereign of the Britons 107

Refusal of the Britons to submit to the Pope   .   .   288
Alleged Reply of Dunawd to St. Augustin   .   .   289
Silence of Bede respecting an Archbishoprick in Wales   .   291
Commissions received by St. Augustin from Pope Gregory   291
Seven Bishops of the British Church at this time   .   292
Massacre of the Monks of Bangor by Ethelfrith   .   293
Legend of Gwenfrewi or St. Winefred   .   .   295

SECTION XIV.

THE WELSH SAINTS FROM THE DEATH OF CADWALLON A. D. 634 TO THE DEATH OF CADWALADR A. D. 664.

Reign of Cadwaladr   299
Confounded with Ceadwalla, King of Wessex   .   300
Cadwaladr esteemed a Saint   .   .   .   301
Peris   302
Edwen   303

SECTION XV.

THE WELSH SAINTS FROM THE DEATH OF CADWALADR A. D. 664 TO THE END OF THE SEVENTH CENTURY, INCLUDING THOSE OF UNCERTAIN DATE.

Little known of the history of this Generation   .   304
Degeman or St. Decumanus   .   .   .   305
Saints after the Conformity of the Welsh to the Church
    of Rome   305
Welsh Saints of uncertain date   .   .   .   306
Curig Lwyd   807
Objection respecting the number of Saints   .   .   309
Epistle of St. Aldhelm to Geruntius respecting the Ton-
    sure and Paschal Cycle   .   .   .   311
The Britons at this time not under Papal Jurisdiction   .   312
Concluding Observations   313

APPENDIX, No. I.—Saints of Britain from Cressy's "Church History
    of Brittany"   315
APPENDIX, No. II.—Anglo-Saxon Saints to whom Churches have
    been dedicated in Wales   322
APPENDIX, No. III.—A List of Churches and Chapels in Wales, in-
    cluding the County of Monmouth and part of the County of
    Hereford   323
INDEX   353

SECTION I.

The comparative Antiquity of the Foundation of Churches and Chapels
in Wales ascertained from the nature of their Endowments.

ACCORDING to popular opinion, many of the churches in
Wales were founded by certain holy persons or Saints whose
names they retain, as if Llangadog and Llandeilo,* or the
Churches of Cadog and Teilo, were not so called in consequence of any formal dedication, but named after their
founders, who are alleged to have lived in the fifth and sixth
centuries. Lest however it should be urged that the Welsh
Records and Traditions, which support this opinion of their
high antiquity, are of insufficient authority, it may be proved
that churches of the class alluded to are necessarily, from the
nature of their endowments, the most ancient† in the Principality, if indeed they were not founded in the early age to
which they are attributed.

In the absence of positive evidence to the fact, it will
readily be granted that the Welsh churches were at first few,
and that they were afterwards multiplied to serve the occasions that required them. How soon certain districts were
apportioned for their maintenance, cannot well be determined.
It is, however, probable that the districts first appropriated

---

* Usually written " Llangadock" and "Llandilo," but the Welsh mode of
spelling is here preferred, in order to render the meaning of the names
more obvious.

† These observations apply to churches as regards their original establishment, the antiquity of the edifices which now exist, being more of an
architectural question, does not belong to the purpose of this Essay.

were extensive; but when once they were attached to particular churches, the sacred nature of ecclesiastical property would tend to preserve their limits inviolate. If therefore any such extensive appropriations can be discovered, it may be presumed that the churches to which they belong are those of the earliest date. An example may be taken from the northern part of Radnorshire, where the churches of Nantmel, Llangynllo, and Llanbister are ascribed or dedicated to Cynllo. This tract of country was probably the scene of his ministry, or it will be sufficient if it be allowed that he possessed some influence over it. Whenever tithes would be assigned for the support of the clergy, this tract would be divided into three districts, which should maintain the ministers of the three churches mentioned. It would afterwards be found that these churches were insufficient for the accommodation of districts so extensive. Chapels of Ease were therefore built in the more remote parts; and whenever the minister of the mother church found it inconvenient to attend in person, he would appoint Curates, to whom he allowed a certain stipend out of his own income; for he still maintained his right to the tithes of the whole district as before. In process of time the district would be subdivided, and certain parts assigned to the Curacies, which would thus become Parochial Chapelries; and though the Curacy might become Perpetual, the minister still retained the right of nomination. He also maintained his right, though perhaps little more than nominal, to the tithes of the several parts which would together constitute so many parishes according to their modern arrangement.

At this day the district of Nantmel, in the county of Radnor, includes the several parishes of Nantmel, Llanfihangel-Helygen, Llanyre, and Rhayader. Nantmel is a Vicarage in the patronage of the Bishop of St. David's; Llanfihangel and Rhayader are Perpetual Curacies in the gift of the Vicar of Nantmel, and the Curacy or Chapelry of

Llanyre is vested in the Vicar himself, who thus, either directly or indirectly, provides for the religious instruction of the whole district. The Vicar, it is true, does not possess a share of the tithes of all the four parishes, but this right is still claimed and exercised by the Impropriator, who, as regards the original founder, must be considered as one and the same person with the Vicar: for it is agreed by ecclesiastical historians, that the subdivision of tithes into rectorial and vicarial was an arrangement posterior to the foundation, and first made to suit the convenience of the minister. Originally the Incumbent of every parish was a Rector, and under him the Vicar held a situation precisely analogous to that of Assistant Curate in modern times. When it was found that the Vicar could perform the whole of the duty for a part of the emolument, so much was given him by way of endowment, and the remainder was applied to the maintenance of a Monastery or the Cathedral of the Diocese. The Vicar would readily consent to this arrangement, as, instead of having a precarious stipend and being removable at pleasure, his place and salary were made permanent. The same fate befel the clergy who performed service in the remote chapels; certain portions of the parish were assigned them for their separate ministry, out of which they received a certain small allowance as a fixed stipend, but, as an equivalent, their Curacies were made Perpetual; while the far greater portion of the tithes of the entire district maintained some distant religious establishment, which thus continued to represent the original Rector. This arrangement was not without its evils. Jealousies broke out between the monastic and parochial clergy; and, at the Reformation, the tithes, which had been attached to Monasteries, passed from them, by an easy transition, into the hands of Lay-impropriators. Those tithes, however, which had been assigned for the support of Cathedrals and Collegiate Chapters were suffered to remain, and are still an illustration of the system here described.

There are also instances of parishes appropriated to a monastic institution, where the parochial duties were left to be performed by a Perpetual Curate without the intervention of a Vicar; but such parishes are generally smaller than those now under consideration.

The expression "mother church" can only mean that the edifice so designated is of older foundation than the several chapels dependent upon it, and this rule is very generally admitted. But if the view of ecclesiastical foundations, just described, be correct, the chapels mentioned as subordinate to Nantmel, must not only have been built after the mother church, but at a time when its endowment was fully recognized and established. If the chapels were of older date, it is not likely that the founder of Nantmel would have endowed his church with the tithes of an extensive district, to the prejudice of places of worship already existing in the country; but, the tithes being once disposed of, no provision would remain for the support of additional churches, except as dependent upon the Rector of the first establishment.[*]

The district of Llanbister, also in the county of Radnor, comprises the parishes of Llanbister, Llananno, Llanbadarn-Fynydd, Llanddewi Ystrad Enni, and Llanfihangel Rhydeithon; the last four are chapelries subject to the former; they are also Perpetual Curacies in the patronage of the Chancellor of Brecon, or his Lessee, who represents the

---

[*] "The Constitutions of Egbert, Archbishop of York, in the year 750, do take care that churches of ancient institution should not be deprived of tithes, or any other rights, by giving or allotting any part to new oratories." (*Vide* Burn's Ecclesiastical Law, Vol. I. *sub voce* Chapel.)

If existing rights were so well defined in England as early as A. D. 750, it is not too much to expect that they were equally well defined about the same period in Wales, where Christianity had been longer and more permanently settled. In the Principality the integrity of benefices appears to have been first disturbed by foreigners, though it must be regretted that the new arrangement introduced by them was not adopted generally by the native princes.

Rector, and who still claims and receives the whole tithes of the five parishes, except the vicarial tithes of Llanbister. The district of Llangynllo extends over the parishes of Llangynllo and Pilleth, and it probably included originally one or two small parishes adjoining, which are now separate benefices. As these districts are very extensive it may safely be concluded, that the places of worship to which they are appropriated were first built when churches were few. Leaving therefore the question of chapelries for a future consideration, it may be assumed, that Nantmel, Llanbister, Llangynllo, and other churches of a similar endowment, are churches of the first or oldest foundation.

As Christianity became more general, the want of places of worship in districts unappropriated would come next to be considered. The necessity of multiplying churches would now be felt, and the tithes to be attached to them would necessarily extend over tracts of country varying much in extent according to the nature of the ground before unoccupied. These parishes cannot be formed into a separate class from the preceding, for their extent alone will not determine the order of their foundation; and, though the largest endowments are *necessarily* ancient, there is nothing to prevent a small endowment from being of equal antiquity. But when parishes of very unequal limits are intermingled together, their arrangement must be attributed to the natural obligation of circumstances.

So far the endowments of churches proceed systematically, without any prejudice to existing rights. There are, however, districts of the Principality where the system is broken up, and the country is studded with numerous churches, all of them small rectories, as if the chapelries which before existed had been converted into separate benefices. A slight acquaintance with the history of these localities will show that this new arrangement is the result of foreign conquest. These churches are principally found in the southern part of Pem-

...ie of Glamorgan,† and on the borders
....ic the system of subordinate chapelries is
...ose parts of the country where the inde-
...atives was of longest continuance. The
...otwithstanding their endless dissensions,
...ed rights of their churches;‡ but the
...ings, asserting the claims of conquest,

...by of Flemings about A. D. 1100.
...adventurers about A. D. 1090.
...ured from the existing state of churches in Wales,
...ess, who wrote his " Cambriæ Descriptio" in the reign
...this particular as if it were a national characteristic.
...is extracted from that work as translated by Sir

...ity show a greater respect than other nations to
...persons, to the relics of saints, bells, holy books,
...they devoutly revere; and hence their churches enjoy
...quility. For peace is not only preserved towards all
...yards, but at a great distance beyond them, where
...riches have been appointed by the Bishops in order
...of the sanctuary. But the principal churches, to
...the greater reverence, extend their protection to
...go to feed in the morning and return at night."

...remarkable as it shows that there existed in the
...churches distinguished for their antiquity; and
...most extensively endowed, it will readily appear
...principal." So tenacious were the Welsh of the
...that, even when they were inconvenient from their
...situate them, they appointed several clergymen
...be says,—
...almost as many parsons and parties as there are
...rish; the sons, after the death of their fathers,
...benefices, not by election, but by hereditary right
...sanctuary of God. And if a prelate should by
...or institute any other person, the people would
...upon the institutor and instituted." (Description
...ed.)
...as Archdeacon of Brecknock, and in one of his
...church in Radnorshire as having six or seven

would establish churches where they thought expedient. All churches of this description may be considered as of the last foundation, leaving those which are intermediate in un- certainty for the present.

It may be objected by some, that the extent of benefices depends not so much upon their subjection to Welsh Princes, or Norman Lords, as upon the barrenness, or fertility of the country in which they are situate. A glance at the map of Wales will be sufficient to show, that though *parishes* may be large or small for the reason specified, the objection does not apply to endowments. The fertile vale of Towy, in the county of Carmarthen, is filled with endowments of the first class, which are subdivided into parishes, of greater or less extent, to suit the nature of the country; and on the other hand, places of worship are sometimes numerous in districts the most barren. The recesses of the mountains appear to have been more populous formerly than at present, for the in- habitants of Wales chose to live in such situations as were most secure from foreign aggression; and thus the county of Carnarvon contains more churches than the larger and more fertile county of Montgomery.

Though churches, strictly so called, were few, it was not on account of the scantiness of population, for chapels of every description were scattered over the Principality, which would

---

clergymen. ("Clerici sex vel septem, more Walensium, participes Ecclesiæ illius.") The custom of dividing a benefice between several portionists, without compromising its integrity, continued in some of parts of the Diocese of St. Asaph until after the subjugation of Wales; several instances may be found in the Taxation of Pope Nicholas, A. D. 1291, but the following extract, relating to the church of Corwén, Merionethshire, will suffice.

	Porcio Gynon ap Ednefed....	8	13	4
	Porcio Kenewyrc'	5	0	0
Ecclia de Corvaen.	Porcio Gwyn ap Twdyr	5	0	0
	Porcio Gregor p'bri	3	6	8
	Porcio Vicar'	6	0	0

c

not have been requisite unless the country were well peopled.
From what has been already written, it will appear that the
definition of "church" has been considered to be a place of
worship endowed with tithes. A "chapel," on the contrary,
is considered to be a place of worship without any such endowment. It has been already stated that chapels are of
later erection than the churches to which they are subject.
Some of them are ancient; and an attempt will be made to
form such a classification of them as will assist in determining
generally the eras in which they were built.

Parochial Chapels are considered to be the most ancient,
being a necessary consequence of the great extent of the
district assigned to the mother church, which was soon found
insufficient for the instruction of people spread over so wide
a territory. There is reason for supposing that chapels of
this description are coeval with churches of the intermediate
foundation. They were erected before the division of the
country into parishes as at present constituted, for such a
subdivision of the older districts could have been of no
utility unless chapels were already built; and the existence
of these places of worship, which at first were only chapels of
ease, suggested the division for the sake of convenience.

Between Parochial Chapels and Chapels of Ease there was
at first no distinction, but the latter are now known from the
circumstance that they have no separate districts assigned
them, being always situate in the same parish as the mother
church. As a general rule, these chapels are of later erection
than the former, being the result of a demand for an increased
supply of places of worship. They belong to a time when
the boundaries of parishes were so far permanently settled
that it was not expedient to disturb them.

There is reason, however, to believe that the Normans and
Flemings, wherever they made their settlements, converted
such chapels as they found in the country into separate
benefices. But they also built many churches in addition,

making a new distribution of parishes. Thus the Rectories in the Deaneries of Rhos and Castlemartin, Pembrokeshire; in the peninsula of Gower, and the Vale of Glamorgan, average at about half the extent of parochial chapelries in most of the other districts of Wales. This distribution, however, belongs to a period in which so much information may be collected from history, as will serve to distinguish the older churches from their more modern neighbours.

There are also other Chapels, which do not appear to have been used for the purposes of public, or congregational worship; such as Cells, Oratories, and Hermitages, where prayers and offerings were made in private. They are sometimes distinguished from public churches by their situation, either in the solitude of an island, or promontory, over the well of a favourite Saint, or adjoining to a church where provision was already made for public worship; and were so small that they could contain but few persons. They may also be distinguished by their present state, being all of them in ruin, and the situations of most of them are known only by tradition. Being of no use as public churches, and the offerings to them ceasing, they were suffered to fall to decay soon after the Reformation. Nearly all parochial chapels, inasmuch as they are repaired at the cost of their respective parishes, have been preserved entire to the present time. Several chapels of ease, however, for want of a similar provision, have become ruinated, and in some cases their situation is almost forgotten; yet the names of most of them may be recovered from various ecclesiastical documents and editions of the "Liber Regis."

In treating of the Saints, it is intended to give such notices of cells, and oratories, as may be supplied from the vague information which remains respecting them. If there were any small chapels of this description in ancient times, the veneration attached to them would suggest their enlargement into churches or parochial chapels, whenever a

demand might be made for an increased number of public
places of worship; unless their situations were such as to
render the change useless or impracticable.* It may be
presumed that the earliest oratories, founded after the final
settlement of parishes, were frequently converted into chapels
of ease; and while it is the tendency of ecclesiastical establishments gradually to rise in importance,† it may be concluded that those, which as a class have remained in the
lowest rank, were the latest. Chapels erected over wells owe
their origin to the superstition of the middle ages, and those
which are contiguous to a larger church, or cathedral, have
their antiquity limited by the date of the fabric to which
they are adjoined.

At this stage of proceeding, it will be proper to observe
that the Welsh word "Llan" was at first applied to churches
and chapels indiscriminately; in determining the antiquity
of chapels, it may be considered that such as have their
names compounded with this word are of the older kind.
The word "Capel" appears to be of subsequent introduction,
as it is seldom attached to the names of parochial chapels,
but applied principally to chapels of ease and decayed oratories. Another designation applied to chapels in Wales is
"Bettws;" and though several places so named have been
formed into independent benefices, there are proofs remaining sufficient to show that they were originally subject to
other churches in their neighbourhood. Sometimes the two
latter appellations are used together, as Capel Bettws Lleicu,

---

* The exception applies principally to cells said to have been founded by
the primitive Christians of Wales in certain small islands, to which they
retired for the sake of security.

† This observation, though intended to apply to churches and chapels, is
also true of monastic institutions; Priories, being of later foundation than
Abbeys, remained unequal to them in revenues and importance : it may also
be noticed that the relationship subsisting between a superior convent and
its cells is in some degree analogous to that between a church and its chapels.

Cardiganshire, and Capel Bettws, subject to Trelech, Carmarthenshire.[*]

Great stress has been laid upon parochial divisions, for the reason that they determine the comparative antiquity of the churches to which they belong. The idea that parishes in Wales were established by a general Act of the Legislature can never be maintained. Without entering further into the question, it is sufficient to say that they existed in the times of of Welsh independency, when no Acts of the English Parliament could affect them; and the Welsh annals record no ordinance for their arrangement, which in the state of the country, divided between contending Princes, was almost impossible. Their establishment was gradual, and their limits were determined by the territory of the person who endowed each church with tithes. This is the only way to account for their unequal extent, and the inconvenience of their distribution. A chieftain might divide his lands between his his sons, and this arrangement might form some criterion for the division of an endowment of the first class into parochial chapelries; but he could make no partition of the tithes, for as they had been already given away, they were no longer in his power; and it rested with the minister[†] of the mother church to make his own arrangements with the curates of the chapelries.

Property in Wales descended by the law of Gavelkind,

---

[*] Llan appears to be indigenous in the Welsh language, meaning not only the church, but the sacred spot which surrounds it, and in this sense it corresponds with the Greek word "τεμενος." The idea of "enclosure" is also observable in its compounds, gwinllan, perllan, corlan, ydlan, &c. Capel is derived from "Capella," a Latin word of modern invention. The derivation of Bettws is uncertain. Qu. from the Anglo-Saxon—"Bead-house." .

[†] Giraldus Cambrensis does not inform us by what scale the tithes were divided between a plurality of Rectors, but he loudly declaims against the whole system as an abuse.

which ordained that sons should inherit their father's territory in equal proportions. Such was the theory of the
institution, but in practice it was very defective. Feuds
always arose about the distribution. Might would overcome
right, and as a necessary consequence the divisions were very
unequal, and sometimes intermixed with each other. Tracts
of country may therefore be found, where the church appears
to have been endowed when affairs were in the state described. In the Rural Deanery of Maelienydd in the county
of Radnor, which contained the districts of Nantmel, Llanbister, and Llangynllo, the division was regular; but it was
otherwise in the Deanery of Builth in the county of Brecon.
In the latter, the district of Llanafan includes the continuous
parishes of Llanafan Fawr, Llanfechan, Llanfihangel Bryn
Pabûan, and Llanfihangel Abergwesin; and also the parish
of Alltmawr, which is separated from the others by the inter-
vening parishes of Llanddewi'r Cwm and Builth. The
district of Llangammarch includes the parishes of Llangammarch, Llanwrtyd, and Llanddewi Abergwesin, and there
is reason to suspect that Llanddulas ought to be added to
the number. But what is more surprising, there is docu-
mentary evidence[*] to prove that it formerly included the
extensive parish of Llansanffraid Cwmmwd Deuddwr[†] though

---

[*] The authority alluded to is the "Valor Ecclesiasticus" of Henry VIII.
under the heads of "Llangammarch" and "Llanseyntffrede." The connexion is also proved by another authority more ancient; in a Deed of
Agreement with the Abbey of Strata Florida, to which the Chapter of
Abergwilly was a party, dated March 21, 1339, mention is made of the
Prebendary of "Llangammarch Readr" alluding to the town of Rhayader,
in a suburb of which the church of Llansanffraid is situated.

[†] The name "Cwmmwd Deuddwr" is restored from a passage in the
Valor Ecclesiasticus, where it is said to be a part of the possessions of
Strata Florida. (See also the enumeration of parishes in the second Vol.
of the Myvyrian Archaiology.) It is now generally written "Cwm
y Toyddwr."

divided from it by the interposition of Llanafan Fawr. The parishes of Llanfihangel Bryn Pabûan and Llanafan Fawr intervene between Llanwrthwl and its subordinate parish of Llanlleonfel; and Llanganten is in a similar manner separated by Maesmynys and Llanddewi'r Cwm from its chapelry of Llangynog. When it is added that Llanddewi'r Cwm* is the mother church of Builth, and Maesmynys† the mother church of Llanynys, all the parishes in the Deanery are enumerated, and the last two districts alone are entirely continuous.

If it be objected that chapelries may have been originally separate benefices which were afterwards consolidated, it may be replied that the extinction of a benefice and its conversion into a chapelry is contrary to the progress of ecclesiastical polity. So far from the fact of churches uniting together to form one benefice, the tendency is the reverse; chapels are frequently detached from the older church and become independent benefices. Even when the whole tithes of a living were appropriated to a Monastery or Collegiate Chapter, the benefice did not lose its existence and become subject to some neighbouring parish, but it continued its independence under the name of prebend or curacy. Whenever, from the smallness of their value, two rectories or vicarages are consolidated, neither of them merges into the other, or becomes a chapel; but they preserve their original designation as separate benefices, and are only said to be annexed. These points do not depend upon accident, as they affect the interests of every clergyman upon his institution to a living. Churches, which are described as benefices in the survey of Pope Nicholas in the reign of Edward the First, continued to be, for the most part, so described in the surveys of Henry the Eighth, and Queen Anne, and are found to be similar with

* Taxation of Pope Nicholas, and Jones's Brecknockshire, Vol. II. p. 298.
† Taxation of Pope Nicholas.

a few exceptions at this present time.* Sometimes, from
being a larger edifice or more favourably situated, the chapel
may take precedence of the parent church; but this accident
does not compromise the integrity of the benefice. It has
been the interest of every incumbent to observe that his
rights were not infringed upon by his neighbour; and if he
held a plurality of livings, they were generally separated
upon his decease.

Should ever such a consolidation, or rather extinction of
benefices have taken place; it may naturally be supposed
that it was formed for the purpose of aggrandizing Monasteries, or the dignitaries of collegiate bodies. But the system of
subordination is of older date; for the foundation Charters of
Abbeys in Wales describe it as already existing. Chapels
are enumerated under their respective churches as at present,
with the exception, as may be expected, that some of them
have since been converted into separate benefices, but this is
a proceeding the reverse of consolidation. In Dugdale's
Monasticon is a Charter† of Edw. III. confirming a prior
Grant made by certain Princes of South Wales in the time of
Henry III. to the Abbey of Talley in Carmarthenshire.

---

* In examining ecclesiastical documents, care must be taken to ascertain whether the word "ecclesia" be used generically or specifically,
and irregularities must be rectified by a comparison with other authorities.

† The information, to be derived from a perusal of documents of this
nature, may be demonstrated by another example from the Monasticon,
in the words of the original.—" A. D. 1141, Mauritius de London, filius
Willielmi de London, dedit ecclesiæ Sancti Petri Glouc. ecclesiam S. Michaelis de Ewenny, ecclesiam S. Brigidæ, cum capella de Ugemor de
Lanfey. Ecclesiam S. Michaelis de Colveston cum terris, &c,—ita ut
conventus Monachorum fiat."—The Grant of these churches to the
Monastery of St. Peter's Gloucester was made with a view to the establishment of a Priory, subject to that society, at Ewenny in the county
of Glamorgan. The church of St. Bridget, mentioned therein, is St.
Bride's Major in the same county. The capella de Ugemor was probably

These Welsh Princes were the founders of the Abbey, and in their Grant the churches of Llansadwrn, Llanwrda, Llansawel, and Pumsant are mentioned as chapels under Cynwyl Gaio. Of these, Llansadwrn now forms a separate vicarage, having Llanwrda annexed to it as a chapelry; Llansawel is still subject to Cynwyl Gaio, and Pumsant is the name of a place in the parish of Caio, where tradition states there was formerly a chapel, of which no vestiges now remain.

The subordination of churches, described as prevailing to so great an extent in Wales, may at first appear surprising; it is however no theory, for it actually exists at this very day, and all that has been done is to endeavour to account for the causes which produced it. The arrangement made will be found intimately connected with the Saints to whom the Welsh churches are dedicated; for if any of them were founded by the persons whose names they bear, they must be those which retain the greatest evidences of antiquity.

in the castle of Ogmore, on the bank of a river of the same name, as the curacy of Wick, now subject to St. Bride's, is too far from the river to merit the appellation, and most large castles had formerly a chapel within their precincts. The chapel of Llamphey must have been situate in the hamlet so called in the parish of St. Bride's, and the omission of Wick affords a presumption that it was founded after the date of the Grant. In those documents, however, where chapels are altogether omitted, it must follow, that if they existed in the time of the record, the name of the mother church was considered sufficient to include its dependencies.

SECTION II.

The Subordination of Churches and Chapels considered in reference to
the Saints to whom they are dedicated.

In an enquiry into the question, by whom and at what
time the several churches of Wales were founded, great
assistance may be derived from the names of the Saints to
whom they are dedicated. In forming a classification, two
grand divisions immediately present themselves;—the Saints
which have been admitted into the Romish Calendar, and
those who are natives of the country, or otherwise connected
with its history. The characteristics of both kinds are so
different, that they can hardly be conceived to belong to the
same people, or indeed to the same religion. In the time of
St. Augustin the Monk,* there was already in Wales a
Christian Church, furnished with Bishops, Monasteries, stated
places of worship, and other appendages of a religious establishment.† It refused to submit to the authority of the
Pope, and proofs are not wanting to show that it continued
its independence for some time afterwards, until, from the
intercourse of foreigners, and the gradual subjugation of the
Welsh people, it merged into Catholicism. It might naturally
be concluded that the native Saints belonged to the primitive
Church of the country, and that the places of worship called
after their names were of older foundation than those dedicated to Saints of the Catholic Calendar. It will not be
amiss, therefore, to give the result of an examination of all

* A. D. 600.
† Bede's Ecclesiastical History, Book II. Chap. 2.

the dedications in Wales, according to Ecton's Thesaurus, edited by Browne Willis;* and greater pleasure is felt in appealing to that book, as it is of generally received authority, and its Editor was utterly unconscious of the conclusions that are here sought to be maintained.

The Saints, to whom the greatest number of churches are dedicated, are St. Mary the Virgin, St. Michael, and St. David. Those dedicated to St. Mary are as follow, and it should be observed that care is taken to distinguish chapelries from benefices.†

DIOCESE OF ST. DAVID'S.

PEMBROKESHIRE.

Hayscastle, V.—1 *Chapel, Forde.*
Fishguard, V.
Llanfair,—chapel to Letterstone
   (St. Giles.)
Maenor Nawen, C.
Ambleston, V.
Maenclochog, V.
Spittle, C.
Walton-East, C.
Wiston, C.
Herbranston, R.
St. Mary's, Haverford West, V.
Roch, V.
Talbenny, R.

Nangle, R. & V.
Pwllcrochan, R.
Tenby, R. & V.
St. Mary's, Pembroke, V.—1
   Chapel, St. Anne's, in ruins.
Warren, V.
Coedcanlas,—chapel to Martletwy
   (St. Marcellus.)
Newport, R.
Puncheston, R.
Cilgwyn,—chapel to Nevern (St.
   Brynach.)
Llanfair Nantgwyn,—chapel to
   Whitchurch (St. Michael.)

* Bacon, in his "Liber Regis," appears to follow the authority of Browne Willis, with a few corrections.

† The letters R. V. P. and C. affixed to benefices, denote Rectory, Vicarage, Prebend, and Curacy; and it must be noticed that those Curacies only are so designated which do not acknowledge a dependence upon any other church. The chapels, subject to churches of St. Mary, are printed in Italics; and their Saints, as well as those of parent churches, connected with the names in the list, are added, except where omitted by Browne Willis.

BRECKNOCKSHIRE.

Aberyscyr. V.
St. Mary's, Brecon,—chapel to
St. John's.
Ystrad Feltte,—chapel to Dyfrn-
og (St. Cynog.)
Cantref. R.—1 *Chapel, Nant Du.*
Llanywern. C.
Freuddyn. V.
Talachddin. R.

Hay. V.—1 *Chapel, St. John's,
in ruins.*
Aberllyfni. or Pipton, ruinated,
—chapel to Glasebury. (St.
Peter.)
Cragcadarn.—chapel to Llan-
dyfalle (St. Matthew.)
Llanfair in Builth, C.

HEREFORDSHIRE.

Creswell,—chapel to Clodock, Walterstone, C.
(St. Clydog.)

MONTGOMERYSHIRE.

Kerry, V.*

RADNORSHIRE.

Bleddfa, R.
Abbey Cwm-Hir,—chapel to
Llanbister (St. Cynllo.)
Pilleth,—chapel to Llangynllo
(St. Cynllo.)
Gladestry, R.

Newchurch, R.
Bettws,—chapel to Diserth (St.
Cewydd.)
Llanfaredd,—chapel to Aberedw
(St. Cewydd.)

CARMARTHENSHIRE.

Eglwys Fair a Churig,—chapel
to Henllan Amgoed (St. David.)
Eglwys Fair Lantâf,—chapel to
Llanboidy (St. Brynach.)
Kidwelly, V.—5 *ruinated Chap-
els.*—*Capel Trilo (St. Teilo;)
Llanfihangel (St. Michael;)*

*Coker; Cadog (St. Cadog;)
and St. Thomas.*
Llanfair ar y Bryn,—chapel to
Llandingad (St. Dingad.)
Capel Mair, in ruins,—chapel to
Talley (St. Michael.)

* Kerry is dedicated to St. Michael; but the authority of Browne
Willis is followed, in order to preserve the proportion which this and
the two succeeding lists bear to each other, including all inaccuracies.

GLAMORGANSHIRE.

Rhosili, R.
Penard, or Penarth, V.

St. Mary's, Swansea, V.—1 *Chapel, St. John's.*
Penrice, C.

CARDIGANSHIRE.

St. Mary's, Cardigan, V.
Llanfair Orllwyn, R.
Bryngwyn,—chapel to Penbryn (St. Michael.)

Llanfair Trefhelygen,—chapel to Llandyfriog (St. Tyfriog.)
Llanfair Clydogau, C.
Strata Florida, or Ystrad Flur, C.

SUMMARY OF ST. DAVID'S.

Pembrokeshire	- - - -	23
Brecknockshire	- - - -	11
Herefordshire	- - - -	2
Montgomeryshire	- - - -	1
Radnorshire	- - -	7

Carmarthenshire	- - - -	5
Glamorganshire	- - - -	4
Cardiganshire	- - - -	6
		—
In the Diocese	- - - -	59

DIOCESE OF ST. ASAPH.

FLINTSHIRE

Ysgeifiog, R. & V.
Halkin, or Helygen, R.
Kilken, R. & V.
Rhuddlan, V.
Whitford, R. & V.
Gwaunesgor, R.
Nannerch, R. & V.

St. Mary's, Flint,—chapel to Northop (St. Peter.)
St. Mary's, Mold, V.—2 *Chapels, Nerquis and Treuddin.*
Nerquis,—chapel to Mold.
Treuddin,—chapel to Mold.
Overton,—chapel to Bangor in Maelor (St. Dunawd.)

MONTGOMERYSHIRE.

Llanfair Caereinion, R.
Welsh Pool, V.—1 *Chapel, Buttington (All Saints) Salop.*

Newtown, R.
Llanllugan, C.
Llanbrynmair, R. & V.

MERIONETHSHIRE.

Gloddaeth,*—a free chapel.   Bettws Gwerfyl Goch, R.

DENBIGHSHIRE.

Penrhyn,*—a free chapel.   Rhiwfabon, V.
Llannefydd, V.   Chirk, or Eglwys y Waun, V.
Llanfair Talhaiarn, C.

SHROPSHIRE.

Syllatyn, R.   Knocking, R.
Kinnersley, V.

Total in St. Asaph - - - - - 27.

DIOCESE OF BANGOR.

CARNARVONSHIRE.

Llanfair Isgaer, V.—1 *Chapel,*   Trefriw, R.—*2 Chapels, Llan-*
Bettws Garmon (St. German-   *rhychwyn, (St. Rhychwyn;)*
us.)   *and Bettws y Coed (St. Mi-*
St. Mary's, Carnarvon,—chapel   *chael.)*
to Llanbeblig (St. Peblig.)   Penllech,—chapel to Llaniestin
Caer-rhun, V.   (St. Iestin.)
Conway, V.   Beddgelert, C.
Llanfair Fechan, R.

MERIONETHSHIRE.

Dolgelleu, R.   Llanfair juxta Harlech, R.
Llanegryn, V.   Tal y Llyn,—chapel to Towyn
Maentwrog,—chapel to Festiniog   (All Saints.)
(St. Michael.)

* Properly speaking, Gloddaeth and Penrhyn are chapels in the parish
of Eglwys Rhos, Carnarvonshire.

DENBIGHSHIRE.

Derwen yn Ial, R.
Llanfair Dyffryn Clwyd, V.

Cyffylliog,—chapel to Llanynys (St. Saeran.)

ANGLESEY.

Gwaredog,—chapel to Llantrisant (St. Sanan, Afran, and Iefan.)
Llanfair Ynghornwy,—chapel to Llanddeusant (St. Marcellus and Marcellinus.)
Llannerch y Medd,—chapel to Llanbeulan (St. Peulan.)
Tal y Llyn.—chapel to Llanbeulan (St. Peulan.)
Llanfair is Cwmmwd,—chapel to Llannidan (St. Aidan.)

Llanfair Pwll Gwyngyll, R.—1 Chapel, Llandyssilio (St. Tyssilio.)
Beaumaris,—chapel to Llandegfan (St. Tydecho.)
Bodewrid,—chapel to Llanelian (St. Elian.)
Pentraeth,—chapel to Llanddyfnan (St. Dyfnan.)
Llanfair Mathafarn,—chapel to Llanddyfnan (St. Dyfnan.)

Total in Bangor - - - - - - - - - 26.

DIOCESE OF LLANDAFF.

GLAMORGANSHIRE.

Bonvilleston, C.
Penmark, V.
Wenvo, R.
St. Mary's, Cardiff, (originally the parish church,)—1 Chapel, St. John's.
Caerau, C.
Whitchurch,—chapel to Llandaff (St. Teilo & St. Peter.)
Coetty, R.—1 Chapel, Nolton.

Nolton Bridgend,—chapel to Coetty.
Aberafon, V.—1 Chapel, Baglan (St. Baglan.)
Cowbridge,—chapel to Llanbleddian (St. John the Baptist.)
St. Mary Hill, R.
St. Mary-church, R.
Margam, C.
Monknash, C.

MONMOUTHSHIRE.

Llanfair Cilgedin, R.
Abergavenny, V.—1 Chapel, St. John's.

Dynstow, V.—1 Chapel, Tregaer.
Tregaer, chapel to Dynstow.
Chepstow, V.

Llanwern, R.
Magor, V.
Nash,—chapel to Goldcliff (St. Mary Magdalen.)
Parsenet, alias Porthskewit, R.

Llanfair Discoed, C.
Malpas, C.
Pautedge, R. (Qu. Pant-teg.)
Usk, V.

Total in Llandaff - - - - - - 27.

OUTLYING PARISHES OF WALES.

DIOCESE OF HEREFORD.

Newton Wallica, C. Monmouth-shire.
St. Mary's, Monmouth, V.

New Radnor, V. Radnorshire.
Kenarton, alias Keynarth,—chapel to Old Radnor (St. Stephen.)

SUMMARY.

St. David's - - - - - - 59	Churches* - - - - - - 98
St. Asaph - - - - - - 27	Chapels - - - - - - 45
Bangor - - - - - - 26	
Llandaff - - - - - - 27	
Other parishes - - - - - 4	
143	143

The list, notwithstanding its apparently large amount, bears but a small proportion to the churches dedicated to this Saint over the same extent of territory in England; and it must not be forgotten that the great majority is to be found in such parts of Wales as became first subject to the English

* If it were allowable to amend the list given from Ecton, it might be shown, from the Taxation of Pope Nicholas, that Llanbrynmair was once a chapel under Darowain, though it now forms a separate benefice ; Builth was formerly subject to Llanddewi'r Cwm; Strata Florida is in the parish of Caron, and therefore subordinate to the church of Tregaron. Other corrections might be adduced; and if decayed chapels and oratories not mentioned by Ecton were included, the number of chapels dedicated to the Virgin would be considerably augmented.

or Flemings. Forty five out of the number are chapels, and therefore of later date than the churches to which they belong. The remainder are, nearly all of them, churches of the last foundation; and in those parts of Wales which preserved their independence longest, the proportion is very small. This would almost induce a suspicion that the homage paid to the Virgin was not of native growth, but was forced upon the inhabitants of the Principality by their English neighbours. But with the aid of a map, and some knowledge of the history of the country, the subject may be examined more narrowly.

The number in Pembrokeshire alone is twenty three, but many of these parishes do not even possess a Welsh name, and in the greatest part of the county the system of Welsh endowments is entirely subverted. This tract was colonized about A. D. 1100 by English and Flemings, whose descendants still remain; and the churches enumerated probably date their origin from that period. In the adjoining counties of Carmarthen and Cardigan, the numbers are only five and six, being the smallest proportions of any, and four of the former are chapels; but these counties preserved their independence down to the time of Edw. I. In Glamorganshire, the number is eighteen, but the same reasons apply to this county as to Pembrokeshire, it being conquered by Norman adventurers from England, who divided the county between them about A. D. 1090. The proportions in Brecknockshire and Monmouthshire must be referred to the conquest of both of them by Bernard Newmarch and others. Out of eight, the number in Radnorshire,* five are chapels. In Carnarvonshire also, the number is eight, two of which are chapels; and if these churches were not founded after the death of the last Llewelyn, they at least present a fair specimen of the number to be looked for under the supremacy

* Including that portion of the county which forms a part of the Diocese of Hereford.

E

of the Welsh Princes. In Montgomery, Merioneth, and
Denbigh the proportion is small. Out of ten, the number for
Anglesey, there are nine chapels; while in Flint, being a
border county, and at one time an appendage of the Earldom
of Chester, the proportion is large,*

Most of the towns in Wales are of late origin, being built
to suit the convenience of castles in their vicinity, which are
known to have been erected by Norman and other adventurers. It might, therefore, be expected that the churches of
these would present the features of a late foundation. Upon
referring to the list, churches are found at Fishguard,† Newport, Haverford West, Tenby, Pembroke, Brecon, Hay,
Builth, Kidwelly, Swansea, Cardigan, Rhuddlan, Flint, Mold,
Llanfair Caereinion, Welsh Pool, Newtown, Carnarvon, Conway, Dolgelleu, Beaumaris, Cardiff, Bridgend, Cowbridge,
Abergavenny, Chepstow, Usk, Monmouth, and New Radnor,
dedicated to St. Mary, comprising nearly half the towns in
the Principality. Several others, as Roch, Brwynllys, and
Coetty, are in the neighbourhood of Norman castles, where
no towns have been built; and a few more, as Abbey Cwm
Hir, Strata Florida, Margam, Beddgelert, and Creswell, owe
their dedications to the Monasteries which formerly existed
on their sites.

The late introduction of the homage of St. Mary may be
proved by another mode of computation. Forty five of her
places of worship are chapels, while only sixteen of her
churches are of sufficient antiquity or importance to have
chapels under them. Again, twenty four‡ chapels, dedicated

---

* Three churches in the list are in the county of Salop, and four more,
including one chapelry, are in the Diocese of Hereford.

† In Carlisle's Topographical Dictionary of Wales, reasons are given
for the supposition that the parish of Fishguard was formed upon the
dissolution of two others more ancient.

‡ By an amendment of the list, without the introduction of any new
names, this number may be increased to thirty three. The five ex-

to St. Mary, are found subordinate to churches ascribed to Welsh Saints; while only five chapels named after Welsh Saints are subordinate to churches of St. Mary. The inference is, that the custom of ascribing churches or chapels to Welsh Saints had nearly ceased before that of dedicating to St. Mary had commenced; and perhaps the exceptions to the rule may be referred to an accident, where the chapel had taken precedence of the mother church.

The justness of these conclusions, as regards one county, can be verified from a document of unquestionable authority. In the preceding list, the county of Flint has a proportion about three times greater than any of the rest; as the entire number of its churches and chapels is only twenty eight, twelve of which are dedicated to St. Mary; and of these twelve, eight are in the ancient Lordship of Tegeingl, or Englefield. It happens that this Lordship, as being part of the Palatinate of Chester, is included in the Survey of Domesday Book, made by order of William the Conqueror; and in the enumeration of its churches, two* only of those dedicated to St. Mary are mentioned as then existing. It must therefore be concluded that the remainder were built at a later period; and as the same document describes this Lordship, which it calls the Hundred of Atiscros, as if it had been some time in the occupation of the Saxons, the dedication of the two churches mentioned may be attributed to their influence.

ceptions are the chapels of Cadog and Teilo under Kidwelly, Llanrhychwyn subject to Trefriw, Llandyssilio subject to Llanfihangel Pwll Gwyngyll, and Baglan subject to Aberafon. As the church of Kidwelly is presumed to be of a date subsequent to the erection of a castle there by William de Londres, a Norman adventurer, A. D. 1094, the parish church before that time was probably the chapel of Cadog, or, as it is called, Llangadog, to which the chapel of Teilo might have been subordinate. A similar reason may perhaps be found to account for the three remaining irregularities.

* "Widford" (Whitford,) and "Roeland" (Rhuddlan.)

The next Saint, to whom the largest number of churches is dedicated, is St. Michael, the Archangel.

DIOCESE OF ST. DAVID'S.

PEMBROKESHIRE.

Rudbacston, R.
Stackpoole Boscher, alias Bosheston, R.
Castle Martin, V.—1 *Chapel, Flimston.*
Cosheston, R.

St. Michael's, Pembroke, V.
Whitchurch, R.—1 *Chapel, Llanfair Nantgwyn, (St. Mary.)*
Castle Beith, R.
Llanfihangel Penbedw, R.

BRECKNOCKSHIRE.

Llanfihangel Nant Bran, C.
Llanfihangel Fechan,—chapel to Llandyfaelog (St. Maelog.)
Llanfihangel Cwm Du, R. & V.—1 *Chapel, Tretwr.*
Cathedin, R.

Llanfihangel Tal y Llyn, R.
Llanfihangel Abergwesin,—chapel to Llanafan Fawr, (St. Afan.)
Llanfihangel Bryn Pabûan,—chapel to Llanafan Fawr, (St. Afan.)

HEREFORDSHIRE.

Dulas, C.
Ewyas Harold, C.

Michael-church, Eskley, C.

RADNORSHIRE.

Cefn Llys, R.
Bugeildy, V.
Cascob, R.
Bryngwyn, R.
Clyro, P. & V.—1 *Chapel, Bettws Clyro.*

Llanfihangel Nant Melan, V.
Llanfihangel Rhydeithon,—chapel to Llanbister, (St. Cynllo.)
Llanfihangel Helygen,—chapel to Nantmel, (St. Cynllo.)

CARMARTHENSHIRE.

Egermond, C.
Llanfihangel Abercywyn,—chapel to Meidrym (St. David.)
Llanfihangel, in ruins,—chapel to St. Mary's, Kidwelly.
Cil y Cwm, V.
Llanfihangel Fach Cilfargen, R.
Llangathen, V.
Llanfihangel Ararth, V.—1 Chapel, *Pencadair.*
Llanfihangel Uwch Gwyli,—chapel to Abergwyli, (St. David.)

Llanfihangel Rhos y Corn,—chapel to Llanllwni, (St. Llwni.)
Llanfihangel Aberbythych, C.
Talley, C.—5 *Chapels, all in ruins, Capel Crist (Holy Trinity;) Capel Mair, (St. Mary;) Llanfihangel, (St. Michael;) Cynhwm and Teilo, (St. Teilo.)*
Llanfihangel, in ruins,—chapel to Talley, (St. Michael.)
Myddfai, V.

GLAMORGANSHIRE.

Llwchwr, or Loughor, R.

CARDIGANSHIRE.

Llanfihangel Ystrad, P. & V.
Llanfihangel Penbryn, V.—2 *Chapels, Bettws Ifan, (St. John,) and Bryngwyn, (St. Mary.)*
Troedyraur, R.

Tremain, C.
Llanfihangel Geneu'r Glyn, V.
Llanfihangel y Creuddin.——1 *Chapel, Eglwys Newydd.*
Lledroed, P.
Rhosdeiau, R.

Total in St. David's - - - - - - - 48.

DIOCESE OF ST. ASAPH.

FLINTSHIRE.

Caerwys, R. & V.   Rhelofnoid, C.

MONTGOMERYSHIRE.

Llanfihangel y Gwynt, R.   Manafon, R.

DENBIGHSHIRE.

Abergele, V.   Llanfihangel, R.
Bettws, V.*

SHROPSHIRE.

Llanyblodwel, R.—1 *Chapel, Morton.*

Total in St. Asaph - - - - - - - - - 8.

DIOCESE OF BANGOR.

CARNARVONSHIRE.

Llanrug, R.   Llanfihangel y Pennant, C.
Bettws y Coed,—chapel to Tref-   Treflys,—chapel to Criccieth
  riw (St. Mary.)   (St. Catherine.)
Llanfihangel Bachellaeth,—chap-
  el to Llanbedrog (St. Pedrog.)

MERIONETHSHIRE.

Ffestiniog, R.—1 *Chapel, Maen-* Llanfihangel y Traeth,—chapel
  twrog (St. Mary.)   to Llandecwyn (St. Tecwyn.)
Llanfihangel y Pennant,—chapel
  to Tywyn (All Saints.)

MONTGOMERYSHIRE.

Trefeglwys, R.

DENBIGHSHIRE.

Efenechtyd, R.

* Bettws was formerly a chapel to Abergele.—See Edwards's "Cathedral of St. Asaph."

ANGLESEY.

Llanfihangel yn Nhywyn,—chapel to Rhoscolyn, (St. Gwenfaen.)

Llanfihangel Ysgeifiog, C.—1 *Chapel, Llanffinan (St. Ffinan.)*

Llanfihangel Tinsilwy,—chapel to Llaniestin (St. Iestin.)

Llanfihangel Tre'r Beirdd,--chapel to Llandyfrydog (St. Dyfrydog.)

Llugwy,—chapel to Llaneigrad (St. Eigrad.)

Penrhos, C.

Total in Bangor - - - - - - - - 16.

DIOCESE OF LLANDAFF.

GLAMORGANSHIRE.

Michaelston le Pit, R.
St. Michael's upon Ely, R.
Colwinston, V.
Fleminston, R.

Michaelston, alias Llanfihangel, near Cowbridge, R.
Ewenny, C.
Michaelston, super Afon, C.

MONMOUTHSHIRE.

Llanfihangel Istern Llewern, R.
Llanfihangel juxta Usk, R.
Llanfihangel Crug corneu, V.
Llanfihangel, R. (in Deanery of Nether Went.)
Tintern Parva, R.
Machan, or Maghen, R.
St. Michael's near Rumney, or Michaelston Vedo, R.

Troy, or Mitchel Troy, R.—1 *Chapel, Cwmcarfan.*
Kemmys, (Cemmaes,) R.
Gwernesey, R.
Llanfihangel Tormynydd, R.
Llanfihangel Pontymoel, C.
Llanfihangel juxta Llantarnam, C.

Total in Llandaff - - - - - - 20.

OUTLYING PARISHES OF WALES.

DIOCESE OF HEREFORD.

Discoed,—chapel to Presteign (St. Andrew,) Radnorshire.

Michaelchurch upon Arrow,—chapel to Kington (St. Mary.)

SUMMARY.

St. David's - - - - - - 48	Churches - - - - - - 73
St. Asaph - - - - - - 8	Chapels - - - - - - 21
Bangor - - - - - 16	
Llandaff - - - - - 20	
Other parishes - - - - - 2	
____	____
94	94

These churches, unlike those dedicated to St. Mary, do not crowd the English districts, but are dispersed over the country with greater regularity. They are found in the interior as well as in the outskirts, and are so far characteristic of the Principality, that the proportion they bear to other churches is twice as great as that of those dedicated to St. Michael in England.* This national distinction would show that they were mostly founded by the native princes, and their more general dispersion would indicate that they belonged to an era prior to the permanent occupation of parts of Wales by foreigners. Another mark of nationality, as well as of higher antiquity, is the greater number of Welsh names in the list of St. Michael than in that of St. Mary.† But the best criterion, in the absence of historical records, is the arrangement of parishes. Except in those parts where English and Norman settlers may have made a new distribution, the parishes dedicated to St. Michael are generally of much larger extent than those dedicated to St. Mary, some of them being eight, and even ten miles in length. While only nine out of

---

* According to Ecton, or Browne Willis, there are in the Diocese of Lincoln about 1520 churches, including extinct chapelries, sixty of which are dedicated to St. Michael. According to the same authority, there are in the Dioceses of St. David's and Bangor 720 churches, or less than half the number in Lincoln, *sixty four* of which are dedicated to St. Michael.

† Only two churches situate in towns, St. Michael's Pembroke, and Caerwys, occur in the list.

eighty five places of worship, in the Dioceses of St. David's and Bangor, named in the first list, were of sufficient antiquity or importance to have chapelries under them; the proportion in the list of St. Michael, for the same Dioceses, is ten out of sixty four. Four chapels of St. Mary are subject to churches of St. Michael, and two* *vice versâ*. Out of nineteen chapels dedicated to St. Michael, fourteen are parochial,† which for reasons already stated are more ancient than chapels of ease; while of those consecrated to St. Mary, the proportion is less, being twenty out of thirty three. From these calculations the Dioceses of St. Asaph and Llandaff are excluded, owing to the singular circumstance that, according to the authority of Ecton, there are no chapels dedicated to St. Michael in either of them.

These Dioceses therefore require a separate consideration, and the circumstance alluded to is an illustration of the truth of Welsh history. The Diocese of St. Asaph extends more along the English frontier than the rest; and long before the Norman conquest, according to the Welsh Annals, it appears to have suffered severely from the ravages of the Anglo-Saxons, who are even recorded to have taken possession of the territories comprised in it;‡ and though they could not

---

* Namely, Llanfihangel, in ruins, subject to St. Mary's Kidwelly, and Bettws y Coed subject to Trefriw; but the irregular situations of both the superior churches has been already noticed, in note page 35. Another irregularity is Michael-church upon Arrow subordinate to Kington; both these churches however are in the Diocese of Hereford.

† This particular is ascertained from Carlisle's Topographical Dictionary.

‡ Between A. D. 810 and 820, as stated in two Chronicles printed in the Myvyrian Archaiology, the Saxons took possession of Rhufoniog, or the western part of Denbighshire. In about ten years afterwards, according to three Chronicles in the same collection, they took possession of the "kingdom" or principality of Powys, comprising the county of Montgomery, with the remainder of Denbigh, and parts of Flint, Merioneth,

maintain their footing, their continual inroads must have desolated the country. To this cause may be attributed the
fact that all the churches dedicated to St. Michael in this
Diocese are only eight; and also, that though it is, perhaps,
the second of the Welsh Dioceses in point of extent, it contains fewer churches considerably than either of the other
three.* In Llandaff, the least extensive Diocese in Wales,
the number of churches dedicated to St. Michael is twenty,
not one of which is a chapel; but the Normans formed their
settlements in this district at a later period, and it may be
presumed that, according to their usual rule, they converted
such chapels as existed in the country into independent
benefices.

On the other hand, the churches of St. Michael, though
more ancient than those of St. Mary, are not the most ancient
in the Principality. One† only of the chapels subordinate to
them is dedicated to a Welsh Saint; while fourteen of the
chapels dedicated to St. Michael are subordinate to churches
ascribed to Welsh Saints; and this want of reciprocity can be
accounted for on no other principle than that the commemoration of the native Saints is of older date. The parishes dedicated to St. Michael vary considerably in extent, according
to the nature of the ground unoccupied by previous endowments; but even the most extensive of them do not
possess the characteristics of endowments of the first class.
That which approaches nearest is Llanfihangel Penbryn in
Cardiganshire, which contains the subordinate parishes of

and Salop. The occupation of the remaining part of Flintshire by the
Saxons has been already noticed, and it will be observed that the terri-
tories described are situated principally in the Diocese of St. Asaph.
(Myvyrian Archaiology, Vol. II. pp. 392, 475, & 476.)

* The number of churches in St. David's, including extinct chapelries,
as far as can be collected from Browne Willis, is 598; in Llandaff 275;
Bangor 194; and St. Asaph 145.

† Capel Teilo, a decayed chapel under Talley, Carmarthenshire.

Bettws Ifan and Bryngwyn. But this district, the only one in the list which possesses a plurality of *parochial* chapelries, shows the marks of a later origin so far that its chapels have not been formed into Perpetual Curacies, and continue to be served by the Vicar of Penbryn, or his stipendiary Curate.

The next Saint, whose churches were to be considered, was St. David, and the list according to Ecton is as follows.—

DIOCESE OF ST. DAVID'S.

PEMBROKESHIRE.

The Cathedral (St. David and St. Andrew.)--5 *Chapels, Gwrhyd; Non, (St. Non;) Padrig, (St. Patrick:) Pistyll; and Stinan, (St. Justinian.)*
Brawdy, V.
Whitchurch, V.
Prendergast, R.

Hubberston, R.
Bridell, R.
Llanuchllwydog, R.—1 *Chapel, Llanllawen.*
Llanychaer, R.
Llanddewi Felffre, R. & V.
Maenor Deifi, R.

CARDIGANSHIRE.

Llanddewi Brefi, C.—4 *Chapels, Bettws Lleicu; Blaenpennal, (St. David;) Gartheli; Gwenfyl, (St. Gwenfyl.)*
Blaenporth, P.
Bangor, R.—1 *Chapel, Henllan, (St. David.)*

Henfynyw, C,
Llanddewi Aberarth, P.
Henllan,—chapel to Bangor (St. David.)
Blaenpennal,—chapel to Llanddewi Brefi (St. David.)

CARMARTHENSHIRE.

Henllan Amgoed, R.—1 *Chapel, Eglwys Fair a Churig.*
Meidrym, V.—1 *Chapel, LlanhangelAbercywyn(St. Michael.*
Capel Dewi,—chapel to Llanelly (St. Ellyw.)
Llanarthneu, P. & V.—1 *Chapel, Llanlleian.*

Abergwilly, or Abergwyli, V.— 3 *Chapels, Llanfihangel Uwch Gwyli, (St. Michael;) Llanpumsant; and Llanllawddog, (St. Llawddog.)*
Bettws, C.
Llanycrwys, C.
Llandyfeisant, C.

BRECKNOCKSHIRE.

Garthbrengi, P.
Trallwng, P.
Llywel, V.—1 *Chapel, Rhydy-briw.*
Llanfaes, V.
Maesmynys, R.

Llanddewi Abergwesin,—chapel to Llangammarch (St. Cammarch.)
Llanwrtyd,—chapel to Llangammarch (St. Cammarch.)
Llanddewi'r Cwm, C.

RADNORSHIRE.

Heyop, R.
Whitton, R.
Llanddewi Ystrad Enni,—chapel to Llanbister (St. Cynllo.)
Cregruna, R.—1 *Chapel, Llanbadarn y Garreg, (St.Padarn.)*
Glascwm, V.—*2 Chapels, Colfa, (St. David;) and Rhiwlen, (St. David.)*

Colfa,—chapel to Glascwm (St. David.)
Llanddewi Fach,—chapel to Llywes (St. Meilig.)
Rhiwlen,—chapel to Glascwm (St. David.)

GLAMORGANSHIRE.

Llanddewi in Gower.

DIOCESE OF LLANDAFF.

GLAMORGANSHIRE.

Bettws,—chapel to Newcastle (St. Illtyd.)

Laleston,—chapel to Newcastle (St Illtyd.)

MONMOUTHSHIRE.

Llanddewi Sgyryd, R.
Llanddewi Rhydderch, V.
Llanddewi Fach, C.

Bettws,—chapel to Newport (St. Gwynllyw.)
Trostrey, alias Trawsdre, C.
Llangyniow, C. Qu. Llangyfyw?

DIOCESE OF HEREFORD.

HEREFORDSHIRE.

Kilpeck, C. (St. Mary & St. David.)
Dewchurch Magna, V.

Little Dewchurch,——chapel to Lugwardine (St. Peter.)

SUMMARY.

Pembrokeshire	- - - -	10	Glamorganshire - - - -	2
Cardiganshire	- - - -	7	Monmouthshire - - - -	6
Carmarthenshire	- - - -	8		—
Brecknock	- - - - -	8	Diocese of Llandaff - - -	8
Radnor	- - - - - -	8	Diocese of Hereford - - -	3
Glamorgan	- - - - - -	1		
		—		—
Diocese of St. David's	- -	42	Total - - - - - - -	53

Churches 40, Chapels 13.—53.

It is remarkable that there is not one church or chapel, dedicated to St. David, in the whole of North Wales. The nationality of these churches will not be questioned, as the person, to whom they are dedicated, was the tutelar Saint of the country. Their antiquity appears from the fact that they are dispersed without reference to the petty conquests, or to the towns of later ages; and as they are to be found, in a certain quarter, beyond the borders of the Principality, they belong to an era when its limits were more extensive than at present. Their foundation is popularly ascribed to St. David himself; but in order to shew whether any of them can advance a plausible claim to so early a date, they must be submitted to the same kind of examination as the preceding; and the test is the more necessary, because, from the circumstance of his being canonized by the Pope in the twelfth century, he was adopted into the Romish Calendar, and several churches may have been dedicated to his memory in later times. Four endowments, in the list, are of the first class, having a plurality of chapels dependent on them; seven more have one chapel each; and most of these subordinate chapels are dedicated to St. David himself, or to Welsh Saints, his contemporaries. The chapels dedicated to St. David, and, for that reason, allowed a place in the front of the list, are subject to churches attributed to the same person, or to other Welsh Saints of contemporary or older date. Their relative situation would therefore show that both churches and chapels where founded in an age, when indiscriminate dedications had not become customary; for, according to Ecton, only one* of the chapels, dedicated to St. David, is subordinate to a church dedicated to one of the Apostles, and this exception does not occur within the present limits of Wales. Out of the thirteen chapelries assigned to St. David, eleven are parochial,† being a larger proportion than appears in the lists of those of St. Mary, or St. Michael. But it may be urged against the antiquity of the beneficed churches, that only four out of forty have endowments of the first foundation. A review of the list, however, compared with a map of the country, and some knowledge of its localities, will show that the majority of these benefices do not stand singly in their situations, but are joined by two, and sometimes by three together. Thus Whitchurch is contiguous to St. David's, Llanuchllwydog and Llanychaer are adjoining parishes, and the same may be said of Maenor Deifi and Bridell. Henfynyw and Llanddewi Aberarth are contiguous; so are Trallwng and Llywel; Maesmynys and Llanddewi'r Cwm; as well as Glascwm and Cregruna. The number of benefices, which stand alone and without chapels, is therefore reduced to twenty. To proceed,

* Little Dewchurch, subject to Lugwardine, (St. Peter,) in the Diocese and county of Hereford.

† Ascertained from the Population Returns for 1831, printed by order of the House of Commons.

Brawdy and Whitchurch, though not contiguous, are nearer to each other than many detached chapelries. The same may be said of Henllan Amgoed and Llanddewi Felffre, and also of Llanddewi Brefi and Llanycrwys; Garthbrengi and Llanfaes are so situate with respect to each other,* that is probable they were first separated by the arrangements of the followers of Bernard Newmarch.† In Monmouthshire, Llanddewi Sgyryd and Llanddewi Rhydderch are near each other; as are also Trostre and Llangyniow; and the same rule will apply to the three churches in Herefordshire. The single churches which remain, are only nine; of which number, Prendergast, Hubberston, and Llanddewi in Gower, are situate in districts avowedly Flemish; so that it cannot be said what was the original extent of their endowments, and what churches might have been detached from them. Heyop and Whitton‡ are so situated, that there is reason to suppose they were once subordinate to the neighbouring church of Llangynllo: their churches are very small, and belong to a district which was one of the first to become subject to the Lords Marchers. Blaenporth, Cardiganshire, and Llanddewi Fach, Monmouthshire, may perhaps be ancient, but they afford no criterion to prove their antiquity.

* The author of the "History of Brecknockshire" (Vol. II. p. 147.) gives his reasons for the supposition that Llanfaes was originally a chapel under Llanddew, a parish which intervenes between it and Garthbrengi. He further supposes Llanddew to be an abbreviation of Llanddewi; but while the connexion between the several parishes is admitted, there are certain objections to his etymology, into which it is at present unnecessary to enter. (See Appendix.)

† A Norman adventurer, who took forcible possession of the county of Brecknock about A. D. 1090.

‡ The district around Whitton is included in the Survey of Domesday Book, and while the names of the surrounding churches are mentioned, that of Whitton is omitted; from which it may be inferred that the latter was founded after the Conquest, and the tract, assigned for its endowment, must have been taken from one of the adjoining parishes.

The almost uniform disposition of these churches in clusters is too remarkable to be the effect of accident. From the analogy of other cases, there is reason to suppose that the parishes of each cluster formed originally a single endowment, in support of one, or perhaps two churches, to which the rest served as so many chapels; and the supposition is confirmed from the analogy of Glascwm, and other districts, where the chapels are dedicated to the same Saint as the mother church. But great light may be borrowed from the testimony of Gwynfardd Brycheiniog, a Bard, who is stated to have lived between the years 1160 and 1230. In a poem composed by him in honour of Dewi, or St. David, and inserted in the Welsh Archaiology, Vol. I. page 270, occurs a passage, which is thus translated by Williams in his " Dissertation upon the Pelagian Heresy."—

> " Dewi* the great of Menevia, the wise sage ;
> And Dewi of Brefi near the plains ;
> And Dewi is the owner of the superb church of Cyfelach,
> Where there is joy and great piety.
> And Dewi owns the choir that is
> At Meidrym, a place affording sepulture to multitudes ;
> And Bangor Esgor ; and the choir of Henllan,
> Which is a place of fame for sheltering yews ;
> And Maenor Deifi, void of steep declivities ;
> And Abergwilly, containing mildness and modesty ;
> And fair Henfynyw, by the side of the Glens of Aeron,
> Fields prolific in trefoil, and oaks productive of acorns.

* The following is the original, adapted by Williams to the orthography now current in the principality.—

" Dewi mawr *Mynyw*, syw Sywedydd,   A *Bangor Esgor* ; a Bangelbyr *Henllan*,
A Dewi *Brefi*, ger ei broydd ;   Y sydd i'r clod-fan y clyd Ywydd ;
A Dewi bieu balch *lan Gyfelach*,   *Maenawr Deifi* di-orfynydd ;
Lle mae morach, a mawr grefydd.   *Abergwyli* bieu gwyl-wlydd ;
A Dewi bieu Bangelbyr y sydd   *Henfynw* deg o du glennydd Aeron,
Meidrym, le a'i mynwent i luossydd ;   Hyfaes ei meilliou, hyfes goedydd ;

Llanarth, Llanadneu, churches of the Patron Saint;
Llangadog, a privileged place, enriched by chiefs:
Llanfaes, a lofty place, shall not suffer by war;
Nor the church in Llywel from any hostile band;
Garthbrengi, the hill of Dewi, void of disgrace;
And Trallwng Cynfyn by the dales;
And Llanddewi of the Cross, with a new chancel;
And Glascwm, and its church by Glas Fynydd, (the
    green mountain,)
A lofty sylvan retreat, where sanctuary fails not;
The rock of Vuruna fair is here, and fair its hilly pros-
    pects;
And Ystrad-fynydd, and its uncontrouled liberty."

In these verses, the Bard considers St. David to be " the
owner" of twenty churches, fifteen of which are ascribed to
him in the foregoing list. But as not one of those enumerated
happens to be a chapelry, it is probable the Bard mentions
such out of every cluster as were endowed at the time the
poem was written, and the rest, being chapels, are omitted.
Thus the Cathedral church of St. David's, then called Mynyw
or Menevia, is mentioned without Whitchurch and Brawdy;
Llanddewi Brefi without its chapels; Maenor Deifi without
Bridell; Abergwyli without its chapels; and Henfynyw
without Llanddewi Aberarth. In the Brecknock cluster, the
churches are more numerous; and there are two in the cluster
of Radnorshire. But what is most remarkable is the fact, that
with the exception of Brecknock, his native district, the Bard
mentions nothing of the churches of those parts which, in that
or the preceding generation, had been occupied by the En-

Llanarth, Llan-adneu, llannau llywydd;   A Thrallwng Cynfyn ger y dolydd;
Llangadawg, lle breiniawg rannawg ri-   A Llanddewi y Croys, Llogawd newydd;
    hydd;   A Glascwm a'i eglwys ger glas fynydd,
Nis arfeidd rhyfel Llanfaes, lle uchel;   Gwydd-elfod aruchel, nawdd ni achwydd;
Na'r llan yn Llywel, gan neb lluydd;   Craig Furuna deg yma, teg ym mynydd;
Garthbrengt, bryn Dewi, digywilydd;   Ac Ystrad-fynydd, a'i ryddid rydd."

G

glish, Normans, and Flemings;—were they destroyed, or did
he omit them from patriotic indignation, because Dewi was
not then the owner of them? The multiplied number near
Brecon may be due to Bernard Newmarch, who, according to
the usual mode, may have subdivided the endowment, and
converted the chapels into churches; and even the Bard
alludes to certain circumstances of hostility, from which he
either hopes, or predicts, that the churches of Llanfaes and
Llywel should be spared. Gwynfardd ascribes also to St.
David the churches of Llangyfelach, Glamorganshire, Llanarth, Cardiganshire, and Llangadog, Carmarthenshire; but
if any dependence can be placed on the names of these
churches, the first and last must have had a double dedication. With respect to Llangadog this is highly probable, as
there is a place in the parish called Llwyndewi; but there
is evidence to the fact in the "Greefes of Rees Vachan of
Stratywy,"* printed in Latin and English at the end of Warrington's History of Wales, in which occurs the following
passage:—

"In the *church of S. Dauid, which they call Lhangadoc,* they
made stables, * * * * and took awaie all the goods of the
said church, and burning all the houses, wounded the preest
of the said church before the high altar, and left him there
as dead."

Cyfelach† was the name of the twenty second Bishop of
Llandaff, but whether Llangyfelach is so called from him, or

* Rees Vachan, or rather Rhys Fychan, was a chieftain of the Vale of
Towy, who, in the reign of Edward the First, presented to the Archbishop of Canterbury a statement of grievances, or acts of oppression
committed in his territories by the English.

† See Godwin, De Præsulibus Angliæ, who calls him "Cimeliauc,"
and states that he died A. D. 927. A chronicle in the Welsh Archaiology
(Vol. II. page 473,) states that he was killed in battle at Hereford A. D.
754; but this assertion is probably a mistake, as it is unsupported by the
testimony of three other chronicles in the same collection.

from another person, is doubtful, as he lived about three centuries after the era in which nearly all the Welsh Saints flourished; it is possible, however, that he either rebuilt the church, or enlarged its privileges: but the connexion of St. David with that place is more certain, for it is recorded by Giraldus Cambrensis, and Ricemarchus,* a still older authority, that he was the founder of the "Monastery of Llangyfelach in Gower." Browne Willis attributes Llanarth to St. Vystygy, which is, perhaps, an error, as the name does not occur elsewhere.† For the "Llanadneu" of Gwynfardd may be read Llanarthneu from Ecton's list, as it harmonizes admirably with the preceding word in the original, according to the laws of the metre; and there is no place in the Principality which bears the name of Llanadneu. By Henllan in Gwynfardd may be understood Henllan Amgoed, and not the chapel of that name subject to Bangor. Llanddewi y Crwys is Llanycrwys in Carmarthenshire, which, in the Charter of the Abbey of Talley, is called "Landewicrus." The rock of Vuruna, or Craig Furuna, is Cregruna in Radnorshire; and the order of succession would lead to the supposition, that by Ystrad Fynydd is meant the cluster in the neighbourhood of Builth. The cluster of Llanuchllwydog, being in the territory of the Lords of Cemmaes, is omitted‡. The clusters of Hereford and Abergavenny‡ were at that time subject to the Lacies, Lords of Ewyas, and the cluster of Trostrey‡ was probably in a similar situation.

* Ricemarchus, or Rhyddmarch, was Bishop of St. David's from A. D. 1088 to 1098. A Life of St. David by Giraldus, and fragments of another by Ricemarchus, are printed in the second volume of Wharton's Anglia Sacra.

† It has been remarked that modern fairs have, in many instances, succeeded to wakes or festivals; and, in support of the testimony of Gwynfardd, it may be stated that a fair is held at Llanarth on the twelfth of March, or St. David's Day, Old Style.

‡ Qu. Was not the circumstance of their being included in the Diocese of Llandaff, the reason of their omission?

The list compiled from Ecton is very imperfect, and use
has been made of it in order to shew that the inferences of
this Essay are drawn from premises generally acknowledged.
The list, as proposed to be amended, is as follows.—

The Cathedral of St. David's.
>Whitchurch, V. (St. David.) Brawdy, V. (St. David.)
Capel Gwrhyd; * *Capel Non* (St. Non.) *Capel Padrig*
(St. Patrick.) *Capel y Pistyll; Capel Stinan* (St. Justin-
ian.)

Llanuchlwydog, R.
>Llanychaer, R. (St. David.) Llanllawen chapel.

Maenor Deifi, R.
>Bridell, R. (St. David. *Cilfywyr chapel.*

Llanddewi Brefi, C.
>Llanycrwys, C. (St David.) Blaenpennal chapel (St. Da-
vid.) Capel Bettws Lleicu (St. Lucia.) Capel Gartheli
(St. Gartheli.) *Capel Gwenfyl* (St. Gwenfyl.)

Bangor Esgor, R.
>Henllan chapel (St. David.)

Henfynyw, C.
>Llanddewi Aberarth, P. (St. David.)

Llanarth, V.
>Llanina chapel (St. Ina.) *Capel Crist* (Holy Cross.)

Henllan Amgoed, R.
>Eglwys Fair a Churig (St. Mary & St. Curig, or Cyrique.)
Llanddewi Felffre, R. & V. (St. David.) *Henllan,* in the
parish of Llanddewi.

Meidrym, V.
>Llanfihangel Abercywyn, C. (St. Michael.)

Llanarthneu, P. & V.
>Llanlleian chapel ; *Capel Dewi* (St. David.)

Abergwyli, V.
>Llanpumsant (Sts. Celynin, Ceitho, Gwyn, Gwynno, and
Gwynnoro.) Llanllawddog (St. Llawddog.) Llanfihangel
Uwch Gwyli (St. Michael.) *Bettws Ystum Gwyli; Capel
Bach.*

Llangadog, V.
>Llanddeusant, (St. Simon & St. Jude.) Capel Gwynfai;
Capel Tydyst.

Llangyfelach, V.
>Llansamled, C.

---

* The chapels printed in Italics are decayed or extinct.

Garthbrengi, P.
Llanddew, C. (Holy Trinity.)   Llanfaes V. (St. David.)
St. Nicholas's church.

Llywel, V.
Trallwng, P. (St. David.)   Capel Rhydybriw ;   *Dolhywel**
(St. David.)

Maesmynys, R.
Llanynys, R. (St. David.)   Llanddewi'r Cwm, C. (St. David.)   Llanfair in Builth, C. (St. Mary.)

Glascwm, V.
Colfa chapel (St. David.)   Rhiwlen chapel (St. David.)

Cregruna, R.
Llanbadarn y Garreg chapel (St. Padarn.)   *Llannon* (St. Non.)

Llanddewi Sgyryd, R,
Llanddewi Rhydderch, R. (St. David.)

Rhaglan, or Ragland, V.† Monmouthshire.
Trostrey, or Trawsdre, C. (St. David.)   Llangyfyw.   Qu.

Dewchurch Magna, V. Herefordshire.
Little Dewchurch (St. David.)   Kilpeck, C. (St. David.)   Dewshall, V. (St. David.)   Callow, (St. Michael,) chapel to Dewshall.

Prendergast, R. in the country of the Flemings, chapels unknown.
Hubberston, R.   ditto
Llanddewi in Gower   ditto
Blaenporth, P.
Llanddewi Fach, C. Monmouthshire.
Llanthony, or Llanddewi Nant Honddu, C. Monmouthshire.‡

---

* The hamlet of Dolhywel is now included in the parish of Myddfai; but in the foundation Charter of Talley, the church is called, "Ecclesia sancti David de Dolhowel," as if it was formerly an independent benefice. It was situated on the confines of the parish of Llywel. (See Dugdale's Monasticon.)

† According to Browne Willis, Ragland is dedicated to St. Cadocus; but it is here assigned to St. David on the authority of Ricemarchus and Giraldus Cambrensis.

‡ Llandyfeisant, C. Carmarthenshire, is omitted in this list, as there are grounds for the supposition that it was so called from Tyfei, the nephew of St. Teilo. There was formerly a chapel, dedicated to St. David, in the castle of Dinefwr, in the same parish; which, in the Charter of Talley, is called " Ecclesia sancti David de Dinewr," and is mentioned separately from " Ecclesia de Lantevassan." The former, from the circumstance of

The chapels of St. David, subject to churches of other Saints, are also occasionally grouped.—

Llanddewi Abergwesin, Llanwrtyd, and another *Llanddewi* in ruins are subject to Llangammarch, (St. Cammarch,) Brecknockshire.

Bettws, and Laleston, subject to Newcastle, (St. Illtyd,) Glamorganshire.

Heyop, and Whitton, subject to Llangynllo, (St. Cynllo,) Radnorshire.

Llanddewi Ystrad Enni, to Llanbister, (St. Cynllo,) Radnorshire.

Capel Dewi, to Llanelly, (St. Ellyw,) Carmarthenshire.

Bettws, C. Carmarthenshire. The original parish church destroyed; dedication uncertain.

St. David's chapel, in the castle of Dinefwr, subject to Llandyfeisant, (St. Tyfei,) Carmarthenshire.

Capel Dewi, subject to Llandyssul, (St. Tyssul,) Cardiganshire.

Llauddewi Fach, chapel to Llywes, (St. Maelog,) Radnorshire.

Bettws, chapel to Newport, (St. Gwynllyw Filwr,) Monmouthshire.

This list, if its arrangements be correct, presents a series of extensive endowments; and it will readily be allowed that the churches, which, in the several groups, are considered as the parents of the rest, belong to a class of foundations the most ancient in the Principality. In what age, or by whom, these parent churches were endowed with the tithes of the surrounding districts is unknown; for none of the documents extant, which relate to the history of Wales, have recorded the event. But the precise period is immaterial to the present question, for the original church might have been supported by the offerings of the people long before a perpetual endowment was granted. The way is, therefore, clear for the belief, that the most ancient churches of Wales were founded by the persons to whom they are usually attributed; and the word "foundation" may be taken to mean the first erection of a

its being called "ecclesia," must have been a free chapel, or exempt from ordinary jurisdiction. (See the word "Chapel" in Burn's Ecclesiastical Law.)

building devoted to the purposes of religion, though some time may elapse before a revenue is appropriated for its maintenance. Chapels, on the contrary, were erected after the endowment became a vested right, for upon this principle, as already shown, depends the circumstance of their subordination. It will, therefore, follow that the chapels and subordinate churches, which are assigned to St. David, in the preceding list, were not founded by him, but dedicated to his memory after his decease; and though the distinction is not carefully observed in popular opinion, it may be stated in confirmation of the view here given, that, in the writings of the middle ages, specific mention occurs of only one of these chapels as founded by the Saint to whom it is ascribed. The instance alluded to is that of Colfa, subject to Glascwm, which Ricemarchus and Giraldus* describe as one of the Monasteries founded by St. David; but, as the passages in which it occurs are very corrupt, the statement may be a mistake. It is inconsistent with analogy, as well as with the testimony of Gwynfardd; but allowing its correctness, the solitary exception will not invalidate the general rule.

St. David is stated to have been canonized by Pope Calixtus, between A. D. 1119 and 1124; it might, therefore, be expected that churches were dedicated to his memory after that event; and also that, according to the practice with other Saints of the Romish Calendar, churches were called after his name in places which had no connexion with his history, the selection of the patron Saint being left arbitrarily to the founder of the building. His canonization appears, however, to have resulted from, rather than have caused the celebrity in which he was held by his countrymen; and upon the churches of Wales it appears to have had no further effect than perhaps to increase the number of his chapels; but numerous as these may be, it will be inferred, from the following considerations,

* Life of St. David, in Wharton's Anglia Sacra.

that the great majority of them are more ancient, and belong
to a time when arbitrary dedication was not the usual practice.
Many of them are dedicated to the same Saint as the mother
church; but this, it will be observed, is an extension of the
principle of subordination. The remainder are almost uni-
formly subordinate to churches of Welsh Saints of contemporary or older date. If it were the custom to build chapels
and dedicate them to St. David in later ages, they would be
found occasionally subordinate to Saints of a later generation,
or to those of the Romish Calendar; but such is not the case.
If it were the custom to dedicate churches to St. David as to
St. Peter, St. John, and others, it would be expected that they
were dispersed over the country indiscriminately; but, on the
contrary, they are strictly local, being grouped together in
certain districts, over which his personal influence must have
extended. In the six counties of North Wales there is not one
church that bears his name. In the original Diocese of Llandaff he has but two chapels, and only three in what is supposed to have been the original Diocese of Llanbadarn; all
the rest, including every one of the endowments, are in the
district of which, as Archbishop of Caerleon, or Menevia, he
was himself the Diocesan. The Cathedral of St. David's is
in the territory of his maternal grandfather, the neighbourhood of Henfynyw appears to have been the property of his
father, and Llanddewi Brefi is situated on the spot where he
refuted the Pelagian Heresy.

SECTION III.

General Observations on the Welsh Saints, as distinguished from those
of the Roman Catholic Church.

THE three Saints,[*] whose churches have been examined,
happen to be the best specimens that could have been selected
to represent so many classes of foundations; and it is hoped
the arrangement will not prove inconsistent with the testimony of ecclesiastical historians. The oldest churches in
Wales are called after the names of certain holy persons, who
are reputed to have been their founders; but a difficulty
presents itself in the question—to whom were they dedicated?
for their patron Saints are unknown, and it cannot be supposed that their founders would raise churches in honour of
themselves. The objection, that they must have been erected
to the memory of these persons after their decease, would
perhaps be admitted as insuperable, if it could not be shown
from authentic documents, that the belief current in the Principality since the eleventh century has been to the contrary.
The popular explanation is, that they were called after the
names of their founders, upon the principle that a house is

---

[*] The pre-eminence of these Saints did not escape the notice of Gwynfardd; the concluding lines of his poem are,—

"Cyfodwn, archwn arch ddlommedd,   Drwy eirioledd *Mair*, mam radlonedd,
Drwy eirioledd *Dewi*, a Duw a fedd.   A *Mihangel*, mawr ym mhob arfedd.
Gwae a nâd gwen-wlad gwedi masw-   Dychyfarfyddwn ei lu am ei lariedd;
    edd.   Dychyfarfyddwn ninnau am drugaredd."

H

frequently named after its builder; and if they never had any
other patron Saints, the inference naturally follows, that they
must have been founded before formal dedications were customary. It must have remained for the superstition of succeeding generations to dignify these founders with the title
of Saints; but, as they flourished in the fifth and sixth centuries, it may be urged that formal dedications were at that time
usually practised on the continent. The superstitions of
Britain, however, were those prevalent in the Catholic or
Universal Church in the fourth century; for shortly after the
commencement of the fifth, the communication between the
Britons and their continental neighbours was interrupted; so
that while the Catholic Church was inventing new ceremonies,
the Britons continued stationary; and in the seventh century
the discrepancy was so great, that the Christians of Wales
would hold no communion with the Saxons, who had adopted
the Roman ritual.* In Italy and the Eastern Empire, instances occur of churches formally named after Saints as early
as the time of Constantine; how rapidly this practice may
have spread westwards is uncertain; but Bede mentions two
churches so dedicated in Britain in the beginning of the fifth
century. The first is the church of St. Martin at Canterbury,
which however is intimated to have been built by the Romans
rather than the Britons.† The second is the church of Candida Casa, or Whithern, in Galloway, North Britain, dedicated
also to St. Martin; but it is stated that Ninia, its founder,
received his religious education at Rome, and it is added that
this church was built of stone contrary to the usual custom of
the Britons.‡ About A. D. 710, Naiton, king of the Picts,
upon conforming to the Romish ritual, desired that architects
should be sent him, to build a church of stone in his country
according to the fashion of the Romans, which he promised to

---

* Bede's Eccl. Hist.   † Ibid. Book I. Chap. 26.   ‡ Book III. Chap. 4.

dedicate to the prince of the Apostles, adding that thenceforward he and his people would adopt the customs of the holy Roman and Apostolic Church, so far as they could be learnt by persons so distant from the language and nation of Rome.* Though the Britons of Wales were not so remote from Rome as their brethren of Scotland, they persisted more obstinately in their non-conformity, and are described by Bede, in his own time, as celebrating the Passover without fellowship with the church of Christ.† The full amount of difference is not stated, but it is a satisfaction to remark that the historian does not charge them with errors of doctrine. That their religious ceremonies were conducted with a degree of. primitive simplicity might be expected from their poverty and seclusion. It is evident, however, that the churches of the Britons were built of wood, and covered with reeds, or straw ; and from the situation of their representatives in Wales, it would further appear that they were not formally dedicated to Saints. The grounds upon which this opinion rests are, that the churches, which from their endowments are shown to be the most ancient, have no other patron Saints than the persons alleged to have been their founders; the next in point of antiquity are called after St. Michael, the Archangel, being the first advance in the way of superstition; afterwards follow those dedicated to the Apostles and other Saints, still retaining certain marks of distinction. But not to depend entirely upon speculation, however well supported by existing circumstances, two passages in the writings of Bede will perhaps decide the question. The first is to the following effect.

" Aidan, the Bishop, having departed this life,‡ Finan, who had been ordained and sent by the Scots to succeed him in his Bishoprick, built, in the island of Lindisfarne, a church fit for an Episcopal See; which however, after the manner of the

* Bede, V. 21.   † Eccl. Hist. V. 21.
‡ A. D. 652.

Scots, he did not erect of stone, but of sawn timber, covering it with reeds. At a later time, it was dedicated by the most reverend Archbishop Theodore in honour of the blessed Apostle, Peter. But Eadbert, Bishop of that place, stripping off the reeds, covered the entire building, both roof and sides, with sheets of lead." (Eccl. Hist. III. 25.)

From this passage it is clear that Finan, who was a Christian of the British school, founded a church of cathedral rank without appointing a patron Saint; and though he presided over the See of Lindisfarne ten years, and was succeeded by Colman, one of his countrymen, it may be collected that four years intervened between the resignation of the latter and the arrival of Archbishop Theodore in Britain.*

The next passage is important, as it describes the mode of consecration practised by the Scots. It must be premised that the historian is speaking of Cedd, Bishop of the East Saxons,† to whom Oidivald, King of Deira, had given a spot of ground for the purpose of founding a Monastery.—

" The man of God, wishing by prayer and fasting to purge the place of its former pollution of wickedness, and so to lay the foundations of the Monastery, entreated the king that he would grant him the means and permission to dwell there, for that purpose, during the whole time of Lent, which was then at hand. In all the days of this time, except on the Sabbath, he always prolonged his fast, according to custom, until the evening; and even then he took only a small piece of bread, and one egg, with a little milk mixed with water. He said that this was the custom of those from whom he had learned a rule of regular discipline, that they should first consecrate with prayer and fasting those places which had been newly obtained for founding a Monastery, or church.

* Bede's Eccl. Hist. III. 25, 26, and IV. 2. The Saxon Chronicle translated by Dr. Ingram, A. D. 664 and 688.
† From A. D. 653 to 664.

When ten of the forty days were remaining, a person came, and summoned him to the king; but that the sacred work might not be discontinued on account of the king's business, he desired his presbyter, Cynibill, who was also his own brother, to complete the pious beginning; who having readily complied, and the exercise of fasting and prayer being completed, he (Cedd) built there a Monastery, which is now called Laestingaeu, and established it with religious customs, according to the practice of Lindisfarne, where he had been educated. After he had held his Bishoprick for many years in the aforesaid province, and by appointing superintendents had conducted also the management of this Monastery; it happened that he arrived at the Monastery about the time of his mortality, and, being taken with infirmity of body, he died. He was at first buried without; but in process of time, when a church was built of stone in the Monastery, in honour of the blessed Mother of God, his body was laid within, at the right side of the altar." (Eccl. Hist. III. 23.)

This mode of consecration was so different from that practised in the Romish Church, that Bede thought proper to describe it at length; and from the analogy of their situation, it may be presumed that the practice of the southern Britons was similar. No patron Saint is mentioned, and the church of stone, in honour of the Virgin, was not built until after the death of the original founder of the Monastery. If the consecration of a place depended upon the residence of a person of presumed sanctity, who for a given time should perform certain religious exercises upon the spot, it will at once appear how the Primitive Christians of Wales were, at first, the founders, and afterwards, in default of the usual mode of dedication, were considered to be the Saints of the churches which bear their names.

In the Eastern Empire, the invocation of angels commenced so early that the Council of Laodicea had occasion to condemn it in A. D. 366. It was a more easy deflection from the purity –

of Christianity than the invocation of Saints ; the latter, however, soon followed ; but the custom of dedicating churches to
them arose from purely local circumstances. About the end
of the fourth century, it was a practice to erect a church in
memory of a martyr over his grave. St. Augustine, who died
A. D. 430, says,—" We do not erect temples to our martyrs,
as if they were Gods ; but memories as to dead men, whose
spirits live with God." This extract is given on the authority
of Bishop Burnet in his Exposition of the twenty second
Article, who in a preceding part of the same Exposition
says,—

"It was a remnant both of Judaism and Gentilism, that the
souls of the martyrs hovered about their tombs, called their
memories; and that therefore they might be called upon and
spoke to there. St. Basil, and the other Fathers, that do so
often mention the going to their memories, do very plainly
insinuate their being present at them, and hearing themselves
called upon. This may be the reason, why among all the
Saints that are so much magnified in that age,* we never find
the blessed Virgin so much as once mentioned. They knew
not where her body was laid, they had no tomb for her, no,
nor any of her relicks or utensils. But upon the occasion of
Nestorius's denying her to be the *Mother of God,* and by carrying the opposition to that too far, a superstition to her was
set on foot, it made a progress sufficient to balance the slow-
ness of its beginning; the whole world was then filled with
very extravagant devotions for her."

If this view of the learned Prelate be correct, the churches
generally founded in the fourth century were those called by
ecclesiastical historians "martyria," or "memoriæ martyrum."†
They were necessarily confined to the spot where the Saint
was buried, in honour of whom, therefore, only one church of

* The fourth century.
† Bingham's Antiquities of the Christian Church, VIII. Chap. 1. Section 8.

this description could be erected. The custom would, however, lead to the erection of churches to the memory of Saints
in other indifferent places; and the belief, that martyrs could
hear themselves called upon over their graves, would lead to
the practice of invocation generally. But the concurrence of
the view, here taken, with the preceding arrangement of
Welsh foundations, is most obvious in the late introduction of
the homage of St. Mary. The heresy of Nestorius occupied
the attention of the Church, in the East, from the third
General Council at Ephesus A. D. 431 to the fourth General
Council at Chalcedon A. D. 451. Sufficient time must be allowed for the spread of these superstitions, and they would
hardly reach Britain before most churches of the earliest
foundation were built. The secluded state of the Britons, and
their refusal to submit to the authority of the Pope, inter-
posed a further delay, until long after the conversion of the
Saxons.*

To the class of St. David belong all the foundations of
churches erected by the Primitive Christians of Wales, from
the earliest period to the middle of the seventh century. The
mean peirod of their establishment is from the year 500 to 550.

---

* In the works of the "Cynfeirdd," or Primitive Bards, the second
person in the Trinity is often called "mab Mair," or the son of Mary;
which would indicate the side the Britons would have taken in the Nes-
torian controversy if it had reached them. But in the poems, which,
there is reason to suppose from their style, were written before the year
900, the *intercession* of the Virgin is mentioned only in an ode the author
of which is not known. (Myvyrian Archaiology, Vol. I. pp. 187, 188.)
Her name is spoken of in terms expressive of superstition in three other
poems which have been attributed to the earlier Bards, but the language
in which they are composed is too modern to allow them to be genuine.
(Myv. Archaiol. Vol. I. pp. 16, 26, 552.) In the Ecclesiastical History
of Bede, the Virgin does not occupy the pre-eminent situation to which
she afterwards attained; the favourite Saint of the Anglo-Saxons, in the
infancy of their Church, being St. Peter.

Their general antiquity may be shown by the methods of proof already employed, and accords well with the notion that they were founded by the persons to whom they are ascribed, who are also ascertained to have lived principally in the fifth and sixth centuries. Very few of these persons have been admitted into the Romish Calendar; and, if credit be given to the authority of the Welsh Triads, only six of them were canonized.* They also differ from Roman Catholic Saints in one important particular, that few of them have been dignified with the title of martyr. They lived at a time when Christianity was the common religion of their country; and if some individuals of their number met with a violent death, it appears to have been at the hands of the enemies of their nation rather than their faith. That they were men of holy lives is recorded in all the scanty accounts which remain respecting them; and it is evident that many of them made a formal profession of religion according to the system of Monachism prevalent in the early ages of Christianity. But the character, in which, more especially, their names have been handed down to posterity, is that of founders of churches. Many of them had more than ordinary opportunities of conferring this blessing upon their country; for they were related to its chieftains, and the churches they founded were often situate within the territories of the head of their tribe. Others, not so fortunate as to birth, are ascertained to have founded churches in places connected with ther own history, and probably they depended upon their influence with some neighbouring chieftain. In nearly all cases, the assumption of their names, so far from depending upon chance, is attributable to local causes.

The second class of foundations, or those dedicated to St. Michael, commenced when the Britons were beginning to

* Cambrian Biography, *vocibus* Gwrthefyr, & Teilo.

conform to the religious observances of their neighbours, and the mean period of their establishment may, for various reasons, be assigned to the time from A. D. 800 to 850. Shortly before this period, it is recorded that the affairs of the Church made unusual progress. Charlemagne had established the civil obligation of tithes over his dominions in France, Germany, and Italy; and a similar ordinance had been passed by Offa in England. It is probable that the example of these might so far have had effect upon the people of Wales, as to cause generally the erection of churches in places not yet supplied with them, and to assign for their maintenance the tithes of lands not appropriated by previous endowments. This notion, though highly probable, is only a supposition; but it is recorded, that in the latter part of the eighth century the Welsh were brought gradually into communion with the Church of Rome, for during the time the primitive founders flourished the British Church was independent. The first public act, which acknowledged a submission to the Papal See, has been thought to have been the resignation of his kingdom by Cadwaladr, that he might make a pilgrimage to the eternal city, where it is said he died in 688. But great obscurity seems to hang over the accounts of this performance; and as this, and other actions in the life of that Prince, are related in almost the same words of his contemporary, Ceadwalla, King of the West Saxons, who died at Rome in that year, there is reason to believe that the monkish historians[*] have confounded the one with the other. It is clear, however, that the Welsh did not conform to the Romish time of the celebration of Easter till the year 755. The Britons had been accustomed to calculate this festival from a cycle, according to which it was generally held a week earlier than it was observed at Rome; and the subject, though trifling in itself, was considered to be of such importance that it was made the test

[*] Walter de Mapes, Geoffrey of Monmouth, and their followers.

I

of difference, and those who refused to adopt the Romish computation were deemed without the pale of the Catholic Church.*
In 755, Elfod, or Elbodius, became Archbishop of Bangor.
A modern writer† states that he was appointed by the Pope ;
and though the assertion is not supported by a reference to
authority, the circumstance is by no means improbable. Upon
his accession, he induced the people of North Wales to adopt
the Romish cycle. The Bishops of South Wales, however,
refused to comply ; in consequence of which the Saxons in-
vaded their country, and a battle was fought at a place called
Coed Marchan, in which the Welsh gained an honourable
victory.‡ What further measures were taken is not recorded,
but in 777 the time of Easter was altered in South Wales.§
In this state it appears to have continued until the death of
Elbodius in 809, when the South-Welsh Bishops refused
to acknowledge the authority of his successor.|| The con-
troversy of the celebration of Easter was again renewed,
and though it is not stated how soon it subsided into compliance with the Romish computation, there is reason to
suppose that the Welsh were still slow to surrender their
ancient custom.*

Those Welsh Chronicles, which are generally deemed authentic, commence about A. D. 700 ; and it is to be regretted,

* Bede's Eccl. Hist. *passim.*

† Warrington ; in his account of the Church at the end of the "History
of Wales."

‡ Brut y Tywysogion, or Chronicle of the Princes, the second copy,
Archaiology of Wales, Vol. II. page 473.

§ Archaiology of Wales, Vol. II. p. 474.

|| Ibid. Vol. II. pp. 474, 475.

* The following is extracted from Hughes's Horæ Britannicæ.—" We
find in the Greek life of St. Chrysostom, that certain clergymen, who
dwelt in the isles of the ocean, repaired from the utmost borders of the
habitable world to Constantinople, in the days of Methodius, (who was

that, for the first century after their commencement, they are
so brief that they afford but few *data* for tracing the progress
of superstition. But the introduction of the custom of dedicating churches to Saints, after the Catholic method, would
have been so remarkable an innovation that it could hardly
pass unobserved. Accordingly, in two of these Chronicles,
the following curious notices occur. In Brut y Tywysogion,
or the Chronicle of the Princes, it is stated that between
A. D. 710 and 720 "a church of Llanfihangel was consecrated;" and in Brut y Saeson, or the Chronicle of the Saxons, it
is said "in 717 was consecrated a church of Michael."* Neither of the Chronicles offers any further explanation, but as
there is no church of St. Michael in Wales of eminence sufficient to deserve this special notice, the most rational interpretation of the record is, that the church alluded to was the
first, in the Principality, dedicated to the Archangel, and the
date alleged occurs at a time when such a circumstance might
reasonably be expected.

It must not, however, be denied that in the works of
Bards who flourished before A. D. 700, some traces may be
found of the corruptions of Christianity; for to state, that the
Welsh Church was entirely free from them, would be an
assertion which it would be impossible to maintain. But
these traces are slight. Allusions to religious subjects are
very frequent, and it would appear that some respect was paid
to the memory of Saints; but on the supposition that *all* the

patriarch there, from the year 842 to 847,) to enquire of *certain eccles-*
tical traditions, and the perfect and exact computation of Easter. It is
to be inferred from hence, that as there can be no doubt that the British
isles are referred to, that the disputes respecting Easter were not yet laid
to rest; and that our Britons, not being satisfied with the determination of
the Pope of Rome, resorted to the decision of the bishop of Constantinople." (Vol. II. p. 317.)

    * Archaiology of Wales, Vol. II. p. 300.   † Ibid. Vol. II. p. 471.

poems ascribed to that age are genuine,* a point which is
more than questionable, the intercession of Saints is noticed
only three times ; namely, once respectively in two compositions which an ancient MS. attributes, with an expression
of doubt, to Taliesin ; and the third instance occurs in a poem,
ascribed in the Archaiology of Wales to the same author, but
since acknowledged to be modern.† The oldest composition,
in which the *Welsh* Saints are spoken of superstitiously, is
attributed to Golyddan, a contemporary of Cadwaladr, near
the close of the period in question.

The dedication of churches to St. Michael, doubtless, led
the way to the erection of others in honour of St. Peter and
the rest of the Apostles, which were founded as occasions
required them until modern times. In arranging the latter,
those, which from the nature of their endowments show that
they have some claim for consideration on the score of antiquity, may be ranked in the same class with the former ; and
the list may also include those dedicated to St. John the
Baptist, St. Stephen, and St. Mary Magdalene, as well as the
older churches of St. Mary the Virgin.‡ But the churches

---

* The number in the Archaiology of Wales is upwards of a hundred,
and those which are spurious may be distinguished from the rest by the
modern style in which they are written.

† The acknowledgment is made by one of the editors of the Archaiology, who thus explains the rule observed during its publication.—

"The editors of the Myvyrian Archaiology were bound to give to the
world all the pieces, whatever their origin, which were ascribed to the
poets whose works were comprised in that collection, leaving it to the
critic to elucidate the various styles, and pronounce upon the authenticity
of the productions—this department was not within the scope of their
undertaking." (Dr. Owen Pughe, in the Cambrian Quarterly Magazine,
Vol. V. p. 109 & 204.) The first two poems, alluded to above, are inserted
in the Archaiology, Vol. I. pp. 76—77 and 169—170, and the last in p. 83
of the same Volume.

‡ The time when the dedication of churches to the Virgin first commenced in Wales cannot be ascertained ; but the earliest instance upon

dedicated to the Apostles, in Wales, are not many; and of those enumerated by Ecton, nearly one half can be shown to have had Welsh Saints for their original founders.

The mean period of the erection of churches of the last foundation is the twelfth century. To this class belong, besides the remainder of the Apostolic churches, all such as are dedicated to inferior Saints of the Roman Catholic Calendar, such as St. Nicholas, St. Lawrence, &c. which were erected principally by foreign adventurers. But the great preponderance at this period of churches dedicated to St. Mary,* may in some degree be attributed to the Cistercian monks, whose order was the most prevalent in Wales; and it was a rule of the fraternity that their religious houses should be dedicated to the Virgin.†

As formal dedication in honour of Saints was not the original custom of the Welsh, the question which remains is, the era of those *chapels* which have been built in honour of natives of Wales; that they are ancient may be shown from the fact that the great majority of them are parochial, and few of them are subject to churches dedicated to the Apostles and other Saints whose homage was introduced at a later period. When the Welsh began to honour Saints after the Catholic method, they would naturally direct their attention to those who deserved that respect among their own countrymen. But it appears to have been under certain limitations; and compared with the Apostles, and other celebrated names, the holy men

record is that of a church, near the Cathedral of Bangor, which was founded, in honour of St. Mary, in A. D. 973, by Edgar, King of England. (Wynne's History of Wales,—Beauties of North Wales, p. 443.)

* An examination of the poems of the Welsh Bards, in the order in which they stand in the Myvyrian Archaiology, will show that St. Mary began to receive distinguished attention about A. D. 1200, which preeminence appears to have continued until the Reformation. Vol. I. pp. 315, 324.

† Tanner's Notitia Monastica.

of Wales could only rank as saints of an inferior class. To regard the founders in the character of tutelar Saints of their respective churches was an obvious mode of proceeding; but in the establishment of new foundations preference would be given to Saints of more extensive reputation; and the only edifices, erected in honour of Welshmen, would be chapels in places where they had lived, or subject to churches connected with their history. In other countries where the Romish Church has prevailed, many persons who never were canonised have been allowed the honours of sanctity in their immediate neighbourhood, and in this local character the saints of Wales must be considered. Accordingly many of the chapels called after Welshmen are found to be dedicated to the Saint of the mother church, to his relatives, or to persons whom tradition has connected with the place; and the prevalence of known cases of the last kind is sufficiently great to justify a similar inference being drawn where the tradition has been entirely forgotten. Chapels of this description must generally have been erected while the memory of their Saints was comparatively recent, and may therefore be deemed coeval with churches of the second foundation. The perishable nature of tradition, and the occupation of several parts of Wales by foreigners will sufficiently explain why no material increase was afterwards made to their number.

That the Roman Catholics, or, at least, the various conquerors of Wales, all of whom professed that religion, hardly considered the primitive founders in the light of Saints, will further appear from the circumstance that in many instances they gave their churches a new dedication. To show how far the practice prevailed the following list is adduced.

St. David's Cathedral, Pembrokeshire, St. David and St. Andrew.
Stainton, Pembrokeshire, (St. Kewill in the Monasticon,) St. Peter.
Stackpool Elider, Pembrokeshire, St. Elider, St. James.
Llantoni, Monmouthshire, St. David, St. John the Baptist.
Llanveuno, Herefordshire, St. Beuno, St. Peter.

- Llansilloe, Herefordshire, St. Tyssilio, St. Peter.
Llangathen, Carmarthenshire, St. Cathen, St. Michael and All Saints.
St. Thomas, alias St. Dogmael's, Pembrokeshire.
Northop, (Llaneurgain,) Flintshire, St. Eugain, St. Peter.
Llangynyw, Montgomeryshire, St. Cynyw, All Saints.
Llanegryn, Merionethshire, St. Egryn, St. Mary.
Llandaff Cathedral, Glamorganshire, St. Teilo and St. Peter.
Llanbleddian, Glamorganshire, St. Bleiddian, St. John the Baptist.
Llanfabon, Glamorganshire, St. Mabon, St. Constantine.
Dynstow, or Dyngestow, Monmouthshire, St. Dingad, St, Mary.
Llangyniow, Monmouthshire, St. Cynyw, St. David.
Kilpeck, Herefordshire, St. David and St. Mary.

It is not necessary to extend the list further, but the hypothesis must depend upon the supposition that Ecton is correct in assigning those dedications which differ from the Welsh names of the churches, or from the known history of their founders. It can, however, be verified in certain cases. For instance, the church of Llantoni, which was originally founded by St. David and called after his name, is now stated to be dedicated to St. John the Baptist. But in A. D. 1108, a Priory of Black Canons was built on the spot, by Hugh Lacy, to the honour of St. John the Baptist, which accounts for its present dedication. The second dedication of the two Cathedrals is well attested. And of all the religious houses founded in Wales since the tenth century, not one, except perhaps the Collegiate church of Llanddewi Brefi, was dedicated to a Welshman.

The Romish Church was however determined to have its martyrology of Britain; and out of "Cressy," the Catholic historian of this kingdom, may be enlisted about a hundred British Saints and Martyrs, from the first dawn of Christianity to the close of the sixth century. A few only of their names are to be found in the Welsh accounts, and as for the rest, persons acquainted merely with the history of Wales might well wonder from whence they came. Their legends, however,

were at one time regularly read, and their martyrdoms duly
commemorated in the Catholic Church. They are not so
much distinguished for the churches they founded, as for their
miracles and the sufferings they underwent for the spread of
the Gospel. They claim for their names a most remote antiquity, prior to the age of the Welsh founders; but it will be
no part of this Essay to substantiate their pretensions, or
indeed to maintain their existence. It will therefore be deemed sufficient to append to these pages a list of them, chronologically disposed, according to Cressy.

The catalogue of founders is less pretending, and has reference generally to a later period; and though the persons
contained in it have been dignified from an early time with
the title of Saints by their grateful countrymen, there are
but few notices in the Welsh language of miracles performed
by them.* Such marvellous relations as exist were nearly all
of them written in Latin, and from the silence of the Welsh
Bards upon the subject it may be presumed they were better
known abroad than at home. It will be allowed that these
legends were the productions of the monks, if they were not
of foreign manufacture. The accounts of renowned Britons,
current in Cornwall and Armorica, and in England and
France generally, have been more extravagant than in Wales.
In the latter country, Lucius, Merlin, Arthur, and St. David

---

* The poem ascribed to Golyddan is the oldest composition in which
it is intimated that a Welsh Saint wrought miracles; and, if it were
genuine, it would prove, that in about a century after the death of
St. David, a belief was current that he was possessed of miraculous
powers. There is, however, sufficient evidence to prove that the poem,
though ancient, was written after the time of Golyddan, (A. D. 660,) but it
is not necessary to enter into the question, as, at the period alluded to, the
era of the Welsh Saints was passing by, and had nearly terminated.
Mr. Sharon Turner, in his "Vindication of the Ancient British Poems,"
p. 269, supposes the composition of Golyddan to have been written in the
eighth century.

are reduced to reasonable dimensions. The grand parent of these absurdities, the Chronicle of Geoffrey of Monmouth, with its long line of British Trojan kings, is acknowledged to have been borrowed from Armorica. There are, it is true, a few stories current in the mouths of the peasantry, but the fact that they never have been written, is a proof that the Bards of the middle ages did not think them worthy of credit. It is, however, not an unlikely supposition that these stories were derived from such accounts as the monks would take care to publish.

In a subject so likely to be mixed up with fable as the history of Saints, it is of the greatest importance to ascertain what accounts relative to the Saints of Wales may be depended upon as true. The Welsh authorities, upon which the greatest reliance has been placed, are the catalogues or genealogies, usually called " Bonedd," or "Achau y Saint." The fondness of the Welsh for pedigrees has always been acknowledged, and genealogies are a species of record in which, owing to the complicated nature of the details, forgery is most easily detected. Owing to intermarriages and descents from a common ancestor, family connexions are so interwoven, that a variety of pedigrees, derived from different sources, would be contradictory unless their statements were true. To record these affinities, while they were well known, was the office of an order of Bards called "Arwyddfeirdd" or Heralds; a great part of whose multifarious productions have survived the ravages of time, and a fair specimen of them may be seen in Jones's History of Brecknockshire. It is not likely that such persons would neglect the genealogy of the founders of churches, related as so many of them were to the chieftains of the country. Accordingly a variety of catalogues of Saints, with their more immediate ancestors, have been collected from different sources and apparently in different parts of the Principality. Two only of these catalogues have been published. The first, called "Bonedd Saint Ynys

K

Prydain,"* is inserted in the Welsh Archaiology, where it is
professed to have been taken from the book of Hafod Ychh-
dryd. Its orthography is ancient, and from the names it
contains it would appear to have been formed in Cardiganshire.† The second is also published in the same Archaiology, under the name of "Bonedd, neu Achau Saint Ynys
Prydain,"‡ being a collection by Lewis Morris from various
old MSS. in North Wales, some of which are still in
existence.§ There is also a third catalogue which has not
been printed in an entire form, but a great part of its
contents have been made known to the world in detached
notices. It is styled "Achau Saint Ynys Prydain,"|| and
gives a more full account of such Saints as lived in Siluria, where it seems to have been collected. Each of these
catalogues contains a variety of detail not to be found in the
others ; but they also contain a great many names in common,
and, in treating of them, their statements are seldom so con-
flicting but that they may be reconciled. With the exception
of some interesting historical notices in the Silurian record,
the information they supply is but meagre ; but it is so far

---

* " The Gentility of the Saints of the Isle of Britain."
† A short list of Saints, without reference to their genealogy, has been
published in the Cambrian Register, Vol. III. p. 219. It appears to have
originated in Cardiganshire, but it is perfectly distinct from the above, and
contains a few curious notices not to be found elsewhere.
‡ " Gentility, or Pedigrees of the Saints of the Isle of Britain."
§ The MSS. consulted by Lewis Morris, amounting to nine in number,
are specified in the Welsh Archaiology, Vol. II. p. 26.
|| The attention of the public was first directed to this catalogue by the
late Mr. Edw. Williams, the distinguished antiquary of Glamorganshire,
by whom it was transcribed from a MS. written, about A. D. 1670, by
Thomas ab Ievan of Tre-bryn in the same county. As this appears to be
one of the most interesting of the Welsh records, its publication, accompanied with various readings and additions from other MSS. known to
exist in the same part of the Principality, is a desideratum which it is
hoped will not long be left unsupplied.

valuable that it is capable of chronological arrangement. If the period, when any one mentioned in the list is said to have flourished, be known, the usual computation of thirty three years to a generation, or a century to three generations, will assign within reasonable limits the era of his kindred both ascending and descending.* And if any one of another line be found contemporary with either of these, the same computation will avail with sufficient accuracy to determine the order of succession. The circumstances of their history may next be collected together, and embodied forth from other sources of information. The principal of these are the Triads, a species of record not to be relied upon implicitly, but deserving of consideration as they give a fair representation of such traditions, relating to the history of the Welsh nation, as existed prior to the inventions of the monks. Some collateral testimony may also be derived from the poetry of the Welsh Bards, though, as already observed, there are few allusions to Saints in poems which are of early date. The Romish legends will be used but sparingly, and only when their statements are within the verge of probability.

* In forming an artificial chronology, computation by generations is much more satisfactory than by a succession of kings, whose reigns for various reasons are of uncertain duration. Sir Isaac Newton objects to the chronology of the kings of Rome, and other ancient nations, upon the plea that the reigns, averaging at about thirty five years each, are too long; and the following is the result of his observations after a careful examination of different authorities.—

"Generations from father to son may be reckoned one with another at about thirty three or thirty four years apiece, or about three generations to a hundred years; but if the reckoning proceed by the eldest sons, they are shorter, so that three of them may be reckoned at about seventy five or eighty years; and the reigns of kings are still shorter, because kings are succeeded not only by their eldest sons, but sometimes by their brethren, and sometimes they are slain or deposed; and succeeded by others of an equal or greater age, especially in elective or turbulent kingdoms." (Remarks prefixed to Hooke's History of Rome.)

Where the materials of history are scanty, the deficiency may, in part, be supplied by existing monuments, provided they are sufficiently numerous to allow of inferences being drawn upon fair principles of induction; and in support of the genealogies it may be stated, that the order of succession deduced from them is, to a certain extent, observable in the arrangement of churches. As the chapels called after Welsh Saints have been dedicated to them for local reasons, so it is found that they are named after relatives, or contemporaries, possibly companions, of the founder of the mother church; and where this is not the case, they are dedicated to persons of a *later* generation, who perhaps enlarged the foundation, or were distinguished ministers at the place. The occasional recurrence of the same names together is also a circumstance which could not have happened, unless some connexion, of the nature alluded to, originally subsisted between them. On the other hand, chapels are but seldom dedicated to persons of a generation *earlier* than the founder, for the first Saint who resided in the district was the most likely to establish its place of worship; persons, however, of the generation immediately preceding may be deemed contemporary, for a great part of their lives may have been concurrent. The few chapels, named after native Saints, which are subject to churches dedicated to the Apostles, are of a date comparatively modern; and, with others founded at a similar period, may be known by the technical appellatives of "Capel" and "Bettws," in contradistinction to " Llan," which in an earlier age was applied to churches and chapels indiscriminately.

SECTION IV.

To proceed chronologically with the notices of such Saints as are to be found in the Welsh accounts, the commencement should be made with the introduction of the Gospel into Britain.

The credit of this glorious work has been claimed for the Apostles—St. Peter, St. Paul, St. James, and Simon Zelotes, as well as for Joseph of Arimathea; but without entering further into the subject, it will be sufficient to observe that the Welsh records and traditions are silent as to their pretensions, and their claims must rest upon the support they receive from testimonies in other languages. According to the Triads,* and more especially the Silurian copies of Achau y Saint, the blessed instrument was " Bran ab Llyr," the father of Caradog or Caractacus. It is said that he and his son were betrayed to the Romans through the treachery of Aregwedd Foeddog, generally understood to be Cartismandua. He was detained at Rome as a hostage for his son seven years, and by this means obtained an opportunity of embracing the Christian faith. Upon his return, he brought with him three, or according to others, four teachers of the names of Ilid, Cyndaf, Arwystli Hen, and Mawan; and through their instrumentality the Gospel was first preached in this country. Such is the collective statement of the Welsh authorities, and it is so far plausible, that Stillingfleet, without being aware of this testi-

* Triads 18 and 35, Third Series, Myv. Archaiol. Vol. II.

mony, conjectured that a similar circumstance was likely
to have taken place.* If the account were correct, the return
of Bran must have happened in A. D. 58, allowing seven years
to elapse from the capture of Caractacus, which occurred in
A. D. 51.† It is, however, beset with difficulties which it is
to be feared are insurmountable. In the first place, Tacitus,
who mentions the capture or surrender of the several members
of the family of Caractacus, and describes the appearance of
the same persons *seriatim* before the Emperor Claudius,‡ says
nothing of Bran. When the historian particularizes twice the
wife, daughter, and brothers of the captive chieftain, the
omission of so important a personage as his father affords a
strong presumption that he was not at Rome, and had not
been taken prisoner. If an attempt were made to account for
the omission, it would be met by another difficulty. Dion
Cassius states that the father of Caractacus§ was Cunobelinus,
who died before the war with the Romans had commenced,
and was succeeded in his kingdom by two sons, of whom
Caractacus was one, the name of the other being Togodumnus.
The latter testimony precludes the possibility of Bran being
Cunobelinus under another name; and would imply that
Caractacus was not originally a chieftain of Siluria, but of the
Trinobantes in the neighbourhood of London, where he is
said to have fought a battle with the Romans in the first year
of their invasion. In the ninth year following‖ he was taken

* Origines Britannicæ.

† Tacitus's Annals, XII. 17.

‡ Ibid. Annals, XII. 35 and 36.

§ Dio, or Dion Cassius composed his History of Rome in Greek; and,
according to the usual practice, altered the name of Caractacus to Katara-
takos, to accommodate it to the sound of the language in which he wrote.
(Lib LX.)

‖ "Nono post anno, quam bellum *in Britannia* cœptum." (Taciti
Annales, Lib. XII. cap. 36.)

prisoner, having opposed the Roman arms the whole of the interval, in the latter part of which the war had reached the Silures.

In a conflict with classical historians the Welsh traditions must give way, and if the foregoing prove a correct interpretation of the meaning of Tacitus and Dion Cassius, the claims of Bran ab Llyr to be considered the founder of Christianity in Britain must be surrendered. That traditions which relate to so early a period as the first and second century should prove inaccurate might be expected; but as they may have originated in an obscure notion of facts, they are deserving of respect, and should not be relinquished without a careful examination. That the story of Bran is not a modern forgery is clear, as the inventor would have taken care to avoid the difficulties presented by classical writers, which, if he were unacquainted with the original languages, he could have learnt from various histories of England. The Triads which support it, are professed to be taken originally from the Book of Caradog of Llancarfan,* who died in A. D. 1156; so that the opinion may have been current in Wales before the publication of the romance of Geoffrey of Monmouth. When these and other Triads were first written does not appear; but as they relate principally to circumstances which took place in the sixth century, most of them must have been formed after that time. They, however, belong to different dates, being a method of arranging ancient traditions together, as they occurred to the mind of the inventor; and as they are insulated compositions, the incorrectness of some of them does not necessarily affect the authenticity of the rest. If Bran were the first British Christian, it might be expected that the Bards of the sixth century would celebrate him in that character. The only poem of that era in which his name occurs, is attributed to Taliesin, in which he is alluded to as the hero of a mytho-

* Myv. Archaiology, Vol. II. p. 75.

logical story or romance now extant.* After this there is no
mention of his name in an authenticated composition until the
twelfth century, when he is described by Cynddelw as a distinguished warrior.† The weight of evidence would show
that if the Triads, which relate to his character as a Saint,
were as ancient as the twelfth century, they were then comparatively recent and not generally received.

Bran, on account of the supposed introduction of Christianity, has had the epithet of " Bendigaid" or Blessed attached to
his name; and in the Triads he is classed with Prydain and
Dyfnwal, as one who consolidated the form of elective sovereignty in Britain.‡ Nothing further is related of him, except
as the subject of romance. In the "Mabinogion," or Juvenile
Tales, is described an expedition of Bran to Ireland to re-
venge an insult offered to his sister, Bronwen, by Matholwch,
the Irishman. From this expedition, only seven returned,
after having destroyed nearly all the people of the country;
and Bran, being mortally wounded, ordered his companions
who survived to carry his head to be interred in the White Hill
in London, as a protection against all future invasions, so long

* "Bum i gan Vran yn Iwerddon." (Kerdd am Veib Llyr ab Brych-
wel. Myv. Archaiology, Vol. I. p. 66. See also Turner's Vindication,
p. 284.)

† "Rhudd ongyr Bran fab Llyr Llediaith,
    Rhwydd ei glod o gludaw anrhaith."

The bloody spears of Bran, the son of Llyr Llediaith,
Of unrestrained fame as the bearer of the spoil.

                                    Myv. Archaiol. Vol. I. p. 212.

"Rhybu Fran fab Llyr, llu rwymadur mad,
    Ynghamp, ynghywlad, ynghâd, ynghûr."

Bran the son of Llyr has been,—the excellent commander of the host,
In the games, in the assembly of the country, in battle, in anxious care.
                                    Ibid. Vol. I. p. 248.

‡ No. 36, Third Series, and Cambrian Biography voce Bran.

as it remained there.* It was afterwards removed by Arthur, who would not have this island defended by other means than his own prowess.†

Ilid and Cyndaf, the reputed companions of Bran from Rome, are said to have been "men of Israel," which would imply that they were converted Jews; while Arwystli is styled "a man of Italy," or a Roman. In the Silurian catalogue he is said to have been the confessor or spiritual instructor (periglor) of Bran; and by some modern commentators he is identified with Aristobulus, mentioned in the Epistle to the Romans, xvi. 10. It is, however, remarkable that according to the Greek Martyrology, as cited by Archbishop Usher,‡ Aristobulus was ordained by St. Paul as a Bishop for the Britons. Cressy also says that St. Aristobulus, a disciple of St. Peter, or St. Paul at Rome, was sent as an Apostle to the Britons, and was the first Bishop in Britain; that he died at Glastonbury A. D. 99, and that his Commemoration or Saint's day was kept in the Church, March 15.

Two of Lewis Morris's authorities§ state that Meigent or Meugant, was the son of Cyndaf, "a man of Israel;" but this is probably a mistake, as the catalogues of North Wales make no other allusion to Bran or his companions.|| The Saint intended appears to be Mawan, who according to one of the copies of the Silurian catalogue is said to have been a son of Cyndaf, and to have accompanied Bran from Rome to Britain.

The descendants of Bran are styled in the Triads, one of the three holy families of Britain. It is not stated that Caractacus himself embraced Christianity; but Eigen, a daughter of Caradog ab Bran, or Caractacus, is recorded as the first female

* Dr. O. Pughe, in Preface to Gunn's Nennius.
† Triads.
‡ De Britannicarum Ecclesiarum Primordiis, page 9.
§ Myv. Archaiology, Vol. II. 47.
|| Qu. Is there any notice of Bran in the Regestum Landavense?

L

Saint among the Britons. " She lived in the close of the first
— century, and was married to Sarllog, who was lord of Caer
Sarllog, or the present Old Sarum."* Cyllin, the son of Caradog, is also called a Saint, and with him is closed the list of
primitive Christians of the first century; none of whom, except Arwystli, have been noticed by the monkish writers,
and no churches in the Principality are known to bear their
names.†

That Christianity, however introduced, had taken deep root
in Britain in the second century is clear from the testimony of
Tertullian, a contemporary writer, who states that certain
parts inaccessible to the Romans were subdued by Christ.‡
The first Saint of this period, mentioned in the Welsh accounts, is Lleurwg, or Lleufer Mawr, the grandson of Cyllin.
One Triad states that he was the person " who erected the
first church at Llandaff, which was the first in the Isle of
Britain; and he bestowed the freedom of country and nation,
with the privilege of judgment and surety upon those who
might be of the faith in Christ."§ Another Triad, speaking
of the three Archbishopricks of the Isle of the Britons, says,
" the earliest was Llandaff, of the foundation of Lleurwg ab
Coel ab Cyllin, who gave lands and civil privileges to such as
first embraced the faith in Christ."‖ And the Silurian catalogues of Saints further relate that he applied to Rome for
spiritual instruction; upon which, four persons, named Dyfan,

* Cambrian Biography.—Claudia, the wife of Pudens and reputed
daughter of Caractacus, is not noticed in the Welsh records.

† Llanilid, Glamorganshire, supposed by some to have been called after
Ilid, is dedicated to Julitta and Cyrique. See the List of Parishes, at the
end of the Myvyrian Archaiology, Vol. II. with Iolo Morganwg's note.

‡ " Britannorum inaccessa Romanis loca, Christo verò subdita."

§ Triad 35, Third Series.—The privileges, which are scarcely intel-
ligible, appear to mean redress in courts of justice, and the obligation of
contracts made by a Christian.

‖ No. 62, Third Series.—The title of Archbishop was not known until
after the council of Nice, A. D. 325.

Ffagan, Medwy, and Elfan, were sent him by Eleutherius,
Bishop of that See.   This is all the account the Welsh authorities give respecting a person about whom so much has been
written under the name of Lucius, or Lles ab Coel.   Not content with these statements, Walter de Mapes, and Geoffrey of
Monmouth, whose authority, as observed, is not Welsh but
Armorican, must make him the king of all Britain; and
gravely relate, that by a decree of his sovereign power he converted all the heathen temples in the kingdom into churches,
that he transformed the Sees of twenty eight Flamens and
three Archiflamens into so many Bishopricks and Archbishopricks, and in fact established a national religion more complete
in its provisions than that which is the pride of England at
this day.   But this was not sufficient to satisfy some Catholic
writers; they must needs add, that after he had Christianized
the whole of his dominions, he laid aside his crown; and, in
company with his sister, St. Emerita, he toiled his weary way,
as a missionary, through Bavaria, Rhætia, and Vindelicia,
until at last he suffered martyrdom near Curia in Germany.*

After this extravagance of fiction, it can be no wonder that
some modern writers have denied altogether the existence of
Lucius; and it must be admitted that his history, though
upon the whole better attested than that of Bran, is, with its
most confined limitations, involved in uncertainty.   The
Welsh accounts authorize no further supposition than that he
was the chieftain of that part of Siluria, which was afterwards
known by the joint names of Gwent and Morganwg.   But
even these accounts must be received with caution.   The
second Triad, just quoted, as it would appear from the remainder of its contents, is of no higher date than the seventh
century;† and some of its statements are so manifestly inaccurate that it must be rejected entirely.   The statement of the

* Cressy's Church History of Brittany.

† It speaks of the Archbishopricks of Canterbury and York: the latter,
as a Saxon church, was not founded till A. D. 625.

first Triad is not incredible, only that the privileges, which
could have been granted by a chieftain retaining his patrimony under the Roman jurisdiction, must have been limited.
As for the mission to Rome, the Welsh authorities make no
mention of an alleged epistle of Eleutherius, still extant; and
it may be observed that the four names Dyfan, Ffagan,
Medwy, and Elfan are not Roman, but British. Some accounts* state that Medwy and Elfan were Britons, and that
being sent to Rome with the message, they brought Dyfan†
and Ffagan with them on their return. Amid these doubts
and contradictions, the reader must exercise his own judgment, and perhaps he will reject the idea of a mission to Rome
as a monkish fabrication. There are, however, local indications in the neighbourhood of Llandaff which support the
belief of the *existence* of these persons. Four churches have
been called after the names of Lleurwg, Dyfan, Ffagan, and
Medwy; and their locality not only determines the situation
of the patrimony of Lucius, but, in some respects, the confined sphere to which the labours of these Christian teachers
were limited; for in no other part of Wales has a tradition of
their presence remained, a fact inconsistent with the notion
that they evangelized the whole of Britain.

Lleurwg was also called " Lleufer Mawr," or the Great Lu-
minary, which probably was an epithet bestowed upon him at
at a later age in consideration of his having promoted the
cause of Christianity. The Latin name corresponding to this
epithet was Lucius from *Lux*. Lles, on the other hand, first
occurs in the fabulous chronicles, and is perhaps due to those
later authors who formed a Welsh imitation of Lucius. Geoffrey of Monmouth also gives him a different pedigree to that

* The Latin Book of Llandaff, and the Life of St. Dubricius in John of
Teignmouth and Capgrave. (See Usher de Primordiis, pp. 49, 50.)

† If any dependence could be placed upon the genealogies of this period,
it would appear that Dyfan was a Briton by descent; his pedigree is
given under his name in the "Cambrian Biography."

in Achau y Saint and the Triads; for he makes his grandfather to be Meirig, King of Britain, instead of Cyllin, the
Saint; and thus carries his genealogy to Brute and the
Trojans. As for the time in which he lived, Archbishop
Usher* has cited above fifty Latin authorities with a view to
ascertain the year of his conversion, a few only of whom agree
together; and even the name of the Bishop of Rome with
whom he is said to have corresponded is differently mentioned,
some saying it was Euaristus, while a more numerous party
maintain it was Eleutherius. But most of them agree in
saying that Lucius flourished in the latter part of the second
century, which is rather later than the order of generations in
the Welsh account from the known date of Caractacus. If
the Welsh computation be correct, he must have flourished
about the *middle* of the second century, in the reign of either
of the two Antonines, whose edicts in favour of the Christians
would give him the opportunity of promoting the new religion. That a native chieftain was allowed to exercise some
degree of power, is probable from the known policy of the
Romans in Britain and elsewhere. And Tacitus† indeed
relates that such was their conduct in this country in the time
of Ostorius, the captor of Caractacus.

Under these circumstances it is certainly possible, if it be
not probable, that, according to the first of the two Triads
last quoted, some place might have been set apart for the
purposes of religious worship by Lucius at Llandaff. But
the declaration of the second Triad, that he gave lands to the
faithful, cannot be admitted. According to the general testi-

* De Brit. Eccl. Primordiis, Cap. III.

† His words are—" Consularium primus Aulus Plautius præpositus, ac
subinde Ostorius Scapula, uterque bello egregius: redactaque paulatim in
formam provinciæ proxima pars Britanniæ, addita insuper veteranorum
colonia; *quædam civitates Cogiduno regi donatæ, vetere ac jam pridem
recepta populi Romani consuetudine, ut haberet instrumenta servitutis
et reges.*" Life of Agricola, Cap. XIV.

mony of ecclesiastical historians, endowments for the maintenance of religion did not commence until several generations
afterwards; and from another Triad* in the same collection is
seen that they did not commence in Britain until about the
end of the fourth century.   If any reliance can be placed upon
Welsh traditions which relate to so early a period, it will be
sufficient to acquiesce in the testimony of the first Triad,
which implies no more than that he built a church, said to
have been the first erected in Britain.   That Llandaff was one
of the oldest churches in this country is not improbable, as the
circumstance would afterwards be a reason for the selection of
the place to be the seat of a Bishoprick; but, whether true or
false, in the simple statement of the Triad may be recognised
the germ of that story which afterwards grew to be the wonder of Christendom.†

As for the other four churches which have passed under the
names of Lleurwg, Dyfan, Ffagan, and Medwy, there is
nothing in the present state of their endowments from which
they may be judged to belong to the most ancient class.   It
might be said that in this age places of worship were supported by the voluntary contributions of the people; and
though there is every reason to believe that such was the fact,
still had these churches existed at so early a period, the veneration attached to their antiquity would, in some way or other,
have distinguished them from their neighbours; but there are
not any traces of pre-eminence to be observed.   That they
were built long after the time of the persons whose names

* Triad 18, Third Series.   Archaiology of Wales, Vol. II.
† In the Catholic Church, the anniversary of the Baptism of Lucius was
celebrated May 26, and that of his martyrdom Dec. 3.   The festival of
Dyfan was held April 8, and of Ffagan August 8; they were also com-
memorated together May 24.   The Saint's day of Elfan was held Sept.
26; that of Medwy is unknown, except it be identified with the festival of
Medwyr, which according to some Calendars occurred Jan. 1.   (Cressy.—
Sir Harris Nicolas's Chronology of History.)

they bear is evident in the instance of Merthyr Dyfan, the
designation of which implies that it was a *martyrium*, and the
erection of places of worship of this description did not commence before the fourth century. Ecton, or rather Browne
Willis, asserts that the patron Saint of Merthyr Dyfan was
Teilo; it is not known upon what authority he gives the
name, but if he were correct, it might be said that the church
was founded *in memoriam martyris Duviani* by Teilo in the
sixth century. The most safe conclusion is that these four
churches were built at a later age to the memory of the persons whose names they bear, and in situations which tradition
reported to have been the scene of their labours.

The monkish historians mention that Elfan was the second
Bishop of London; and, according to the authors of the Latin
account of the origin of the church of Llandaff, it would appear that he was ordained a Bishop at the time of his visit to
Rome, while his companion Medwy, was created a Doctor.
Upon these points the Welsh authorities are silent; and all
that is related of Elfan is that he presided over a congregation
of Christians at Glastonbury; but this allusion to the church
founded by Joseph of Arimathea savours of a monkish origin.
The monks are also prolix in their detail of the acts of Dyfan
and Ffagan in various parts of Britain; but setting the
legends aside, it will be sufficient to add, to the little information to be gleaned from the Welsh historical remains,
the supposition that the former suffered martyrdom at the
place now called " Merthyr Dyfan;" and as for Ffagan and
the rest, the conjecture may be hazarded that they lived and
died in Glamorganshire, as in this county alone they seem
to retain traces of

" A local habitation and a name."

SECTION V.

An Examination of the early Welsh Pedigrees, with a view to ascertain the period about which the commencement of their authenticity may be dated.

WITH the foregoing Saints is concluded the list for the second century. From the age of Lleurwg, the Triads and the Poems of the Bards present a perfect blank until the time of Macsen Wledig, generally supposed to be Maximus, Emperor of Rome, who began to reign A. D. 383. But not so the Genealogists, for they carry the ancestry of the British Chieftains and Saints, without interruption, through the period of Roman ascendancy. The alleged descendants of Bran Fendigaid are, therefore, drawn up in a tabular form, as it appears on the opposite side.

This pedigree is arranged according to the " Cambrian Biography,"* where each connecting link may be found upon reference to most of the names included, but more especially under the names Caradog ab Iestin, Cadfrawd, Tudwal Befr, and Eldad. The names printed in Italics are those of reputed Saints, and the rest are introduced for the sake of preserving the lineage unbroken. It has been already stated that genealogy, if its details be at all complicated, can hardly fail of betraying itself whenever it is not founded in fact. Thus Ystrafael, the daughter of Cadfan, is said to have been the wife of Coel Godebog; and she is placed in the pedigree in the

---

* It is to be regretted that Dr. Owen Pughe, to whom Welsh literature is already under greater obligations than to any other individual, does not favour the public with a new and enlarged edition of this useful work.

[TABLE I.]

LLYR LLEDIAITH.

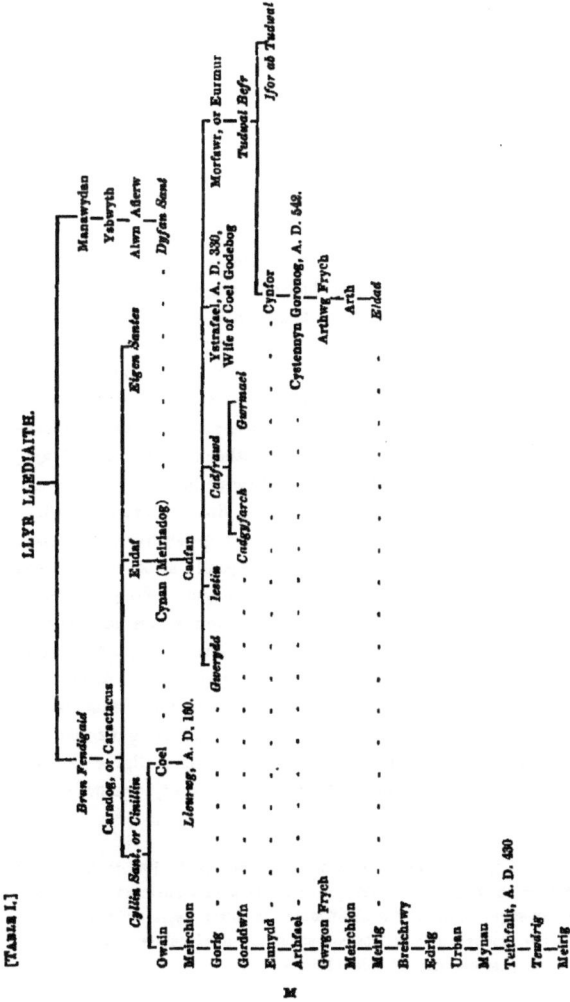

seventh generation from Llyr Llediaith inclusive. The ancestry of Coel Godebog is also given under his name in the
Cambrian Biography, and the number of generations there
enumerated agrees with the statements usually given. The
ancestor of Coel, according to that list contemporary with Llyr
Llediaith was Afallach; but from Afallach to Coel there are
fourteen generations, precisely double the number of those
from Llyr Llediaith to Ystrafael, the wife of Coel; and this
large discrepancy must have happened in the short space of
250 years, for Afallach and Llyr Llediaith were of a generation commencing with the Christian era, while Coel Godebog
is stated to have lived about the middle of the third century.
There are reasons for placing Coel a few generations later than
the date usually assigned him; but Ystrafael must also be
brought down to the same period, and, early or late, both
lineages cannot be true together. It is possible and often happens that a son is born after his father is fifty years of age,
but the accident must be repeated twice before a century can
pass with only two generations; the line of Ystrafael would
render it necessary for the accident to happen five or six times
in regular succession. It happens equally as often that a son
is born when his father is twenty five years of age or under,
but this accident must be repeated four times successively
before a century can pass with four generations; in the line of
Coel the accident must have happened about fourteen times
in about three centuries and a half. But in every examination
of well authenticated genealogies the accidents generally correct each other, and the average in a long pedigree is three
generations to a century.* In this respect, whenever the

---

* From the birth of William the Conqueror A. D. 1027 to the birth of
William the Fourth A. D. 1765, twenty four generations may be reckoned,
the average duration of each of which is thirty years and nine months;
and the proportion is maintained under the disadvantage of a succession,
in every possible case, of elder children.

Welsh pedigrees attempt to penetrate the Roman-British period they are all of them faulty.* With the exception of the line of Eudaf ab Caradog ab Bran, already given, they are during this period a mere string of names, without a single marriage, plurality of issue, or reference to historical events, by which their correctness may be determined. Those which pass through the period in question are five in number, two of which have been given already, and the remainder may be added by way of illustration.

[Table II.]

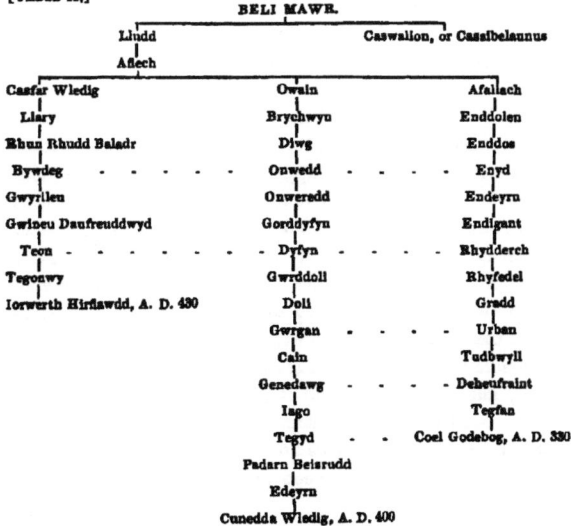

BELI MAWR.

| Lludd | | Caswallon, or Cassibelaunus |
| Afiech | | |

Casfar Wledig	Owain	Afallach
Llary	Brychwyn	Enddolen
Rhun Rhudd Baladr	Diwg	Enddos
Bywdeg	Onwedd	Enyd
Gwyrlleu	Onweredd	Endeyrn
Gwineu Daufreuddwyd	Gorddyfyn	Endigant
Teon	Dyfyn	Rhydderch
Tegonwy	Gwrddoll	Rhyfedel
Iorwerth Hirflawdd, A. D. 430	Doli	Gradd
	Gwrgan	Urban
	Cain	Tudbwyll
	Genedawg	Deheufraint
	Iago	Tegfan
	Tegyd	Coel Godebog, A. D. 330
	Padarn Beisrudd	
	Edeyrn	
	Cunedda Wledig, A. D. 400	

* In the first table it may be noticed, that the date of Teithfallt, the *seventeenth* descendant from Llyr Llediaith in one line is A. D. 430; while that of Cystennyn Goronog, the *ninth* descendant in another line, is A. D. 542.

These pedigrees are generally given without any variation; but to say nothing of the improbability that such memorials should be preserved during the three centuries and upwards of Roman ascendancy, they receive no confirmation from other authorities until the lower dates affixed, being the first that could be ascertained with any tolerable degree of accuracy. From those dates downwards, however, these pedigrees divide into several branches; their relationships multiply, and are so complex and interwoven that they could not have been traced with any degree of correctness unless they were recorded soon after the times in which they occurred, and it should not be forgotten that they are almost always reconcilable with chronology. It will be observed that the dates in question, to which may be added Teithfallt A. D. 430, and Ystrafael A. D. 330 from the first table, occur shortly before or soon after the departure of the Romans from Britain. May it not, therefore, be supposed that all the generations from thence upwards were invented to support the pretensions of those chieftains, who rose into power upon the decline of the Roman interest; for that they were forged at an early time is probable from the fact that they are at variance with the monkish stories respecting the British parentage of Constantine the Great. These worthies were likely to owe their influence to the system of clanship prevalent among the Celtic nations, and they would find it politic to show their descent from the families of Cassibelaunus and Caractacus, of whose existence and prowess they could be informed by their Roman masters, even if there had been no native traditions remaining.

The line of Eudaf ab Caradog, in the first table, demands a more especial attention upon the present occasion, inasmuch as it contains the names of several Saints; and as its details are more complicated, it presents features very different from the rest. Cadfrawd, the son of Cadfan, appears in a generation immediately succeeding that of Lleurwg; and upon reference to the Cambrian Biography, it is seen that this person was "a Saint and Bishop who lived about the beginning of the *third* century." It would appear that the editor of that work employed as his authority the Silurian catalogue of Saints, and that he calculated the dates accordingly; but in a lower part of the line the dates of other members of the family may be ascertained from the known era of their contemporaries in history. These dates, however, are so much at variance with the former that the whole chronology is confused. There is reason to think that the inconsistency has arisen from a very simple mistake on the part of some compilers of genealogies in the middle ages; and to explain it a third table may be produced on the authority of George Owen Harry.—

[TABLE III.]

BRAN FENDIGAID.

1 Caradog.

2 Eudaf, or Euddaf

3 Cynan

4 Cadfan   1 Caradog

Stradwen, wife of Coel   2 Eudaf   (Caradog)

Ceneu   Gwawl, wife of Edeyrn   Elen, wife of   3 Cynan Meiriadog, A. D. 380
                         Maximus

Gwrwst   Cunedda Wledig   4 Cadfan

Meirchion   Morfawr

Cynfarch Oer   Tudwal

Llew, married Anna, daughter of Uther, A. D. 500 to 550   -   -   (Cynfor)

Constantine, A. D. 433   Androenus

Coustans   Emrys or Ambrosius   Uther   Emyr Llydaw

Arthur   Anna, wife of Llew
               ab Cynfarch

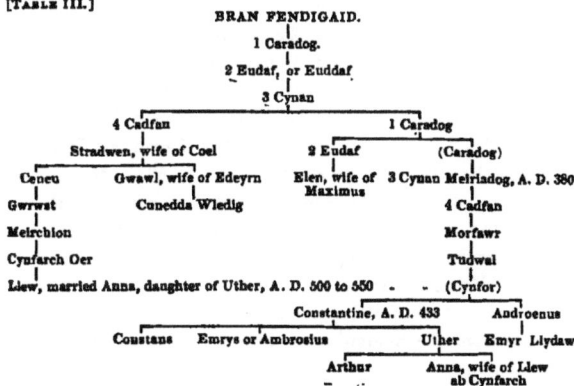

In this table it is necessary first to point out an error. In the Triads, Cynan Meiriadog is invariably said to be the brother of Elen; and if she was the daughter of Eudaf, Cynan must also have been the son of Eudaf. The name of Caradog may have slipt into the place of Eudaf from the generation

preceding. If this arrangement be the correct one, it will
immediately be observed that the names marked 1, 2, 3, and
4, are repeated twice over, and the mistake alluded to is
simply this:—Cadfan the father of Stradwen, and Cadfan the
father of Morfawr have been thought to be the same person,
and the ancestry of the latter has been given to the former.
Cadfan, the father of Stradwen,* which is only another name
for Ystrafael, must be considered the first person or founder
of his family, and the time in which he lived will depend
upon the known date of his descendant Llew ab Cynfarch,
who was contemporary with Arthur. Cadfrawd and Ystrafael
will thus be placed in the first part of the *fourth* century ; and
Coel Godebog will be coeval with Constantine the Great,
instead of being his grandfather, as reported in the legends.
The pedigree of Cynan Meiriadog must commence with his
grandfather Caradog,† and the notion that he was a descendant of the great Caractacus must be set aside. The general
period in which he lived may be known from his connexion
with the emperor Maximus, the date of whose usurpation is
A. D. 383. But if Cynan Meiriadog was living in A. D. 380,
it is impossible that his descendant in the fourth or fifth
degree should be king of the Britons in A. D. 433. It appears, however, that George Owen Harry has confounded
Constantine, the father of Ambrosius, with Cystennyn Goronog, a descendant of Cynan, and who succeeded to the
sovereignty of Britain on the death of Arthur A. D. 542.

So much may be said for the sake of establishing the order
of succession from the beginning of the fourth century, so as

* George Owen Harry, to fill up the chronology, has heaped the presumed ancestors of Stradwen and Morfawr, one upon the other; but notwithstanding this accumulation, the pedigree falls short of the era of
Caractacus by a whole century.

† According to the first table, Caractacus and Caradog the grandfather
of Cynan were the same person, which cannot be admitted without com-
mitting an anachronism of *two* centuries.

to include the immediate ancestors of those chieftains who
rose into power upon the departure of the Romans. It has
been already observed that the Triads and the poems of the
Bards allude to no affairs which were transacted in the *third*
century; and if the arrangements just made be correct, the
genealogies afford no information as to the Saints who lived in
the same period. This chasm in Welsh tradition is due to the
quiet submission of the people under a foreign power; and if
those accounts which relate to the age preceding prove uncertain, and occasionally incorrect, the remoteness of the time,
as well as the interruption, must in fairness be sufficient to
account for their inaccuracy and uncertainty. The third and
early part of the fourth centuries include the usurpation of
Carausius and the accession of Constantine, both of which
happened in Britain, but these events more especially concerned the Romans. As regarded the history of the Britons
as a nation, this was an eventful period. The Christian
religion, doubtless, continued to make progress; but as for
those who were engaged in the work of promoting it, no
friendly Bard has preserved their names.

> —— Omnes illachrymabiles
> Urgentur, ignotique longâ
> Nocte, carent quia vate sacro.

SECTION VI.

The Welsh Saints from A. D. 300 to A. D. 400.

In the year 303 occurred the persecution under Dioclesian, in which St. Alban, the Proto-martyr of England, and his contemporaries, Amphibalus, Aaron, and Julius, are said to have suffered martyrdom; and though their history is obscured with fable, the credit of their existence may be maintained upon the testimony of writers of great antiquity;[*] but as their names are not noticed in any catalogue of Welsh Saints, it will not be necessary to say much respecting them. They appear to have been Romans rather than Britons, which may account for the circumstance of their having passed almost unregarded by the Welsh people. There is no church in Wales dedicated to Alban, or Amphibalus. Julius and Aaron are said to have been inhabitants of the Roman city of Caerleon upon Usk, where, according to Walter de Mapes, Geoffrey of Monmouth, as well as Giraldus Cambrensis, two illustrious churches were dedicated to their memory, and adorned with a convent of nuns and a society of regular canons. But as those authors, who flourished from A. D. 1150 to 1200, admit that these establishments did not exist in their time, but were among the glories of Caerleon which had passed away, the whole account may be regarded as a monkish fable, it being inconsistent with the history of the age to which it is referred. Soon after the Norman Conquest there was an ordinary church at Caerleon, dedicated to Julius and Aaron jointly,

* Constantius of Lyons, who wrote the life of St. Germanus about A. D. 500, Venantius Fortunatus, and Bede.

which was about the same time granted by Robert de Candos
to the priory of Goldcliff.* According to Bishop Godwin,
there existed, in the recollection of the generation preceding
that in which he wrote,† two chapels called after Julius and
Aaron, on the east and west side of the town, and about two
miles distant from each other; but so little respect appears to
have been paid to these edifices that antiquaries are not quite
agreed as to their situations. Llanharan in Glamorganshire,
considered to be dedicated to Julius and Aaron, is but a
chapel; and its mother church, Llanilid, is also of late dedication, being consecrated to Julitta and Cyrique, French
Saints‡ whose homage was introduced probably by the
Normans.

In A. D. 306 Constantine was proclaimed Emperor of Rome
upon the death of his father Constantius, an event which took
place in Britain. From this circumstance the Armorican
chronicle has taken occasion to fill the world with the story,
that he was a native of this island, and that his mother, Helen,
was the daughter of Coel, a British king. This tale has been
much controverted, and since the time of Gibbon the decision
of most historical writers is in the negative. The best authorities in support of it are, the following passage from
Eumenius, the Rhetorician,—" O fortunate Britain, and now
happier than all countries, which hast first seen Constantine
Cæsar:" and the following from another panegyrist;—" He
(thy father Constantius) delivered Britain from bondage, but
thou by arising from thence hast made it illustrious."‡ But
these passages can surely mean no more than his accession, as

* Dugdale's Monasticon.
† Sometimes called Julietta and Cyr, their Welsh names are Ilid and
Curig.
‡ These passages are originally thus :—" O fortunata, et nunc omnibus
beatior terris Britannia, quæ Constantinum *Cæsarem* prima vidisti."——
" Liberavit ille (pater videlicet Constantius) Britannias servitute, tu etiam
nobiles illic *oriendo* fecisti."—With respect to the meaning of " oriendo,"

N

Cæsar, to a share of the Imperial government. The opinion
of Archbishop Usher is to the contrary,* but it is surprising
that the learned Primate should not have examined the subject
with his usual chronological skill. Constantine was of full age
A. D. 306, when he was proclaimed Emperor upon the death
of his father ; indeed Usher produces authorities to show that
he was created Cæsar before that time. ' Now Constantius
visited Britain, for the first time, in 296; and allowing that
Constantine was born that year, he could only have been ten
years old at the time of his accession to the empire; he was,
therefore, not born in Britain. Besides, Helen was the wife
of Constantius's younger years, and, as she was divorced by
him as early as A. D. 286, ten years before his arrival in this
country, she was not likely to have been a Briton. But chronology and the monkish historians are always at variance, and
the attempt to reconcile them would be a fruitless undertaking. A modern writer† asks, how has it happened that
such a tradition, as that of the British parentage of Constantine, should become perfectly national? To this it may be
replied, that in all the works of the earlier Bards, the catalogues of Saints, the older pedigrees, and all the Triads,
except one, there is not the slightest allusion to the circumstance ;‡ and the omission of a fact, which would have gra-
tified the national pride of the Welsh, is a presumptive proof
that they were not acquainted with it. When the story was
communicated to them by the monks in the middle ages, they
received it with avidity. The solitary Triad to the contrary
is No. 6, second series, in the Myvyrian Archaiology ; but a

---

it is sufficient to say that Eumenius describes the accession of Constantius,
the father of Constantine, in similar terms.

   * De Brit. Eccl. Primordiis, Cap. VIII.

   † Roberts, in his Chronicle of the Kings of Britain.

   ‡ It appears to have been unknown to Bede, to the author of the composition ascribed to Gildas, and to the compilers of the Saxon Chronicle
translated by Dr. Ingram.

single reading of it will discover its monkish origin. The only Triad besides, in which even the name of Constantine is mentioned, is the Triad respecting Archbishopricks,* which may also be referred to the same manufactory.

Helen and Constantine were canonized by the Romanists; but the name of the latter does not occur in any Welsh list of Saints, and that of the former is omitted in almost all the existing catalogues.† There is a church in Glamorganshire, called Eglwys Ilan, which is supposed by Browne Willis to be dedicated to Helen; and to render the dedication more complete, the subordinate church of Llanfabon, despite the name it bears, is attributed to Constantine.‡ Another church, in Cardiganshire, is called Tref Ilan; but the identity of Ilan with Helen is, at least, questionable, as in all the current stories respecting the latter the name is never corrupted. A church in Monmouthshire is called distinctly Llanelen; but not to lay too great a stress upon names, it may be allowed that these churches, as well as a chapel of St. Helen§ which once existed at Carnarvon, were dedicated to her in the middle ages; and if the story of her British origin were true, it would be surprising that such dedications were not more numerous. A church in Carnarvonshire, called Llangysten-nyn,‖ is perhaps dedicated to Constantine the Great; but this must be uncertain, as soon after the departure of the Romans there was a sainted king in Britain, called Cystennyn Fendigaid, or Constantine the Blessed.

* No. 62, Third Series, Myv. Archaiology.

† It is mentioned in only two of the MSS. cited in the Myvyrian Archaiology.

‡ Llanfabon is called after Mabon, the brother of Teilo, Bishop of Llandaff; and Eglwys Ilan may derive its name from a Welsh Saint, of whom all other memorials have perished.

§ Rowlands's Mona Antiqua, Section XI.

‖ This church does not appear to be ancient, as in the time of Edw. I. it was a chapel under Abergele (St. Michael.)

During this vacuity of Welsh tradition, which later legends
have endeavoured to occupy with fable, it is gratifying to
learn, from testimonies of another kind, that Christianity must
have made considerable progress. Of this the most irrefragable proofs remain in the fact on record, that there were
British Bishops present at the Councils—of Arles in Gaul
A. D. 314, of Sardica in Illyria A. D. 347, and of Ariminum
in Italy A. D. 359. The Council of Arles was convened by
Constantine for the sake of suppressing the heresy of the
Donatists; and it is satisfactory to know that at that time,
seventeen years before the general edict in favour of Christianity, there were at least three Bishops in Britain. The names
of those who attended upon that occasion, as given by Usher,
and Spelman, were:—

"Eborius Episcopus, de civitate Eboracensi, provinciâ
Britanniâ.

Restitutus Episcopus, de civitate Londinensi, provinciâ
suprascriptâ.

Adelfius Episcopus, de civitate Coloniâ Londinensium :—
exinde Sacerdos Presbyter, Arminius Diaconus."

None of these Bishops are mentioned in any catalogue of
Welsh Saints, unless it be admitted that Adelfius is identical
with *Cadfrawd*, for the names are almost a translation of each
other.* The British rendering of Eborius and Restitutus
would be Efrog and Rhystyd, both which names were in use
in Wales a few generations later. Colonia Londinensium is
evidently an error, as there was no place place known by
that name in Britain, and the Bishop of London is already
mentioned. Stillingfleet proposes, therefore, to read "Legion-
ensium" for Caerleon upon Usk; Urbs Legionis being the
name by which that town was known to Latin writers in the

---

* Adelfius appears to be formed from the Greek word Ἀδελφὸς,
a brother; and the Welsh Scholar will recognise Brawd in the composition of Cadfrawd.

middle ages. The same place was also in the Roman division of the country* the capital of the province of Britannia Secunda, as London was of Britannia Prima, and York of Maxima Cæsariensis. Welsh tradition has always reported it to have been a Bishop's see from the earliest times; and the importance of these three places enabled their Diocesans in a subsequent age to assume the title of Archbishop. No further information can be gleaned respecting Sacerdos and Arminius, but they attended probably as representatives of the different orders of priesthood.

The list of the Bishops, who subscribed the articles of the Council of Sardica, is not preserved; but it is asserted by Athanasius that Bishops from Britain were present, and that they joined in the condemnation of Arius and vindication of himself. In a few years afterwards, Hilary, Bishop of Poictiers, in an epistle from Phrygia, congratulates the Britons, amongst others, on their freedom from heresy.†

The Council of Ariminum was convened by Constantius, the son of Constantine, to decide, like the preceding, upon the Arian heresy, to which the Emperor himself was favourable. Sulpitius Severus relates that more than four hundred Bishops of the Western Church were assembled together upon the occasion, and adds—"unto all of whom the Emperor had ordered provisions and apartments to be given. But that was deemed unbecoming by the Aquitans, Gauls, and Britons; and refusing the imperial offer, they preferred to live at their own expense. Three only from Britain, on account of poverty, made use of the public gift, after they had rejected the contribution offered by the others; considering it more pro-

---

* "It plainly appears that the Church was divided into Dioceses and Provinces much after the same manner as the Empire, having a Metropolitan or Primate in every Province."—(Bingham's Antiquities, Book IX. Chap. I.)—Under each of these provincial Bishops were several Chorepiscopi or Suffragans.

† Usher de Brit. Eccl. Primordiis, Cap. VIII.

per to burden the exchequer than individuals.*"—This passage
has been, by a mistake, adduced to show the poverty of the
Bishops of Britain in general, when it states, that such was
their sense of propriety that they had rather defray their own
costs and charges than subsist upon the Emperor's bounty.
The three, who did partake of it, are mentioned only as an
exception, as if the independent Bishops were the more numerous party.   Out of four hundred, which number included
only those of the *Western* Church, a proportion of ten or
upwards may well be allowed for Britain, whose distance from
Italy must have added greatly to the expense of their journey.
The prelates assembled at this Council were forced to submit
to the doctrines of Arius through the undue influence of the
Emperor; but in the year 353, Athanasius describes the
churches of Britain, and other churches in the west, as adhering to the faith of the council of Nice.†

Besides Cadfrawd, already mentioned, the period just
passed over includes Gwerydd and Iestyn, brothers, and Cad-
gyfarch and Gwrmael, sons, of Cadfrawd; all of whom are
said to have been Saints, but their feast-days are unknown,
and no churches have been dedicated to them.

Coel Godebog was a chieftain who flourished in the former
part of this century. He married Ystrafael or Stradwen, the
sister of Cadfrawd, by whom he had a son, Ceneu, whose
name appears in the catalogues of Saints, and a daughter,
Gwawl, who married Edeyrn, the father of Cunedda Wledig.
According to the fabulous chroniclers he had only one child, a

---

* The original words are these,—"Quibus omnibus annonas et cellaria
dare Imperator præceperat. Sed id Aquitanis, Gallis, ac Britannis in-
decens visum; repudiatis fiscalibus, propriis sumptibus vivere maluerunt.
Tres tantùm ex Britanniâ, inopiâ proprii, publico usi sunt, cum oblatam a
cæteris collationem respuissent; sanctius putantes fiscum gravare, quam
singulos."—Sulpitii Severi Sacræ Historiæ, Lib. II. Cap. LV.

† Usher, de Brit. Eccl. Primordiis, Cap. VIII.

[TABLE IV.]

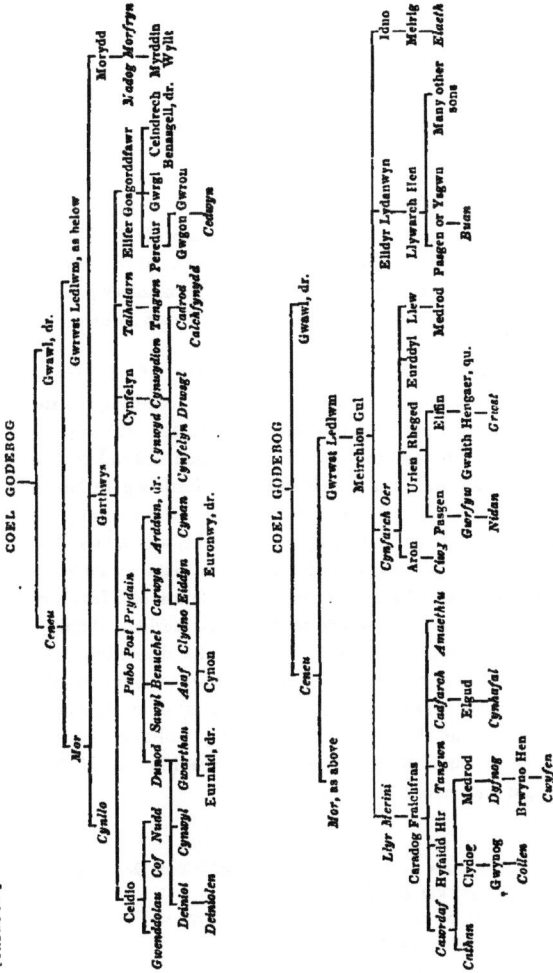

daughter,* who was afterwards the mother of Constantine the Great. But setting fable aside, no transactions of his life have been recorded, and to the Welsh genealogists he is known only as the founder of a large family of descendants. He was probably regarded as the head of a tribe in the system of clanship, which, as it is found flourishing in full vigour upon the departure of the Romans, must have been maintained in some degree under their supremacy.

Ceneu, the son of Coel,† probably spent his life in the service of religion, for which reason he has been called a Saint; but no churches have been consecrated to his memory; Llangeneu in Brecknockshire being assigned to Ceneu, a daughter or grand-daughter of Brychan.

With Cynan Meiriadog and Macsen Wledig, who flourished about A. D. 380, the history of Britain according to the Triads may be said to recommence. Macsen Wledig, or Maximus, is reported to have married Elen Luyddog, the sister of Cynan, who was the chieftain of Meiriadog in North Wales; and in this story may be recognised the prototype of the fable that Helen, the daughter of Coel, was married to Constantius. It is further said, that Cynan led over an army of 60,000 men into Gaul to support the claims of Maximus, and that this army afterwards settled in Armorica. Though some modern French writers find reasons for discrediting the whole of the story,‡ it should not, upon that account, be dismissed without examination; but as its truth or falsehood forms no part of the present enquiry, it is only necessary in this place to establish the date of the expedition, A. D. 383, so far as it may affect subsequent events.

---

* "Nyt oed o plant oy that namyn hy ehunan."—Brut Gr. ab Arthur, Myv. Archaiology, Vol. II. p. 207.

† He is not to be confounded with another Ceneu ab Coel, a warrior who flourished in the time of Arthur.

‡ Turner's Anglo Saxons, Appendix to Book VI. Chap. II.

The monkish chronologists thought that these 60,000 men would, of course, be in want of wives; and therefore they appended the tale of St. Ursula and the eleven thousand, nay seventy thousand virgins, who, on their voyage from Britain to Armorica, were captured by pagan pirates, and all suffered for their faith. But this grave narration is so improbable throughout, that the whole may, without scruple, be pronounced a fiction.*

There is a church in Cardiganshire called Llanygwyryfon, or Llanygweryddon, which is supposed to be dedicated to St. Ursula and the virgins; and if so, it is obviously of late foundation.

Before the end of this century the celebrated Pelagius, who was a Briton, commenced his career; but as the name of this person has not been enrolled in any catalogue of Saints, it will be enough to observe that his heresy was first promulgated in Italy, and was soon afterwards brought to Britain by his disciple, Agricola.

* The story may be seen at length in Cressy's " Church History of Brittany."

SECTION VII.

THE list of primitive Christians has reached the beginning of the fifth century, and it may be stated that of all those hitherto mentioned, none, with the exception perhaps of Lleurwg, were founders of churches in the usual sense of the term. But the reader is now about to enter upon a time, when, in consequence of the distresses of the Romans, the Britons threw off their yoke, and the affairs of the island underwent a complete revolution. From the Welsh genealogies it would seem as if the country came at once into the possession of several chieftains, who rose into power, either as elders of tribes according to a system of clanship, or from their activity in resisting the northern invaders.

This event took place, according to Zosimus, in A. D. 408 or 409; and he says it happened in consequence of an irruption of barbarians into Gaul, which cut off the communication between Britain and the rest of the Roman empire. His words may thus be rendered :—

"The barbarians above the Rhine, invading all parts with unrestrained freedom, forced, of necessity, the inhabitants of the island of Britain, and some of the Celtic tribes, to revolt from the dominion of the Romans, and to live independent, no longer obeying the Roman laws. The Britons, therefore, armed themselves, and, facing the danger on their own account, delivered their cities from the barbarians that infested them. And all Armorica and other provinces of Gaul, imitating the example of the Britons, set themselves free in like manner; expelling the Roman governors, and setting up a native form of government at their own liberty. This revolt of Britain and the Celtic tribes happened during the time of the usurpation of Constantine, when the barbarians had made an incursion through his neglect of the affairs of the empire."[*]

This is the statement of a contemporary historian, for Zosimus died A. D. 420; and though it does not enter into particulars as much as could be wished, it is of incomparably greater value than all the dreaming of Gildas and the monkish writers about the "groans of the Britons," whom they represent as the most imbecile of the nations of antiquity. It is pleasing, however, to find historians of such eminence as Gibbon, Mr. Sharon Turner, and Dr. Lingard, giving to the testimony of Zosimus the respect to which it is entitled; and they proceed to describe the state of Britain after its emancipation, in terms perfectly consistent with the information to be gleaned from the Welsh authorities. Gibbon indeed quotes[†] a passage from Procopius to show that the Romans could never recover possesssion of the island, which continued from that time under the government of tyrants; and by the latter term, in the original ὑπο τυραννοις, which is not always used in a bad sense, it is obvious the writer intended to designate the native chieftains.

From the Triads it would appear that the emperor Maximus left a son in Britain, called Owain ab Macsen Wledig, who was by national convention elected to the chief sovereignty of the Britons. It is said that under him Britain was restored to a state of independence, and the annual tribute which had been paid to the Romans from the time of Julius Cæsar was discontinued. It is added that the Romans, under pretence of consenting to these proceedings, withdrew their troops, and

* Zosimi Historiarum Lib. VI. Cap. 5, 6.
† Decline and Fall, Chap. XXXI. Notes 177 and 186.

brought away at the same time the best of the Britons who were able to bear arms, by which means the country was so weakened that it became a prey to its enemies.*—In this traditional account may be perceived a confused notion of the events which took place as related by Zosimus; and if the Roman and Greek writers make no mention of so distinguished a person as Owain the son of Maximus, it was because all communication with Britain had been intercepted.   One of the Triads† states that Owain was raised to the dignity of Pendragon or chief sovereign of the Britons, though he was not an *elder*, from which it may be concluded that he was a young man at the time of his election.   The editor of the Cambrian Biography says that he was also called Owain Finddu, and that he has been considered · a Saint by his countrymen; but there are no churches existing which bear his name.

[TABLE V.]

MACSEN WLEDIG married ELEN, daughter of Euddaf.

Owain	Peblig		Ednyfed	Cystennyn
Madog			Dyfnwal Hen	
Gafran	Ceitig		Gortynion	Gwrwst Briodor
Aeddan Fradog	Tudwal Tudglyd		Senyllt Gwyddno Garanhir	Elidyr Mwynfawr
Gafran	Rhydderch Hael *Melangell* Gwenfron		Nudd Hael *Elffin*	
Llidnerth		Dingad m. Tonwy dr. of Llewddyn Luyddog		
Lleuddad	Buglan Gwytherin Tygwy		Tyfriog Eleri, dr.	

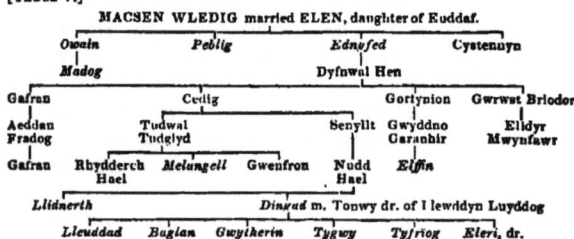

According to the Welsh accounts, one of the most distinguished chieftains of this time was Cunedda Wledig. His territory is said to have been in the north, an expression used indefinitely for any part of the tract reaching from the

* Triads 21 and 34. Third Series, Myv. Archaiology.

† No. 17. Third Series. Qu. Was not his disqualification owing to the *foreign* origin of his father, which prevented him from being the elder of a clan of native Britons?

Humber to the Clyde; the particular district is not mentioned, but owing to the remoteness of the country from Wales it cannot be expected that the tradition should be precise. In right of his mother, Gwawl, Cunedda was also entitled to the headship of the clan of Coel Godebog in the south ; Ceneu and Mor, the proper representatives of that tribe, being ecclesiastics.* Soon after the departure of Maximus to the continent, a people, called Gwyddyl Ffichti, or Irish Picts, to distinguish them the Picts of the north, landed on the western coasts of Britain,† and occupied the whole of North Wales, as well as the Dimetian counties‡ of South Wales. At a later time, the northern Picts made one of their irruptions into the country of their more civilized neighbours ; and Cunedda, being unable to resist them, was forced to seek an asylum to the southward. The probability is that he retired to his maternal kindred. He was the father of a numerous family ; and his sons, being reduced to the condition of adventurers, undertook the enterprise of delivering Wales from the Irish marauders. In this it is presumed they were assisted by the rightful inhabitants; and they were so far successful that they recovered a great part of South Wales, and the whole of North Wales, except Anglesey and some portions of Denbighshire. The country recovered was divided between them, and they became the founders of so many clans which gave names to the districts that they occupied, some of which names are retained to this day. Thus Ceredig had Ceredigion, comprising the present county of Cardigan with a great part of Carmarthenshire ; the word, Ceredigion, being the

---

* Saints.

† In this statement the Welsh authorities are confirmed by the Irish historians, who relate that an invasion of Britain, on an extensive and formidable scale, took place towards the close of the fourth century under the auspices of a king of Ireland, called Nial of the Nine Hostages.— Moore's History of Ireland, Chap. VII.

‡ The present counties of Cardigan, Pembroke, and Carmarthen.

plural of Ceredig, and meaning his followers. Arwystl had
Arwystli, or the western part of Montgomeryshire. Dunod
had Dunodig, or the northern part of Merioneth with part of
Carnarvonshire. Edeyrn had Edeyrnion, and Mael had Dinmael, both in the eastern part of Merioneth. Coel had Coel-
eion, and Dogfael had Dogfeilin, both in Denbighshire.
Rhufon had Rhufoniog, in Denbigh and Carnarvonshires.
Einion had Caereinion in Montgomery, and Oswal had Os-
weilin on the borders of Shropshire. Tibion, the eldest son of
Cunedda, died in the Isle of Man; but his son, Meirion, was
one of these adventurers, and had Cantref Meirion. The date
which may be assigned to this expulsion of the Irish is the
period between A. D. 420 and 430.*

Another chieftain, contemporary with Owain ab Macsen
and Cunedda, was Brychan, the regulus of Brecknock. It is
said that his mother was Marchell, the daughter of Tudur or
Tewdrig, who is styled the king of Garthmadryn, by which is
conceived to be meant the present county of Brecknock southward of the Eppynt hills.† The genealogy of Tewdrig is
carried up to Gwraldeg, king of Garthmadryn, who is computed to have lived about A. D. 230. But here the same
process may be detected at work which has been demonstrated
in the case of Cadfrawd ab Cadfan and Cynan Meiriadog.‡
Two, if not three pedigrees show that the ancestry of Meirig
ab Tewdrig, who lived about A. D. 500, has been given to
Tewdrig of Garthmadryn, who must have flourished about
A. D. 370. The majority of authorities, it is true, give the
older names differently, but they all agree in saying that the
father of both the persons named Tewdrig was Teithfallt or
Teithffaltim. Notwithstanding the opinion of the historian of

* The Silurian Achau y Saint, and Nennius.
† According to Nennius, the hundred of Builth, or the northern part
of the county was included in the possessions of Vortigern.
‡ Page 94 of this Essay.

[TABLE VI.]

CUNEDDA WLEDIG

Tiblon — Meirion — Arwystl — Ceredig — Dunod — Mael — Coel — Dogfael — Four other sons as below.

Cedig
Bleiddyd — Afan — Doged — Tybiul Caranaog Pedrun — Corun — Pedr — Tyrnog Cyndeyrn — Arthog — Ithel Senılle Hydwn Dwn
Cynfelyn Cynudyn — Cyndeyra Cynwr — Dogfael DEWI Enlleu
Gwynllieu — Telio Mabon

CUNEDDA WLEDIG

Seven sons as above. — Rhufon — Einiou Yrth — Owal — Gwron

Gwenasedh, dr. — Caswallon Lawhir — Owain Danwyn — Meigr Medyr Cynyr Farfdrwch
Maelgwn Gwynedd — Einion Frenhin Scirtol Meirion — Cal Celynin Ceitho Gwpn Gwynne Gwynnoro
Eurgain dr,
Rhun
Bell
Iago — Nudd
Rhun — Cadfan — Edeyrn
Lindd — Cadwallon
Cadfael — Cadwaladr Fendigaid
Tangno
Collwyn

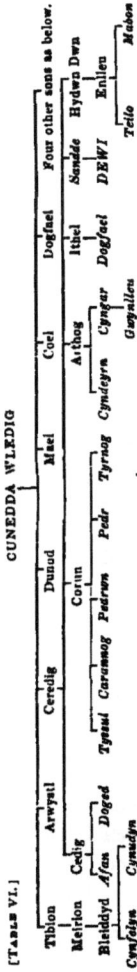

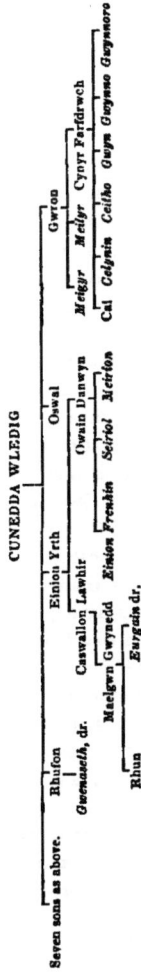

N. B. This and the other pedigrees do not contain all the names that might be introduced, but only so many as are sufficient to determine the era and genealogy of the Saints.

Brecknockshire,* there is reason to conclude, as shown by the minority, that one Tewdrig has been mistaken for the other ; since the alternative would render it necessary to explain how the ancestry of the elder Tewdrig could have been preserved at so early a time ; and it should be noticed that the pedigree is disjointed within two generations of the departure of the Romans, about the very period at which the authority of other genealogies seems to commence. The claims of clanship were, doubtless, acknowledged by the Britons, as they are by most nations in a rude state of society ; but as the heads of families were in a state of dependency, there could have been no great inducement to preserve the memory of their affinities. From the departure of the Romans, downwards, the celebrity and independence of the chieftains, together with the claims of their descendants to the inheritance of their territories, are a sufficient reason to account for the preservation of the record.

Marchell, the daughter of Tewdrig, is said to have been married to Anllech Goronog, " Brenhin Ewerddon," or, according to others, to Aulach, the son of Cormac mac Cairbre, one of the kings of Ireland. He was, probably, the captain of a band of Irish rovers who infested the coast of Wales after the departure of Maximus, and might have penetrated into the interior. The fruit of this union was Brychan. In the " History of Brecknockshire" may be found a long legend respecting the visit of Marchell to Ireland, and her marriage there, attended with the parade which a writer of romance might deem necessary upon such an occasion ; but as the story, which has been recorded in Latin and English, has never appeared in the Welsh language, it may be said that the silence of the earlier Welsh writers, as to events which concerned the honour of their country, affords a presumption that such events were either unknown or discredited.

* Mr. Theophilus Jones, in Vol. I. Chap. II. of his "History" of that country.

† Vol. 1. Chap. II, and Appendix No. VI.

Brychan is computed to have *reigned,* such is the term, from
A. D. 400 to A. D. 450.* The computation may, however,
be altered so far as to bring down the commencement of his
reign to about A. D. 410, in order to allow a sufficient interval,
after the departure of Maximus in 383, for the marriage of his
mother with an Irish adventurer, as well as for his own
growth to manhood. That he commenced his reign later than
A. D. 410 is not likely from the chronology which it is necessary to give to his descendants. His grandfather and
mother must have lived in the Roman time, and therefore in a
state of dependence, if not of obscurity; for, that Brychan attained to power not possessed by his ancestors is probable
from his having given his name to the district where he —
exercised his authority;† and the date here assigned to his
accession agrees well with the time in which, according to
Zosimus, the Britons threw off the Roman yoke.

A fourth chieftain, contemporary with the preceding, was
Cystennyn Gorneu, the founder of a family in Cornwall.
No further particulars are known respecting him; but the
pedigree of his descendants, which includes several Saints, is
given as follows.—

[TABLE VII.]

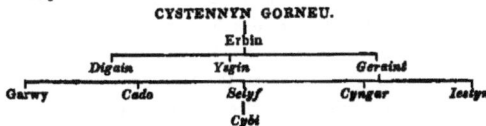

A fifth chieftain of this time was Cadell, who is often confounded with Cadell Deyrnllug. From the pedigree of his

* Jones's Brecknockshire, Vol. I. Chap. III.
† The names "Brecon and Brecknock" are but English modifications of
"Brychan and Brycheiniog."

P

family it may be concluded that his territories lay in Glamorganshire and Monmouthshire.

[TABLE VIII.]

CADELL
|
Tegyd
|
Glywys of Glewyseg
|
Gwynllyw Filwr of Gwynllwg

Cattwg Ddoeth	Cammaroh	Glywys Cerniw	Hywgu	Maches	Cynfyw or Cyfyw	Gwyddleu
		Gwodloew	Beuno			Camnen

Cadrod Calchfynydd is the last that may be mentioned of
this early date. His territories were situated about the middle
of England.

Of these contemporary chieftains there are reasons for
adjudging the seniority in respect of age to Cunedda.* But
he is deserving of notice more especially, as the Triads record
that he was the first who gave lands and privileges to God and
the Saints in the island of Britain; by which may be understood that this was the first time the Church received temporal
possessions and endowments in this country. It is not stated
what particular churches were thus endowed by Cunedda,
but they probably existed in his northern territories, or in
England, and subsequent revolutions have swept away every
trace of them. Before this time the British chieftains were
not in a condition to give lands to the Church, and perhaps
the practice did not commence elsewhere before the con-

* An elegy on the death of Cunedda is printed in the Myvyrian Archaiology of Wales, Vol. I. p. 71, from which his character as a warrior
and some particulars of his history may be collected. It was composed
by a Taliesin, older than the Bard usually known by that name, and is
perhaps the earliest specimen of Welsh poetry extant. An English
translation of it is given in Davies's Claims of Ossian, Section I, accompanied by several interesting and appropriate remarks.

version of Constantine; but before the end of the fourth century it was not uncommon.

It has been observed that no church in Wales bears the name of Owain ab Macsen; the same may be said of his brother, Ednyfed, who is also included in the catalogue of Saints. The church of Llanbeblig near Carnarvon is called after Peblig, another brother of Owain; and this is the first instance of a church in Wales bearing the name of a Saint not admitted into the Romish Calendar. The circumstance of the name may, therefore, be attributed to the supposition that he was the founder, having previously consecrated the place by the performance of certain religious exercises, after the manner which Bede describes as customary among the Christians of North Britain.* It is necessary, however, to suppose that this church was founded after the expulsion of the Irish, and it would not require that Peblig should be more than sixty years of age to extend his life down to the time; since Maximus left Britain in 383, and the Irish were driven from North Wales before A. D. 430. The first churches would naturally be erected in towns, where the greatest population was collected; an opinion which ecclesiastical writers in general maintain. Llanbeblig is the parish church of Carnarvon, but it is not situate in that town, nor at the neighbouring Roman station of Segontium. The Romans had quitted the country, and whatever buildings were left at Segontium were likely to have been destroyed by the Irish. Carnarvon, on the other hand, is of later origin, though of very ancient date. The inference drawn is, that Llanbeblig was founded before the existence of Carnarvon. But another circumstance which might have contributed to the foundation of this and other churches in the age of Peblig, was the visit of St. Germanus to Britain in 429, and that he visited Carnarvonshire is pro-

* See page 60 of this Essay.

bable from the traces of his name which still remain in that county.*

The chapels subject to Llanbeblig are, St. Mary's, or the present church of Carnarvon; and St. Helen's, which formerly existed in that town. The author of Mona Antiqua supposes the latter to be dedicated† to Helen, the wife of Maximus, and the conjecture is supported by the circumstance that she was also the mother of Peblig. The coincidence might be thought sufficient to determine the question, if it could be shown that the wife of Maximus has ever been considered a Saint; and the cause of doubt is increased by the equally plausible conjecture, supported by similar local reasons, that the person intended was the elder Helen, whose saintship is undisputed. A belief, though founded on insufficient grounds, is known to have existed so early as the time of Nennius, that either Constantius, the emperor, or his grandson of the same name, was buried at Carnarvon; and, in proof, it was alleged that a stone with a certain inscription pointed out the place of his grave.‡ This, however, is contradictory to the testimony of classical writers, who state that the first Constantius was buried at York, and the second at Mopsuestia in Cilicia; but

* Llanarmon (St. Germanus) chapel to Llangybi; and Bettws Garmon, subject to Llanfair Isgaer, all in Carnarvonshire.

† The editor of the Beauties of North Wales, carrying the popular opinion too far, states that this chapel was *founded* by Helen. Had this been the case, according to the principles laid down in the first Section of this Essay, it would, at the time of the institution of tithes and the division of parishes, have received its separate endowment; but, being founded after that time, no means remained for its maintenance except as dependent upon the church of the parish in which it was situated.

‡ Nennius, who flourished in the ninth century, says that the person commemorated was Constantius, the *son* of Constantine; while Matthew of Westminster states that A. D. 1283 the body of Constantius, the *father* of that emperor was found by digging, and was, by order of Edward the First, honourably interred in the adjacent church. See also Hanes Gruffudd ab Cynan, Myv. Archaiology, Vol. II. 595.

as the words of the words of the inscription have not been
preserved, and as the name Constantius can be proved to have
been common in Britain for some time after the retirement of
the Romans, the stone probably commemorated some other
person, who was afterwards mistaken for the emperor.

As Mor, the son of Ceneu ab Coel, was a Saint contemporary with Cunedda and Peblig, he may be considered the
founder of the churches of Llannor or Llanfor in Carnarvonshire, and Llanfor in Penllyn, Merionethshire. The first of
these may claim a higher antiquity than the town of Pwllheli,
which is situate at the distance of three miles in a subordinate
chapelry.* Had the town existed first, the probability is that
the mother church would have been built in it. Llanfor in
Merioneth is said by Browne Willis to be dedicated to St.
Deiniol, and the names of both these churches have been
thought to be corruptions of Llan-fawr, *anglicè* "the great
church ;" but to set aside etymological conjectures, both of
them were known by the name of Llanfor as early as the
time of Llywarch Hen, a Bard who died about A. D. 660, and
the verses in which he speaks of them may thus be translated :†—

> Trust not Bran, trust not Dunawd,
> That thou shalt not find wounded by them
> The pastor of the flock of Llanfor who guides our path.
>
> There is a Llanfor beyond the tide,
> To whom the sea pours forth its praises,
> Whether she be equal to ours I know not.

* The chapel of Pwllheli, alias Denio, is dedicated to St. Beuno, who
flourished A. D. 580.

† The following is the original, from the Myv. Archaiology, Vol. I.
page 120,—

Na chred Vrân na chred Dunawd	Yssydd Lanvor dra gweilgi
Na chai ganthudd yn fosawd	Y gwna môr molud wrthi
Bugail liol Llanvor llwybrawd.	Llaliogan ni wn ai hi.

There is a Llanfor, towering aloft,
Where the Clwyd flows into Clywedog,
And I know not whether she be her equal.

The Dee winds within her borders,
From Meloch to Traweryn;
The pastor of the flock of Llanfor is our conductor.

Here three churches are mentioned together in such a way
that their enumeration may best be attributed to the circumstance of their being founded by the same Saint, since the
descriptive term—"great church"—was not likely in those
days to have passed for a proper name. The Bard spent the
latter part of his life at Llanfor in Merionethshire, where he
died, and in these stanzas he appears to warn his spiritual
instructor against some impending danger. Situated where
he was, unless he was a good topographer, he could easily
conceive that the upper part of Cardigan Bay intervened
between him and Llanfor in Lleyn Carnarvonshire, the parish-
ioners of which place are near enough to the sea to hear the
music of the waves. The Bard mentions also another church
which is conceived to be Llanynys* in Denbighshire, the
name of which, in English "the church of the island," is descriptive of its situation between the rivers Clwyd and Clywedog. This church has been ascribed to St. Saeran from the
circumstance of his having been buried there;† but as Welsh
churches are sometimes found to claim the honour of two
Saints,‡ this will interpose no difficulty, since the oldest Saint
may be allowed to be the founder, and the younger may have

Yssydd Llanvor tra bânawg   Hela Dyvyrdwy yn ei thervyn
Ydd aa Clwyd yn Nghlywedawg   O Veloch hyd Traweryn
Ac ni wn ai hi llallawg.   Bugail lloi Llanvor llwybryn.

* Chapel to Llanynys—Cyffylliog, St. Mary.

† Myv. Archaiology, Vol. II. page 51.

‡ The two Saints are rather a proof that there was no formal dedication,
and that the church was called after the name of the person whose memory was most associated with it.

been a distinguished minister, or one who increased the privileges of the church. In the last stanza, the Bard returns to his own parish; and the Dee, Meloch, and Traweryn, are rivers in that neighbourhood which still retain those names.

About this time (A. D. 420 to 430) it is said that the Church in Britain was infected with the Pelagian heresy; and that the orthodox clergy, being unable to stem its progress, sent to Gaul desiring assistance. Upon which it was determined in a full synod of the Gallican Church, that Germanus, Bishop of Auxerre, and Lupus, Bishop of Troyes, should be sent to Britain to confute the heretics. The date assigned to this event by Prosper, a contemporary writer, is A. D. 429; but he speaks of Germanus only, who, he says, was sent by Pope Celestine at the suit of Palladius, the Apostle of Scotland. Constantius of Lyons, the biographer of St. Grrmanus, who wrote while several persons who had been acquainted with that Prelate were living, relates the affair differently; and his words may be rendered as follows.*—"At that time a deputation, direct from Britain, announced to the Gallican Bishops, that the Pelagian heresy was gaining an extensive hold upon the people in that country; and that assistance ought to be given as soon as possible to the Catholic faith. For which reason a large synod was convened, and with one consent the prayers of the whole assembly were directed to those bright luminaries of religion, Germanus and Lupus, Apostolic priests, who while their bodies were on earth had their minds fixed on heaven. And inasmuch as the necessity appeared the more

---

* The original, as given by Archbishop Usher, is,—"Eodem tempore ex Britanniis directa legatio Gallicanis Episcopis nunclavit, Pelagianam perversitatem latè populos occupàsse, et quamprimum fidei catholicæ debere succurri. Ob quam causam Synodus numerosa collecta est: omniumque judicio duo præclara religionis lumina universorum precibus ambiuntur, Germanus et Lupus, Apostolici sacerdotes, terram corporibus, cœlum meritis, (seu mentibus) possidentes. Et quanto necessitas laboros-

urgent, so much the more readily did those devoted heroes undertake the task, hastening thé despatch of the business, to which they were stimulated by their faith."—This narrative amounts to a full contradiction of the other as regards the interference of the Pope, or Palladius. Baronius endeavours to reconcile the statements by supposing that Celestine might have entrusted the affair to the Gallican synod, and approved of their choice. But the *haste* with which, according to Constantius, the business was transacted will allow of no such supposition. Besides which, Baronius ought to have known that at that time the Pope and the Gallican Church were at variance. The latter were charged with Semi-Pelagianism, and Celestine was not likely to trust the suppression of Pelagianism to those persons whom he himself accused of an approximation to it. It would appear that when Prosper found that the mission of Germanus and Lupus had been attended with unwonted success, he wished to claim a share of the credit for his friend, the Pope; for he was himself also one of the greatest opponents of the Semi-Pelagians, and perhaps the reason why he omits the name of Lupus is because that person was brother to Vincentius Lirinensis, who was a distinguished leader of the adverse party.*

Stress is laid upon these particulars because Prosper would insinuate that Britain was brought under the Papal jurisdiction; but, unfortunately for his pious fraud, the clearest proofs of British independence appear after his time. The historian Bede, who was a zealous Catholic, gives an account of this transaction in nearly the same words as Constantius. In the latter writer may also be found an inflated account of

ior apparebat, tanto eam promptius heroes devotissimi susceperunt, celeritatem negotii fidei stimulis maturantes."—De Brit. Eccl. Primordiis, Cap. XI.

* Usher de Primordiis, Cap. XI. and XII.   Hughes's Horæ Britannicæ, Vol. II. Cap. VII.

the zeal, and success of the preaching of Germanus and Lupus
until the Pelagians were triumphantly vanquished at a general
conference, supposed to have been held at Verulam. Then
follows the discovery of the relicks of St. Alban, and a description of a mass of earth still reeking with his blood, which
Germanus carried away to Gaul. The next occurrence is the
miraculous victory obtained by the Britons, under Germanus,
over the Saxons and Picts, by suddenly shouting the word
"Alleluia," upon which the enemy fled in great consternation. It seems strange that Constantius should describe
such miracles within fifty years after the death of the Saint,
but this was the age of religious imposture, and stories could
be related at Lyons, with perfect safety, of events which took
place in an obscure corner of Britain. It does not appear
that any of these tales are to be found in Welsh MSS. and it
was the occurrence of the name of "Maesgarmon,"* in the
parish of Mold, Flintshire, that led Archbishop Usher to fix
upon that spot for the "Alleluiatic Victory." That a battle
was fought there, under circumstances which were afterwards
improved into a miracle, is not improbable; and there are
names of places in that neighbourhood, which show that the
district has, for some reason or other, been tenacious of the
memory of the Saint. The alliance of the Saxons and Picts†
about a score of years before the landing of Hengist, is
possibly a mistake, into which Constantius was led for want
of the means of accurate information.

The mission of St. Germanus, or as he is called by the
Welsh, Garmon, may have lasted about two or three years,
and, according to Constantius, he visited Britain a second
time, upon which occasion he was accompanied by Severus,
Bishop of Triers. Archbishop Usher calculates that the
second mission was performed A. D. 447, and that it was of
short continuance. On the other hand, the Welsh authorities
would imply that he visited this country but once, which was

* "The field of Germanus." † Qu. Gwyddyl Ffichti?

Q

about the time of the last date,* when he was accompanied by
Lupus, for they make no mention whatever of Severus. Par-
tiality for national traditions must give way in a point in
which Constantius could not easily have been mistaken; besides which, there is an incongruity in the Welsh accounts
themselves which ought to be rectified. The following is
extracted from Achau y Saint, as translated in the Horæ
Britannicæ. (Vol. II. page 161.)

"Garmon was a Saint and a bishop, the son of Ridigius
from the land of Gallia; and it was in the time of Constantine
of Armorica that he came there; and continued here to the
time of Vortigern; and then he returned back to France
where he died. He formed two choirs of saints, and placed
bishops and divines in them, that they might teach the
Christian faith to the nation of the Cymry, where they were
become degenerate in the faith. One choir he formed in
Llan Carvan, where Dyfric (Dubricius) the Saint was the
principal, and he himself was bishop there. The other was
near Caer Worgorn,† where he appointed Iltutus to be principal; and Lupus (called Bleiddan) was the chief bishop there.
After which he placed bishops in Llandaff; he constituted
Dubricius archbishop there; and Cadoc, the Saint, the son of
Gwynlliw, took his place in the choir at Llancarvan, and the
archbishop of Llandaff was bishop there also."

Now it happens that another note in Achau y Saint says
that the College‡ of Caerworgorn was founded by Cystennyn
Fendigaid, and soon afterwards destroyed by the Irish. At
that time its principal was Padrig. It might be said that
Germanus restored the foundation in A. D. 447, when he ap-

* "Garmon ap Redgitus o Ffrainc i'r henyw, ac yn amser Gwrtheym
Gwrthenau i doeth i'r ynys hon."—Myv. Archaiology, Vol. II. p. 43.
† Llancarvan and Caerworgorn, the latter of which is now known by
the name of Llanilltyd or Lantwit, are both in Glamorganshire.
‡ "College"—so the word Bangor—the Welsh term for the monastic
institutions of the fifth and sixth centuries, is generally rendered.

pointed Iltutus to be its principal.   But the genealogies show that Iltutus must have been at that time too young for the office, since about eighty years afterwards he is known to have flourished in the court of Arthur, and in his younger days he was not an ecclesiastic but a soldier.   The relationship in which he stood to Germanus was that of sister's grandson, as will appear from the following scale.—

[TABLE IX.]

	CYNFOR			RHEDYW		
Constantine			Aldor married .... dr.			*Garmon*
Uther	Emyr Llydaw			Rhiain m. to Bicanus		
Arthur	Tewdwr	Hywel	*Gwyndaf*	*Illtyd*	*Sadwrn* m. Canna	
	Canna		*Meugan*		*Crallo*	

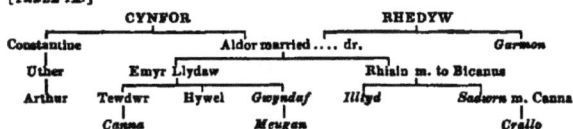

It does not follow that these generations should be necessarily parallel, but the Chronicles and Triads state that Arthur, Hywel, and Iltutus or Illtyd were contemporary ; and if it be said that Iltutus was appointed by St. Germanus in his *first* visit, the inconsistency will appear more glaring.* But while all other accounts agree that Iltutus was the first principal of the College which afterwards bore his name, the Book of Llandaff decides the question by saying that he received his appointment from St. Dubricius† who lived in an age succeeding that of Germanus.   If the foregoing extract be compared with the narration of Constantius, its incongruities increase.   Lupus did not accompany Germanus the second time, and therefore could not have been Bishop of Caerworgorn.   The same note

---

* The anachronism did not escape the acuteness of Archbishop Usher— "Iltutus S. Germani fuisse discipulum, et in Vincentii Speculo Historiali, et in Landavensium Regesto legimus ; *licet id ægre temporum ratio patiatur.*" Cap. XIII.

† "A Dubricio Landavensi episcopo in loco, qui ab illo Lan-iltut, id est Ecclesiæ Iltuti accepit nomen, est constitutus." Usher, from the Regestum Landavense.

implies that Germanus lived to remove Dubricius to Llandaff, and place Cadog or Cattwg in his room; but Archbishop Usher puts an end to this idea, by showing that Germanus returned to Gaul, and died in the second year of his last mission. That Dubricius received any appointment from St. Germanus, except perhaps the bishoprick of Llandaff, is questionable; and, by the order of time, it would appear that the connexion of Germanus and Lupus with the institutions of Caerworgorn and Llancarvan was altogether apocryphal.

Authorities are not wanting to show that Germanus was the founder of the Universities of Oxford and Cambridge, but they are not worthy of a serious refutation, and even the credulous Constantius does not make mention of any schools founded at this time in Britain. That Germanus made regulations for the stability of the British Church is very probable; and if credit be given to an anonymous treatise which Usher says was written in the eighth century, he introduced the Gallic liturgy into this country. It is certain, however, that his visit was the commencement of a frequent intercourse which subsisted for some time afterwards between the Cambrian and Armorican Churches; and it was by no means unlikely that the one Church should adopt some of the regulations of the other.

In the Welsh accounts Garmon or St. Germanus is called the son of Rhedyw, Rhedygus, Ridicus, or Redgitus; and notwithstanding the variety of names in different MSS. there can be little doubt that the same person is intended.* It is further stated that he was a native of Armorica; and as proofs remain that his countrymen spoke the same language as the Britons, he may have derived from that circumstance one of the qualifications which fitted him for his mission. His sister is said to have been the mother of Emyr Llydaw, an Armorican prince; but as Usher does not quote this relationship

* From other authorities it appears that the correct name was Rusticus.

from Constantius, it is probable the prince did not aspire to a higher rank than that of an ordinary chieftain.

Several churches in Wales bear the name of Garmon; but as he visited this country twice, only one of them can be distinctly referred to his first mission, namely Llanarmon in Iâl, Denbighshire. It is singular that the parish attached to it adjoins that of Mold, in which the "Alleluiatic Victory" is said to have been gained; and if Archbishop Usher has correctly determined the locality of the engagement, the church in question is possibly situated on the spot where Germanus is described to have raised a sacred edifice,* formed of the branches of trees interwoven together, in which he and his followers celebrated the services of Easter, and baptized the

---

* From the manner in which the story is related it may be gathered that the mode of consecration used upon the occasion was no other than the performance of the religious exercises of Lent; and though it does not appear that the consecration of ground for the erection of churches was necessarily confined to that season, yet the time when a similar occurrence took place, as described by Bede, is a remarkable coincidence. The following is a close version of the words of Constantius which relate to this particular.—"The sacred days of Lent were at hand, which the presence of the divines rendered more solemn, insomuch that those instructed by their daily preaching flocked eagerly to the grace of Baptism. For the great multitude of the army was desirous of the water of the laver of salvation. A church, formed of interwoven branches of trees (frondibus contexta) is prepared against the day of the resurrection of our Lord, and though the expedition was encamped in the field, is fitted up like that of a city. The army, wet with baptism, advances, the people are fervent in faith, and neglecting the protection of arms, they await the assistance of the Deity. In the mean time this plan of proceeding, or state of the camp, is reported to the enemy, who, anticipating a victory over an unarmed multitude, hasten with alacrity. But their approach is discovered by the scouts; and when, after concluding the solemnities of Easter, the greater part of the army, fresh from their baptism, were preparing to take up arms and give battle, Germanus offers himself as the leader of the war."—An exaggerated description follows of the rout of the enemy, who were thrown into consternation upon hearing the word Alleluia shouted thrice by the Britons.

greater part of the army of the Britons, before they proceeded
to meet their enemies.

Lupus, it would appear, was the younger and less obtrusive
of the two legates, as nothing is related of him in which the
other does not bear a part. His name is rendered in Welsh by
Bleiddian, a word of similar import. The churches ascribed
to him are, Llanfleiddian Fawr in Glamorganshire, which
bears the same relation to the town of Cowbridge as Llanbeblig and Llannor do to Carnarvon and Pwllheli;—and Llanfleiddian Fach, or St. Lythian's, in the same county. The
latter is a small parish, but probably some parts have been
detached from it by the Normans; and the occurrence of these
names perhaps gave rise to the tradition, that Lupus was connected with the College afterwards founded at Caerworgorn.
The chapels subject to Llanfleiddian Fawr are, Cowbridge
(St. Mary,) and Welsh St. Donat's (Dunwyd:) and, according
to the Martyrology of Bede, the commemoration or festival of
St. Lupus was held on the twenty ninth of July.

The foregoing are all the churches whose foundations may
be attributed to this generation, ending with the accession of
Constantine the Blessed, A. D. 433; most of which are situate
in the territories of the sons of Cunedda, under whose protection it is obvious they were established. Nearly all the
parishes annexed to them are of considerable extent, and have
their subordinate chapelries, in which the Saints of the Catholic, or more modern character, predominate. For the support
which they gave to the cause of Christianity, the children of
Cunedda are called, in the Triads, the second holy family of
Britain ; the first being that of Bran ab Llyr Llediaith.

SECTION VIII.

IT is proposed that the next generation shall commence with the accession of Constantine A. D. 433, and terminate with the deposition of Vortigern A. D. 464; not that any reliance can be placed upon the history or chronology of the "Kings of Britain," but, since it has been generally received, it will give the reader a clearer idea of the succession of events.

The chronicles of Walter and Geoffrey relate that about this time, the Britons were so oppressed with the inroads of barbarians, that they applied to Aldor, king of Armorica, for assistance; upon which he sent them his brother Constantine with a large body of troops; and it would appear that Constantine performed such important services after his arrival that he was elected to the headship of the confederated states of the island. The Triads confirm this account so far as to say that Cystennyn Fendigaid, or Constantine the Blessed,* was one of the three foreign princes of Britain; and the "Genealogy of the Saints" calls him Cystennyn Llydaw, or Constantine of Armorica. In his person the office of Pendragon of the Britons assumed, for the first time, the appearance of a monarchy, but it still continued to be elective. Upon his death in 443, his son Constans was elected to succeed him. This person was in 448 murdered by Vortigern, who usurped the kingdom until 464, when he was deposed and his son Vortimer chosen in his room.

* He is distinguished from Constantine the Great, who is called Cystennyn Amherawdwr and Cystennyn ab Elen.

Constantine has been surnamed "the Blessed" in consequence of being considered a Saint of the British Church, and
Llangystennyn near Conway is perhaps dedicated to his memory. In "Achau y. Saint" the following curious notice
occurs respecting him:—"It was the glory of the emperor
Theodosius in conjunction with Cystennyn Llydaw, surnamed
the Blessed, to have first founded the College of Illtyd, which
was regulated by Balerus, a man from Rome; and Padrig,
the son of Mawon, was the first principal of it, before he was
carried away captive by the Irishmen."*—The College here
mentioned was that of Caerworgorn, which was also called
Côr Tewdws; but what authority Theodosius the Second,
who was at this time emperor of Rome, or rather of the East,
could have exercised in Britain is more than can be explained;
unless it be supposed that the name was given to the College
in compliment to him because Balerus was a Roman. The
account will not justify the supposition that it was founded by
Theodosius the Elder, or by Theodosius the Great, neither of
whom was a contemporary of Cystennyn Llydaw. But the
most remarkable part of the statement is a Welsh tradition
respecting the great Apostle of Ireland, who, according to the
Silurian catalogue of Saints, was the son of Mawon, and a
native of the country of Gŵyr or Gower in Glamorganshire.
He was also called Padrig Maenwyn; and as Caerworgorn
was situated near the sea coast, the story that he was carried
away from thence by the Irish in one of their expeditions
would be thought by no means improbable, if it were supported
by other testimonies. In a composition acknowledged to be a
genuine production of St. Patrick, and entitled his "Confession," he states that he was but sixteen years of age when
he was made captive; his youth, therefore, precludes the idea
that he was at that time the principal of a College. He
further explains that his father was Calpurnius, a deacon, who

* Cambrian Biography, voce Padrig.

lived at " Bonavem Taberniæ," near to which was the village
of " Enon," from which he was himself taken into captivity.
The situation of these last places is disputed; and while they
are generally considered to have been in North Britain, others
contend that they should be looked for in Armorica. To
enter into the circumstances of his life would be needless
upon the present occasion, and, until the evidence of his
connexion with the Principality were better supported, all
further investigation would be deemed irrelevant. Ricemarchus, Giraldus Cambrensis, and John of Teignmouth relate that
he settled at one time in a small valley at Menevia, called
Vallis Rosina, where he built a monastery and intended to pass
his days in religious seclusion. But an angel, appearing, commanded him to preach the Gospel in Ireland; and, in confirmation of his mission, displayed to him the whole of that country
in a vision from the spot where he stood. The legend adds that
the same angel foretold that Menevia should be famed for
another Saint, who should be born there thirty years after that
day. The Saint predicted was St. David; and absurd as the
whole fable may appear, the latter part of it was embodied in
one of the collects of the Breviary of Salisbury, and devoutly
repeated over a great part of England before the Reformation.
The only religious edifice in Wales, known to have been dedicated to St. Patrick, was a chapel, which once existed in the
parish of St. David's Pembrokeshire; and, according to John
of Teignmouth, was situated close to the spot where the angel
showed him the vision of Ireland.*

The year 447 is the date of the second mission of St. Germanus to Britain. His stay was short, as, according to the
computation of Usher, he died in Italy the following year.
His former colleague, Lupus, survived him thirty years, but
upon this occasion he was accompanied by Severus, Bishop of

* Llanbadrig in Anglesey is reported to have been named from another
Padrig, the son of Aelfryd ab Goronwy.

R

Triers. Several fables are related by Nennius and others as
to the acts of his second mission, the whole circumstances of
which are too absurd to repeat. One of them is in brief:—
Ketelus, or Cadellus, the swineherd of Benly, king of Powys,
offered the Saint that hospitality which had been refused by
his master ; in consequence of which Benly was deposed by
the Saint, and the swineherd was elected in his room, whose
descendants continued afterwards to possess the territory.[*]
It so happens that the Welsh accounts mention the name of
Benlli Gawr, who, according to Mr. Owen,[†] was a chieftain of
a district in the present county of Denbigh about the middle
of the fifth century ; but he was succeeded by his son Beli.
By Ketelus is meant Cadell Deyrnllug,[‡] " a prince of the Vale
Royal and part of Powys," who rose into power about this
time. These facts show that there is some foundation for the
story, though they are no proof of its correctness. It is remarkable that there is a church dedicated to St. Germanus,
called Llanarmon Dyffryn Ceiriog, in the district which might
have been part of the possessions of either Cadell or Benlli ;
and a chapel, subject to the church of an adjoining parish, is
called Llanarmon Fach.

Another story relates that Vortigern endeavoured in a
council of the Britons, held in Gwrtheyrnion, to palm upon
the Saint the fruit of his own incest ; for which he was cursed
by the Saint and the whole body of the clergy assembled ; and
that afterwards Vortimer, the son of Vortigern, to appease the
Saint, gave him the lands upon which he suffered the insult to
be his for ever. Gwrtheyrnion is a district of Radnorshire,

* See Usher, De Primordiis, Cap. XI, who attributes this tale to the
first mission ; but the arrangement here attempted is more consistent with
chronology. The names are given according to Gildas, as of better
authority than Ranulphus Cestrensis.

† Cambrian Biography.

‡ Nennius, as quoted in Jones's Brecknockshire, Vol. I page 52, says
that Cadell Deyrnllug was converted and baptized by St. Germanus.

forming the present hundred of Rhayader; and there is in it at this day a church, which under the name of St. Harmon's is ascribed to St. Germanus. Whether these stories were invented to account for the origin of the churches, or whether the churches owe their dedications to the previous existence of the stories, is more than can be determined; but the coincidence is singular.

The festival of St. Germanus was observed July 31, or, according to other authorities, August 1. The churches, the foundations of which may be ascribed to him, are—Llanarmon in Iâl, Denbighshire, Llanarmon Dyffryn Ceiriog, ditto, St. Harmon's, Radnorshire, and Llanfechain, Montgomeryshire; and the chapels dedicated to him are—Llanarmon under Llangybi, Carnarvonshire, Bettws Garmon under Llanfair Isgaer, ditto, Capel Garmon under Llanrwst, Denbighshire, and Llanarmon Fach under Llandegfan, ditto.

That Germanus effected a great change in the religious condition of the Britons is not unlikely from the respect so generally paid to his name; and it may be observed that there are no parish churches in Wales which can be traced to a higher date than his first visit, and even those that may be so ancient are few. Parochial churches did not belong to the early ages of Christianity. According to the concurring testimony of ecclesiastical writers, the clergy lived for some time in towns in communities under their Bishop, from whence they itinerated about the country, and on their return brought with them the offerings which they had collected for the common support of the society. But about the beginning of this century the ecclesiastical system was undergoing a change, and Germanus would regulate the British Church after the model of the Gallican. Accordingly, in the Council of Vaison in Gaul A. D. 442, a decree was made "that country parishes should have presbyters to preach in them as well as the city-churches;"*—and to the influence of this circumstance,

* Bingham's Ecclesiastical Antiquities, Book IX. Chap. 8. Section 1.

the origin of country churches in Wales may perhaps be traced.

About the commencement of this generation, Gwrtheyrn, or Vortigern, first appears among the chiefs of the Britons. According to Nennius his territories included the northern part of the present counties of Radnor and Brecon, and some of the Welsh genealogists state also that he was the regulus of Erging or Erchenfield in Herefordshire. From these two points being considered together it would appear that his dominions, as the leader of a clan, extended along the vale of the river Wye. But in 448, or about the time of the second visit of Germanus, he became by treachery or otherwise the Pendragon or chief ruler of Britain. To trace the various circumstances of his history would require a separate treatise; for they have been obscured with the extravagancies of romance, and a careful investigation would be necessary to distinguish the truth from fable.* Suffice it for the present purpose to say that his ancestors, as given in the mutilated orthography of Nennius, were " Guortheneu,† Mᶜ Guitaul, Mᶜ Guitolin, Mᶜ ap Glou ;" and the following is the pedigree of his descendants according to Achau y Saint:—

[TABLE X.]

GWRTHEYRN GWRTHENEU

Gwrthefyr Fendigaid, or Vortimer	Cyndeyrn	Pasgen	A daughter, and other sons as below.

Anna dr. married to Cynyr of Caergawch		Madrun dr. m. to Ynyr Gwent	
Ceidio	Tegiwg dr.	Iddon	Caradog	Cynheiddion

GWRTHEYRN GWRTHENEU

Edeyrn	Aerdeyrn	Ell-leyrn	Gotta, son of Rhonwen or Rowena

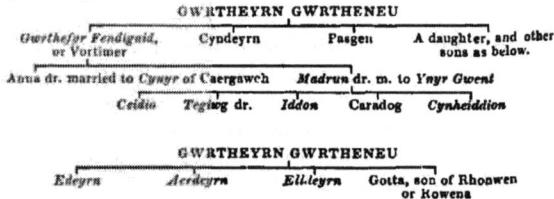

* Instances of the confusion, with which Geoffrey of Monmouth has clouded the life of Vortigern, have been shown by Mr. S. Turner in his " History of the Anglo Saxons," Vol. I. Book II. Chap. VII.

† While nearly all accounts agree that the father of Gwrtheyrn was Gwrthenau, some modern pedigrees state that his grandfather was Rhy-

In passing through the different families *seriatim*, and observing the Saints whose names fall in with this generation, the only one that occurs in the line of Macsen Wledig is Madog, the son of Owain; but as other persons of the name of Madog have received the honours of sanctity, the churches to be assigned to each of them separately are uncertain.

In the line of Coel Godebog, Cynllo, the son of Mor, presents himself to notice. He was the tutelar Saint or founder of the three churches in Radnorshire, whose extensive endowments have been already described. He was also the founder of Llangynllo, and Llangoedmor, in Cardiganshire; to the latter of which, the neighbouring churches of Mount and Llechryd, both dedicated to the Holy Cross, were formerly subject. Cynllo is commemorated in the Calendar, July 17, under the name of Cynllo Frenhin,* or the King; and as he belonged to a powerful family it is probable that he was originally a chieftain, and might afterwards, according to the practice of the age, have embraced a life of religion. The Pseudo-Taliesin says of him—

" The prayer of Cynllo shall not be in vain."†

—a proof that in after times his intercession was considered efficacious.

In the line of Cynan Meiriadog occurs the name of Tudwal Befr,‡ who is described as a Saint and Bishop; and as his diocese is not mentioned, it is possible that he was a Chorepis-

deyrn, whose descent is traced in the ninth, or according to others in the fifteenth degree from Beli Mawr; but the older and better supported authority of Nennius must be preferred. The discrepancy coincides with the time of the retirement of the Romans, and the names given by Nennius are no more than might easily have been retained from the period before that crisis.

* See the old Editions of the Welsh Common Prayer.

† "Ni bydd coeg gweddi Cynllo." Dyhuddiant Elphin. Myvyrian Archaiology, Vol. II. p. 83.

‡ Son of Morfawr ab Cadfan ab Cynan, in Table I.

copus or local Bishop, an office which was at this time not
uncommon. An island off the coast of Carnarvonshire is
called after him, in which are the ruins of a small chapel,
dedicated to the same person,* and subject, as it would seem,
to the church of Llaneingion Frenhin on the main land.
Another church in the neighbourhood is named Tudweiliog,
but the word is more descriptive of a district or clan of followers than of a religious edifice; and Carlisle† says that the
parish festival is that of St. Cwyfen, which is holden on the
third of June. Tudwal Befr was married to Nefydd, daughter of Brychan, and is reported to have had a son, Ifor ab
Tudwal, who is said to have been a Saint, but no churches
are ascribed to him.‡

The Saints of the family of Cystennyn Gorneu are, Erbin
ab Cystennyn Gorneu, and Digain his brother;§ to the latter
of whom the foundation of Llangerniw, or the "church of the
Cornishman," in Denbighshire, is attributed. His festival is
held Nov. 21.

The date of some of the descendants of Vortigern renders it
necessary to place the age of his son, Gwrthefyr or Vortimer,
in this generation; and though this arrangement differs from
the chronology which has been generally followed, it is agreed
on all hands that both these persons were engaged in active
life together, and the inference to be drawn is that Vortimer
was born when his father had scarcely passed the time of
youth. It would appear, however, that the monkish chronologists have placed the era of Vortigern several years too late;

---

* Is there any tradition that this chapel was actually founded by St.
Tudwal; its peculiar situation would prevent it from becoming afterwards a parish church?

† Topographical Dictionary.—Browne Willis states that Tudweiliog is
a chapel, subordinate to Llangwynodl, and dedicated to St. Cwyfen.

‡ Qu. Is not Llanstadwel, Pembrokeshire, an abbreviation of Llansant-
tudwal?

§ In Table VII. Digain was erroneously shown to be a son of Erbin.

for they extend his reign from A. D. 448 to 464, when he is superseded by his son for four years, after which he unaccountably reigns again until A. D. 481. All this is inconsistent with their statement that Vortimer, who is known from a respectable authority* to have died before the battle of Crayford in 457, was of age to take the chief command of the Britons in the field so early as 455; and though it is uncertain how long Vortigern may have survived his son, it is probable that the date usually assigned to his deposition is in truth the date of his decease. Vortimer, who has been surnamed "Bendigaid, or the Blessed," has been accounted a Saint; and as he was not an ecclesiastic, the honour is perhaps due to his care in restoring those churches which had been destroyed by the Saxons, and the respect which he paid to men of religion.† In the Triads he is styled one of the three canonized kings of Britain.

The sons of Cunedda were all of them warriors, and though several of his grandchildren might have flourished in this generation, the order of succession would be better preserved by referring them to the next. The name of Ceredig ab Cunedda, the time in which he lived, and the situation of his territories, determine him to be the hero of the following rencounter with St. Patrick; and the circumstances of the incident, which exhibit a curious picture of the manners of the age, are thus related by Mr. Moore in his " History of

---

* Henry of Huntingdon.

† Matthæus Florilegus says—"Vortimerus, victoriam adeptus, cœpit possessiones amissas civibus indigenis restituere, ipsosque diligere, Ecclesias destructas restaurare, atque viros Ecclesiasticos, præcipuè religiosos, honorare."—(Usher De Primordiis, Cap. XII.) "Gwedy kaffael o Werthyfyr e wudugolyaeth dechreu a oruc talw y pawb tref y dat ac eu kyvoeth or ar rydugassey e sayson y arnadunt. ac y gyt a henny hevyt karu y wyrda ac eu hanrydedu ac o arch Garmawn ae kynghor adnewydhau er eglwyseu."—Brut G. ab Arthur. Myv. Archaiology, Vol. II. p. 252.

Ireland."—" The event, in consequence of which the Saint addressed his indignant letter to Coroticus,* the only authentic writing, besides the Confession, we have from his hand, is supposed to have taken place during his stay on the Munster coast, about the year 450. A British prince, named Coroticus, who, though professing to be a Christian, was not the less, as appears from his conduct, a pirate and persecutor, had landed with a party of armed followers, while St. Patrick was on the coast, and set about plundering a large district in which, on the very day before, the Saint had baptized and confirmed a vast number of converts. Having murdered several of these persons, the pirates carried off a considerable number of captives, and then sold them as slaves to the Picts and Scots, who were at that time engaged in their last joint excursion into Britain. A letter despatched by the Saint to the marauders, requesting them to restore the baptized captives, and part of the booty, having been treated with contumely, he found himself under the necessity of forthwith issuing the solemn epistle which has come down to us, in which, denouncing Coroticus and his followers as robbers and marauders, he in his capacity of ' Bishop established in Ireland' declares them to be excommunicated."

The family most distinguished in the Church during the present interval was that of Brychan, who is said, in Bonedd y Saint, to have been the father of twenty four sons and twenty five daughters, in all forty nine children !! Statements, however, vary, of which this is the largest. The smallest statement is twenty four for the whole number. In explanation it is said that he had three wives,† though it is not mentioned that they were living at the same time ; and it appears

---

* In some printed accounts of St. Patrick, this name is spelled—Coreticus, and Cereticus,—the latter of which is but a slight deviation from the Welsh orthography.

† Eurbrawst, Rhybrawst, and Peresgrl.

that four, at least, of his sons were illegitimate. It is, however, supposed by the Historian of Brecknockshire and the
Author of the Horæ Britannicæ that the names of the grandchildren of Brychan have crept into the list of his children;
and, in confirmation of this opinion, it may be stated that the
Triads record that Brychan "brought up his children and
grandchildren in learning and the liberal arts, that they might
be able to show the faith in Christ to the nation of the Cymry,
wherever they were without the faith:" from which it would
be inferred that the grandchildren of Brychan were Saints,
and it might be expected that their names were inserted in
the existing catalogues. But as few such names appear,[*]
when the grandchildren would naturally be the most numerous, the supposition, that they have been included in the list
of children, is the most rational way of accounting for the
deficiency. Their intermarriages also show that they belong
to times a considerable distance asunder; and though generations are never strictly concurrent, it is too much to suppose
that two daughters of the same man should be married to
persons who flourished two thirds of a century apart from
each other. Those alluded to are, Gwrgon, wife of Cadrod
Calchfynydd who flourished about A. D. 410, and Gwladus,
wife of Gwynllyw Filwr who flourished about A. D. 480;
but if the latter be considered a grand-daughter of Brychan,
no difficulty will appear in the case. Between the wife of
Ceredig who flourished about 430, and the wife of Cyngen
ab Cadell who flourished about 500, the discrepancy is equally
as great.

This being the case, Bonedd y Saint leaves the antiquarian
at liberty to acquiesce in the authority of the legend, entitled "Cognacio Brychan," in which several of the children and grandchildren are actually distinguished. But in
treating of the family seriatim, it is proposed to follow the

---

* Only five or six, and those mentioned incidentally.

s

list in the Myvyrian Archaiology of Wales, which, allowance
being made for the intermixture of two generations, appears
to give the names most correctly. It is supported by a
greater number of authorities than the list to which the Historian of Brecknockshire has given a preference, and the
names included are more consonant with the names of
churches now existing. But in this part of the subject it is
impossible to proceed with the satisfaction that can be wished;
all the lists of this family are evidently so corrupt that the
result of a comparison of them can be only a distant approach
to the truth, and a great number of cases must be left un-
decided.

1. Cynawg or Cynog, according to all the lists, the eldest
son of Brychan, by Banhadlwedd the daughter of Banhadle
of Banhadla in Powys. "Soon after his birth he was put
under the care of a holy man named Gastayn, by whom he
was baptized."[*] Cressy says—"the fame of his sanctity was
most eminent among the Silures; his name is consigned
among our English Martyrology on the eleventh of February,[†] where he flourished in all virtues about the year of
Christ 492."—The latter part of the sentence is ambiguously
expressed, but the year mentioned may be taken for the date
of his death, which is more agreeable to the chronology of the
family than that he should have flourished in the prime of life
at that time. The Truman MS.[‡] states that he was murdered

[*] Jones's Brecknockshire, Vol. I. Chap. III. and Cognacio Brychan.

[†] Sir Harris Nicolas, in his Chronology of History, gives Oct. 7 as the
festival of St. Cynog; which would seem to be correct, as the wake of
that Saint was formerly held in the month of October in the parish of
Defynog, Brecknockshire. According to Edwards's Cathedral of St. Asaph,
the wake of Llangynog, Montgomeryshire, should be held Oct. 8, the
difference between which and the authority of Sir H. Nicolas arises only
from an error of computation, where Edwards should have deducted a
day from the reckoning at the commencement of the present century.

[‡] Cited in Jones's Brecknockshire, Vol. I. Chap. III.

by the Pagan Saxons, upon a mountain called the Van, in the parish of Merthyr Cynog in Brecknockshire; and if so, it may be concluded that the church of Merthyr was erected as a *martyrium* to his memory, and built over his grave.* But it does not appear how the Saxons could have penetrated so far westward at so early a date,† unless it be supposed that in their piratical excursions they occasionally landed upon the coast of Wales, and the MS. just quoted mentions an instance in which they joined arms with the Gwyddyl Ffichti.

To Cynog are to be attributed the churches of Defynog, Ystrad Gynlais, and Penderin, in Brecknockshire, forming with their parishes and chapelries three extensive and continuous endowments of the first class. To Defynog the following chapels are subject—Capel Illtyd, (St. Iltutus;) Llanulid, (St. Julitta;) Capel Callwen, (St. Callwen;‡) and Ystrad Fellte, (St. Mary.) Ystrad Gynlais has but one chapel, Capel Coelbren. Penderin stands alone. The parish of Merthyr Cynog, which, like that of Defynog, is of sufficient importance to give name to the Hundred in which it lies, formerly included the church of Llanfihangel Nant Bran, (St. Michael,‖) as well as the chapelry of Dyffryn Honddu. Battel chapel, now independent, and Llangynog subject to Llanganten, (St. Cannen,) are also dedicated to Cynog;§ and it

* This inference from a general custom, explained in page 62 of this Essay, is confirmed by Cognacio Brychan, which says—"Sepulchrum Cynawc in Merthyr Cynawc in Brechenawc."—The words of Bonedd y Saint are to the same purpose—"Kynawc ap Brychan, Merthyr, ac ym Merthyr Cynawc ym Mrecheiniog y mae'n Gorwedd."

† Hengist is usually believed to have carried devastation into the remotest corners of the island, but Mr. Sharon Turner has well observed that all his battles, particularized by the Saxon authorities, were fought in Kent.

‡ In one list of Saints, Callwen is said to have been a daughter of Brychan, and was therefore a sister of Cynog.

‖ Jones's Brecknockshire, Vol. II. page 193.

§ There are reason for supposing that Llangunog, a chapel in Carmar-

may be observed that all these religious edifices are situated in the territory of his father Brychan, a circumstance sufficient to account for his influence as a founder. Llangynog in the county of Montgomery is also attributed to him.

2. Clydwyn, the second, or as others will have it, the third son of Brychan, embraced a military life, and it is said that he conquered South Wales;* but this assertion must be taken with great limitation, as it would seem to contradict the traditional accounts of Glamorganshire, Cardiganshire, and Radnorshire, where the native princes of this generation are known to have maintained possession. It may, therefore, be understood to mean that he established his dominion over the Gwyddyl Ffichti, who still remained in Carmarthenshire and Pembrokeshire; and, to confirm the explanation, it may be shown that the churches dedicated to his family are more numerous in that district than in any other, and one church, Llanglydwyn, upon the confines of the two counties included, bears the name of the warrior himself. According to Mr. Theophilus Jones, he succeeded his father in the government of the western and more mountainous parts of Brecknockshire. His commemoration or festival is Nov. 1.

3. Dingad, son of Brychan, the founder of a church in Carmarthenshire called Llandingad, and of another called Llaningad or Dingatstowe† in Monmouthshire, where it is said he was buried. "He was of the congregation of Cattwg,‡ but like many others he must have entered that society in his old age. He is not to be confounded with another Saint, called Dingad ab Nudd Hael. The commemoration of Dingad ab Brychan is Nov. 1; and the chapels subject to Llan-

---

thenshire, is dedicated to another Cynog, who succeeded St. David as Archbishop of Menevia.

* Cognacio, and Bonedd y Saint.
† Generally written Dingestow or Dynstow.
‡ Cambrian Biography.

dingad are Llanfair ar y Bryn (St. Mary,) Capel Peulin (St. Paulinus,) Capel Cynfab (St. Cynfab,) and Eglwys Newydd, the last two of which have been some time in ruins. Dingatstowe has one chapel, Tregaer (St. Mary.)

4. Arthen, the fourth son, is stated in Bonedd y Saint to have been buried in the Isle of Man ;* and according to the Truman MS. there was a church dedicated to him in Gwynllwg, Monmouthshire, which was demolished by the Saxons. The Cognacio says he was the father of Cynon who lived near Llynsafaddan, or Llangorse Pool, Brecknockshire.

5. Cyflefyr;—as the Cognacio and the MS. of Llewelyn Offeiriad† state that he was the son of Dingad and *grandson* of Brychan, he may, upon their authority, be considered as such, and restored to his proper generation. The Cognacio intimates that he suffered martyrdom at a place since called Merthyr Cyflefyr, and the Truman MS. says that he was murdered by the Saxons in Cardiganshire ;‡ but it does not appear where Merthyr Cyflefyr is situated, as no place is known by that name in the county which the two authorities taken together would indicate.||

6. Rhain, surnamed Dremrudd, was the only son of Brychad, who, besides Clydwyn, embraced a military life. He succeeded to the eastern part of his father's possessions, which he transmitted to his descendants; and according to the Cog-

* Qu. Mona, Anglesey?

† In the archives of Jesus College, Oxford.

‡ Jones's Brecknockshire, Vol. I. p. 59.

|| There is, or was lately, a stone in the parish of Crickhowel, Brecknockshire, with an inscription, part of which a writer in the Gentleman's Magazine for 1768 conjectured to be—VERI TR FILIUS DUNOCATI, and if this reading were correct, it might point out the burying-place of Cyflefyr the son of Dingad; but the Historian of Brecknockshire says those letters may be " any thing the antiquary supposes or wishes them to be," and another part of the inscription, more legible, shows that the stone was erected over the grave of Turpilius.—Jones's Brecknockshire, Vol. II. p. 433, and Plate VI. Fig. 4.

nacio, as explained by Mr. Theophilus Jones,* he was buried
at Llandefaelog Fach near Brecon. The catalogue in the
Archaiology of Wales, which says he was a saint in Lincoln-
shire, is therefore mistaken, the solitary instance of connexion
with so distant a county being of itself improbable ; and when
it is stated by the same authority that he had a church in the
Isle of Man, he appears to be confounded with one of his
brothers, named Rhwfan or Rhawin.

7. Dyfnan son of Brychan, was the founder of Llanddyfnan
in Anglesey, where he was buried.† Its chapels are Llanbedr
Goch (St. Peter,) Pentraeth (St. Mary,) and Llanfair ym
Mathafarn Eithaf (St. Mary.) The festival of St. Dyfnan is
April 23.

8. Gerwyn, or as others Berwyn, son of Brychan, a saint
who settled in Cornwall. Mr. Owen, from Achau y Saint,
says he was slain in the isle of Gerwyn ; but as it is also
recorded that there was another Gerwyn, the son of Brynach
Wyddel, by Corth one of the daughters of Brychan, it may
be concluded that they were the same person, and that the
latter account is the true one, thus adding one more to the list
of grandchildren. Gerwyn, the son of Brynach Wyddel, is
said to have had three sisters—Mwynen, Gwennan, and
Gwenlliw, who in one MS. are all called daughters of Brychan,‡ affording another instance of the confusion of two generations, though their names do not appear in the list of
children in the Myvyrian Archaiology.

9. Cadog, the son of Brychan, is said to have been buried
in France, which identifies him with Rheidiog in the Cognacio
and Llewelyn Offeiriad. He is not to be confounded with
Cattwg the abbot of Llancarfan, who was a descendant of

---

* History of Brecknockshire, Vol. I. p. 61, and Vol. II. p. 174.

† Myv. Archaiology, Vol. II. p. 39.

‡ Compare "Mwynen" in the Myv. Archaiology, Vol. II. p. 40. with the
two names " Gerwyn" in the Cambrian Biography.

Brychan in the second, if not in the third, degree.   The distinction did not escape Cressy, who falls into a great part of
the confusion, though he warns his reader against it.   According to this author, he died A. D. 490, and is commemorated in the Calendar Jan. 24.   The churches founded by him
are—Llanspyddyd, Brecknockshire, subject to which is the
chapel of Bettws or Penpont ;   and Llangadog Fawr, Carmarthenshire, under which are Llanddeusant (St. Simon and St.
Jude,) Capel Gwynfai, and Capel Tydyst now in ruins.
There was formerly a chapel in the parish of Kidwelly dedicated to Cadog, and perhaps one or two churches, which have
been confounded with those attributed to Cattwg, ought to be
added to the number.

10. Mathaiarn was a saint in Cardiganshire, or, according
to the Cognacio and Llewelyn Offeiriad, in Cyfeiliog, Montgomeryshire, where there is a place still called Mathafarn.
In the list of Llewelyn this saint is called Marchai.

11. Pasgen, Neffai, and Pabiali, according to Bonedd y
Saint, were all of them sons of Brychan by a Spanish woman,
and they went to Spain, where they became saints and legis-
lators ; but as the distance of Spain renders this story unlikely, those authorities are more probable which say that
Pasgen was the son of Dingad, and therefore a *grandson*
of Brychan.*

12. Neffai is not mentioned in the Cognacio and Llewelyn's
MS. unless he be the same as Dedyn or Neubedd, the son
of Clydwyn.

---

* It has been suggested that a stone, which formerly existed in the
church-yard of Tywyn, Merionethshire, having on it the letters PAS-
CANT without any further explanation, was a monument to the memory
of the son of Dingad ; and though the circumstance of other persons,
named Pasgen, occurring in Welsh history, may so far render the fact
uncertain, the coincidence that Gwenddydd, a daughter of Brychan, is recorded as one of the Saints of the place, seems to offer a strong con.
firmation of the supposition.

13. Pabiali is called Papai by the Cognacio and Llewelyn.
He is described as the son of Brychan, and it is added that
the Irish call him Pianno, Pivannus, and Piapponus.

14. Llecheu lived at Tregaian in Anglesey, or, as others, at
Llanllecheu, in Ewyas, Herefordshire.*

15. Cynbryd was the founder of Llanddulas, Denbighshire,
and was slain by the Saxons at a place called Bwlch Cynbryd.
His commemoration is March 19.

16. Cynfran, the founder of Llysfaen in Rhos, Denbighshire, where, according to Edward Llwyd, there is a well
called Ffynnon Gynfran, at which offerings used to be made
to the saint to procure his blessing upon cattle.

17. Hychan, the saint of Llanhychan in the vale of Clwyd.
No further particulars are known of him; but as neither this,
nor the three saints preceding, are to be found in the lists of
the Cognacio and Llewelyn Offeiriad, it may be suspected
they were grandsons of the Brecknockshire chieftain. The
festival of Hychan is Aug. 8.

18. Dyfrig; the Truman MS. says, with the appearance of
correctness, that he was Dubricius, the Archbishop of Llandaff,
and the time, in which the latter flourished, agrees with the
probable date of the grandchildren of Brychan; but the particulars of his life must be reserved for the next generation.
Another authority,† which says he was a saint in Cardiganshire, appears to have mistaken him for the saint of Llandyfriog in that county, who was the son of Dingad ab
Nudd Hael.

19. Cynin, according to the Cognacio, was the son of Tudwal
Befr by a daughter of Brychan. He was the founder of
Llangynin near St. Clears, Carmarthenshire.‡   Achau y Saint

* Jones's Brecknockshire, Vol. I. p. 59.
†Myvyrian Archaiology, Vol. II. p. 39.
‡ Llangynin is now a chapel subject to St. Clears, but as the latter is
of Norman dedication, the chapel and church have probably changed
their relationship.

says moreover that he was a bishop; and as the church, which he founded, has been called Llangynin a'i Weision neu a'i Feibion,* the additional designation of "his servants or his sons" may mean the clergy in attendance upon him.

20. Dogfan, according to the Silurian MSS. was slain by the pagan Saxons at Merthyr Dogfan in Dyfed, or Pembroke-shire, where a church was consecrated to his memory, the particular situation of which is at present unknown. He is also the patron saint or founder of Llanrhaiadr ym Mochnant, Denbighshire, to which are subject—Llanarmon Mynydd Mawr (St. Germanus,) Llangedwyn (St. Cedwyn,) Llanwddin (St. Gwddin,) and Llangadwaladr (St. Cadwaladr.) His commemoration is July 13.

21. Rhawin, a son of Brychan, whom Llewelyn Offeiriad calls Rhwfan, and states that he settled in the Isle of Man, where there was a church dedicated to him; but the Silurian MSS. record that he, and one of his brothers named Rhun, were slain on a bridge called Penrhun at Merthyr Tydfyl, while defending it against the Saxons; which, if both accounts were true, would imply that he had returned from the Isle of Man, and that persons, who have obtained the honours of sanctity in Wales, occasionally took up arms in defence of their country.

22. Rhun, a son of Brychan, of whom the Cognacio records that he was a saint near Mara, or Llangorse Pool, Brecknock-shire, and the Silurian MSS. state that he was slain together with Rhawin by the Saxons at Merthyr Tydfyl. He appears to have had two sons, Nefydd and Andras, both of whom were saints; and the surname of Dremrudd has been occa-sionally given him, apparently by confounding him with Rhain already mentioned.

23. Cledog or Clydog, "it is agreed by all the MSS. was buried at Clodock in Herefordshire,"† of which church he is

* See Cynin in the Myvyrian Archaiology, Vol. II. p. 35.
† Jones's Brecknockshire, Vol. II. p. 59.

supposed to be the founder. The Cognacio and Llewelyn mention that he was the son of Clydwyn and grandson of Brychan; he appears to have had a brother, whom different MSS. call Dedyn or Neubedd, and a sister, St. Pedita. Cressy states that he suffered martyrdom A. D. 492, and is commemorated in the martyrology on the nineteenth of August. The chapels to Clodock are—Llanfeuno (St. Beuno,) Longtown (St. Peter,) and Cresswell (St. Mary.)

24. Caian, perhaps a grandson of Brychan, as his name is omitted in the Cognacio and Llewelyn's MS. Tregaian, a chapel under Llangefni in Anglesey is dedicated to him, and his festival occurs in the Calendar on the twenty fifth of September.* The Silurian catalogue of Saints omits this name, and inserts in its stead, Nefydd, who was the son of Rhun ab Brychan.

It is recorded† that Nefydd, in his younger days, collected a party of followers, and put to flight the Saxons who had killed his father at Merthyr Tydfyl. He was afterwards a bishop in North Britain, where he was slain by the Picts and Saxons. Andras, a son of Rhun and brother of Nefydd, is also described as the founder of St. Andrew's or Dinas Powys near Cardiff, and should therefore be considered as its patron saint instead of St. Andrew the Apostle.

The alleged daughters of Brychan are the following:

1. Gwladus, the wife of Gwynllyw Filwr ab Glywys of Glywyseg or Gwynllwg in Monmouthshire. From the dates of her husband and children, which are easily computed, it would appear that she was a grand-daughter, rather than a daughter, of Brychan.

2. Arianwen, called by Llewelyn Offeiriad, Wrgren, probably another grand-daughter, married Iorwerth Hirflawdd of Powys, son of Tegonwy ab Teon. She was the mother of

* Sir Harris Nicolas's Chronology of History.
† Achau y Saint.

Caenog Mawr, to whom Clog-caenog in Denbighshire is ascribed.*

3. Tanglwst, Tudglyd, or Gwtfil, married to Cyngen, the son of Cadell Deyrnllug. She was mother to Brochwel Ysgythrog; and without bringing the life of her son down to A. D. 600, about which time he is alleged to have commanded the Britons in the battle of Bangor Iscoed, the era of her husband would render it necessary to consider her a grand-daughter of Brychan. She had two other sons, Maig and Ieuaf.

4. Mechell, according to some MSS. the eldest daughter of Brychan, was married to Gynyr of Caergawch near Menevia.†

5. Nefyn, probably a grand-daughter, was married to Cynfarch Oer, the father of Urien Rheged; and may perhaps be accounted the founder or patron saint of Nefyn,‡ Carnarvonshire.

6. Gwawr, seemingly a grand-daughter, was the wife of Elidyr Lydanwyn, by whom she was the mother of the bard Llywarch Hên.

7. Gwrgon, daughter of Brychan, was married to Cadrod Calchfynydd, who flourished about A. D. 430.

8. Eleri, daughter of Brychan, married to Ceredig ab Cunedda, of the same generation as the preceding. She was the paternal grandmother of St. David.

9. Lleian, the wife of Gafran ab Dyfnwal Hên, by whom she was the mother of Aeddan Fradog, who after his defeat in the battle of Arderydd, in North Britain, was compelled to fly for safety to the Isle of Man. The Cognacio says that Lleian herself settled in that island, and the era of her son§

* Myv. Archaiology *sub voce* Arianwen.

† Cambrian Biography.

‡ The modern saint of this church is St. Mary the Virgin.

§ " On the death of Conal, king of the British Scots, in the year 572-3, Aidan, the son of Gauran, succeeded to the throne; and it is mentioned as

which is determined by the concurrent testimony of the Irish and Welsh authorities, would indicate that she was one of the youngest of the grand-daughters of Brychan. There is a chapel subject to Llanarthne in Carmarthenshire, called Capel Llanlleian, and probably named in honour of this person, unless the words be taken to mean simply "the chapel of the nun."

10. Nefydd, daughter of Brychan, and wife of Tudwal Befr. One of the authorities in the Myvyrian Archaiology says she was a saint at Llechgelyddon in North Britain; but this statement arose probably from confounding her with Nefydd, the grandson of Brychan, already mentioned, and it is, perhaps, the same mistake which led Llwyd to say that Tudwal was " a prince of some territory in Scotland."* The connexions of Nefydd and her husband appear to have been confined to Wales. The churches ascribed to Tudwal have been enumerated already, and to Nefydd may be attributed the foundation of Llannefydd in Denbighshire. Besides her son, Cynin, who was the founder of Llangynin in Carmarthenshire, she appears to have had another, called Ifor ab Tudwal, of whom nothing more is recorded than that he was a saint. The Cognacio confounds Nefydd with Goleu or Goleuddydd.

11. Rhiengar, or according to others, Cyngar, is said to have been a saint at Llech in Maelienydd, and to have been the mother of Cynidr, a saint of Maelienydd;† but there are no means of deciding whether she ought to be placed in the list of the daughters, or the grand-daughters. Maelienydd is the ancient name of a district in Radnorshire, a subdivision of which, or of the adjoining district of Elfael, was

a proof of the general veneration, in which Columba was then held, as well by sovereigns as by the clergy and the people, that he was the person selected to perform the ceremony of inauguration on the accession of the new king."—Moore's History of Ireland, Chap. XII. The defeat of Aeddan at Arderydd probably took place some years before his elevation to the kingdom of the Scots.

† Jones's Brecknockshire, Vol. I. p. 58.

once called Llech Ddyfnog ;* and though the situation of the latter is uncertain, the statement on record† that Cynidr was buried at Glasebury, may assist in determining it. Llangynidr,‡ and Aberyscir, two churches in Brecknockshire, of which Cynidr may have been the founder, are dedicated to him jointly with the Virgin Mary ; and under the former of them there was once a chapel called Eglwys Vesei.

12. Goleuddydd, a saint at Llanhesgin in Gwent, the modern designation of which place is unknown ; and it would appear from the Cognaçio and Llewelyn Offeiriad, that Goleuddydd was only another name for Nefydd, the wife of Tudwal Befr.

13. Gwenddydd, a saint at Tywyn in Merionethshire ;§ but other authorities, who give her the name of Gwawrddydd, state that she was the wife of Cadell Deyrnllug,‖ and consequently the mother of Cyngen, who is already described as having married one of the grand-daughters of Brychan.

14. Tydïe, a saint "yñ y Tri gabelogwar,"* which the Historian of Brecknockshire interprets to mean that she lived at Capel Ogwr or Ogmore Chapel, formerly subject to St. Bride's Major, Glamorganshire.

15. Elined, the Almedha of Giraldus Cambrensis, who says that she suffered martyrdom upon a hill called Penginger near Brecknock, which the Historian of that county, so often

* Ancient Surveys of Wales in the Myv. Archaiology, Vol. II.

† Jones's Brecknockshire, Vol. I. p. 47, & 343.

‡ Called Llanfair a Chynidr, or the church of St. Mary and Cynidr, in the list of Parishes in Wales in the Myv. Archaiology. The double dedication of Aberyscir may be learnt from Jones's Brecknockshire, Vol. I. p. 47; where it may be observed that Cressy and others have confounded Cynidr with Cenydd or St. Kenneth.

§ See Cadfan, *infra*

‖ Myv. Archaiology, Vol. II. p. 48.

* Ibid. Vol. II. p. 54.

quoted, identifies with Slwch. "Crug gorseddawl,"* mentioned
after the name of Elined in the Myvyrian Archaiology, has
been taken for Wyddgrug or Mold in Flintshire; but it may
be no more than a descriptive appellation of Slwch, on which
there were lately some remains of a British Camp.† Cressy,
speaking of St. Almedha, says " This devout virgin, rejecting
the proposals of an earthly prince, who sought her in marriage, and espousing herself to the eternal king, consummated
her life by a triumphant martyrdom. The day of her solemnity is celebrated every year on the first day of August."

16. Ceindrych, or according to Bonedd y Saint, Ceindreg,
lived at Caergodolaur, a place at present unknown; but the
Cognacio states that Kerdech lived at Llandegwyn, which is
the name of a church dedicated to another saint in Merionethshire.

17. Gwen, grand-daughter of Brychan, and wife of Llyr
Merini, by whom she was the mother of Caradog Fraichfras.
Llewelyn Offeiriad says she was buried at Talgarth, Brecknockshire, where according to the Truman MS. she was murdered by the Saxons. Ecton calls her St. Gwendeline.

18. Cenedlon, " a saint on the mountain of Cymorth." It
does not appear where this mountain is situated, but from the
association of Cenedlon, Cymorth, and their sister Clydai, it
may be looked for in the neighbourhood of Newcastle in
Emlyn.

19. Cymorth, from whom the mountain just mentioned derives its name, was a daughter of Brychan, and is said to have
lived in Emlyn,‡ a district divided between the present
counties of Carmarthen and Pembroke. In the Cambrian

---

* Crug gorseddawl—"the hill of judicature."—Dr. Pughe's Welsh
Dictionary.

† "Elyned in monte Gorsavael, quæ pro amore castitatis martyrizata
est."—Cognacio, in Jones's Brecknockshire.

‡ "Cymorth 'ch Brychan a'i chwaer Clydai gyda hi yn Emlyn." Myv.
Archaiology, Vol. II. p. 35.

Biography* she is called Corth, and stated to have been the wife of Brynach Wyddel, by whom she was the mother of Gerwyn, already mentioned, together with his sisters, Mwynen, Gwennan, and Gwenlliw.

20. Clydai, the sister of Cymorth and Cenedlon, and the reputed founder of a church, called Clydai, in Emlyn. Her festival is Nov. 1.†

21. Dwynwen, the founder of a church in Anglesey called Llanddwynwen or Llanddwyn. By the Welsh bards she has been considered the patron saint of lovers. Her commemoration occurs on the twenty fifth of January.

22. Ceinwen, a saint to whom the churches of Llangeinwen and Cerrig Ceinwen in Anglesey are ascribed. As this and the preceding person are omitted in several of the lists of the children of Brychan, it may be presumed they were his granddaughters. The wake of Ceinwen was observed on the eighth of October, which is also the feast day of Ceneu, another member of this redoubtable family. Llangeinwen has one chapel, Llangaffo (St. Caffo.)

23. Tydfyl, a daughter of Brychan, is by some authorities confounded with Tanglwst already mentioned. . She suffered martyrdom at a place, which from that circumstance has been called Merthyr Tydfyl. According to the Cambrian Biography,‡ upon the authority of the Truman MS. she met her father, when he was an old man, attended by some of her brothers, whereupon they were beset by a party of Saxons and Gwyddyl Ffichti, and she, her father, and her brother Rhun Dremrudd, were murdered; but Nefydd the son of Rhun, then a youth, exerted himself in raising the force of the country, and afterwards put the enemy to flight.—Such is the

---

* *Voce* Gerwyn.

+ The list in Bonedd y Saint is corrupt in this place, and omits Clydai, which is restored from a separate notice in the same record, thereby increasing the number of reputed children to fifty.

‡ *Voce* Tydfyl.

brief account; but it is remarkable that no memorials have
been preserved of these early inroads of the Saxons into South
Wales, except a few scattered notices in the Welsh genealogies.
They appear to have been repeated at various intervals from
about the year 460 to 500, during which time it is generally
agreed that the Saxons and Picts were in alliance; and the
former, whose piratical character is acknowledged, were not
unlikely to land on the western coasts of the island, where the
Gwyddyl Ffichti, or Irish Picts, would aid their progress into
the interior. But this is merely a suggestion in support of
accounts not inconsistent in themselves; and if it be too much
to insist at once that the notices alluded to are authentic, the
possibility of their truth is a subject worthy of investigation.
The day of the commemoration of St. Tydfyl is the twenty
third of August.

24. Enfail, a saint at Merthyr Enfail, which a writer in the
Cambro Briton states is in Carmarthenshire; and if his as-
sertion be correct, the place in question may be the church of
Merthyr near Carmarthen.

25. Hawystl—lived at Caer Hawystl, supposed by the Historian of Brecknockshire to be Awst in the county of Gloucester.

26. Tybïe, a saint, of whom it is recorded that she was
murdered by pagans at a place in Carmarthenshire, where
there is a church still called Llandybïe. Her festival is January 30.

The last specified terminates the lengthy catalogue of the
children of Brychan according to Bonedd y Saint. The Cognacio, however, mentions two names which cannot be identified with any of the preceding;—"Keneython at Kidwelly on
the mountain of Kyfor," and "Keurbreit at Caslogwr."[*] The
first has reference to Llangynheiddon, an extinct chapel in the

---

[*] "Keneython apud Kydwely in monte Kyfor, Keurbreit apud Caslogwr." Jones's Brecknockshire, Vol. I. p. 343.

parish of Llandyfaelog, Carmarthenshire, near to which is a hill called Mynydd Cyfor; and the other is perhaps the saint of Lloughor, or, as it is vernacularly called, Casllwchwr, Glamorganshire, the church of which place is generally understood to be dedicated to St. Michael. Upon this authority they may both be regarded as belonging to the family of the Brecknockshire chieftain; and Llewelyn Offeiriad, whq calls the former "Rhyneidon of Cydweli," says she was his daughter.

To such a length has the practice been carried of ranking all the members of this tribe as the immediate offspring of its founder, that in a short list of Saints, published in the Cambrian Register,* two sons, Gwynau and Gwynws, and two daughters, Callwen and Gwenfyl, are added to the number. It is quite enough to suppose they were descendants without enquiring into the degree of their descent. The festival of the first pair is Dec. 13, and that of the second Nov. 1. Gwynws is the saint of Llanwnws, Cardiganshire, and may be deemed its founder; a chapel, now extinct, subject to Llanddewi Brefi in the same county, bore the name of Gwenfyl; and another in the parish of Defynog, Brecknockshire, is dedicated to Callwen.

Cressy, the Catholic writer, treats his readers with a wondrous tale of "St. Keyna the daughter of Braganus," evidently the same person as Ceneu, which appears in some of the lists, but her identity with Ceinwen already mentioned is doubtful. He relates that "when she came to ripe years, many nobles sought her in marriage, but she utterly refused that state; having consecrated her virginity to our Lord by a perpetual vow; for which cause she was afterwards by the Britons called Keyn wiri,† that is Keyna the virgin: at length she determined to forsake her country and find out some desert place, where she might attend to contemplation. Therefore

* Vol. III. p. 219.   † Cein-wyryf.

U

directing her journey beyond Severn, and there meeting a
woody place, she made her request to the prince of that
country, that she might be permitted to serve God in that
solitude. His answer was, that he was very willing to grant
her request, but that the place did so swarm with serpents
that neither man nor beast could inhabit it: but she constantly
replied, that her firm trust was in the name and assistance of
Almighty God to drive all that poisonous brood out of that
region. Hereupon the place was granted to the holy virgin,
who presently prostrating herself to God obtained of him to
change the serpents and vipers into stones; and to this day,
the stones in that region do resemble the windings of serpents
through all the fields and villages, as if they had been framed
so by the hand of the engraver."—From the appearance of the
fossils, called by geologists, "Ammonites," Camden identifies
the place with Keynsham in Somersetshire, and describes a
specimen from that neighbourhood which he had seen.—It is
related afterwards that "her nephew St. Cadoc, performing a
pilgrimage to the Mount of St. Michael, met there with his
blessed Aunt St. Keyna, at whose sight he being replenished
with joy, and being desirous to bring her back to her own
country, the inhabitants of that region would not permit him;
but afterwards, by the admonition of an angel, the holy maid
returned to the place of her nativity; where, on the top of a
hillock, seated at the foot of a high mountain, she made a
little habitation for herself, and by her prayers to God obtained a spring there to flow out of the earth, which by the
merits of the holy virgin affordeth health to divers infirmities.
She is said to have departed this life on the eighth day of the
Ides of October, A. D. 490, and to have been buried in her
own oratory by her nephew St. Cadoc."—The latter part of
the story has reference to certain places on the borders of the
Principality. The Mount of St. Michael is the name of a hill
near Abergavenny, which still maintains its sacred character.
In the same neighbourhood is the parish of Llangeneu, in

which, according to Mr. Theophilus Jones, is to be found the
well of the saint, and the situation of her oratory may yet be
traced. The St. Cadoc here mentioned was Cattwg, the son
of Gwynllyw Filwr and founder of Llangattock Crickhowel,
of which Llangeneu is one of the subordinate chapelries.
From the omission of Ceneu in several of the lists, it may be
inferred that she was a grand-daughter, and in that case
Cattwg would be her sister's son; but if she were a daughter
of Brychan, and Cattwg were her great nephew, it would by
no means violate the unity of the story; and it is obvious that
Cadog, the *son* of Brychan, was not the person intended, as he •
must have been either the brother or uncle of Ceneu, and not
her nephew. The oratory alluded to was situated on a hill at
some distance from the present church of Llangeneu; and if it
were founded by the saint herself, as the legend would imply,
its subordinate condition, for its modern representative is only
a chapelry, would seem to violate the principle laid down in
the first section of this Essay, namely, that upon the institution of tithes, and consequent division of the country into
parishes, every primitive religious edifice received a separate
endowment. It is clear, however, that the legend is a fabrication, for it does not appear why an oratory, of such high
antiquity and honoured with so many sacred recollections,
should afterwards be neglected, and its very name transferred
to a church in another situation; but the following passage
from the tale, in the words of Cressy, will explain that it was
of late erection, and built by some foreign devotees who pre-
tended to discover the burying-place of the saint.—" Some
time before her death she had a prospect of her eternal happiness in a future world in a vision, being ministered to and
comforted by angels, when she thus prophesied to her nephew
St. Cadoc;—this is the place of all others beloved by me, here
my memory shall be perpetuated, this place will I often visit
in spirit if it may be permitted me, and I am assured it shall
be permitted me, because the Lord hath granted me this place

as a certain inheritance. The time will come when this place shall be inhabited by a sinful people, which, notwithstanding, I will violently root out of this seat. *My tomb shall lie a long time unknown, until the coming of other people, whom by my prayers I shall bring hither ;* them will I protect and defend, and in this place shall the name of the Lord be blessed for ever."

According to Jones's Brecknockshire, Ellyw or Elyw, whose name is not mentioned in any of the lists, was a grand-daughter of Brychan. With her may have originated the establishment of Llanelly, Carmarthenshire, subject to which are Llangennech and the extinct chapels of Dewi, (St. David,) Ifan, (St. John,) and Berwick or Dyddgen chapel. The church of Llanelieu, Brecknockshire, is called after her ; and she is also the patron of Llanelly, subject to Llangattock Crickhowel in the same county, where her wake is held on the Sunday next before the first of August O. S. and renders it probable that her name is only an abbreviation of Elined, already noticed, upon whose festival the wake depends.*

The legends† relate that the spiritual instructor of Brychan was Drichan or Brynach, who is called in the Triads Brynach Wyddel or the Irishman, and is said to have married Corth or Cymorth, one of the daughters of Brychan, by whom he had four children already mentioned. He is considered to be the founder of Llanfrynach, Brecknockshire, Llanfrynach alias Penllin, Glamorganshire, Llanboidy, Carmarthenshire, and Llanfernach, Dinas, and Nefern, Pembrokeshire.‡ It may also be inferred, from the analogy of similar cases, that Henry's Moat, and Pontfaen, in the neighbourhood of the three latter, which Ecton ascribes to St. Bernard, should be

---

* History of Brecknockshire, Vol. II. p. 473.

† The Cognacio, and an English legend cited in the History of Brecknockshire, Vol. I.

‡ Eglwys Fair Lan Tâf. (St. Mary,) chapel to Llanboidy ; and Cilgwyn, (St. Mary,) chapel to Nefern.

attributed to Brynach, whose parishes would thus form a continuous endowment which was afterwards disturbedby the Norman Lords of Cemmaes. The parish of Clydai, and the localities of Cymorth and Cenedlon, are immediately adjoining, if not partly included in, the district. Cressy states that " St. Bernach" was an abbot, and that he is commemorated in the Church on the seventh of the Ides of April.

According to the Cognacio, the spiritual instructor of Cynog, the eldest son of Brychan, was a holy man named Gastayn, to whom the same document attributes the church of Llangasty Tal y Llyn, Brecknockshire. This name may conclude the connexions of a family of saints, which for its celebrity has been styled the third holy family of Britain.

It is stated in the Triads that Brychan educated his children and grandchildren to qualify them " to show the faith in Christ to the nation of the Cymry where they were without faith ;"* and upon this statement an argument has been grounded to show that there were parts of Wales which had not yet embraced Christianity. Evident proofs remain that the Britons had not entirely emerged from heathenism, and Druidical superstitions were rooted in the minds of the people until late in the following century, which the foundation of churches about this time must have tended mainly to eradicate; still the allegation, that the Welsh race should have been converted by missionaries from a family whose origin was Irish, is so singular as to demand some inquiry into the correctness of the original assertion. The question may be determined by considering the districts in which the churches and chapels dedicated to the family of Brychan, including those of Brynach and Gastayn, are distributed. They are about fifty five in number, out of which twenty two are in Brecknockshire, or

* " Brychan Brycheiniog, a ddug ei blant a'i wyrion ar ddysg a bonedd, fal y gallent ddangos y Ffydd yng Nghrist i Genedl y Cymry, lle ydd oeddynt yn ddiffydd." Triad 18, Third Series.

immediately upon its borders. Those situated in Carmarthenshire and Pembrokeshire, at that time occupied by the
Gwyddyl Ffichti, are sixteen, Five more are in Anglesey,
and three of the family settled in the Isle of Man, both occupied by the same tribe. Most of the remaining churches are
situated together in Denbighshire ; and as parts of North
Wales are said to have still continued in the possession of the
Irish,* it may be judged by analogy that this was one of the
districts so retained. The conclusion presented by a consideration of these localities, is, that the people without the faith,
who from their settlement in Wales have been mistaken for
the nation of the Cymry, were not Welshmen but Irish. The
latter race had not received the truths of the Gospel, for this
was the age in which St. Patrick was employed in imparting
Christianity to their countrymen in Ireland, and in Wales the
hostility of the native inhabitants would prevent them from
obtaining that blessing: but upon the family of Brychan they
could prefer the claim of a kindred origin; and to this, together with the territorial influence of Clydwyn, it may be
added, that Brynach, who was adopted into the family, and
who for a single member seems to have founded the greatest
number of churches, was himself an Irishman.

Saintship in Wales was already a profession, and those who
belonged to it were persons, who, in the character of ecclesiastics of various grades, devoted their lives to the service of
religion. In the next generation it will be discovered that
many of them belonged to an order of primitive monks, such
as flourished in Gaul in the fifth century,† and the foundation
of several monasteries will soon be noticed. But it is remark-

* Cambrian Biography, *sub voce* Melgyr, from Achau y Saint.

† "That there were monks in Gaul long before the time of St. Benedict is evident from the unquestionable authority of Gregory of Tours.
It is, however, certain that prior to the sixth century there was no common observance among them ; and that though the men, who fled from
the world to practise unusual austerities were held in reverence, the new

able that no nunnery is known to have been established in the
Principality for several hundred years later than the period
under consideration.   It is, therefore, an interesting inquiry—
what rank did female saints hold in the Church of the ancient
Britons?   They were not numerous compared with those of
the other sex, and by far the largest quota seems to have been
furnished by the progeny of Brychan.   A review of the list
will show that only half the reputed daughters of that prince
have received the honours of sanctity.   No churches bear the
names of the remaining half, no festivals have been kept to
their memory, and they are known only as the wives of chieftains.   Some, even of those particularized as saints, are described as having married, and become the mothers of children ;
but it does not appear whether they afterwards renounced the
marriage state, or whether, as is more probable, they devoted
themselves to religion upon the death of their husbands.   A
few individuals, however, are specified in the legends as
having made a vow of virginity in their youth ; and from the
contemporary practice of Gaul it may be learned that, before
the institution of nunneries, they were consecrated by bishops,
and led religious lives in the society of their kindred.   The
fact on record, that St. Germanus, while proceeding upon his
mission, was a party to a consecration of the nature described,
leaves a fair inference that he introduced the custom into
Britain.*   On the other hand, it was by no means uncommon
for *men*, in this age, to exchange the state of matrimony for

mode of life did not rise to the dignity of an institute, nor obtain any
degree of organization."—Europe in the Middle Ages, by S. A. Dunham, Esq. Vol. II. Chap. II.

* " In Gaul, as in other parts of the Christian world, women, previous
to the establishment of nunneries, were consecrated to God by bishops;
and they led religious lives in the houses of their parents or nearest kindred.   There is something peculiarly striking in the manner in which
Genevieve, when in her fifteenth year, assumed the irrevocable obligation.
She was among the inhabitants of Paris who went forth to receive the two

that of monachism ; and St. Lupus, after he had been married
seven years, became an inmate of the monastery of Lerins ;
but celibacy formed no part of the discipline of the *secular*
Welsh clergy as late as the thirteenth century.

The natives of Wales may be surprized to find that Leland
has given, out of the life of St. Nectan, a list of the children
of Brychan, twenty four in number, two only of which, or at
most three, can be identified with the names in the Welsh
lists.   They are as follow :—

"Nectanus, Joannes, Endelient, Menfre, Dilic, Tedda,
Maben, Weneu, Wensent, Merewenna, Wenna, Juliana, Yse,
Morwenna, Wymp, Wenheder, Cleder, Keri, Jona, Kananc,
Kerhender, Adwen, Helic, Tamalanc. All these sons and
daughters were afterwards holy martyrs and confessors in
Devon and Cornwall, where they led an eremitical life."

It is perhaps sufficient to decide the fate of this list to say
that it depends solely upon the authority of one or two monkish writers, and the compiler has forgotten to explain why all
these saints should have quitted their country in a body, and
settled in Devon and Cornwall.   In Wales, with the exception
of the two or three who may be recognised in spite of their
disguise, they have left not even a memento of their existence.

---

saints, Germanus and Lupus, then on a mission to Britain. Her devotion,
during the exhortation of the former, and the enthusiastic zeal which there
was in her countenance, principally attracted his notice. He caused her
to approach him; and, on enquiring into her sentiments and feelings,
found that she was resolved to consecrate her virginity to God, a resolu-
tion which he was not backward to strengthen. They entered the church,
and joined in certain prayers and hymns suited to the occasion; but Germanus would not give her the veil until she had passed the night in vigils,
in self-examination."   Europe in the Middle Ages, Vol. II. Chap. II.

SECTION IX.

The Welsh Saints from the Accession of Vortimer A. D. 464. to the
Death of Ambrosius A. D. 500.

THE founders of new families which appear for the first
time in this generation, are Cadell Deyrnllug, Gynyr of Caer
Gawch, Ynyr Gwent, Tewdrig ab Teithfallt, Emyr Llydaw,
and Ithel Hael. Cadell's descendants are as follow :—

[TABLE XI.]

CADELL DEYRNLLUG married Gwawrddydd, daughter of Brychan

Cynan Glodrydd				Cyngen *Sant* m. Tanglwst, grand-daughter of Brychan			
Cleddyfgar	Maig	Ieuaf	*Mawan*	Brochwel Ysgythrog m. Arddun, daughter of Pabo Post Prydain			
Caranog			*Ystyffan*	*Tysilio*	Cynan	Garwyn	Llyr
Geraint			Gwedrog	Selyf		*Enghenel*	
Eldad	*Ystag*	Gwrydr Drwm	Mael Mynan		*Dona*		
		Egryn	Beli				
			Cynllo				
			Elisau				
			Brochwel				

Cadell, obiit A. D. 804.

Nest, mother of Merfyn Frych.	Cyngen, murdered at Rome A. D. 854.

Cadell Deyrnllug flourished partly in the preceding generation, and the legend of his accession to power has been already
related. He married Gwawrddydd, one of the daughters of
Brychan, and his domains lay in the Vale Royal and the
upper part of Powys. Before the close of this generation he
appears to have been succeeded by his son, Cyngen, who is
distinguished for the patronage which he afforded to the
saints, and for the liberal endowments which he gave to
the Church.

v

The order of birth would also determine Gynyr of Caer Gawch to belong to the preceding generation, but he is introduced in the present in order that he may be placed with his family. He appears to have been the chieftain of a district in Pembrokeshire, since called Pebidiog or Dewsland, in which the town of St. David's is situated ; and he probably rose into power upon the reduction of the Gwyddyl Ffichti by Clydwyn. His first wife was Mechell, daughter of Brychan, by whom he had issue a daughter called Danadlwen; whose husband, Dirdan, is included in the catalogue of saints, but no churches are ascribed to him. The second wife of Gynyr was Anna, daughter of Gwrthefyr Fendigaid, or Vortimer, king of Britain ; and the fruit of this union was a son, named Gistlianus,* together with two daughters, Non, the mother of St. David,† and Gwen, the mother of St Cybi. From confounding Anna, the' daughter of Gwrthefyr Fendigaid, with Anna, the daughter of Uther Pendragon, arose probably the legendary story that St. David was related to king Arthur, but this tale is at variance with all the pedigrees.

Gynyr of Caer Gawch, is said to have embraced a religious life, having given all his lands to the Church, for which reason he has been enrolled among the saints. It may be learned from Giraldus Cambrensis that his son, Gistlianus, was a bishop at Menevia some time before the elevation of St. David to that dignity, and his residence or see, which was perhaps the particular establishment endowed by Gynyr, was situated at some distance from the present cathedral. It was afterwards removed by him to the valley of " Rosina," where the cathedral now stands, at the instance of St. David ; who, as the legend relates, had received a warning from an angel to

---

* Giustilianus, according to the orthography of Ricemarchus; the Welsh form of the name is not preserved.

† The succession from Vortimer to St. David is rapid, and allows scarcely more than twenty years to a generation.

the effect, that the place first chosen was not accepted by the
Deity, for he foresaw that little or no fruit would be produced
from it; but there was another place, not far from thence,
more suitable for devotion and the purposes of a holy congregation.*—This brief narrative, the miraculous part being set
aside, is not unlikely to be true; and if, as the same author
asserts elsewhere, a monastery had been founded by St. Patrick
in the valley of Rosina, thirty years before the birth of St.
David,† it would have furnished Gistlianus with a more
obvious reason for changing his residence; but an appointment less than divine would ill become the hallowed glories of
a spot regarded by the Welsh as the most sacred in Britain.

It would appear from the "Genealogy of the Saints" that
Gynyr had a grandson, Ailfyw, the son of Dirdan by Danadlwen, who might have flourished about the end of this generation or the beginning of the following; and a church near the
town of St. David's, called Llanailfyw or St. Elfeis, is considered
to be dedicated to him. He derived his name most probably
from St. Albeus or Ailbe, bishop of Munster in Ireland; who
visited this district, and is recorded to have baptized St. David, the other grandson of Gynyr.

Non, the daughter of Gynyr, was married to Sandde the son
of Ceredig ab Cunedda; and the following religious edifices

---

* "Post longa tam discendi primo, quam postea quoque docendi tempora, ad locum unde discesserat, Meneviam scilicet, demum vir sanctus
(David) repatriavit. Erat autem eodem tempore ibidem Episcopus avun-
culus ejus, vir venerabilis, cui nomen Gistlianus. Huic igitur Angelica,
quæ jam susceperat, monita nepos in hunc modum recitavit. Locus, inquit
Angelus, in quo Deo servire proponis, non est ei acceptus. Modicum enim
vel nullum sibi futurum fructum inde providit. Veruntamen est alius non
procul hinc locus, ostendens Vallem Rosinam, ubi sacrum hodie Cimiter-
ium extat, longè religioni et sanctæ congregationi competentior."—Giraldus
Cambrensis de Vitâ S. Davidis, apud Wharton, Tom. II.

† The residence of St. Patrick at Menevia, though noticed by Gwynfardd, is at variance with chronology and the most approved histories of
his life.

have been dedicated to her memory:—Llan Uwch Aeron, a church in Cardiganshire; Llannon, a chapel under Pembre, Carmarthenshire, St. Nun's chapel in the parish of St. David's, Pembrokeshire; and Llannon, formerly a chapel under Llansanffraid, Cardiganshire; all of which are situated in the immediate neighbourhood of churches ascribed to St. David. The festival of St. Non was kept on the third of March.

The next founder of a family, that may be noticed, is Ynyr Gwent, who married Madrun, another daughter of Gwrthefyr or Vortimer. His territories consisted of a part of the present county of Monmouth, and he is considered a saint, probably on account of having founded a college or monastery at Caerwent under the superintendence of St. Tathan. His wife, Madrun, in conjunction with Anhun her handmaid, is said to have been the foundress of the church of Trawsfynydd, Merionethshire.*

Tewdrig, the son of Teithfallt ab Nynio, was a prince, or king as he is called, of Glamorgan; the sovereignty of which was retained by his descendants until it was wrested from them by the Normans in the eleventh century. The era of his life belongs to the past generation, but the first particulars, which are known of him, occur in the present. According to the most consistent authorities his pedigree commences with his grandfather, Nynio, whose age immediately precedes the departure of the Romans; while others, who state that his grandfather's name was Mynan, derive his descent from Caractacus.

TABLE XII.

TEWDRIG

	Meirig, king of Glamorgan		
Arthwys	Anna, dr. married to Amwn Ddu	Gwenonwy, dr. married to Gwyndaf Hên	
Morgan	Samson	Tathan	Meigant	Hywyn

Eunydd, ancestor of Iestyn ab Gwrgan.

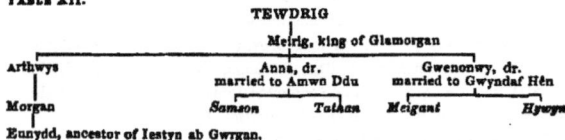

* For the children of Ynyr, see Table X. p. 132

Emyr Llydaw was the prince of a certain territory in Armorica, and nephew to St. Germanus. He flourished in the early part of this generation, and is noticed here on account of his descendants, whose names appear conspicuous in the catalogue of saints.

TABLE XIII.

		EMYR LLYDAW					
Gwenteirbron, dr. m. to Eneas Lydewig			Hywel			Others as below	
Cadfan	Hywel Fychan	Derfel Gadarn	Dwywau	Cristiolus	Rhystyd	Sulien.	

	EMYR LLYDAW				
Amwn Ddu		Pedredin or Petrwn		Alan	
Tydecho	Samson	Tathan	Padarn	Lleuddad	Lionio	Llynab.

	EMYR LLYDAW			
Gwyndaf Hén	Difwng	Tewdwr Mawr		Gwyddno
Meigant	Hywyn	Trinio	Canna, dr.	Meilyr	Maelrys
			Crallo.		

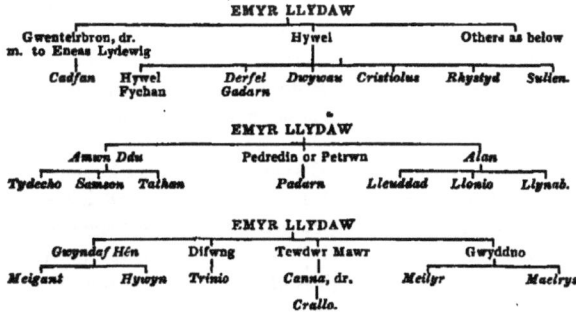

Ithel Hael o Lydaw was another Armorican prince, whose children in this and the following generation accompanied Illtyd and Cadfan to Britain, and became saints of the Welsh Church.

To return to the older families, the distinguished hero of the line of Cunedda, during this period, was Caswallon Lawhir. His history as related in Achau y Saint, under the head of Meigyr, is as follows:—"Meigyr, with his brothers, Cynyr and Meilyr, accompanied Caswallon Lawhir, their cousin, to drive the Ffichti out of Mona,* to which island they had retreated from the sons of Cunedda, and had strengthened themselves there. After cruel fighting they drove the Gwyddelians out of Mona, in which Caswallon slew Serigi, the Gwyddelian, with his own hand. This Serigi was the leader

* Anglesey.

of the Gwyddelians and the Ffichti that had overrun Gwynedd* from the time of Macsen Wledig. And after driving
the strangers out of Mona, the Cymry took courage, and
chased them from every part of Gwynedd, so that none remained in the country but such of them as were made
slaves."†—This account is important as it records the final
expulsion of the Gwyddyl Ffichti from North Wales; and
though the precise time of the event is not mentioned, there
are reasons for supposing that it took place near the close of
the century. There was formerly a chapel near the church of
Holyhead, called Eglwys y Bedd or Llanygwyddyl, which, as
reported by tradition, had been erected over the grave of
Serigi.‡

Meigyr was the son of Gwron ab Cunedda; he and his
brother, Meilyr, are included in the Silurian catalogue of
saints, though there are no churches which bear their names.
The same may also be said of Sandde ab Ceredig ab Cunedda,
who married Non, the daughter of Gynyr of Caer Gawch, by
whom he became the father of St. David. The only remaining
saint of the family, for this generation, was Gwenaseth,
daughter of Rhufon ab Cunedda, who was married to
Pabo Post Prydain: but in connexion with the tribe
may be mentioned, Tegwedd, the daughter of Tegid Foel
of Penllyn, Merionethshire. She was married, first to
Cedig ab Ceredig ab Cunedda, by whom she became the
mother of Afan of Buallt; and secondly to Enlleu ab Hydwn

---

* North Wales.

† Translated in the Cambrian Biography.

‡ The author of a "History of Anglesey," London, 1775, says,—"The
ruins of it a few years ago were removed in order to render the way to the
church more commodious. Here formerly was the shrine of Sirigi, who
was canonized by the Irish. It seem to have been held in exceeding great
repute for several very wonderful qualities and cures: but according to an
old Irish chronicle, it was carried off by some Irish rovers, and deposited
in the cathedral of Christ Church, in Dublin."

Dwn ab Ceredig, by whom she had Teilo, bishop of Llandaff. A church in Monmouthshire, called Llandegfyth, is ascribed to her, at which place, according to Achau y Saint, she was murdered by the Saxons.

It appears that upon the progress of the Saxon arms in the south of Britain, the families of Coel Godebog and many others retreated to the north,* where, as in Wales, the Britons endeavoured to concentrate themselves. Here, however, they were obliged to maintain an unequal contest with the Picts on one side and the Saxons on the other. And though the Britons of Cumberland, and more especially those of Strath Clyde, maintained their independence for some two or three centuries, the chieftains of other districts were not equally fortunate; and when stripped of their territories by the continual aggressions of the invaders, their practice was to seek an asylum in Wales, and, in several instances, to devote their lives to the service of religion. Of the latter description was Pabo Post Prydain, the descendant of Coel in the fourth degree. He first distinguished himself as a brave warrior, but eventually he was obliged to give way and leave his territory in the north. He sought refuge in Wales, and was hospitably received by Cyngen ab Cadell, the prince of Powys, by whom he had lands given to him. He afterwards lived a holy life, and was accounted a saint of the British Church. To these

---

* The cause of this migration, which is more probably due to internal warfare, is here given in accordance with popular opinion, as the subject requires a more extensive investigation than could be included within the limits of this Essay. The slow progress of the Saxons has been well described, according to their own authorities, by Mr. Sharon Turner; and it is remarkable that the Welsh records of the sixth century allude to but few instances of conflict with that people. Between them and the Cymry from whom the Welsh are descended, another race of Britons, alike hostile to both, intervened. They were called Lloegrwys, and appear to have been incorporated with the Saxons upon the establishment of the kingdom of Mercia.

particulars may be added, from the Cambrian Biography, that he married Gwenaseth, daughter of Rhufon of Rhufoniog; which is more consistent with chronology than the statement of others who assert that Gwenaseth was the wife of Sawyl, his son.* Pabo is considered to be the founder of Llanbabo in Anglesey,† where a stone still remains, bearing his effigy, with the following inscription,—HIC JACET PABO POST PRUD COR- PORS......TE......PRIMA.   The author of Mona Antiqua is of opinion that he was the earliest saint in that island, though it is clear from other authorities that some of the children of Brychan must have preceded him.   His commemoration is November 9.

Talhaiarn, the son of Garthwys of the line of Coel, was a celebrated bard and saint of the congregation of Cattwg.   "He composed a prayer which has always been the formula used in the Gorsedd Morganwg or Session of the bards of Glamor- gan."‡   His residence was originally at Caerleon, where he was chaplain to Emrys Wledig or Ambrosius, king of Britain; but when that prince was slain, he lived as a hermit at a place in Denbighshire since called Llanfair Talhaiarn, where a church was founded and dedicated to him in conjunction with the Virgin Mary.

In another branch of the family of Coel, occurs the name of Cynfarch Oer, a chieftain of North Britain; but who after- wards became a saint in Wales.   He is said to have been the

---

* Cambrian Biography, *voce* Gwenaseth; and "Asaph" in Bonedd y Saint, Myv. Archaiology, Vol. II.

† As Llanbabo is now a chapel subject to Llanddeusant, it must be sup- posed that some change has taken place in the relative condition of these edifices if Pabo was the founder of the first of them.   It is possible, how- ever, that the chapel was built over his grave at a later period, and dedi- cated to him.   The stone monument alluded to was discovered, in the reign of Charles the Second, by the sexton while digging a grave; and an engraving of it is given in Rowlands's Mona Antiqua, Second Edition.

‡ Cambrian Biography.

founder of Llangynfarch in Maelor, Flintshire, which was
destroyed by the Saxons in the battle of Bangor Orchard
A. D. 603 ;* and he is associated with the Virgin Mary as the
patron of Llanfair Dyffryn Clwyd,† Denbighshire. His wife
was Nefyn, a grand-daughter of Brychan, by whom he was
the father of Urien Rheged.

Llyr Merini, of the line of Coel and father of Caradog
Fraich Fras, is classed among the saints. Llanllyr, now called
Llanyre, a chapel to Nantmel in Radnorshire ; and Llanllyr,
formerly a nunnery in Cardiganshire, are dedicated either to
him, or to another saint of the name of Llyr, a virgin, whose
commemoration was kept Oct. 21. Llyr Merini married
Gwen, a grand-daughter of Brychan.

The last saint to be mentioned, of the line of Coel, was
Madog Morfryn, whose life must have extended into the
following century. He was a member of the congregation or
monastery of Illtyd, where he is said to have distinguished
himself as a teacher ;‡ but he is more generally known as the
father of the bard, Myrddin Wyllt.

In the line of Cystennyn Gorneu occurs Geraint ab Erbin, a
chieftain of Dyfnaint or Devon, who is called a saint. It does
not appear how he merited the distinction; for he was not an
ecclesiastic, and it is recorded that he fell fighting at the head
of his men in the following century. It is said that there was
a church dedicated to him at Caerffawydd or Hereford. An
elegy to his memory by Llywarch Hên is published in the
Myvyrian Archaiology ; and the following passage, according to " Owen's Translation," describes his death :—

> In Llongborth I saw hard toiling
> Amidst the stones, ravens feasting on entrails,
> And on the chieftain's brow a crimson gash.

* Cambrian Biography.
† Bonedd y Saint, Myv. Archaiology.—Qu. Is not St. Kinemark's,
Monmouthshire, dedicated to Cynfarch ?
‡ Triad 96, Third Series.

w

In Llongborth I saw a confused conflict,
Men striving together and blood to the knees,
From the assault of the great son of Erbin.

At Llongborth was Geraint slain,
A strenuous warrior from the woodland of Dyfnaint,
Slaughtering his foes as he fell.

Ysgin ab Erbin, brother of the preceding, is mentioned in
Bonedd y Saint; and to him, perhaps, the name of Llanhesgin, Monmouthshire, may be traced.

To this generation belongs Gwynllyw Filwr, the son of
Glywys ab Tegid ab Cadell, and chieftain of Gwynllwg or
Gwentloog in Monmouthshire, which is supposed to take its
name from him. He is called by the Latin writers of the middle ages St. Gundleus, and according to John of Teignmouth he
was the eldest of seven brothers, who, in compliance with the
custom of gavel-kind, divided the territories of their father
between them, the six younger paying homage to Gwynllyw
as the elder. He married Gwladus, a grand-daughter of
Brychan; and was the father of a large family of children,
most of whom resigned their temporal possessions and embraced a life of religion. From the epithet attached to his
name it may be judged that he was originally a warrior, but
in course of time he surrendered his dominions to his son
Cattwg, and built a church where he passed the remainder of
his life in great abstinence and devotion.* The church alluded
to is supposed to be that of Newport, Monmouthshire, situated
in the hundred of Gwentloog, and dedicated to him under the
name of St. Woolos. His festival was held on the twenty
ninth of March.

All the family of Brychan for obvious reasons were described in the last generation, except Dyfrig or St. Dubricius,

* "Regno Cadoco filio suo commendato, Ecclesiam construxit, ibique
in magnâ abstinentiâ et vitæ sanctimoniâ vivere cœpit."—Johannes Tinmuthensis, apud Usher.

who for his celebrity deserved a more particular notice. Two localities rather ill defined contend for the honour of his birth, namely the banks of the Gwain near Fishguard, Pembrokeshire,* and the banks of the Wye in Herefordshire. On the part of the former it has been contended that he has been called " Dyfrig of Langweyn, Gwaynianus, and Vaginensis," —*vagina* being the Latin translation of the Welsh name " Gwain." On behalf of the latter, the Life of Dubricius by John of Teignmouth, and another by Benedict of Gloucester,† affirm, that he was born at Miserbdil on the Wye, and that the name was afterwards changed by Dubricius to Mochros. The claims of either place would be equally consistent with the idea that he was a grandson of Brychan, but the Welsh genealogies are silent upon the subject. The weight of evidence is in favour of the latter, as there happen to be in a part of Herefordshire, called Erchenfield, a church (Whitchurch) and two chapels (Ballingham and Hentland, subject to Lugwardine,) which are dedicated to Dubricius, all of which are situated near the Wye.‡ While in Pembrokeshire there is not a single church which bears the name of the saint. As for the translation of Gwain into Vagina, it should not be forgotten that the Latin name of the Wye was " Vaga," from which in the corrupt state of the Latin language there would be no difficulty in forming the adjective Vaginensis. John of Teignmouth says that his mother was Eurdila,§ the daughter of Peiban, a certain regulus of Cambria, but that his father's name was unknown. One of the Warwick chroniclers says that his father was a king of Erging or Erchenfield, by name

* Cambrian Register, Vol. II. p. 202.

† Benedict was a monk of Gloucester, and his Life of St. Dubricius, written about A. D. 1120, is published in Wharton's Anglia Sacra.

‡ Qu. Is not St. Devereux, Herefordshire, a Norman rendering of Dubricius?

§ Eurddyl.

Pepiau ;* and an old commentator upon the Book of Llandaff asserts that the same statement originally appeared in that document, but that a later hand, wishing to make a correction, had mutilated the manuscript.† If these authorities can be depended upon, the unknown person is discovered, for Pabiali, the son of Brychan, is also called Papai; and the hypothesis that Dyfrig was a grandson of Brychan is satisfactorily explained.   It is said that he founded a college at Henllan on the Wye, where he remained seven years before he removed to Mochros on the same river; and in support of the assertion it may be said that Hentland in Erchenfield, where on a farm called Lanfrother traces of former importance were lately remaining, is dedicated to St. Dubricius. The other place is supposed to be Moccas, in the same district and not many miles distant. John of Teignmouth gives a list of his most distinguished disciples at Henllan, which it is needless to transcribe as it is not chronologically correct. According to Achau y Saint he was consecrated bishop of Llandaff by St. Germanus, which can hardly be admitted, for Germanus died A. D. 448. and Dubricius was living in 520, so that he must have held his episcopal honours for the improbable period of seventy years. The utmost that can be granted is to suppose with Archbishop Usher, that he was appointed bishop of Llandaff about A. D. 470, which however is rather too early; and that he was raised by Ambrosius to the archbishoprick of Caerleon, upon the death of Tremounus or Tremorinus, in 490.‡

* Usher de Primordiis, Cap. XIII.

† De Jure et Fundatione Landavensis Ecclesiæ a Registro Landavensi.
—"Supra dictus rex Ergic, Peipiau nomine, fuit pater Sancti Dubricii; prout habetur in Chronicis apud Collegium de Warwick; et supra nomen dicti Regis patris Sancti Dubricii prius rectè scribebatur antiquâ manu, et quidam novellus voluit corrigere, sed scripturam antiquam corripuit et malefecit." (Additamentum recentius.) Wharton's Anglia Sacra.

‡ Usher de Primordiis, Cap. V. et Index Chronologicus.

In this part of the subject, it is necessary to pause awhile to consider the general state of the Church. It does not appear that the Principality of Wales was in this age divided into dioceses, or that there were any established bishops' sees; for it is generally agreed upon that the bishopricks of St. David's, Llanbadarn, Bangor, and St. Asaph, were not founded till some time in the following century.* The archbishoprick of Caerleon was the only exception, and its permanency depended upon the importance which that place had maintained from the time it was occupied by the Romans. The jurisdiction of its archbishop, according to the rule observable in other parts of the Empire, would be co-extensive with the Roman province of Britannia Secunda; and his suffragans were so many " *Chorepiscopi*" without any settled place of residence;† thus the names occur of Tudwal in Carnarvonshire, Cynin at Llangynin, Gistlianus at Menevia, Paulinus at Tygwyn, all of whom are called bishops, and to their number may be added Dubricius, bishop of Llandaff. The influence of the latter, together with the liberality of Meurig ab Tewdrig, king of Glamorgan, was the means of making the see of Llandaff permanent;‡ whence Dubricius is said to have been its first bishop. It appears, however, that after his promotion to the archbishoprick of Caerleon, he still retained the bishoprick of Llandaff; and that he mostly resided at the latter place, from which he is called archbishop of Llandaff.§ But that the title still belonged to Caerleon, is clear from the fact that St. David, his successor in the primacy, was appointed archbishop of Caerleon; and though the bishoprick of Llan-

* In strictness the see of St. David's may be said to have commenced with Gistlianus, but as it had no diocese until it is was formed into an archbishoprick by St. David, its existence is usually dated from that event.

† Bingham's Antiquities of the Christian Church, Book II; and Stillingfleet's Origines Britannicæ, Chap. II.

‡ Registrum Landavense apud Godwin et Usher.

§ Achau y Saint, Registrum Landavense, and Godwin's Bishops.

daff merged into the archbishoprick in the person of Dubricius, it was not extinguished ; for, upon his resignation of the primacy, Teilo was appointed bishop of Llandaff, as if the title had been kept distinct.   St. David, after his election, removed the archiepiscopal see from Caerleon to Menevia, where he had lived before as Chorepiscopus.   His successor was Cynog, who was translated to Menevia from Llanbadarn.*
The third primate after Dubricius was Teilo, who, having appointed a suffragan at Menevia, continued his residence at Llandaff;† and is therefore styled its archbishop ;‡ but the migratory nature of the primacy seems to have weakened its stability, and it is not certain who was the next metropolitan. The partizane of the church of Llandaff, at a later time, contended that St. Oudoceus, its third bishop, succeeded to the archiepiscopal honours of Teilo ;§ while the clergy of Menevia, who exhibit the name of Teilo in their own catalogue, maintained that Ceneu, *their* fourth archbishop, transmitted the primacy to a long list of successors.   From a comparison of a variety of testimonies, it appears that upon the death of Teilo, the dignity sunk between contending parties; and at the time of the conference between St. Augustine and the British bishops it does not seem to have retained its existence.‖   The title was, however, occasionally assumed by the different prelates who contended for it ; and in the year 809 there were no less than three candidates for supremacy, a claim having been set up by the bishop of Bangor.*   The bishops of Wales, as well as its princes, were jealous of each

* Giraldus Cambrensis.

† Usher de Primordiis, Cap. XIV. p, 560.

‡ Godwin. Usher, Cap. V.

§ Usher, Cap. V. p. 85.

‖ Bede, Lib. I. Cap. 27, Lib. II. Cap. 2.—Giraldi Retractationes, apud Wharton.

* " Oed Crist 809, y bu farw Elfod Archescob Gwynedd, ac y bu diffyg ar yr haul, ac y bu terfysg mawr ym mhlith y Gwyr Eglwysig achaws y

other's ascendancy; and it is clear that a title so ill defined
could be only a dignity of assumption, but the preponderance
seems generally to have inclined in favour of Menevia or
St. David's. These irregularities, though perplexing to the
antiquary, are important as a proof of the independence of
the ancient British Church; for had it been subject to the see
of Rome, an appointment from the Pope would have settled
all disputes; and Giraldus Cambrensis, upon referring the
question to that tribunal in the twelfth century, was unable to
prove that any Welsh prelate had ever received the pall.* The
constitution of an archbishoprick, in the first instance, was a
continuation of the plan established under the Roman government; but when its authority was once shaken, the intermi-
nable commotions of the people would prevent its effectual
restoration: and in the register of the Catholic Church, exhi-
bited by the Pope to Giraldus, the names of the four Welsh
bishopricks are given simply, without explaining that any one
of them had authority over the rest, or that they were subject
to a foreign metropolitan.† The gradual reduction of Wales
by the English, obliged them to submit to the jurisdiction
of Canterbury.

<hr>

Pasc, canys ni fynnai Escobion Llandaf a Mynyw ymroddi dan Archescob
Gwynedd lle yr oeddynt eu hunain yn Archescobion hŷn o fraint."—Myvyrian Archaiology, Vol. II. p. 474.

* The whole controversy may be seen in Wharton's Anglia Sacra. The
story of Samson, archbishop of St. David's, and the pall, which was vir-
tually surrendered by Giraldus in his chapter of Retractions, is completely
overthrown by Archbishop Usher. Primordia, Cap. V.

† The account of this particular must be given in Giraldus's own words,
as the force of the argument depends upon the construction of Latin.—
"Accidit autem, ut vesperâ quadam, cum ad Papam in camerâ suâ Giraldus
accessisset; cum semper eum benignum satis et benevolum, ut videbatur,
invenire consueverit; tunc forte præter solitum amicabilem magis et
affabilem ipsum invenit. Inter primos igitur affatus, cum de jure Menevensis Ecclesiæ Metropolitico mentio facta fuisset; præcepit Papa Registrum afferri, ubi de universo fidelium orbe singulorum regnorum, tam

Dubricius is distinguished as the founder of colleges; and besides those, already mentioned, on the banks of the Wye, it is more rational to suppose that he, and not St. Germanus, was the founder of the colleges of Llancarfan, Caerworgorn, and Caerleon. At any rate, if the origin of those institutions be referred to this generation, which it is necessary to do to avoid anachronisms, they are situated so closely under the jurisdiction of Dubricius that they could not have been founded without his concurrence. The first principal or abbot of Llancarfan was Cattwg, the eldest son of Gwynllyw Filwr, of whom it is recorded that he chose a life of religion and learning rather than succeed to his father's principality. On account of his wisdom he is generally known by the appellation of Cattwg Ddoeth, or the Wise, and a large collection of his maxims and moral sayings, both in prose and verse, is preserved in the third volume of the Myvyrian Archaiology. His college, like all the rest founded in Wales in the infancy of monastic institutions, seems to have partaken of the characters both of a monastery and a place of education; and several

Metropoles per ordinem, quam earum quoque Suffraganeæ numerantur Ecclesiæ Pontificales. Et cum verteretur ad regnum Anglorum, scriptum in hunc modum ibidem et lectum fuit. "*Cantuariensis Metropolis Suffraganeas habet Ecclesias istas, Roffensem, Londoniensem,*" et cæteras per ordinem. Enumeratis autem singulis Suffraganeis Ecclesiasticis Angliæ; interposita Rubrica tali *De Wallia*, prosequitur in hunc modum. "*In Wallia Menevensis Ecclesia, Landavensis, Bangoriensis, et de Sancto Asaph.*" Quo audito, subjecit Papa quasi insultando et subridendo. Ecce Menevensis Ecclesia connumeratur. Respondit' Giraldus. Sed non eo modo connumeratur ista vel aliæ de Walliâ per accusativam scilicet, sicut Suffraganeæ de Angliâ. Quod si fieret, tunc revera reputari possent subjectæ. Cui Papa. Bene, inquit, hoc notâsti. Sed est et aliud, quod similiter pro vobis et Ecclesiâ vestrâ facit, de Rubricâ sc. interpositâ; quæ quidem in Registro nusquam apponitur, nisi ubi transitus fit, de regno ad regnum, vel Metropoli ad Metropolim. Verum est, inquit Giraldus; Et Wallia quidem portio est regni Anglicani et non per se regnum. Ad quod Papa. Unum sciatis, quod non est contra vos Registrum nostrum.

of the most eminent of the Welsh bards and clergy were ranked among its members. Though it is said to have been situated at Llancarfan, the particular spot on which it stood was called Llanfeithin, for which reason the names are used indiscriminately. It is said that Dubricius was so partial to the society of Cattwg that he made him his companion in his travels; and, that they might be more constantly together, Dubricius continued to live at a place, near Llanfeithin, called Garnllwyd, after he was appointed bishop; but the statement must be received with some qualification, as his usual residence was at Llandaff or Caerleon. Cattwg was an attendant at the court of Arthur; and though for the sake of convenience the particulars of his life are detailed in this generation, his history belongs more properly to the following, as he is said to have lived to the patriarchal age of a hundred and twenty years,[*] and the assertion is in some measure borne out by the great discrepancy in the ages of persons who shared his instructions. He is considered to be the founder of several churches, of which the following is a list.

Llangattock Crickhowell, R. with 2 chapels, Llangeneu (St. Ceneu) and Llanelly (St. Ellyw) Brecknockshire.
Porteinion, R. Glamorganshire.
Gelli Gaer, R.—1 chapel, Brithdir, Glamorgan.
Cadoxton juxta Barry, R. Glam,
Llancarfan, V.—2 chapels, *Llanfeithin*, *Liege Castle*, Glam.
Pendeulwyn, V. Glam.
Pentyrch, R. Glam.
Llanmaes, R. Glam.
Cadoxton juxta Neath, V.—2 chapels, Creinant, Aberpergwm, Glamorganshire.
Llangattock near Usk, R. Monmouthshire.
Llangattock Lenig, V. Monm.
Llangattock Lingoed. V. Monm.
Llangattock Feibion Afel, V.—1 chapel, St. Moughan's (Qu. Meugan?) Monm.
Caerleon upon Usk, V. Monm.

Besides the foregoing, Penrhos, subject to Llandeilo Cresenni, Monmouthshire, and Trefethin under Llanofer, in the

* Myvyrian Archaiology, Vol. III. p. 2.

x

same county, are dedicated to him. None of these require
any particular notice, except Caerleon, which, from its situation, might be suspected to have been the metropolitan
church of Cambria. The cathedral must, however, have been
some other building, as the archbishoprick was founded before
the time of Cattwg, and those who filled the see must have
possessed a church from which they derived their title.
Geoffrey of Monmouth, who, for want of better authority, may
be followed in this instance, says* the cathedral was dedicated
to St. Aaron, the martyr; but it was not in existence in the
time of that writer, and all traces of it have been forgotten.
The epithet of Doeth, attached to the name of Cattwg, has
induced certain Romish writers to confound him with St.
Sophias, bishop of Beneventum in Italy, and the accumulated
history of these persons may be seen in Cressy. Cattwg is
commemorated in the Calendar, Feb. 24.†

   The next college is Caerworgorn, the first principal of
which was Illtyd or St. Iltutus, from which it was called Côr
.or Bangor Illtyd. The place at which it was situated is now
known by the name of Llanilltyd Fawr, or Lantwit Major:
but with respect to the age of Iltutus some uncertainty pre-
vails; for while one account says that he was appointed to
this college by St. Germanus,‡ and therefore before A. D.
450, another account states that he was a soldier in the train of
Arthur, and that he was persuaded by Cattwg Ddoeth to
renounce the world and devote himself to religion.§ The
last statement would bring down the date of his appointment
to A. D. 520. The first date has been already shown to be
wrong, and the last depends upon his legendary life. His

---

   * According to the Latin copy, as quoted by Usher.
   † Mr Sharon Turner cites a Latin Life of Cattwg under the name of
Cadocus, from the Cottonian MSS. Vesp. A. 14. and Titus D. 22.
   ‡ Achau y Saint.
   § Johannes Tinmuthensis, apud Usher.

position in his own genealogy, and the age of persons said to have been members of his college, would show that his appointment took place before the close of this century.* He was by birth an Armorican, being the son of Bicanys by a sister of Emyr Llydaw, whom John of Teignmouth calls Rieniguilida; and was therefore the great nephew of St. Germanus.† As the Welsh authorities call him Illtyd Farchog, or the knight, he was probably distinguished for his military career before he left his native country. Like Cattwg he attended the court of Arthur, and though both of them are said in the Triads to have been knights there, the title must have had reference to their past achievements, for it is immediately added that they were devoted to the law of God and the faith in Christ.‡ According to the Regestum Landavense,§ Iltutus, having built a church, and afterwards a monastery at Lantwit under the patronage of Meirchion, a chieftain of Glamorgan, opened a school, which was filled with a large number of disciples. But as some of those whose names are enumerated, are also known to have studied elsewhere, it may be inferred that it was not an unusual practice to migrate from one college to another. There appears to have been no appointed age at which members were admitted. Besides the youth who resorted to these institutions for instruction, old men often passed the remainder of their days in them, devoting their time to religious exercises; and these contingencies being borne in mind, much apparent contradiction will be obviated.

The name of Illtyd is connected with several churches, besides that of Llanilltyd Fawr or Lantwit; he may be consider-

---

* The Regestum Landavense says he was appointed by St. Dubricius.

† In another account it is said that his mother was Gweryla, daughter of Tewdrig, king of Glamorgan.

‡ Triads 121 & 122, Third Series.

§ Apud Usher, Cap. XIII.

ed the founder of Penbre, Carmarthenshire,* Ilston, and Newcastle, Glamorganshire ;† and also of Llantrisaint in the latter
county in conjunction with St. Tyfodwg and St. Gwynno,
from which circumstance the church derives its name, imply-
ing "the church of the three saints."‡ Ecton records Illtyd
as the patron saint of Llanhary, and Llantryddid, Glamorganshire, as well as of Llanhileth, Monmouthshire, and Llantwood
or Llantwyd, Pembrokeshire. The following chapels are dedicated to him,—Llanilltyd Faerdre under Llantrisaint, and
Lantwit subject to Neath, Glamorganshire, Capel Illtyd subject to Dyfynog, Brecknockshire, and Llanelltyd under Llanfachraith, Merionethshire. Independently of the churches
which he founded, the memory of Illtyd is honoured by the
Welsh on account of his having introduced among them an
improved method of ploughing: before his time they were
accustomed to cultivate their grounds with the mattock and
over-treading plough (aradr arsang,) implements, which, the
compiler of a Triad upon husbandry observes, were still used
by the Irish.§ Mr. Owen says he died about A. D. 480, but
it is evident his life extended through a considerable part of
the sixth century, which may more properly be said to be the
age in which he flourished. According to Cressy his commemoration was held Feb. 7, but the year in which he died

* Chapels to Penbre,—Llannon (St. Non) and Llandurry. There appears also to have been a chapel dedicated to St. Non in the parish of
Ilston.

† Chapels to Newcastle,—Bettws (St. David,) Laleston (St. David,) and
Tithegston (St. Tudwg ab Tyfodwg.)

‡ Chapels to Llantrisaint,—Llanilltyd or Lantwit Faerdre (St. Illtyd,)
Ystrad Dyfodwg (St. Tyfodwg,) Llanwonno (St. Gwynno,) Aberdâr (St.
John the Baptist,) and St. John's chapel (St. John the Baptist.) In the
dedications of the foregoing chapels, some historical allusions may be
traced. Four of them seem to refer to the fact, that St. David, who was
the son of Non, was a pupil of St. Iltutus, and three others have reference
to the founders of the mother church.

§ Triad 56, Third Series.

was uncertain. Tradition affirms that he was buried near the chapel that bears his name in Brecknockshire, where there is a place called Bedd Gwyl Illtyd, or the grave of St. Illtyd's eve, from its having been a custom to watch there during the night previous to the saint's day.* In the church-yard of Lantwit Major a large stone may be seen with three several inscriptions, one of them purporting that it was the cross of Iltutus and Samson, another that Samson raised the cross for his soul, and the third that one Samuel was the carver.†

The last college, the foundation of which may be attributed to Dubricius, was at Caerleon; and, according to some copies of Geoffrey of Monmouth, it contained two hundred philosophers who studied astronomy and other sciences.

The British monastic institutions require further notice. Little is known respecting their internal regulations, but it would appear that choral service formed an important part of their arrangements. The Welsh terms, which have been generally rendered "college or congregation," and by Latin writers invariably "monasterium," are *Côr*, choir; and *Bangor*, high choir.‡ According to the Triads, the three societies of the first class, of which Bangor Illtyd was one,§ contained no less than two thousand four hundred members; one hundred being employed every hour, in order that the praise and service of God might be continued day and night without intermission. The number, however, in other establishments varied exceedingly; and the magnificent scale of those alluded

* Jones's Brecknockshire, Vol. II. p. 683.

† Gibson's Camden, Vol. II.—There is a Life of St. Illtut, abbot, in the Cottonian MSS. Vespasian A. XIV.　•

‡ Sixteen communities in Wales, which bore these appellations, are enumerated by the intelligent author of the Horæ Britannicæ, Vol. II. Chap. VII.

§ The other two were Cor Emrys yng Nghaer Caradawg, probably at Old Sarum; and Bangor Wydrin at Glastonbury. Triad 80, First Series, and 84 Third Series.

to would be thought incredible, if it were not for the authentic
testimony of Bede, who flourished about a century after the
destruction of the monastery of Bangor Iscoed. That author,
whose accuracy is universally admitted, says that the number
of its monks was two thousand one hundred, who were divided into classes, of three hundred each, under their respective superintendents ; and, that his readers might not be
ignorant as to the manner in which so vast a society was
supported, he adds that they all lived by the labour of their
own hands.* Compared with this, the assertion that Dubricius had upwards of a thousand pupils at Henllan,† will
will not appear strange ; and it ie said that Cattwg, who retained a part of his father's territories for the purpose, was
wont to maintain a hundred ecclesiastics, as many paupers,
and the same number of widows, besides strangers and guests,
at his own expense.‡ The traces of extensive ranges of buildings still observable at Bangor Iscoed and Lantwit Major
confirm the asseverations of ancient writers ; and an old manuscript, extant in the reign of Elizabeth, affirmed that the saints
at the latter place had for their habitations seven halls and
four hundred houses.§ The abbots of these institutions are
sometimes styled bishops, and it is not improbable that they
exercised chorepiscopal authority in their respective societies ;
but it is agreed that they were all of them subject to the
bishop of the diocese ; and there is an instance on record of
St. Dubricius interfering to correct certain abuses and jealousies
which had broken out at Lantwit Major.‖ Some of these

* Eccl. Hist. Lib. II. Cap. 2.

† Johannes Tinmuthensis, apud Usher.

‡ Ibid.

§ Horæ Britannicæ, Vol. II. p. 355.

‖ " Vir beatæ memoriæ Dubricius visitavit locum Sti. Ilduti tempore
quadragesimali, ut quæ emendanda erant corrigeret, et servanda consolidet,
ibidem enim conversabantur multi sanctissimi viri, quodam livore de-
cepti."—Liber Landavensis, as quoted in the Horæ Britannicæ.

establishments were not of long continuance, and appear to have declined upon the death of their first abbot; while others, which were endowed with lands, remained for a longer time, but even these dwindled away, or were re-modelled upon the introduction of monasteries of the regular orders in the middle ages. The primitive British institutions followed no uniform rule, and may in some degree have resembled the monasteries of Gaul before the adoption of the rule of St. Benedict; but in borrowing analogies from the continent, to supply the lack of positive information, allowance must be made for the secluded situation of the Britons, and their more partial advance in civilization. The monasteries of Wales appear to have borne a closer resemblance to those of Ireland,* for which reason the writings of Irish historians may be consulted with advantage by the Welsh antiquary.

The abbots of Llancarfan and Lantwit exercised great influence in the diocese of Llandaff; and the records of that see associate with them a third dignitary, the abbot of Docunnus, but the situation of the monastery of that name is at present unknown. It is said to have been founded by Cungarus, who is also called Docwinus ;† and in Achau y Saint it is stated that Cyngar founded a congregation at a place in Glamorgan which, in the time of the compiler, was called Llangenys. But wherever this place may be situated, there is some uncertainty in the accounts which have been received respecting the founder of the community, as in the pedigrees there are two persons of the name of Cyngar ; and both of them are distinguished from Dochdwy, who might be thought to be the same person as Docwinus.

Tewdrig ab Teithfallt has been considered a saint, and is classed with Gwrthefyr and Cadwaladr as one of the three

---

* The monastery of Beanchor in Ulster is reported to have contained three thousand monks under the care of St. Comgallus.

† Capgrave in Vitâ S. Cungari.

canonized kings of Britain. The history of this person and
his family is involved in confusion. One account identifies
him with an ancestor of Brychan Brycheiniog, while others
make him contemporary with St. Oudoceus about the close of
the sixth century; but the only position, that can be assigned
him consistently with his genealogy, would show that he
flourished between A. D. 440 and 470; and this arrangement
is the one best supported by collateral testimony. It is said
that in his old age he resigned the government of Glamorgan
into the hands of his son, Meurig, and retired to lead a religious life in the solitude of Tinteyrn, Monmouthshire. He
was afterwards induced to appear once more in defence of his
country against the Saxons, and, receiving a wound in battle
which he expected to be mortal, he requested that a church
should be raised upon the spot where he should expire. His
request was performed accordingly. The church was called
from the circumstance Merthyr Tewdrig, and is now known
by the name of Mathern.*

Meurig ab Tewdrig, by whom the church just mentioned
was built, was also the prince under whose protection the
bishoprick of Llandaff and the monastery of Llancarfan were
founded. If reliance can be placed upon certain records
of Llandaff, he endowed that see with lands and churches,
from the situations of which it would appear that he held
paramount authority over a tract forming the principal part of
the present county of Glamorgan, the whole of Monmouthshire, and so much of the county of Hereford as lies to the
south-west of the river Wye. Citations from grants securing
these endowments, and other privileges and immunities, to

---

* "His bones lie entoombed, uppon the North side of the sayde Church.
And his sonne not contented therewithall, gaue moreouer the lands and
territory adiacent unto the same to the Bishoppe, whose Successors in
processe of time built a house there, to witte at Mertherne or as now we
tearme it Matherne, beeing the only mansion house now left unto him."—
Godwin, Bp. of Llandaff in 1615.

the bishop and his successors, are still extant.[*] But whatever may be the antiquity of these documents, they certainly do not belong to the fifth century, and seem to describe the diocese of Llandaff and principality of Gwent at a later era. They should not, however, be rejected without examination, as they supply important links of history, which would otherwise have been wanting; and it should not be forgotten, that such grants and charters as were fabricated in the middle ages, were, in every practicable case, palmed upon real personages in order to obtain credit for genuineness.

A proposition has been advanced in the Cambrian Biography, which has been copied into other publications, that the real Uther Pendragon, the father of Arthur, was no other than Meurig ab Tewdrig.[†] It is, however, no more than a genealogical mistake, arising from the supposition that Arthruis,[‡] or Arthwys, a son, and Anna, a daughter of Meurig, were the same persons as Arthur and Anna, two of the children of Uther. The history and connexions of both the families are so different as to render it surprising that such an error should have been committed, were it not for the fact that Meurig and Uther were contemporaries, and that Arthur is reported to have held his court at Caerleon in the territories of the Silurian chieftain. From a comparison of the most ancient authorities extant upon the subject, including the oldest of the Welsh remains, it may be collected that Arthur was a native of Devon or Cornwall, and that his connexion with the Cymry of Wales and North Britain was almost entirely of an intrusive kind. He appears, indeed, to have obtained the chief sovereignty of the Britons, but it was by usurpation, and he was

---

[*] Wharton's Anglia Sacra, Vol. II. and Godwin's Bishops.

[†] Cambrian Biography *vocibus* Anna, Arthur, Meirig, and Uthyr.

[‡] Registrum Landavense, and Godwin's Bishops. He is called "Andros" in the Cambrian Biography, page 40; and "Adras" in Triads 118 and 118, Third Series.

more often engaged in conflict with his own countrymen than
with the Saxons. The documents,* which exhibit Meurig as
the paramount ruler of Gwent, imply that there were several
chieftains subordinate to him. He was succeeded by his son,
Arthruis, who was the father of Morgan Mwynfawr ;† but the
acts and territories of the family are on a scale too small, even
for the limited description of Arthur which may be drawn
from Nennius and the poems of the Welsh bards.‡

The name of Gwrtheyrn, or Vortigern, is more implicated
with the Welsh genealogies than that of Arthur ; and it is recorded that Edeyrn, one of his sons, who was a saint of the
congregation of Cattwg, established a religious community of
three hundred members at a place in Glamorganshire which
was afterwards called Llanedeyrn. Two others of his sons
have obtained the reputation of sanctity in the same county ;—
Aerdeyrn, to whom it is said there was a church dedicated in
Glamorgan ; and Elldeyrn, who is the patron of Llanelldeyrn
or Llaniltern, a chapel under St. Fagan's. Nennius, who does
not mention the three preceding, relates that Faustus, one of
his sons, built a large place on the bank of the river Renis,
which remained till the time in which he wrote. No further
mark of locality is added, and as the Welsh name of Faustus
is unknown, it has been conjectured that he was the same person as Edeyrn, and that the Rhymni which passes by Llanedeyrn is the Renis.§ Faustus was born in his father's old
age ; which it is presumed was the case with the other two, or
it may be three, persons, as they are not noticed in the current

* The records of Llandaff.

† Godwin's Bishops, and Triads 113, 118.

‡ This question is discussed by Mr. Sharon Turner in his "Anglo-Saxons,"
Book III. Chap. III. and by Mr. Ritson in his "Life of King Arthur ;"
but it is to be lamented that the latter person, with all his erudition and
talent, should, in his desire to maintain a favourite position, deform his
work with unfair criticism and reckless abuse.

§ Notes to Gunn's Nennius,—and Usher, p. 1002.

accounts of the life of Vortigern; and their date is therefore referred to this generation.

Paulinus, or Pawl Hên, was originally a North Briton, and it may be inferred from one or two manuscripts that he resided for some time in the Isle of Man.* The cause of his removal is not stated, but his next residence that is known was at Caerworgorn, where he became a saint of the monastery of Iltutus. He afterwards founded a similar institution at Ty-gwyn ar Dâf, or Whitland, in Carmarthenshire, of which he was himself the first abbot, and where he was also styled a bishop,† though it does not appear that he had the care of a diocese. His institution soon became famous as a place of religious education; and as Paulinus was eminent for his acquaintance with the sacred Scriptures, David, Teilo, and other distinguished saints removed to Ty-gwyn to share his instructions.‡ It is said that he placed at the head of his society two persons, named Gredifael and Fflewyn, who as they held office jointly were probably superintendents of classes, similar to those described by Bede in the monastery of Bangor Iscoed. He is the patron saint of the church of Llangors, Brecknockshire, and of Capel Peulin,§ a chapel subordinate to Llandingad, Carmarthenshire. As he lived to attend a synod held at Llanddewi Brefi,‖ the date of which is generally assigned to the year 519, his life must have reached to a considerable part of the sixth century; and it is remarkable that the most lasting traces of his memory remain in the neighbourhood of that place. Capel Peulin, which bears his

---

* Cambrian Biography.

† Life of St. David by Giraldus Cambrensis.

‡ Life of St, Teilo written about A. D. 1120 by Galfridus alias Stephanus, brother of Urban Bp. of Llandaff, and published in Wharton's Anglia Sacra.

§ Called "Capella Sancti Paulini" in one of the charters of the abbey of Strata Florida.

‖ Life of St. David by Giraldus.

name, is on the borders of the parish of Llanddewi Brefi; and in the parish of Caio, adjoining the latter, still exists a stone with the following inscription :—

> SERVATVR FIDÆI
> PATRIEQ: SEMPER
> AMATOR HIC PAVLIN
> VS IACIT CVLTOR PIENT—
> SIMVS ÆQVI

The localities being considered, it would appear that this stone commemorated the interment of Paulinus the saint, and not that of a Roman general as has been supposed.* The expression "Servator Fidei" implies that the person interred was a Christian; and the whole inscription consists of two Hexameter lines which belong to a period when Latin versification was more corrupt than at the time of the departure of the Romans from Britain.† Paulinus was commemorated on the twenty second of November under the name of Polin, Esgob, or the bishop.‡

---

* Cambrian Register, Vol. III. p, 38 and 39.

† A facsimile of the inscription may be seen in the account of Carmarthenshire in Gibson's Camden; and the words when placed in their proper form are:

> Servator fidei, patriæque semper amator,
> Hic Paulinus jacet, cultor pientissimus æqui.

The last syllable of patriæque is an error in prosody, unless the author intended the u for a vowel, and so formed the end of the word into a dactyl. In the second line he appears to have had for his model the poets before the Augustan age, who frequently omitted the final s, and allowed the vowel preceding to assume its natural quantity; the last u in Paulinus is therefore short. The n in pientissimus must have been quiescent, in which case the vowel before it would be short, as in "pietas" from whence the word is derived. This interesting relic of antiquity lay originally at a place called Pant y Polion, obviously a corruption of Pant Polin; and is now removed for preservation to Dolau Cothi, the seat of J. Johnes, Esq.

‡ Cambrian Register, Vol. p. 220.

It would not be proper to close this generation without some notice of Ffraid, for though she was not a Welsh saint, her memory has been held in great respect in the Principality. She is more generally known by the names of St. Bridget or St. Bride, and, according to Llyfr Bodeulwyn,* she was the daughter of Cadwrthai, an Irishman; but other MSS. state that she was of Scottish† parentage, being the daughter of Dwyppws ab Cefyth or Dwpdagws. The Latin life of this saint says that her father, Dubtachus, was an Irishman, and that she was born at Fochart, in the county of Lowth; and Archbishop Usher places the date of her birth in the year 453. The Welsh and Irish accounts agree in describing her as a nun, and it is said that she received the veil from Maccaleus, one of the disciples of St. Patrick. In her native country her celebrity appears to have been exceeded only by that of the great Apostle of Ireland himself, and in Wales no less than eighteen churches and chapels are dedicated to her, as may be seen by the following catalogue.

Diserth, C. Flintshire.
Llansanffraid Glyn Conwy, R. Denbighshire.
Llansanffraid Glyn Ceiriog, C. Denb.
Llansanffraid in Mechain, R.—New Chapel, Montgomeryshire.
Llansanffraid Glyndyfrdwy, R. Merionethshire.
Capel Sanffraid, in ruins, a chapel to Holyhead, Anglesey.
St. Brides, R.—1 chapel, in ruins, Pembrokeshire.
Llansanffraid, V.—1 chapel, Llannon (St. Non.) Cardiganshire.
Llansanffraid Cwmmwd Deuddwr, V.—2 chapels, Llanfadog (St. Madog,) and Nantgwyllt, Radnorshire.
Llansanffraid in Elfael, V. Radn.
Llansanffraid, R. Brecknockshire.
St. Brides Minor upon Ogmor, R. Glamorganshire,
St. Brides Major, V.—3 chapels, Wick, (St. James,) Llamphey (St. Faith,) and "capella de Ugemor," Glam.
St. Brides super Elai, R. Glam.
St. Brides, alias Llansanffraid, R. Monmouthshire.
Skenfreth, or Ysgynfraith, V. Monm.
St. Brides, in Netherwent, R. Monm.
St. Brides Wentloog, C. Monm.

* A manuscript cited in the Myv. Archaiology, Vol. II. p. 51.
† "O rieni Yscotiaid," meaning of course the Scots of Ireland.

From the extent of the parishes attached, it may be inferred, that the foundations of several of these churches are of considerable antiquity, and seem to belong to the class of those dedicated to St. Michael and St. Peter. There is a vague tradition that St. Bridget visited Wales, which may in some degree account for the homage she has received; but veneration for this holy person has, for some unknown cause of preference, been diffused so widely, that she deserves to be called pre-eminently the saint of the British Isles; for churches have been consecrated to her memory throughout England and Scotland, in the Isle of Man, and especially in the Hebrides. Her remembrance, however, was in no place cherished with more fond assiduity than at Kildare in Ireland, where a sacred fire kindled by her own hands was kept perpetually burning, and according to Giraldus Cambrensis had not been extinguished for six hundred years. Her death is supposed to have happened about A. D. 525, and the first of February was held as a festival in her honour.

Colman was a saint who flourished in Ireland about the same time as Ffraid. Llangolman, subject to Maenclochog, and Capel Colman, subject to Llanfihangel Penbedw, both in Pembrokeshire, are dedicated to him, but it is not known whether he had any personal connexion with that county. He is sometimes called Colman the elder, to distinguish him from another Colman, the third bishop of Lindisfarn.

SECTION X.

The Welsh Saints from the Accession of Uther Pendragon A. D. 500, to the Death of Arthur A. D. 542.

THE saints of this generation are exceedingly numerous, and the history of one or two already noticed remains to be concluded.

Dubricius still continued to preside over the see of Caerleon, and it is said that he had the honour of crowning king Arthur. In his time the Pelagian heresy, which for a while had been suppressed by St. Germanus, had increased to such a degree that it required an extraordinary effort to check its progress, and, if possible, to extinguish it. Accordingly a synod of the whole clergy of Wales was convened at Llanddewi Brefi, in Cardiganshire, and the following is the account given of it by Giraldus Cambrensis in his " Life of St. David."—

" The detestable heresy of the Pelagians, although formerly extinguished through the labours of Germanus of Auxerre, and Lupus of Troyes, when they came over to this island; this pestilence, although once suppressed, sprung up anew, and gave occasion for convening a general synod of all the churches of Wales. All the bishops, and abbots, and religious of different orders, together with the princes and laymen, were assembled at Brefi in the county of Cardigan. When many discourses had been delivered in public, and were ineffectual to reclaim the Pelagians from their error, at length Paulinus, a bishop, with whom David had studied in his youth, very earnestly entreated that that holy, discreet, and eloquent man might be sent for. Messengers were therefore despatched to desire his attendance; but their importunity was unavailing with the holy man, he being so fully and intently given up to

contemplation that urgent necessity alone could induce him to
pay any regard to temporal or secular concerns. At last, two
holy men, namely Daniel* and Dubricius, went over to him.
By them he was persuaded to come to the synod; and after
his arrival, such was the grace and eloquence with which he
spoke, that he silenced the opponents, and they were utterly
vanquished.† But Father David, by the common consent of
all, whether clergy or laity, (Dubricius having resigned in his
favour,) was elected primate of the Cambrian Church."—

This is the account generally received, and it is said that St.
Dubricius, worn down with years and longing for retirement,
withdrew to a monastery in the island of Enlli or Bardsey,
where he died A. D. 522. He was buried in the island, where
his remains lay undisturbed till A. D. 1120, when Urban,
bishop of Llandaff, through the favour of Radulphus, archbishop
of Canterbury, obtained the permission of David, bishop of Bangor, and Griffith, prince of North Wales, to remove them.†
They were accordingly translated to Llandaff, where they
were interred with great pomp and solemnity in the cathedral,
which had been rebuilt a short time before from its foundation.
But the most remarkable feature in the history of the pro-

---

* Intended for Daniel, the first bishop of Bangor, whose life, to avoid
an anachronism, should be placed a full generation later.

† Tradition points to the site of the church of Llanddewi Brefi as the
spot where this memorable sermon was preached, and Cressy relates, with
a devout faith, that the following miracles took place upon the occasion.—
" When all the fathers assembled enjoined David to preach, he commanded
a child which attended, and had lately been restored to life by him, to
spread a napkin under his feet, and standing upon it, he began to expound
the Gospel and the Law to the auditory: all the while that this oration
continued, a snow-white dove descending from heaven sat upon his shoul-
ders; and moreover the earth on which he stood raised itself under him
till it became a hill, from whence his voice like a trumpet was clearly
heard, and understood by all, both near and far off; on the top of which
hill a church was afterwards built, and remains to this day."

† Life of St. Dubricius in Wharton.

ceeding is the fact that the bones of the saint were discovered with great difficulty.   Inquiry was made into the monuments of the past, and the oldest writings were searched in order to ascertain where his body had been deposited; by whom, how, and at what time it was buried.   The passage of the Book of Llandaff, which records these particulars, though written when the Romish religion was at its highest ascendency, has therefore, in making this admission, betrayed the inference, that in whatever esteem the Britons of the primitive Church might have held the memory of their holy men, they could not have worshipped their relics.   The body of the great archbishop of Caerleon, whose reputation for sanctity was almost equal to that of St. David, lay unenshrined for six centuries.   His example, however, in retiring to close his life in Bardsey, was so extensively followed, that according to the exaggerations of after ages, no less than twenty thousand saints were interred in the island, the entire surface of which was covered with their ashes; but his remains were so little regarded that other bodies were buried over him, and how his relics were afterwards distinguished from the general heap is a problem which the author of the record has left unexplained.*   His death was commemorated on the fourth of November, and his translation on the twenty ninth of May.

The most eminent saint of Wales must now be introduced to the reader; David, or, as his countrymen call him, Dewi, was the son of Sandde ab Ceredig ab Cunedda, by Non, the daughter of Gynyr of Caergawch.   To repeat all the fabulous legends invented respecting him, would be to heap together a mass of absurdity and profaneness; for the monks, in the

---

* "Quod vero postmodum investigatum est, et adquisitum monumentis seniorum, et antiquissimis scriptis literarum, quo loco sepultus est infra sepulturam sanctorum virorum Enlli ; quoque situ firmiter humatus est; et a quo, et qualiter, quorumque principum tempore."—Lib. Landav. MS. as quoted in Roberts's Chronicle of the Kings of Britain, p. 339.

z

excess of their veneration, have not scrupled to say that his birth was foretold thirty years before the event, and that he was honoured with miracles while yet in the womb. But to pass by these wretched imaginations of a perverted mind, it will be sufficient to notice only those statements of his history which have an appearance of truth. It is said by Giraldus that he was born at the place since called St. David's, and that he was baptized at Porth Clais in that neighbourhood by Ælveus, or rather Albeus, bishop of Munster, " who by divine providence had arrived at that time from Ireland." The same author adds, that he was brought up at a place, the name of which, meaning "the old bush," is in Welsh "Hen-meneu,"* and in Latin " Vetus Menevia."—The locality of Hen-meneu is uncertain, and a claim has been set up on behalf of Henfynyw in Cardiganshire,† which answers to the name, and its church is dedicated to the saint; but it is clear that Giraldus and Ricemarchus, from whom the information is derived, intended to designate some spot near the western promontory of Pembrokeshire, possibly the Roman station of Menapia, for the latter writer intimates that the " Old Bush," as he calls it, was the place where Gistlianus resided before he removed to the valley of Rosina.‡

St. David is reported to have received his religious education in the school of Iltutus; and afterwards in that of Paulinus at Ty-gwyn ar Dâf, where he is said to have spent ten years in the study of the Scriptures, and where Teilo, the second bishop of Llandaff, was one of his fellow-students. It would appear from Giraldus that he was ordained a presbyter before he entered the school of Paulinus, and the same author states that

* His etymology of the word is borrowed from two languages, *hên* being the Welsh for *old*, and *muni*, as he says, is the Irish term for a *bush*.

† Carlisle's Topographical Dictionary of Wales, *voce* Henfynyw.

‡ Various readings to Giraldus, in Wharton Vol. II.—See also page 162 of this Essay.

David, Padarn, and Teilo, visited Jerusalem together, where
they were consecrated to the order of Bishops by the Patriarch.   Whether this event should be considered to have happened before, or after, the time that David became principal of
the monastery in the valley of Rosina is of little consequence,
as the story is so improbable that it may be rejected entirely.
From its construction it appears to have been borrowed by
Giraldus from one of the lost Triads, and it was probably invented by some bard who wished to show that the Welsh
bishops traced their consecration to higher authority than that
of the Pope.   It is, however, admitted that St. David founded
or restored a monastery in the valley of Rosina,* which was
afterwards called Menevia; and as the abbots of similar religious societies were in those days considered to be bishops in
the neighbourhood of their respective communities, St. David
enjoyed the dignity of a *Chorepiscopus* before his elevation to
the archbishoprick of Cambria.   In the retirement of Menevia, he appears to have lived with his disciples, practising
those religious austerities which were sanctioned by the superstition of the times.   He denied himself the enjoyment of
animal food, and his only drink was water.   Except when
compelled by urgent necessity, he rigidly abstained from
every interference in temporal affairs, all his time being devoted to prayer and spiritual contemplation.   It is not stated
how long he continued to practise these exercises; but he is
said to have experienced considerable molestation from a
chieftain of the Gwyddyl Ffichti, named Boia,† who with a
band of followers had occupied the surrounding district.
Such, however, was the patience with which David and his
associates endured this persecution, that the chieftain relin-

* Its Welsh name is Rhôs, and Giraldus, who occasionally indulges
in a pun, says there were no *roses* in the valley,—*rosina non rosea.*

† Ricemarchus calls him a Scot; Galfridus, a Pict; and Gwynfardd intimates that he was an Irishman (Gwyddyl;) the name Gwyddyl Ffichti is
adopted above, as being applicable to the three in common.

quished his hostility, and was at last converted and baptized.[*]
St. David was first roused from his seclusion to · attend the
synod of Brefi in the manner already related. It is recorded
that he accepted the archbishoprick with reluctance ; but after
his entrance into public life he was distinguished for his
activity. As the Pelagian heresy was not entirely suppressed,
he convened another synod, which it would appear from the
Annales Menevenses was held at Caerleon. His exertions
upon this occasion were so successful that the heresy was
exterminated, and the meeting has been named, in consequence,
" the Synod of Victory."

After these councils he is said to have drawn up with his
own hand a code of rules for the regulation of the British
Church, a copy of which remained in the cathedral of St.
David's until it was lost in an incursion of pirates. Under his
presidency the cause of religion attained to great prosperity,
and, to use the words of Giraldus :—" In those times in the
territory of Cambria the Church of God flourished exceedingly,
and ripened with much fruit every day. Monasteries were built
every where ; many congregations of the faithful of various orders were collected to celebrate with fervent devotion the sac-
rifice of Christ. But to all of them, Father David, as if placed
on a lofty eminence, was a mirror and a pattern of life. He informed them by words, and he instructed them by example ;
as a preacher, most powerful through his eloquence, but
more so in his works. He was a doctrine to his hearers, a
guide to the religious, a life to the poor, a support to orphans,
a protection to widows, a father to the fatherless, a rule to

---

* Life of Teilo by Galfridus. Giraldus's version of the story is, that
Boia, attempting to molest the saints, suffered the vengeance of heaven,
being himself afflicted with a fever, and his cattle perishing by disease ;
upon which he solicited the peace of the holy men, and through their intercession obtained a removal of the judgment, his cattle being restored to
life ; but his wife, making a second attempt at molestation, was deprived
of her reason, and Boia was soon afterwards slain by an enemy.

monks, and a path to seculars, becoming all to all, that he might gain all to God."—This character is, of course, overcharged; but it is recorded in the Triads that the three blessed visitors of the Isle of Britain were Dewi, Padarn, and Teilo. —" They were so called because they went as guests to the houses of the noble, the plebeian, the native and the stranger, without accepting either fee or reward, or victuals or drink; but what they did was to teach the faith in Christ to every one without pay or thanks. Besides which, they gave to the poor and needy, gifts of their gold and silver, their raiment and provisions."

After his elevation, St. David appears to have resided for a while at Caerleon, the proper seat of the primate;[*] but his stay was not of long continuance before he obtained the permission of Arthur to remove the see to Menevia. No reason is alleged for this proceeding, and probably it arose from the mere desire of dignifying a place to which he had become attached from early associations.[†] The churches founded by him have been enumerated already,[‡] and the list is worthy of another consideration as it serves to point out the country which, though archbishop, he held under his peculiar jurisdiction. It is generally agreed that Wales was first divided into dioceses in his time, and local indications are exceedingly valuable wherever they are sufficiently numerous to establish an inference upon inductive principles. The diocese of St. David, therefore, as may be judged from the foundations at-

---

[*] Triad 7, First Series.

[†] The Latin copy of Geoffrey says that he loved Menevia above all other monasteries of his diocese, because St. Patrick, by whom his birth had been foretold, had founded it! Bp. Godwyn suggests: " It seemeth he misliked the frequency of people at Caerlegion, as a meanes to withdraw him from contemplation, whereunto that hee might be more free, hee made choice of this place for his See rather than for any fitness of the same otherwise."

[‡] Page 52.

tributed to him, extended over the entire counties of Pembroke and Carmarthen; its northern boundary in Cardiganshire included the parishes of Llanddewi Aberarth, and Llanddewi Brefi; from whence it seems to have followed the course of the Irfon through Brecknockshire,* and in Radnorshire it included the parishes of Cregruna and Glascwm. North of this line was the diocese of Llanbadarn, in which there are no church-foundations attributable to St. David; and the three chapels dedicated to him, as mentioned before,† date in all probability subsequent to the time when this diocese merged into that of Menevia. From Glascwm the boundary of St. David's seems to have passed southwards to the Wye, and to have followed the course of that river to its junction with the Severn, including the districts of Ewyas and Erchenfield in Herefordshire, and the whole of Monmouthshire with the exception of the lordship of Gwynllwg. The southern boundary seems to have commenced, as at present, between the rivers Neath and Tawe, and afterwards to have passed along the hills which naturally divide Brecknockshire from Glamorganshire, as far as Blaenau Gwent; from this point it followed the present limits of Gwynllwg to the mouth of the Usk. South of this line was the original diocese of Teilo; in which the only edifices, dedicated to St. David, are the chapels of Laleston‡ and Bettws, subject to Newcastle, Glamorganshire, and Bettws, subject to Newport, Monmouthshire; but they appear to be of modern origin. The Lordship of Gwynllwg was co-extensive with the present deanery of Newport, and until the Union of England and

* There were formerly not less than six churches and chapels ascribed or dedicated to St. David in the Hundred of Builth, Brecknockshire, and it is remarkable that they were all on the south side of the Irfon. Five of them still remain.

† Llanddewi Ystrad Enni, Heyop, and Whitton.

‡ Built about A. D. 1110, by Lales, architect to Richard Granville, Lord of Neath.

Wales it was considered a part of Glamorgan.* It is singular
that the parishes of Caerleon and Llanddewi Fach, though
west of the Usk, do not form part of this district; and they
remain to this day a confirmation of the arrangement which
would place them in the diocese of St. David's. They are at
no great distance from the town of Llandaff, but David
might have weakened his authority, as archbishop of Menevia,
had he surrendered the place from which he originally derived the title of Metropolitan; and he is, by some writers,
called archbishop of Caerleon to the time of his death.

As it was the custom in the early ages of Christianity for
the bishop to receive a share of the offerings presented in all
the churches under his superintendence, the boundaries of his
diocese would soon be determined with considerable precision;
and he could not intrude into the diocese of another without
an infringement of rights. The tract described includes all
the churches, named after St. David, in Wales and the adjoining counties. There are, however, three churches and a
chapel in Devon and Cornwall, of which he is considered the
patron saint :† and though none of his ancient biographers
have noticed that he passed any portion of his life in that
country, the circumstance that he visited it, probably in the
early part of his life, is intimated in the poetry of Gwynfardd,‡
who says that he received ill-treatment there at the hands of a

---

* Description of Wales, by Sir John Price.
† Bacon's Liber Regis.

‡ "A goddef palfawd, dyrnawd trameint,
   Y gan forwyn ddifwyn, ddiwyl ei deint,
   Dialwys, peirglwys pergig Dyfneint,
   A'r ni lâs llosged———"

He endured buffetings, very hard blows,
From the hands of an uncourteous woman, devoid of modesty,
He took vengeance, he endangered the sceptre of Devon,
And those who were not slain were burned.—

   Myv. Archaiol. Vol. I. p. 270, and Williams's Pelagian Heresy.

female, on account of which the inhabitants suffered his vengeance. The edifices alluded to are the following.—

Tilbruge, alias Thelbridge, R. Devon.
Ashprington, R. with the chapelry of Paimford, Devon.
St. David's, a chapel to Heavitree, in the city of Exeter.
Dewstowe, alias Davidstow, V. Cornwall.

Some of these were possibly founded by the saint; but they
may, at least, be thought to confirm the tradition of his presence, which is further strengthened by the existence, in the
same quarter, of the following, dedicated to St. Non, his
mother.

Bradstone, R. Devon.
Plenynt, alias Pelynt, alias Plint, V. Cornwall.
Alternon, V. Cornwall.

There are three religious edifices dedicated to St. David in
the rest of England,* so few and far between, that no historical
inference can be deduced from them, except that they were
consecrated to his memory long after the conversion of the
Saxons. The county of Devon remained in the possession of
the Britons so late as the year 900.

Geoffrey of Monmouth states that Dewi, archbishop of
Caerleon, died in the monastery which he had founded at
Menevia, where he was honourably buried by order of Maelgwn Gwynedd. This event is recorded by Geoffrey as if it
happened soon after the death of Arthur, who died A. D. 542.
According to the computations of Archbishop Usher, St.
David died A. D. 544, aged eighty two, which is certainly
more probable than the legendary accounts of Giraldus and
others, who assert that the saint lived to the patriarchal age
of a hundred and forty seven years, sixty five of which he presided over his diocese. But it must be allowed that the dates

* Barton David, V. Somersetshire; Moreton in the Marsh, a chapel to
Bourton on the Hill, Gloucestershire; and Armin, a chapel to Snaith,
Yorkshire.

quoted by Usher are very uncertain, and depend upon the authority of writers who lived many centuries after the events which they record. The order of generations, and the names of contemporaries, render it necessary to place the birth of David about twenty years later than it is fixed by Usher; and his life may be protracted to any period short of A. D. 566, to which year the death of Maelgwn Gwynedd is assigned in the Annales Menevenses.*

He was canonized by Pope Calistus about A. D. 1120, and his commemoration was held on the first of March, the anniversary, according to Giraldus, of the day on which he died. It has been lately observed, that the reputation which he has acquired of being the patron saint of Wales, is of modern introduction; and the observation is certainly true in the sense of the words " tutelar saint," as understood by those who compiled the romances of the " Seven Champions of Christendom." It may also be said that the story of the leek, and its adoption as a national emblem, is not noticed by his early biographers. But these remarks should not be made with a view to disparage his memory. He has long maintained the highest station among the saints of his country; and whether the number of churches attributed to him, or his exertions in the overthrow of Pelagianism, be considered, he professes the fairest claim to such a distinction. Since the twelfth century his pre-eminence has been undisputed; and the poem of Gwynfardd, written in that age, lauds him in terms as if he were second only to the Almighty. So famous was his shrine at Menevia, that it attracted votaries, not only from all parts

* Lives of St. David have been written—by Ricemarchus about A. D. 1090, a copy of which is preserved in the British Museum, Cotton MSS. Vespasian A. XIV; by Giraldus Cambrensis about A. D. 1200, published in Wharton's Anglia Sacra; by John of Teignmouth, a contemporary of Giraldus, inserted in Capgrave's collection; and by Leland, in the reign of Henry VIII, which is published in his " Collectanea." There is also an ancient Welsh Life in the British Museum, in MSS. Titus D. XXII.

2 A

of Wales, but also from foreign countries; and even three of
the kings of England* are recorded to have undertaken the
journey, which when twice repeated was deemed equal to one
pilgrimage to Rome.†

To take a short notice of temporal affairs; the Gwyddyl
Ffichti, who were conquered by Clydwyn, the son of Brychan,
are in this generation found to be independent. According to
an authority,‡ cited in Jones's History of the county of Brecon,
Dyfnwal, a Pictish or Caledonian prince, had exterminated
the race of Clydwyn and assumed the soveignty. In consequence of which, Caradog Fraichfras, the son of a grand-
daughter of Brychan, appears to have marched westward from
the Severn, and to have recovered the principal part of
Brecknockshire, which he transmitted to his descendants.
The Irish were also in possession of Carmarthenshire, and the
names of Liethali, and Ceing or Ceianus, two of their chieftains in that county, have been recorded;§ but about the
same time, Urien Rheged, whose father, Cynfarch Oer,‖ had
been obliged to leave his territories in North Britain and seek
a refuge in Wales, undertook to clear the country of these
foreign settlers. He was successful; and accordingly was
allowed to take possession of the district lying between the
rivers Towy and Neath, which his descendants continued
to inherit after him. These events took place in the early

* William the Conqueror, Henry II, and Edward I; the latter of whom
was accompanied by his queen, Eleanor, Nov. 26, 1284.

† This opinion was expressed by the monks in the verse,—

"Roma semel quantum, dat bis Menevia tantum."

and more especially in the following couplet;

"Meneviam si bis, et Romam si semel, ibis,
Merces æqua tibi redditur hic et ibi."

‡ Harleian MSS. No. 6639.
§ Gunn's Nennius; Ca   Britannia.
‖ Of the line of Coel G

part of this century, and they seem to have afforded to St.
David the opportunity of establishing a number of churches
in the country thus recovered,* in which none are found of
older date, except those which were dedicated to the children
of Brychan.   Urien, after performing these services in Wales,
appears to have proceeded to North Britain, where he re-
gained his father's dominions ; and with the assistance of his
sons, supported a long and well contested struggle with Ida,
the king of the Angles.   His exertions against the invaders
in this quarter, which entitle him to be considered one of the
most illustrious Britons of his age, would have succeeded in
their expulsion, had he not been embarassed with the dissensions of his countrymen; and he was at last treacherously
slain while besieging Deoric, the son of Ida, in the island of
Lindisfarne.†   It has been said that he was a saint of the congregation of Cattwg, but the assertion is inconsistent with his
character as a warrior, which he maintained to the close of his
life.   He was the patron of the bards, Llywarch Hên, and
Taliesin ; and his heroic deeds have been celebrated in some
of the best effusions of the Welsh muse.‡

The name " North Britain" is here used indefinitely for any
part of the country reaching from the Humber to the Clyde,
as the writer is unable to determine the location of its princes.
This tract was occupied by the Cymry, or Britons of the
same race as those who now inhabit the Principality of Wales,
and whose name may be traced in the modern appellation of

* That it was not originally under his jurisdiction is strongly implied in
an abrupt passage in his Life by Ricemarchus, which says that Boducat
and Maitrun, two saints of the province of Kidwelly, submitted themselves
to him.—" Duo quoque Sancti, Boducat et Maitrun, in provinciâ Cet-
guell, dederunt sibi manus."

† Nennius, and Poems of Taliesin and Llywarch Hên.

‡ Urien Rheged is the Sir Urience of the ... ces of Arthur, and Caradog Fraichfras is Sir Carados brîs ...

the county of Cumberland.*   Their history, though involved
in obscurity, is capable of investigation ; and it is to be hoped
that the Welsh traditions, which throw light upon the subject,
will not long be left unexamined.   Meanwhile the following
extracts from the pages† of a living historian, having reference
to this people at a later period, may be read with interest.—

"The Britons of Cumbria occupy a tolerably large space on
the map, but a very small one in history ; their annals have
entirely perished ; and nothing authentic remains concerning
them except a very few passages, wholly consisting of incidental notices relating to their subjection and their misfor-
tunes.—From the Ribble in Lancashire, or thereabouts, up to
the Clyde, there existed a dense population, composed of
Britons, who preserved their national language and customs,
agreeing in all respects with the Welsh of the present day.
So that even in the tenth century, the ancient Britons still
inhabited the greater part of the western coast of the island,
however much they had been compelled to yield to the political supremacy of the Saxon invaders. * * * The ' Regnum
Cumbrense' comprehended many districts, probably governed
by petty princes or *Reguli*, in subordination to a chief Monarch
or Pendragon. Reged appears to have been some where in
the vicinity of Annandale. *Strath*-Clyde‡ is, of course, the
district or *vale* of Clydes-*dale*. In this district, or state, was
situated Alcluyd, or *Dunbritton*, now Dumbarton, where the

---

* The portion of Britain to the south of the Humber and east of the Severn, was inhabited by another race of Britons called "Lloegrwys." The
name by which the Welsh have invariably called themselves in their own
language is "Cymry."

† Sir Francis Palgrave's History of the Anglo Saxons; a work which
displays great research, and is illustrated with maps of the territories of
the Britons and Anglo-Saxons at different eras.

‡ The word *strath* is still universally used over all Scotland, highland
and lowland, for *valley*.   grave.) The corresponding word in Wales
is *ystrad*.

British kings usually resided; and the whole Cumbrian kingdom was not unfrequently called 'Strath-Clyde,' from the
ruling or principal state.—Many dependencies of the Cumbrian kingdom extended into modern Yorkshire, and Leeds
was the frontier town between the Britons and the Angles;
but the former were always giving way, and their territory
was broken and intersected by English settlements. Carlisle
had been conquered by the Angles at a very early period;
and Egfrith of Northumbria bestowed that city upon the see
of Lindisfarne. * * * The Britons of Strath-Clyde, and Reged, and Cumbria, gradually melted away into the surrounding population; and, losing their language, ceased to be
discernible as a separate race. Yet it is most probable that
this process was not wholly completed until a comparatively
recent period. The 'Wallenses' or Welsh, are enumerated by
David the Lion amongst his subjects, (A. D. 1124—1153;)
and the laws or usages of the *Brets* or Britons continued in
use until abolished by Edward I. at the period when Scotland,
by his command appeared, by her representatives, in the
English parliament at Westminster; (A. D. 1304.) In the
bishoprick of Glasgow, comprehending the greatest portion of
the ancient Cumbrian kingdom, the 'barbarous' British speech
generally gave way to that dialect of the Saxon English,
which is usually called lowland Scottish, about the thirteenth
century; but in some secluded districts the language is
thought to have lingered until the Reformation, when it was
possibly destroyed by the ministration of the Protestant
clergy. In our English Cumberland and the adjoining
Westmoreland, a few British traditions yet survive
among the people. Pendragon Castle reminds the traveller
of the fabled Uther. Some of the mountains which adorn
the landscape retain the appellations given them by the
original population; and 'Skiddaw' and 'Helvellyn' now
rise, as the sepulchral monuments of a race which has passed
away."—

One of the chiefs of North Britain, contemporary with Urien Rheged, was Dunawd or Dunod Fyr,* the son of Pabo, of the line of Coel Godebog. He appears to have gained some distinction as a warrior, and in the Triads he is called one of the three pillars of his country in battle. It is uncertain whether he accompanied his father, whose retreat to Wales has been already described; but in this generation he is found engaged in the north, where he disgraced his arms by fighting against the sons of Urien.† A reverse of fortune, however, obliged him to leave his territories, and to place himself under the protection of Cyngen ab Cadell, the prince of Powys, who had afforded his father an asylum. He afterwards embraced a life of religion; and under the patronage of Cyngen, he became the founder, in conjunction with his sons, Deiniol, Cynwyl, and Gwarthan, of the celebrated college or monastery of Bangor Iscoed on the banks of the Dee in Flintshire.‡ This institution, over which he presided as abbot, was one of the most eminent in the island; and, according to Bede, such was the number of its monks, that when they were divided into seven classes under their respective superintendents, none of these classes contained less than three hundred persons, all of whom supported themselves by their own labour.§ It furnished a large proportion of the learned men, who attended the Welsh bishops in their conference with St. Augustin, at

* Sometimes called "Dunawd Fawr" and "Dunawd Wr;" but it is uncertain which of the three epithets is the right one. The Latin name is "Dinothus;" and in Bede, "Dinoot Abbas."

† Poems of Llywarch Hên.

‡ Achau y Saint, Silurian copies. The monastery has often been styled, Bangor in Maelor, from its situation in a district of that name; and Bangor Dunod from its founder.

§ "Tantus fertur fuisse numerus Monachorum, ut cum in septem portiones esset cum præpositis sibi Rectoribus Monasterium divisum, nulla harum portio minus quam trecentos homines haberet, qui omnes de labore manuum suarum vivere solebant."—Hist. Eccl. Lib. II. Cap. 2.

which time Dunawd was still its abbot, though he must have been far advanced in years, for the earliest date assigned to that event is A. D. 599. The destruction of the monastery by Ethelfrith, king of Northumbria, soon followed, and it was never afterwards restored. Dunawd is the patron saint of the present church of Bangor in Flintshire,* and his festival was held on the seventh of September. His wife, Dwywe, the daughter of Gwallog ab Llenog, has been classed with the saints, but there are no churches which bear her name.

Cyngen, the son of Cadell, in whose territories the monastery of Bangor Iscoed was situated, is said to have endowed it with lands, for which he has had the reputation of sanctity, and there was once a church, dedicated to him, at Shrewsbury. One of his sons, Mawan ab Cyngen, whose life belongs to this generation, has also been deemed a saint, but nothing further is known respecting him.

Sawyl Benuchel, the brother of Dunawd, is described as an overbearing prince; and on account of his oppression, his party joined alliance with the Saxons, with whom they became one people.† He afterwards devoted himself to the service of religion. which appears to have been the common practice of the British chieftains upon the loss of their dominions, and the growing superstition of the age was favourable to such a custom. He closed his life in the monastery of Bangor Iscoed, and is the patron saint of Llansawel, a chapel under Cynwyl Gaio, Carmarthenshire.

Carwyd, another brother of Dunawd, was also a saint, and an inmate of Bangor Iscoed, where he likewise ended his days.

Arddun Benasgell, the sister of Dunawd, was married to Brochwel Ysgythrog, a son of Cyngen ab Cadell. The Cam-

---

* Chapels to Bangor,—Worthenbury (St. Deiniol ab Dunawd,) and Overton or Orton Madoc (St. Mary.)

† Triad 74, Third Series.

brian Biography says that some Welsh churches are dedicated
to her, but it does not appear where they are situated.   Her
husband, Brochwel, succeeded his father in the principality of
Powys, and lived till after the time of St. Augustin, when he
commanded the reserve left for the protection of the monks of
Bangor upon the advance of Ethelfrith.   The Northumbrian,
however, instead of directing his first attack against the main
army of the Britons as had been expected, proceeded against
the monks, who were praying at some distance; and Brochwel, unprepared with a force sufficient for such an emergency,
was defeated.*

To proceed with the line of Coel; Gwenddolau, Cof, and
Nudd, were the sons of Ceidio ab Garthwys, a chieftain of
North Britain.   They were all instructed in the Christian
faith in the college of Iltutus, but no other reason is alleged
why they should be enumerated among the saints.   Gwenddolau was the patron of the bard, Myrddin the Caledonian,
and was slain at the battle of Arderydd, A. D. 577.

Cynwyd Cynwydion, the son of Cynfelyn ab Garthwys, was
a saint of the congregation of Cattwg, and is presumed to be
the founder of Llangynwyd Fawr, Glamorganshire.†

Tangwn, the son of Talhaiarn ab Garthwys, was the founder
of a church in Somersetshire " which is now called Tangyn-
ton."‡

The saints of the line of Cunedda, besides David, archbishop of Menevia, were :—

Afan Buallt, a son of Cedig ab Ceredig, by Tegwedd,
daughter of Tegid Foel of Penllyn; and, therefore, uterine
brother to Teilo.   He was the founder of Llanafan Fawr in
the county of Brecon, and Llanafan Trawsgoed in Cardiganshire; and was buried at the former place, where his tomb

---

* Bedæ Historia Ecclesiastica, Lib. II. Cap. 2.
† One chapel, Bayden.
‡ Cambrian Biography.   Qu. Taunton ?

still remains, with the following inscription, from which it
may be learned that he was a bishop :—

HIC IACET SANCTVS AVANVS EPISCOPVS

As there are reasons for extending his life into the next
generation, it is not improbable that he was the third bishop of
Llanbadarn; and his churches are situated in the district
which may be assigned to that diocese. Llanfechan, one of
the chapels under Llanafan Fawr, is dedicated to him,* and
his memory has been celebrated on the sixteenth of November.

Doged, sometimes styled Doged Frenhin, or "the king ;"
he was the brother of Afan, and founder of a church in Denbighshire called Llanddoged.

Tyssul, a son of Corun ab Ceredig ; the founder of a church
in Cardiganshire, called Llandyssul,† and of another of the
same name in Montgomeryshire. His festival is Jan. 31.

Carannog, in Latin " Carantocus," a brother of Tyssul, and
the founder of the church of Llangrannog, Cardiganshire.
The day of his commemoration is May 16.‡ John of Teignmouth makes him to be a son, instead of a grandson of Ceredig, and the following extracts from that author, as translated
by Cressy, may be taken as a fair specimen of the manner in
which the lives of saints were written in the middle ages.
After stating that St. Carantac was "by descent and countrey
a Brittain, son of Keredic, Prince of the Province of Cardigan,
Ceretica Regionis;" the translator proceeds:—A certain prince,
named Keredic, had many children; among which, one was
called Carantac, a child of a good disposition, who began early

* For the other chapels, see page 22.

† Chapels to Llandyssul, all in ruins,—*Llandyssulfed* (St. Sylvester,
qu.) *Llanfair* (St. Mary,) *Faerdre, Capel Dewi* (St. David,) *Capel Ffraid*
(St. Bridget,) and *Capel Rorthin.*

‡ There is a Life of St. Carantoc in the British Museum, Cottonian
MSS. Vesp. A. XIV.

2 B

to do those things which he thought would be pleasing to God.
Now in those days the Scotts did grievously vex Brittany,* so
that his father, unable to sustain the weight and troubles of
government, would have resigned the province to Carantac.
But he, who loved the celestial King far more than an earthly
kingdom, fled away; and having bought of a poor man a
wallet and a staff, by God's conduct was brought to a certain
pleasant place, where he, reposing, built an oratory, and there
spent his time in the praises of God. From his childhood he
embraced purity and innocence. At last he passed over into
Ireland, invited by his affection to St. Patrick. Whither being
come, by common advice they determined to separate themselves, and that one of them should travel in preaching the
Gospel toward the right hand, the other toward the left. In
their company there were many Ecclesiastical persons attending them ; and they agreed once every year to meet together
at an appointed place. Whithersoever this holy man went, an
angel of our Lord, in the likeness of a dove, accompanied him,
who changed his name from Carantac into Cernach, which was
an Irish appellation. All along his voyage he wrought great
miracles for the confirmation of the faith preached by him,
and healed many thousand.—The wonderful Gests of this holy
man, Cernach or Carantac, are to be read in Irish historians,
and how the grace at first given to the Apostles was plenti-
fully given to him. He was an admirable soldier and cham-
pion of Christ, a spiritual and devout abbot, and a patient
teacher, not refusing to preach saving truth to every one.
During many years spent by him at that Island, he brought an
incredible number to wash away their sins by Penance, and
both day and night he offered innumerable prayers to God.
After he had converted much people to our Lord, who
wrought many miracles by him, he at last returned to his own
native country in Brittany, where he retired to his former

* Ciessy invariably uses the words—"Brittain" for Briton, and "Brittany" for Great Britain. He styles Armorica " Lesser Brittany."

cave, accompanied by many disciples. There having built a
church he determined to abide. But not long after, being
again admonished by a voice from heaven, he returned to
Ireland, where in a good old age, and full of holy works, he
rested in peace on the seventeenth of the Calends of June,*
and was buried in his own city, which from him was called
Chernach.

Pedrwn, brother of Tyssul, enrolled among the saints, but
there is no church at present called after his name.

Pedr, brother of Tyssul; his churches, if he founded any,
cannot be distinguished from those which are dedicated to
St. Peter, the Apostle.

Tyrnog, or Teyrnog, brother of Tyssul, a saint, but there are
no churches ascribed to him. Llandyrnog, Denbighshire, is
attributed to another person of the same name.

Cyndeyrn, a son of Arthog ab Ceredig; a saint to whom
Llangyndeyrn, formerly subject to Llandyfaelog, Carmarthenshire is dedicated. His festival occurs on the twenty
fifth of July.

Cyngar, the brother of Cyndeyrn; it is said that he " established a congregation in Glamorgan, at a place now called
Llangenys;"† but perhaps the statement is an error, arising
from confounding this person with another Cyngar, who is
said to have founded the college of Cungarus in the diocese
of Llandaff.

Dogfael, the son of Ithel ab Ceredig, was the founder of St.
Dogmael's in Cemmaes, St. Dogwel's in Pebidiog, Monachlog
Ddu, and Melinau, all in Pembrokeshire; and has been ac-
counted the patron saint of Llanddogwel under Llanrhyddlad,
Anglesey, Festival, June 14.

* Corresponding to May 16; eleven days after which, or on the twenty-
seventh of the same month, being the festival of St. Carantoc, Old Style, a
fair is held at Llangrannog in Cardiganshire.

† Cambrian Biography.

Einion, surnamed Frenhin, or the king, was the son of
Owain Danwyn ab Einion Yrth ab Cunedda; and was the
founder of a church in the district of Lleyn, Carnarvonshire,
which has since been called Llanengan, or Llaneingion Frenhin.   He also established the college of Penmon in Anglesey,
over which he placed his brother, Seiriol, as the first principal; and in conjunction with St. Cadfan, he founded a monastery in the Isle of Bardsey, of which that person was the first
abbot.   There was an inscription, now effaced, upon the tower
of the church of Llanengan, the latter part of which, as de-
cyphered by the author of Mona Antiqua, asserted that the
founder of the edifice was a king of Wales:—

ENEANUS REX WALLIÆ FABRICAVIT.

The title, however, must be received with some limitation,
as the presence of contemporary chieftains would show that
the sovereignty of Einion must have been confined to the
neighbourhood of Carnarvonshire.   The form of the letters, as
represented in the Mona Antiqua, is not ancient, and the
name "Wallia" was not employed to describe the territories of
the "Cymry" until the middle ages.   The festival of this
royal saint is February the ninth.

Seiriol, the brother, or according to other accounts, the
nephew, of Einion Frenhin, was the first president of the
college of Penmon, which became so celebrated that "the men
of Llychlyn," or the Scandinavian rovers, resorted there for
religious instruction.   Subordinate to this institution was a
cell in the island of Glanach, or Priestholm, off the coast adjacent, of which Seiriol has been deemed the patron saint.

Meirion, another brother of Einion Frenhin, was a saint,
and Llanfeirion, formerly a chapel of ease under Llangadwaladr, Anglesey, has been dedicated to him.   His wake has
been held on the third of February.

Cynyr Farfdrwch,* the son of Gwron ab Cunedda, lived at
Cynwyl Gaio in Carmarthenshire, and was the father of six

* He is also called Cynyr Farfwyn, and Cynyr Ceinfarfog.

sons, five of whom were saints. The names of the five saints
were Gwyn, Gwynno, Gwynnoro, Celynin, and Ceitho ;* and,
according to the fable reported of them, they were all produced at one birth.   There was formerly a chapel of ease in
the parish of Caio, called Pumsaint, which, as well as Llan-
pumsaint, still existing, subject to Abergwyli, Carmarthenshire,
was dedicated to them.   Their festival is said to have been
held on the day of All-Saints ; but no further information can
be obtained respecting them, except that Ceitho is presumed ک.
to be the founder of Llangeitho in Cardiganshire, and his festival was kept on the fifth of August.

Between the commencement of this century and the synod
of Brefi, may be dated the arrival of Cadfan at the head of a
large company of saints from Armorica.   He appears to have
been a person of distinction, being the son of Eneas Lydewig,
by Gwenteirbron, a daughter of Emyr Llydaw, one of the
princes of that country.   Among his companions are mentioned, Cynon, Padarn, Tydecho, Trinio, Gwyndaf, Dochdwy,
Mael, Sulien, Tanwg, Eithras, Sadwrn, Lleuddad, Tecwyn,
Maelrys, and several others.   As most of these were men of
princely family and relatives of Cadfan, the analogy of other
cases suggests that the reason, which induced them to leave
their country and devote themselves to religion, was the loss
of their territories : for the Armoricans struggled hard to
maintain their independence against the Franks, who, under
Clovis, were at this time establishing their dominion in Gaul.†
Cadfan, after his arrival in Wales, became the founder of the
churches of Tywyn‡ Merionethshire, and Llangadfan, Mont-

* The other son was Cai, who possibly gave name to the district in
which he lived.

† The Welsh accounts do not mention this circumstance, but the chronological coincidence is remarkable. Paris was made the capital of the
dominions of Clovis in the year 510.

‡ Chapels.—Llanfihangel y Pennant (St. Michael,) Pennal (St. Peter,)
and Tal-y-llyn (St. Mary.)

gomeryshire; but he is known more especially as the first
abbot of a monastery, founded by him in conjunction with
Einion Frenhin, in the Isle of Bardsey, off the western promontory of Carnarvonshire. It was, probably, the establishment of this institution that induced St. Dubricius to make
choice of the spot, as the place where, remote from the world,
he might end his days in the uninterrupted practice of devotion. Other holy men retired thither for the same purpose;
in consequence of which, the soil of the island at length acquired a sacred character, and it was deemed meritorious to be
buried there. Its narrow limits, scarcely exceeding three
miles in circumference, were said to enclose the bodies of
twenty thousand saints. Pilgrimages were made to it for the
sake of obtaining the intercession of the departed; and as the
voyage was often attended with danger, several of the bards
have employed their verse in describing its difficulties, not
forgetting to celebrate the guardian influence to which the
faithful owed their protection amid the waves. Nor has the
church of Tywyn remained without its eulogy; in a poem*
written between the years 1230 and 1280, the author asserts
that it possessed three altars,† and was furnished like the
church of David, meaning that of Llanddewi Brefi, where,
according to Gwynfardd, the number of altars was five. He
proceeds to praise "its choir, and sanctuary, and its music, its
warriors, and its waters of grace;" and maintains that it was
not right to pass over the place in silence, for its dwellings
were equal to the mighty mansions of heaven.‡—There were

* Canu i Gaduan, Llywelyn Vart ae cant, Myv. Arch. Vol. p. 360.

† The first belonged to St. Mary, the second to St. Peter; and the third,
"happy was the town in its privilege of possessing it, for it was sent by a
hand from heaven," was dedicated to St. Cadfan.

‡ Cadr y ceidw Cadfan glan glas wellgi,
Cadr fab Eneas, gwanas gweddi,
Cadr fryn yw Tywyn, nid iawn tewi ag ef,
Cadr addef nef ail ei athrefl.

some years ago, in the church-yard of Tywyn, two rude
pillars, one of which, of the form of a wedge, about seven feet
high, and having a cross and inscription upon it, went by the
name of St. Cadfan's stone, and was thought to have been a
part of his tomb. Engravings of the inscription, as copied at
two several periods in the last century,* are given in Gough's
Camden, from which it appears that the letters resembled
those used by the Anglo Saxons, but the only word legible
was the name of Cadfan. As there is a tradition that the
saint was buried in Bardsey, which an obscure passage from
the poem just quoted, would seem to confirm, it may be judged
that the stone was merely a rude cross of which similar
specimens, bearing the names of sainted persons, may be found
in other parts of the Principality. He has been considered to
be the patron of warriors, which countenances the supposition
that he led a military life in Armorica; and his festival has
been celebrated on the first of November. His mother,
Gwenteirbron, is mentioned as a saint in one of the catalogues,
but no churches have been erected to her memory.

Cynon accompanied Cadfan to Bardsey, where he was made
chancellor of the monastery; but whatever was the nature of
this and other offices occasionally attributed to the primitive
Christians, it may be said that the compiler of Achau y Saint
has chosen to call them by names which were familiar in his
own time. Cynon is the reputed founder of the church of
Tregynon, Montgomeryshire; and Capel Cynon subject to
Llandyssilio Gogo, Cardiganshire, is dedicated to him.

Padarn, the son of Pedrwn, or Pedredin, ab Emyr Llydaw,
visited Britain, according to Usher, in the year 516; and
though no ancient authority is given for the date, it may be
presumed upon as the time when Cadfan and his companions
arrived in this country. According to Achau y Saint, Padarn,
after his arrival in Wales, became a member of the college of

---

* By Lhuyd before 1709, and by Dr. Taylor in 1761.

Illtyd. He afterwards established a religious society, consisting of a hundred and twenty members,* at a place in Cardiganshire since called Llanbadarn Fawr;† where he also
founded an episcopal see, of which he became the first bishop.
He was the founder of the churches of Llanbadarn Trefeglwys
or Llanbadarn Fach, and Llanbadarn Odin, Cardiganshire, and
of Llanbadarn Fawr, Radnorshire. The chapels of Llanbadarn
Fynydd under Llanbister, and Llanbadarn y Garreg under
Cregruna, both in Radnorshire, are named after him ; and the
situations of some of these places serve to point out the extent
of his diocese to the southward, along the limits which have
been assigned to the diocese of St. David. To the north its
extent is uncertain, but it probably included a considerable
part of Montgomeryshire. How long Llanbadarn continued
to be the capital of a bishoprick cannot be ascertained, as very
little is known of its history, and the last notice of it, under
that character, in the Welsh Chronicles, is in the year 720 ;
when it is recorded that many of the churches of Llandaff,
Mynyw, and Llanbadarn, meaning the three dioceses of South
Wales, were ravaged by the Saxons.‡ It is reported, however,
to have lost its privileges through the turbulent conduct of
its inhabitants, who killed their bishop ; and the diocese was
in consequence annexed to that of Menevia. From the Latin
Hexameters of Johannes Sulgenus,|| it may be learned that
Padarn presided over the see twenty one years, during which
time he spent his life in the practice of such religious exercises

---

* John of Teignmouth differs from the Welsh accounts, in saying that
this institution contained eight hundred and forty seven monks, who came
with St. Paternus from Armorica; and adds that it was governed by an
œconomus, a provost, and a dean.

† Its Latin name is Mauritania, which Archbishop Usher observes is
derived from Mawr, *great*, an epithet added merely for the purpose of dis-
tinguishing this Church from others of less importance.

‡ Brut y Tywysogion, Myv. Archaiology, Vol. II. p. 472.

|| Son of Sullen, or Sulgen, Bishop of St. David's in 1070.

as were approved in the age ;* and the Triads assert that he went about the country preaching the faith in Christ without pay or reward to all ranks of people, for which reason he was counted one of the three blessed visitors of the Isle of Britain. It is mentioned by John of Teignmouth that he built monasteries and churches throughout the whole region of Ceretica ; and that he rebuked Maelgwn Gwynedd, from whom he had received certain injuries in an excursion of that prince into South Wales : but no other incidents of the time spent at Llanbadarn are recorded, upon the truth of which any reliance may be placed. At the expiration of the twenty one years he returned to his native country, where he was made bishop of Vannes. A dissension, however, broke out between him and the other Armorican bishops ; upon which a synod was convened, and a reconciliation effected. Notwithstanding this, he continued to dread their hostility, and retired to the Franks, among whom he remained till the close of his life. He subscribed the decrees of the council of Paris,† which was held in the year 557, and is commended both as an abbot and a bishop in the writings of Venantius Fortunatus, a Latin poet of Gaul, who was his contemporary.‡ One of his early biographers, quoted by Usher, says that three days were held sacred to his memory ; April 15, being the anniversary of his death ; June 20, in remembrance of his consecration as bishop; and Nov. 1, on account of his reconciliation with the prelates of Armorica.

---

* They are thus summed up by Sulgenus :—

    "Orans, jejunans, vigilans, lachrymansque, gemensque,
      Esuris alimenta simul, nexisque levamen,
      Hospitibus pandens aditum, sitientibus haustum,
      Ægrotis curam, nudis miseratus amictum ;
      Prudens quæque gerens, perfecit cuncta potenter."

† Usher, Cap. XIV.

‡ Cressy; who gives the following references,—l. 7. Epig. 3. and l. 3. Epig. 52.

Tydecho, the son of Amwn Ddu ab Emyr Llydaw, and
cousin to Cadfan, left Armorica, and settled in company with
his sister, Tegfedd, in the district of Mawddwy, Merionethshire, where he founded the church of Llanymmawddwy, to
which the neighbouring churches of Mallwyd and Garthbeibio, both dedicated to him, were formerly subject.* In
this retreat he is said to have suffered from the violence and
oppression of Maelgwn Gwynedd, the prince of North Wales;
upon whom, as the legend relates, he retaliated with such a
host of miracles, that the tyrant was glad to make amends, and
grant him several immunities. Tegfedd also was forcibly
carried away by another chief, named Cynon, who in like
manner was compelled to restore her unhurt, and purchase the
peace of the saint by a grant of the lands of Garthbeibio.† He
is considered to be the patron of Cemmaes, Montgomeryshire,
and a chapel was consecrated to his memory in the parish of
Llandegfan, Anglesey. His festival is Dec. 17.

It is uncertain whether Amwn Ddu, the father of the preceding, left Armorica at the same time with Cadfan, but it is
recorded that he quitted that country, where he had been
sovereign of a district called Graweg; and settling in Wales,
he married Anna, a daughter of Meurig, the prince of Glamorgan, by whom he had two sons, Samson and Tathan, who were
afterwards eminent for their sanctity.‡ It is said that he
enjoyed the friendship of Dubricius, as well as of Iltutus of
whose institution he became a member; and that he resided
in a small island near Llantwit Major, until he removed to a
desert on the shores of the Severn, where he seems to have
passed the remainder of his life. The locality of this desert is
not well defined, but it would appear that Anna settled in the

---

* They now form separate benefices, but are described as chapels to
Llanymmawddwy in the Taxation of Pope Nicholas.

† See a Welsh poem inserted in the Cambrian Register, Vol. II. p. 375.

‡ Achau y Saint, Silurian copies.

same quarter, and built a church there, which was consecrated
for her by Samson.*

Gwyndaf Hên ab Emyr Llydaw, an Armorican and brother
of Amwn Ddu, married Gwenonwy, another daughter of
Meurig, by whom he was the father of St. Meugan. He was
a confessor or chaplain in the monastery of Illtyd, and afterwards superior of the college of Dubricius at Caerleon. In his
old age he retired to Bardsey, where he died. He may be
deemed the founder of Llanwnda in Carnarvonshire, and of
another church of that name in Pembrokeshire.

Hywyn, the son of Gwyndaf Hên, is said to have accompanied Cadfan from Armorica, which makes it probable that
he was the issue of a former marriage. He was confessor to
the congregation of saints assembled in the Isle of Bardsey,
and the foundation of Aberdaron, on the opposite coast of
Carnarvonshire, from whence pilgrims generally crossed over
to the island, is ascribed to him.

According to the Life of St. Maglorius,† Umbrafel, another
brother of Amwn Ddu, married Afrella, a third daughter of
Meurig. He is not noticed by the genealogists, but the
"Book of Llandaff" states that after having been ordained a
priest, he was appointed abbot of a monastery in Ireland, by
his nephew, St. Samson.‡

Trinio, the son of Difwng ab Emyr Llydaw, was a saint
who emigrated with Cadfan, and afterwards settled in the Isle
of Bardsey. He was the founder of Llandrinio, Montgomeryshire.§

Dochdwy, whose genealogy is unknown, accompanied Cadfan to Bardsey, where he was ordained a bishop: it does not

* Liber Landavensis, as quoted by Usher.
† Apud Surium, tom. 5. Oct. 24.
‡ Usher, cap. XIV.
§ Chapels—Llandyssilio (St. Tyssilio,) Melverley (St. Peter,) and New
Chapel (Holy Trinity.)

appear that he derived the title from any particular see; but
it is recorded that he was entrusted with the care of the
diocese of Llandaff during the absence of Teilo, who was invited to Bardsey to regulate the affairs of the monastery upon
the death of Cadfan. He is, perhaps, the founder of two
churches in Glamorganshire, called Llandoch or Llandocha.*

Mael, a companion of Cadfan; he is the saint, in conjunction with Sulien, of the churches of Corwen, Merionethshire,
and Cwm, Flintshire, and their joint festival is May 13.

Sulien, called also Silin, a son of Hywel ab Emyr Llydaw,
is said to have settled in Bardsey. He was the founder of
Llansilin and Wrexham, Denbighshire, and of Eglwys Sulien,
Cardiganshire. The chapels of Capel Silin under Wrexham,
and Capel Sant Silin in the parish of Llanfihangel Ystrad,
Cardiganshire, both in ruins, were called after him. His
commemoration is Sept. 1. which led Browne Willis to confound him with St. Giles, whose festival occurs on the same
day.

Cristiolus, another son of Hywel† ab Emyr Llydaw, and
cousin to Cadfan, is reputed to be the founder of Llangristiolus, Anglesey, and of Eglwys Wrw, and Penrydd, Pembrokeshire. Ecton attributes also to him the church of Clydai,
Pembrokeshire, of which, however, he must have been the
restorer, if it be true that the original founder was Clydai, the
daughter of Brychan. Festival Nov. 3.

Rhystud, a brother of Sulien and Cristiolus, was the founder of Llanrhystud, Cardiganshire; and it is said that he was
for some time bishop of Caerleon upon Usk; in which capacity he must have served as suffragan to the prelates of Menevia or Llandaff; the expression, however, may mean no
more than that he was abbot of the monastery established

---

* *Anglice* Llandough.

† According to some accounts, he was a son of Hywel *Fychan* ab Hywel, ab Emyr Llydaw.

there by Dubricius. His wake was held on the Tuesday before Christmas.

Derfel, called also Derfel Gadarn, a brother of the preceding, was the founder of Llandderfel, Merionethshire; from whence, his image, made of wood, was taken, and burnt at Smithfield at the time of the Reformation. His festival occurs on the fifth of April.

Dwywau, another brother of the preceding, is the patron saint of Llanddwywau, a chapel under Llanenddwyn, Merionethshire.

Alan, an Armorican and one of the sons of Emyr Llydaw, appears to have left his country and become a saint in the college of Illtyd or Iltutus. The three following were his sons :—

Lleuddad ab Alan, a member of the college of Illtyd; after the death of Cadfan he was appointed abbot of the monastery of Bardsey, in consideration of which dignity he was also styled a bishop. Next to his predecessor, he has been esteemed the guardian saint of the island; and there are poems extant, in praise of the protection, which he afforded to pilgrims on their passage to the sacred cemetery.*

Llonio Lawhir ab Alan was a member of the college of Illtyd, and afterwards dean of the college of Padarn at Llanbadarn Fawr. He was also the founder of Llanddinam, Montgomeryshire; and it is said that there was a church dedicated to him in Cardiganshire, which, if it be identified with the modern name " Llanio," must have been a chapel to Llanddewi Brefi.

Llynab ab Alan accompanied Cadfan to Britain, where, like his brothers, he became a member of the college of Illtyd. In his old age he retired to Bardsey. The statement, in Achau y Saint, that he was archbishop of Llandaff, is probably a mistake, as it is inconsistent with all other accounts of that see.

* Myv. Archaiology, Vol. I. p. 360, and Cambrian Register, Vol. III.

Meilyr, and Maelerw, or rather Maelrys, sons of Gwyddno ab Emyr Llydaw, and cousins to Cadfan, were saints who settled in Wales; the latter of whom resided in the Isle of Bardsey, and is the patron of Llanfaelrys, a chapel under Aberdaron, Carnarvonshire.   His commemoration is Jan. 1.

Sadwrn, a son of Bicanys of Armorica, called also Sadwrn Farchog, was the brother of St. Iltutus, and nephew of Emyr Llydaw.   He accompanied Cadfan to Britain in his old age, and is presumed to have been the founder of Llansadwrn in Anglesey.   The church of Llansadwrn in Carmarthenshire, formerly a chapel under Cynwyl Gaio, is called after his name.

Canna, a daughter of Tewdwr Mawr ab Emyr Llydaw, was the wife of Sadwrn, to whom she was related before marriage, but she appears to have been a generation younger. She accompanied her husband from Armorica; and is considered the founder of Llanganna, commonly called Llangan, Glamorganshire, and Llangan, Carmarthenshire.   After the death of Sadwrn she married Gallgu Rieddog, by whom she became the mother of Elian Geimiad.

Crallo, the son of Sadwrn and Canna, probably came over to Britain at the same time with his parents.   He was the founder of Llangrallo, otherwise Coychurch, Glamorganshire.

Besides the tribe of Emyr Llydaw, the children of Ithel Hael, another Armorican prince, are said to have joined in this migration, and taken upon them the profession of sanctity in Wales.   Of these, Tanwg may be deemed the founder of Llandanwg,* Merionethshire.

Gredifael and Fflewyn, sons of Ithel Hael, were appointed superintendents of the monastery of Paulinus at Tygwyn ar Dâf, Carmarthenshire.   Gredifael, whose festival is Nov. 13,

---

* Llanbedr (St. Peter,) and *Harlech* (St. Mary Magdalen,) chapels to Llandanwg.

may be considered the founder of Penmynydd, Anglesey; and Fflewyn is the saint of Llanfflewyn, a chapel subject to Llanrhyddlad in the same county.

Tecwyn ab Ithel Hael, the founder of Llandecwyn, Merionethshire.* Festival Sept. 14.

Trillo ab Ithel Hael, the founder of Llandrillo in Rhos, Denbighshire, and Llandrillo in Edeyrnion, Merionethshire. Festival June 16.

Tegai ab Ithel Hael, the founder of Llandegai, Carnarvonshire, which place it would appear was at one time called called Maes Llanglassawg.

Twrog ab Ithel Hael, the founder of Llandwrog, Carnarvonshire. He is also the patron saint of Maentwrog, a chapel subject to Ffestiniog, Merionethshire, and his festival has been held on the twenty sixth of June.

Baglan, a son of Ithel Hael, has obtained the credit of sanctity; but as there was another saint of the same name, it is uncertain to which of them the patronage of the two chapels following should be ascribed;—Llanfaglan under Llanwnda, Carnarvonshire, and Baglan subject to Aberafon, Glamorganshire.†

Llechid, a daughter of Ithel Hael, was the foundress of Llanllechid, Carnarvonshire, and has been commemorated on the second of December.

Tyfodwg was one of the associates of Cadfan, but the pedigree assigned to him in the Cambrian Biography is inconsistent with chronology. He was the founder of Llandyfodwg, Glamorganshire, and one of the three founders of Llantrisaint in the same county. There is also a chapel under Llantrisaint, called Ystrad Tyfodwg.

---

* Chapel, Llanfihangel y Traethau (St. Michael.)

† Rhychwyn is said in one MS. to have been a son of Ithel Hael, apparently by mistake for one of the sons of Hellg ab Glanog. Myvyrian Archaiology, Vol. II.

Ilar, sometimes styled Ilar Bysgottwr, or "the Fisherman," was the founder of Llanilar, Cardiganshire, and probably of other churches now thought to be dedicated to St. Hilary.

Ust and Dyfnig accompanied Cadfan to Britain, and were the joint-founders of Llanwrin, Montgomeryshire. *

Eithras, Llywan or Llywyn, and Durdan, were companions of Cadfan, of whose lives no particulars can be traced : except that the last mentioned settled in Bardsey, and has been considered one of the presiding saints of the island.

The foregoing list is thought to comprise the entire number of holy persons who emigrated from Armorica in this generation, and it may be interesting to enquire how far the situations of their churches illustrate the history of their settlements. Before the close of the present period, another large emigration is reported to have been made by the children of Caw, who were obliged to leave their dominions in North Britain, and become saints in Wales under similar circumstances.

Caw was the lord of Cwm Cawlwyd or Cowllwg, a district in the North, but its particular situation is uncertain.† According to Achau y Saint, he was deprived of his territories by the Gwyddyl Ffichti, or as the general term may be interpreted, by the Picts and Scots; in consequence of which he and his numerous family retired to Wales. He settled at Twrcelyn in Anglesey, where lands were bestowed upon him by Maelgwn Gwynedd; and it is also said that lands were granted to some of his children by Arthur in Siluria. His name is enrolled in the catalogue of saints; and his children are, in one record,‡ styled the third holy family of Britain; an honour, to which they are fairly entitled if the accounts of

---

* Myv. Archaiology, Vol. II.

† A Life of Gildas, from the Monastery of Fleury in France, published by Johannes a Bosco, and quoted by Usher, says that Caunus (Caw) lived in Arecluta, or Strath Clyde.

‡ Llyfr Bodeulwyn, Myv. Archaiology, Vol. II. p. 29.

Bran ab Llyr, to whom the first place in the Triad is usually assigned, have been proved to be without foundation.

Hywel, the eldest son of Caw, was slain in a civil war by Arthur ;* an event which probably took place before the emigration of his brothers.

Ane ab Caw Cowllwg was a saint, and Coed Ane, a chapel under Llanelian, Anglesey, is called after his name.

Aneurin, a son of Caw, was engaged in the battle of Cattraeth, the disasters of which he deplored in a long poem, called " Y Gododin," still extant, and deemed to be a composition of great merit for the age in which it was written. Out of upwards of three hundred British chieftains who entered the field, only four, of whom the bard was one, escaped with their lives. He was afterwards taken prisoner, loaded with chains, and thrown into a dungeon, from which he was released by Ceneu a son of Llywarch Hên. Upon his deliverance he appears to have retreated to South Wales, where he became a saint of the congregation of Cattwg at Llancarfan, but nothing further is known of him under the name of Aneurin, except that his death was occasioned by the blow of an axe from the hand of an assassin. It has, however, been suggested by two eminent antiquaries,† to whose researches the present writer acknowledges himself greatly indebted, that Aneurin was no other person than the celebrated Gildas. The reasons alleged are :—" Aneurin, as well as Gildas, is reckoned among the children of Caw in our old manuscripts ; but both do not occur as such in the same lists ; for in those where Aneurin is said to be the son of Caw, the other is omitted ; and on the contrary, where Gildas is inserted, the other is left out."‡—Besides which, the name Gildas is a Saxon translation of Aneurin, according to a practice not

* Caradocus Lancarbanensis in Vitâ S. Gildæ.
† Mr. Edward Williams (Iolo Morganwg) and Dr. Owen Pughe.
‡ Cambrian Biography.

uncommon with ecclesiastics in the middle ages ; and even the
various ways in which the names are written—" Gilda, Gildas
y Coed Aur, Aur y Coed Aur, and Aneurin y Coed Aur"—all
of similar signification, confirm their identity. Cennydd, a son,
and Ufelwyn, a grandson, of Gildas, are sometimes called the
son and grandson of Aneurin.* So far, therefore, the point is
clear; that the Welsh genealogists have always considered the
names Gildas and Aneurin convertible. The monkish writers
of the Life of Gildas also state that he was a native of North
Britain, and the son of Cau,† a king of that country. But
here the agreement ends; for they mention nothing of the
battle of Cattraeth, and instead of showing that their saint was
originally a bard and a warrior, they assert that he embraced
the sacred profession at an early age, and was employed in
Ireland, preaching the Gospel, until he heard that his eldest
brother had been slain by Arthur; upon which he came over
to Britain, and was reconciled to the king, who had solicited
his pardon. He then removed to Armorica, where, after a
residence of ten years, he wrote his "Epistle" arraigning the
kings of Britain for their vices. Upon his return, he abode
for some time at Llancarfan, and was requested by St. Cadocus
to direct the studies of the school at that place for one year;
which he undertook, and performed to the great advantage of
the scholars, desiring no other reward than their prayers.
After this the two saints withdrew to two small islands, not
far distant, intending to spend their days in retirement. Gildas, however, was disturbed by pirates, and in consequence
removed to Glastonbury, where he wrote his " History of the
Britons," and remained to the close of his life.‡—Such is a
brief summary of their narrative, divested of several fables and

* Compare Cennydd and Ufelwyn in the Cambrian Biography.

† *Cau*, Capgrave; *Caunus*, Floriacensis; *Nau*, Caradocus Lancarbanensis.

‡ The supposition, that there were two persons called Gildas, the one
surnamed Albanius, and the other Badonicus, is apparently a modern dis-

inconsistencies, for these writers differ in several particulars
with each other; and uncertain as the authority of the genealogists may sometimes appear, it is better supported by
external evidence than that of the monks, who have framed
their account to suit the life of the author of the reputed
works of Gildas; which, though ancient,* are not likely to
have been written by Aneurin, or indeed by any one of British
race. Their spirit is anti-national, and their design is obviously to depreciate the Britons. It is not improbable that they
were intended to pass for the productions of the bard, for
they contain no invective against the princes of the North;
but while Aneurin laments that the confederated chiefs should
have entered the field in a state of intoxication, which he
seems to regard more as a misfortune than a crime, he dwells
upon the praises of his heroes, and treats his countrymen
throughout with a friendly feeling.

Caffo ab Caw, a saint, and the patron of Llangaffo, a chapel
under Llangeinwen, Anglesey.

Ceidio ab Caw; Rhodwydd Geidio, subject to Llantrisaint, Anglesey, and Ceidio, Carnarvonshire, are dedicated
to him.

Aeddan Foeddog, a son of Caw. With respect to the name,
Archbishop Usher observes:—Ædanus, the bishop, is called
by the Irish "Moedhog and Mædog," and by Giraldus Cambrensis "Maidocus."—John of Teignmouth says:—This holy
person is named "Aidanus" in the Life of St. David, but in
his own Life "Aidus;" and at Menevia, in the church of
St. David, he is called "Moedok," which is an Irish name,
and his festival is observed with great veneration at that
place.—All the legends agree that Aeddan was a disciple of

tinction, for the older biographers attribute both titles to the same individual.

* They were extant as early as the time of Bede, who quotes them as
if they were authentic.

St. David at Menevia, from whence he passed over into Ireland, and was appointed the first bishop of Ferns. It was
doubtless a reference to this circumstance that induced the
clergy of Menevia, in a later age, to assert that the bishoprick
of Ferns was once subject to the archbishoprick of St. David's,
a proposition which Usher is not willing to admit. Giraldus
tells a marvellous story of the manner in which St. Aeddan
carried over a swarm of bees to Ireland; for such creatures
were never seen in that country before, and have never been
seen at Menevia since!! Traces of his memory are still retained in Pembrokeshire, as he is the reputed founder of
Llanhuadain or Llawhaden in that county, and the churches
of Nolton and West-Haroldston are ascribed to him under the
name of Madog. His festival is Jan. 31.

Cwyllog, a daughter of Caw, was the wife of Medrawd or
Mordred, the nephew of Arthur; and is thought to have
founded the church of Llangwyllog, Anglesey.

Dirynig, one of the sons of Caw; to whom it is said there
was a church dedicated at York.

Cain, daughter of Caw ; a saint, and the patroness of Llangain, Carmarthenshire.

Eigrad, one of sons of Caw; a member of the society of
Illtyd, and the founder of Llaneigrad, Anglesey.

Samson, a son of Caw, was a saint of the college of Illtyd,
and had a church at Caerefrog or York.—This person has
been magnified by certain legendary writers into an archbishop of York ; and they relate that when the Saxons took
the city, and destroyed its cathedral, the prelate saved himself
by flight ; and carrying with him the ensigns of his dignity to
Armorica, he was, by virtue of their possession, constituted
archbishop of Dole in that country, a see which he continued
to hold until his death, when he was succeeded by another
Samson, who had arrived in the same country from Wales.
The history of the two persons is frequently confounded ; but
if the circumstances related of the archbishoprick of the elder

Samson were true, it is remarkable that the Welsh authorities
should have omitted to mention them; for without allusion to
his station, they merely imply that he retired from the advance of the Saxons, and that, like several of his brothers, he
passed the latter part of his life in the college of Illtyd. There
was, however, another Samson at that college about the same
time, the son of Amwn Ddu, who is recorded in Achau y
Saint to have passed over into Armorica, and to have been
elected bishop of Dole. His history, which is better attested
than that of his namesake, is reserved to the next generation.
But the question of the dignity, as well as the identity, of the
elder Samson derives importance from its having been the
subject of an appeal to Rome, grounded on the assertion that
he had carried *a pall* into the country of his exile; in consideration of which, it was alleged, palls were likewise granted
to his successors at Dole, who exercised archiepiscopal authority until their privileges ceased through the intervention of
the archbishop of Tours.* In the twelfth century, the clergy
of St. David's maintained, that the pall, which was taken to
Armorica, belonged to their church, and that it was carried
over, not by an archbishop of York, but by Samson, the
the twenty-fifth archbishop of Menevia; they, therefore, ap-
pealed to the Pope for the restoration of the dignity, and
claimed to be independent of the jurisdiction of Canterbury.
Their cause was advocated with all the learning and ability of
Giraldus Cambrensis, who made three several journeys to
Rome in its behalf; but after a long hearing, the prerogatives
of Canterbury were confirmed; the evidence, adduced upon
the occasion, not being sufficient to prove, that a pall had been
sent from Rome to Menevia, or to any bishop in Britain
before the mission of St. Augustin.

* " Contigit ut ob Pallii gratiam quod Samson illuc attulerat, succe-
dentes ibi Episcopi usque ad nostra hæc fere tempora (quibus prævalente
Turonorum Archipræsule, adventitia dignitas evanuit) pallia semper ob-
tinuerunt."—Giraldus in Dialogo de Ecclesiâ Menevensi.

Eigron, the son of Caw, is stated to have founded a church in Cornwall.

Gwenafwy, Peillan, and Peithien; daughters of Caw, and saints, but there are no churches which retain their names.

Gallgo ab Caw, a saint, to whom Llanallgo, a chapel sub-ordinate to Llaneigrad, Anglesey, is dedicated. **Festival, Nov. 27.**

Peirio ab Caw, a member of the congregation of Illtyd, after whose death he was elected principal of that society ; but he is said to have died on the following day, and to have been succeeded by Samson ab Amwn Ddu. Rhospeirio, sub-ject to Llanelian, Anglesey, is dedicated to his memory.

Cewydd ab Caw was the founder of Aberedw, and Diserth, Radnorshire, and of Llangewydd, an extinct church near Bridgend, Glamorganshire.

Maelog ab Caw, a saint of the congregation of Cattwg. The following curious notice of him occurs in the Life of Gildas from the Library of Fleury :*—" Caunus, the father of Gildas, is said to have had four other sons; namely, Cuillus,† a man of great prowess in arms, who, upon the death of his father, succeeded to his kingdom; next, Mailocus, who was destined by his father to the study of sacred literature, in which he was well instructed; he left his father, and bidding adieu to his paternal estate, came to ' Lyuhes' in the district of ' Elmail,' where he built a monastery, in which, after having served God incessantly with hymns and orations, with watch-ings and fastings, he rested in peace, illustrious for his virtues and miracles. Egreas, moreover, with Allæcus, his brother, and Peteona, their sister, a virgin consecrated to God, in like manner leaving their father's estate; and renouncing all worldly pomp, withdrew to the farthest part of that country, where, not far from each other, they built their several monas-

---

* For the original, see Usher, Primordia, page 676.
† Hywel, as he is called by other authorities.

teries, placing their sister in the midst."—In this extract
" Lyuhes in the district of Elmail" is obviously Llowes in
Elfael, Radnorshire, which according to Ecton, is dedicated
to St. Meilig. Egreas, Allæcus, and Peteona, are Eigrad,
Gallgo, and Peithien; and "the farthest part of the country"
is the Isle of Anglesey, where Llaneigrad is situated with its
chapel of Llanallgo, and another chapel called Llugwy,* which
possibly may be the one intended for Peteona or Peithien.
Maelog is the reputed founder of Llandyfaelog Tref-y-Graig,
and another Llandyfaelog, Brecknockshire, and Llandyfaelog,
Carmarthenshire; the syllable *dy* in these names being either
epenthetic, or borrowed from the Norman *de*.† Llanfaelog, a
chapel under Llanbeulan, Anglesey, is an instance where the
syllable is omitted.

Meilig ab Caw, a saint to whom no churches are ascribed,
except Llowes, Radnorshire, attributed to Maelog in the preceding notice. It is not improbable that the author of the
Life of Gildas supposed that Maelog and Meilig were merely
two modes of pronouncing the name of one individual; but it
would appear that they belonged to different persons from the
circumstance that Maelog is commemorated on the thirty-first
of December, and Meilig on the fourteenth of November.‡
The latter appears to have been the founder of Llowes, as
there is a place in the parish, called Croes Feilig, or St. Meilig's cross.

Gwrddelw ab Caw, a saint who is said to have had a church
at Caerleon upon Usk.

Gwrhai ab Caw, the founder of Penystrywad in Arwystli,
Montgomeryshire.

---

* Ecton names St. Michael as the patron of Llugwy.

† In the Taxation of Pope Nicholas, Llangadock, Carmarthenshire, is
spelled "Landekadok."

‡ Sir Harris Nicolas's Chronology of History.—The compiler of a "History of Anglesey" says that the festival of St. Maelog is Jan. 30.

Huail ab Caw distinguished himself as a warrior in the service of Arthur. He passed the latter part of his life in the monastery of Cattwg; and it is said that there was a church dedicated to him in Euas, Herefordshire.

In this list of the family of Caw, the names of nine sons, who devoted their lives entirely to war, are not recounted; but the number of children assigned to him is too great to be received with credit, except upon the supposition that it includes his grand-children, and, perhaps, other relatives, who were his followers and composed his clan. The death of Geraint ab Erbin, one of the princes of Devon, who was slain, while fighting under Arthur at the battle of Llongborth, has been noticed already.* Four of his sons, who seem to have imitated the example of the children of Caw, were, Selyf, Cyngar, Iestin, and Cado or Cataw, all of whom were saints of the college of Garmon.

Selyf ab Geraint was the person who is called, in the legendary accounts, Solomon Duke of Cornwall. There are no churches in Wales which bear his name.

According to Capgrave, Cungarus, the founder of a monastery or college in the diocese of Llandaff, came from Cungresbury in the county of Somerset; which suggests the opinion that the founder of the college of Llangenys† was Cyngar ab Geraint, and not Cyngar ab Arthog ab Ceredig. He is the patron saint of Badgworth, and Cungresbury, Somerset; and of Hope, Flintshire, and Llangefni, Anglesey.

Iestin ab Geraint was the founder of Llaniestin in Lleyn, Carnarvonshire; and also of Llaniestin in Anglesey, where a stone was seen in the last century with an inscription purporting that he was buried there.‡

Cado or Cataw ab Geraint, a saint, but there are no churches ascribed to him in Wales.

---

* Page 169.   † Page 183 *antea.*
‡ Mona Antiqua; Myv. Archaiology, Vol. II. p. 46.

Of the sons of Gwynllyw Filwr, chieftain of Gwynllwg, Monmouthshire; Cattwg, the eldest, was the first president of the college of Llancarfan; the rest, who have had the credit of sanctity, were :—

Cammarch ab Gwynllyw, the founder of Llangammarch, Brecknockshire.

Glywys Cerniw, the founder of a church at Coed Cerniw in Gwynllwg, Monmouthshire.

Hywgi, otherwise Bugi, the father of St. Beuno. He gave all his lands for the endowment of his brother's college at Llancarfan, where he spent the latter part of his life.

Cyfyw ab Gwynllyw, an officer in the college of Cattwg, and patron saint of Llangyfyw near Caerleon.

Cynfyw, or Cynyw ab Gwynllyw; possibly another pronunciation of the preceding name, as Llangyfyw is written, by Ecton, "Llangyniow." There is a church, called Llangynyw, in Montgomeryshire, of which he may have been the founder.

Gwyddlew, Cyflewyr, and Cammab; sons of Gwynllyw, and saints, but nothing farther is known respecting them.

Maches, a daughter of Gwynllyw, suffered martyrdom at a place since called Merthyr Maches, or Llanfaches, in Monmouthshire. "She gave alms to all who asked; and a pagan Saxon, who appeared before her as a mendicant, stabbed her with a knife."[*]

The children of Ynyr Gwent by Madrun, daughter of Gwrthefyr Fendigaid, were another Silurian family that flourished about this time. Caradog, the eldest, lived at Caerwent, and succeeded to his father's territories; he married Derwela, one of the sisters of Amwn Ddu.[†]

Iddon ab Ynyr Gwent was a chieftain, who afterwards devoted himself to religion. It is said that he made a grant, to the see of Llandaff, of— "Llanarth with all the landes there,

and Lantelio Porth-halawg with the territory unto the same
belonging, and certaine landes at Lantelio Crissenny; all in
thankfulnèsse to God for a victory obtained against the Saxons."* It is also stated that he made a grant of " Lancoyt;"
and the charters conferring these donations are cited from the
register, or " Book," of Llandaff;† but without attempting to
assert their genuineness,‡ it is right to observe that the alleged
date of these grants is misplaced by Godwin, who says they
were made in the time of Comegern and Argwistill, the eighth
and ninth bishops of the see. The prelate, contemporary with
Iddon, was Teilo; the second on the list, and a principal
witness to the grants in question.§

Ceidio and Cynheiddion, sons, and Tegîwg, a daughter, of
Ynyr Gwent, were saints of whose history no particulars have
been recorded, except that Ceidio was a member of the monastery of Llancarfan.

The period between the years 500 and 550 is believed to
include the date of a calamity on the coast of Wales, of which
the most exaggerated and mystified accounts have reached
posterity :‖ for it is asserted that an irruption of the sea broke
in upon a large tract of country, which it has since continued
to cover, forming the whole of the present Cardigan Bay. It
is not necessary to dwell upon the proofs, that such a calamity
could not have occurred to the extent related; as the testimony of Ptolemy, the geographer, is, so far, conclusive against

---

* Godwin's English Bishops.—These churches, which still retain their
names, are situated in Monmouthshire, and acknowledge Teilo for their
patron saint.

† This record, one or two transcripts of which are reported to be extant,
is still unpublished.

‡ See pp. 184, 185 of this Essay.

§ In Chartis Donationum Idonis regis, filii Ynir Guent, inter testes ê
Clericis, primo loco cernitur Teliaus Archiepiscopus.—Usher, p. 98.

‖ Triad 37, Third Series.—See also Davies's Mythology of the Druids,
page 249, and Cambro Briton, Vol. I. p, 361.

the tradition. That author, who lived in the second century, marks the promontories by which Cardigan Bay is confined, and the mouths of the rivers which it receives, in nearly the same relative situations which they retain at present; giving the latitude and longitude of each place according to his mode of computation. It is not unreasonable, however, to suppose that an event took place, similar to that which laid under water the lands of Earl Godwin on the eastern coast of England. A tract of low land along the coast of Cardiganshire and Merionethshire, of which some vestiges still remain,* was overflowed; and as it had been called Cantref y Gwaelod, it

* " Submarine Forest in Cardigan Bay."—(From the proceedings of the Geological Society in London.) At a Meeting of the Society, held on the 7th of November, 1832, a notice of a submarine Forest in Cardigan Bay, by the Rev. James Yates, M. A., F. G. S. and L. S. was read. The Forest extends along the coast of Merionethshire and Cardiganshire, being divided into two parts by the estuary of the river Dovey, which separates these counties. It is bounded on the land side by a sandy beach and by a wall of shingles. Beyond this wall is a tract of bog and marsh, formed by streams of water, which are partially discharged by oozing through sand and shingles. The author argues that as the position of the wall is liable to change, it may have inclosed the part which is now submarine, and that it is not necessary to suppose a subsidence effected by submarine agency. The remains of the forest are covered by a bed of peat, and are distinguished by an abundance of *Pholas Candida* and *Teredo Nivalis*. Among the trees of which the forest consisted, is the *Pinus Sylvestris* or Scotch Fir; and it is shown that this tree abounded anciently in several northern counties of England. The natural order of the *Coniferæ* may thus be traced from the period of the independent coal formation to the middle of the seventeenth century, although the Scotch Fir is excluded from the native *Flora*. The amentaceous wood presents matter for reflection in consequence of the perfect preservation of its vascular structure, while the contents of its vessels are entirely dissipated. The tract is known to the Welsh under the name of *Cantref y Gwaelod, i. e.* the Lowland Hundred. The author refers to the Triads of Britain, and to the ancient Welsh testimonies, which prove that it was submerged about A. D. 520, and ascribe the disaster to the folly of 'Seithenyn the Drunkard,' who in his drink let the sea over *Cantref y Gwaelod*."

was probably of no greater extent than a "Cantref," or "Hundred," in any other part of Wales. This district had been divided between two chieftains, of the names of Seithenyn and Gwyddno, whose children, in consequence of the loss of their inheritance, were induced to embrace a religious life. The sons of Seithenyn, who were all of them, except Arwystli Glóff, members of the college of Dunawd at Bangor Iscoed, were the following :—

Gwynodl ab Seithenyn, the founder of Llangwynodl, Carnarvonshire. Festival, Jan. 1.

Merin, or Merini ab Seithenyn ; presumed to be the founder of Llanferin, or Llanfetherin, Monmouthshire. Bodferin, the signification of which implies the place of his residence, is the name of a chapel under Llaniestin, Carnarvonshire. Festival, Jan. 6.

Senefyr, or Senewyr ab Seithenyn, a saint.

Tudglyd ab Seithenyn.

Tudno ab Seithenyn, the founder of Llandudno, Carnarvonshire ; his commemoration occurs on the fifth of June.

Tyneio ab Seithenyn ; Deneio, or Pwllheli, a chapel under Llanfor, Carnarvonshire, is supposed to be named after him.*

Arwystli Gloff ab Seithenyn, was an inmate of the monastery of Bardsey, and is said to have been the founder of a church, but its situation is not known.

Elffin, the only son of Gwyddno whose name is preserved, was a saint of the college of Illtyd. A story, which, however, is confessedly a fable, relates that Gwyddno had a fishing wear on the sands between the Dovey and Aberystwyth, the annual profits of which were very considerable. But Elffin was the most unlucky of men and nothing prospered in his hands, insomuch that his father was grieved at his ill successes, and feared that he was born in an evil hour : wishing, however, to

* Myv. Archaiology, Vol. II. pp. 30, 55.

give the fortunes of his son a further trial, he agreed to allow him the profits of the wear for one whole year. On the morrow, Elffin visited the wear, and found nothing, except a leathern bag fastened to one of the poles, He was immediately upbraided for his ill luck by his companions, for he had ruined the good fortune of the wear, which before was wont to produce the value of a hundred pounds on May eve. Nay, replied Elffin, there may yet be here an equivalent for the value of a hundred pounds. The bag was opened, and the face of a child appearing from within, "What a noble forehead," exclaimed the opener. "Taliesin be his name," rejoined Elffin,* and commiserating the hard fate of the infant exposed to the mercies of the sea, he took it in his arms, and mounting his steed, conveyed it to his wife, by whom it was nursed tenderly and affectionately: from that time forward, his wealth increased every day.—Such is the story of the discovery of the chief bard of Wales, committed by his mother to the chances of the tide, and saved in the manner described. In return for the kindness of his benefactor, adds the tale, he composed, while a child, his poem, entitled the "Consolation of Elffin," rousing him from the contemplation of his disappointments and cheering with the prospect of blessings which still awaited him; and afterwards when Elffin was imprisoned in the castle of Dyganwy by Maelgwn Gwynedd, Taliesin, through the influence of his song, procured his release.†

The children of Pawl Hên, or Paulinus, of Ty-gwyn ar Daf, were:—Peulan, the founder of Llanbeulan, Anglesey; Gwyngeneu, to whom Capel Gwyngeneu under Holyhead was dedicated; and Gwenfaen, a daughter, who was the foundress of Rhoscolyn, Anglesey. The festival of St. Gwenfaen is Nov. 5.

* Admirable phrenologists;—the English reader must understand that "noble forehead" is the translation of "Tàl-iesin."

† From the Mabinogion or Welsh Romances;—Cambrian Quarterly Magazine, Vol. V. and Myv. Archaiology, Vol. I.

The only saint of the family of Brychan, who belongs to this generation, is Nefydd, a son of Nefydd Ail ab Rhun Dremrudd.

About this period lived Tegfan, the son of Carcludwys of the line of Cadrod Calchfynydd, and though the number of generations between him and his ancestor exceeds the usual allowance for the interval of time, it does not exceed the bounds of probability. He was the brother of Gallgu Rhieddog, and is said to have been the founder of Llandegfan, Anglesey.

According to Achau y Saint; Teon, and Tegonwy ab Teon, were members of the college of Illtyd; but the statement cannot be admitted without incurring a great anachronism, if it be true that Iorwerth Hirflawdd, a son of Tegonwy, married one of the daughters of Brychan. The mistake seems to have arisen from confounding Teon, who stands at the head of a long pedigree of Welsh chieftains,* with Teon, who, according to Geoffrey of Monmouth, was bishop of Gloucester about A. D. 542, when he was translated to the archbishoprick of London; but, unfortunately for Geoffrey, London was in the possession of the Saxons before the year 542.

Bedwini, another bishop mentioned in the Welsh accounts, is said to have been the primate of Cornwall in the time of Arthur, and to have resided at a place called Celliwig.

Stinan, or Justinian, according to his Life by John of Teignmouth, was born of noble parentage in Lesser Brittany; and having spent his youth in the study of learning, he received the order of priesthood, and was, by a divine oracle, commanded to leave his country. After wandering for a while, he came to the coast of Wales, and landed in a certain island called "Lemeney," where he led a religious life in company with Honorius, the son of king Thefriaucus. Cressy says:—

---

* It would appear, from the dates of his descendants, that he flourished about A. D. 400.

"The authour of his life relates at large the envy and malice
with which the Enemy of mankind impugned the devout and
mortified life of this Holy man, seeking to interrupt it by
severall and frequent illusions, and by suggesting scandalous
lyes concerning him. But in conclusion, when he saw himself every way vanquished by the Holy man, and that neither
by violent assaults nor malicious suggestions he could withdraw
him from the service of God: he attempted other arts and
guilefull machinations: For he infused the poyson of his
malice into the hearts of three of the Holy mans servants : Insomuch as they having been reproved by him for their idlenes
and mispending the time, they were inflamed with fury against
him, insomuch as rushing upon him, they threw him to the
ground, and most cruelly cutt off his head. But in the place
where the sacred head fell to the ground, a fountain of pure
water presently flowd, by drinking of which in following
times many were miraculously restored to health. But miracles greater than these immediately succeeded his death.
For the body of the Blessed Martyr presently rose, and taking
the head between the two arms, went down to the sea shore,
and walking thence on the sea, pass'd over to the port call'd by
his name : and being arrived in the place where a Church is
now built to his Memory, it fell down, and was there buried
by Saint David with spirituall Hymns and Canticles."—Cressy
next proceeds to explain that the island Lemeney—"hath in
English obtain'd a new name being calld Ramsey ;" and that
"It lyes opposite and in sight of Menevia the Episcopall seat
of St. David." The church, mentioned in this most out-
rageous legend, is evidently the chapel of Stinan in the parish
of St. David's, Pembrokeshire; as the church of Llanstinan, in
the same county, is too far distant to answer the description.

Ffinian, an Irish saint, is said to have visited St. David at
Menevia about A. D. 530, and to have remained in Britain
thirty years, in which time he built three churches, but their
names are unknown. There was another Irish saint, and con-

temporary, called Ffinan, whose Welsh name, according to Usher, was Winnin. It is uncertain to which of them, Llan-ffinan, subject to Llanfihangel Ysgeifiog, Anglesey, is dedicated.

Senanus, an Irish saint and bishop, who was intimately acquainted with St. David, died A. D. 544. Llansannan, Denbighshire, and Bedwellty, Monmouthshire, are under his tutelage; and his festival is March 1.*

In ascertaining and verifying the commemorations or saints' days, great assistance may be derived from the list of fairs now held in the Principality; it being an opinion generally received among antiquaries that parochial wakes were the means of assembling people, who afterwards converted the occasion into an opportunity of buying and selling. Many of the village fairs in Wales are held on the saint's day Old Style, or rather *eleven* days later than the proper time according to the Gregorian Calendar; for the Welsh peasantry have seldom taken into account, that since the year 1800 the discrepancy between the Old and New Styles has increased to *twelve* days. Thus it may be learned from a list of saints printed in the Cambrian Register,† and also from the Alphabetical Calendar of Sir Harris Nicolas,‡ that the festival of St. Gwenog should be held on the third of January; eleven days being added to that date will point out to Jan. 14, the day upon which, according to the Welsh almanacks, a fair is held at Llanwenog in the county of Cardigan. By inverting the computation, a satisfactory method is obtained of deciding between contradictory statements; for instance the list in the Cambrian Register states that the festival of St. Tyssul was kept on the third of February, while according to Sir H. Ni-

* "Eodem tempore quo David Menevensis præsul, cui conjunctissimus vixit, lucis hanc usuram reddidisse traditur."—Usher, p. 874.
† Vol. III. p. 219.
‡ Inserted in his Chronology of History.

colas's authorities it was held Jan. 31. A fair, however, is held at Llandyssul, Cardiganshire, Feb. 11 ; and eleven days, reckoned backwards from that time, will bring the calculation to Jan. 31, proving the last of the two statements to be the correct one. Sir H. Nicolas assigns the festival of St. Caron to March the fourth or fifth, as if his authorities were doubtful as to the precise time ; but eleven days, counted backwards from a fair at Tregaron on the sixteenth of March, will show that the commemoration of the saint ought to be kept March 5. The other day, March 4, was fixed apparently by some person, who followed the inverted mode of computation, but reckoned twelve days from the fair. In some villages it has been the custom to hold the fair on the vigil, or eve, before the festival; which is easily ascertained, as in that case the difference of reckoning is only *ten* days. The saints of Llangynidr, Brecknockshire, are Cynidr and St. Mary ; one of its fairs is kept on the fourth of April, or ten days after the twenty fifth of March, the feast of the Annunciation of the Blessed Virgin. In like manner St. Mary is the patron saint of Nefyn, Carnarvonshire, and three of its fairs are held, according to Carlisle's Topographical Dictionary, on the fourth of April, the twenty fifth of August, and the eighteenth of September, being ten days respectively after the feasts of her Annunciation, Assumption, and Nativity.*

In the large families, included in the period of this generation, there must be great disparity of age, and the lives of many of the persons named may be found to extend through the period assigned for the next generation.

---

*.The festivals in this Essay are given principally according to Sir H. Nicolas, but they have not been compared with the fairs in every instance.

2 F

SECTION XI.

The Welsh Saints from the Accession of Cystennyn Goronog A. D. 542
to the Death of Maelgwn Gwynedd A. D. 566.

THIS period includes the reigns of Cystennyn, Cynan
Wledig, Gwrthefyr or Vortimer the Second, and Maelgwn;
who are popularly styled kings of Britain, though it would
appear from the writings ascribed to Gildas, that three, at least,
of them were contemporary princes, reigning at the same time
in separate provinces,* which is more consistent with the view
of affairs presented by the bards and genealogists.

The second bishop of Llanbadarn was Cynog, who was
raised, upon the death of St. David, to the archbishoprick of
Menevia. He appears, however, to have presided but a short
time at both places, as no particulars of his life have been recorded, and his parentage, churches, and festival, are alike
unknown. The short duration of his presidency at Menevia
is shown by the fact that he was in turn succeeded by Teilo,
who had been the associate and fellow-student of his predecessor.

Teilo,† the second bishop of Llandaff, was the son of Enlleu ab Hydwn Dwn ab Ceredig ab Cunedda, by Tegfedd,
daughter of Tegid Foel of Penllyn. His Latin name was
Teliaus, and, by a sort of monkish trifling with the sound of

---

* Namely; Constantinus, the tyrant, as he is called, of the Damnonii, or
people of Devon and Cornwall; Vortiporius, the tyrant of the Dimetæ, or
inhabitants of the western part of South Wales; and Maglocunus, the
tyrant of North Wales.

† "Nai, fab Cefnder i Ddewi."—Myv. Archaiology, Vol. II. p. 53.

of the word, he was also called Ηλιος and Eliud.[*] He was born at a place once called "Eccluis Gunnian," or "Gunniau," in the neighbourhood of Tenby, Pembrokeshire. It is said that he studied first under Dubricius, by whose assistance he attained to great proficiency in the knowledge of the Scriptures; his next instructor was Paulinus, under whom he pursued the same study, and in whose school he was the associate of St. David. Under the patronage of Dubricius, he opened a college at Llandaff, which was called Bangor Deilo; and his settlement at that place may serve to account for his appointment to fill the see of Llandaff upon the retirement of his patron to the Isle of Bardsey. The idea that he was made bishop of Llandaff at the time Dubricius was raised to the archbishoprick of Caerleon is irreconcilable with chronology; and the assertion that he succeeded Dubricius as archbishop, without the intervention of St. David,[†] is contrary to all received history, unless it be supposed that Llandaff was an archbishoprick independent of Caerleon, a position which is certainly untenable. The original diocese governed by Teilo, as ascertained by the absence of churches founded by St. David, was coextensive with the ancient Lordship of Glamorgan, containing the present rural deaneries of Groneath, Llandaff, and Newport. How long he continued to preside over this limited district is uncertain; but in the reign of Maelgwn Gwynedd, a plague, called "Flava pestis," and in Welsh "Y Fall felen," is recorded to have desolated the Principality.

---

[*] "Post incrementum ætatis, virtutum et sapientiæ, congruo nomine Helios a sapientibus nuncupatus est. *Elios* autem Græcè Latinè *Sol* interpretatur. Fulget enim ut Sol ejus doctrina, fidelium illustrando corda. Sed illiteratis hominibus extremum vocabuli corruptè proferentibus, adolevit quod non Helios sed Heliud appellatus est."—Life by Galfridus.— "Non Elios sed Eliud."—John of Teignmouth.

[†] The assertion was made in the Regestum Landavense, at a time when the clergy of Llandaff wished to show that their diocese had never been subordinate to the primacy of Menevia.

Upon this occasion, Teilo, with several others, retired to Cornwall, and afterwards to Armorica, where he was honourably received by Samson, the bishop of Dole. After he had remained seven years and as many months in Armorica, he returned, with several of his disciples, to his native country; and upon his arrival was elected to the archbishoprick of Menevia, then vacant by the death of Cynog. Like St. David, however, he retained a predilection for the seat of his original bishoprick, and, appointing Ismael to the situation of bishop of Menevia, he removed the archbishoprick to Llandaff.* In order to maintain his title to the primacy undisturbed, he appears to have kept under his immediate government the whole of the diocese held before by St. David, with the exception of the part north of the river Tivy, which was henceforth attached to the diocese of Llanbadarn.† In support of this view it may be explained that churches founded by Teilo still exist throughout the whole of the country specified, and that one of them, Llandeloi, is situated within a few miles of the cathedral of St. David's; but north of the Tivy, no church of this description is to be found. The proof, however, does not rest solely upon the analogy of existing monuments; for the records of Llandaff show that its bishops continued for several centuries to claim the whole of the country from the mouth of the Taradr, or extreme point of Monmouthshire, to the mouth of the Tivy,‡ including, of course, Pembrokeshire and so much of Herefordshire as lay to the west of the river Wye. It does not appear that any separate district was apportioned as a diocese for Ismael, who must have been no more than an assisting suffragan, and his name is not inserted

* Regestum Landavense; Life by Galfridus; and Usher pp. 83, 517, 559, 560.

† The extension of the diocese of Llanbadarn confirms the supposition that its bishop at this time was Afan, the brother of Teilo.

‡ There is abundant evidence of this in the formulæ of the Councils of Llandaff, which are inserted at length in Spelman's Concilia.

in the list of prelates of St. David's. In his time, therefore, the diocese of Menevia was united to that of Llandaff; and the circumstance may account for the claim afterwards made by the bishops of Llandaff, which, if maintained, would have involved the existence of the bishoprick of St. David's, which it went to deprive of its entire territory. But in effect it was little better than nominal, though attempts were not wanting to enforce it. There is reason to suppose that Oudoceus, the successor of Teilo at Llandaff, retained Monmouthshire and the adjacent part of Herefordshire under his jurisdiction; but he did not succeed to the bishoprick of St. David's,[*] the affairs of which were administered by Ceneu;[†] and though the extent of its territories at the time of its separation, and for two centuries afterwards, is not determinable, it is clear that from the ninth century, or the establishment of the princes of Dinefwr of the line of Rhodri Mawr, it has maintained, with an occasional intrusion from the bishops of Llandaff, nearly the same limits as at present.

The churches founded by Teilo, or dedicated to him, which still exist, are the following :—

DIOCESE OF ST. DAVID'S.

Llandeilo Fawr, V.—3 chapels, Taliaris (Holy Trinity,) *Capel yr Ywen*, and *Llandyfaen*, Carmarthenshire.

Brechfa, C. Carm.

Llandeilo Abercywyn, C. Carm.

Trelèch a'r Bettws, V.—1 chapel, Capel Bettws, Carm.

Llanddowror, R. Carm.

Cilrhedin, R.—1 chapel, *Capel Ifan* (St. John,) Carm. and Pembrokeshire.

Llandeilo, C. Annexed to Maenclochog, Pemb.

Llandeloi, V.—1 chapel, Llanhywel (St. Hywel,) Pemb.

Llandeilo Graban, C. Radnorshire.

Llandeilo'r Fân, C.—1 *chapel*, in ruins, Brecknockshire.

[*] Usher, p. 1155.

[†] Giraldus, and Records of St. David's quoted by Godwin.

Llandeilo Talybont, V. Glamorganshire.
Bishopston, alias Llandeilo Ferwallt, R.—1 chapel, *Caswel*, Glam.

DIOCESE OF LLANDAFF.

Llandaff Cathedral, (St. Teilo and St. Peter.)—1 chapel, Whitchurch (St. Mary,) Glamorganshire.
Merthyr Dyfan, R. Glam.
Merthyr Mawr, C.—*St. Roque's Chapel*, in ruins, Glam.
Llandeilo Cressenny, V.—1 chapel, Penrhos (St. Cattwg,) Monmouthshire.
Llanarth, V. Monm.
Llandeilo Bertholeu, or Porth-halawg, V. Monm.

The foregoing list, so far as regards the diocese of St. David's, may be compared with another which is curious for its antiquity. Between the years 1022 and 1031, in the reign of Canute, king of England; Rhydderch ab Iestin, a prince of Glamorgan, obtained the sovereignty of South Wales,[*] and taking advantage of the opportunity, made an endeavour to restore the ancient diocese of Teilo. He therefore granted to the church of Llandaff, all such churches in the counties of Carmarthen, Pembroke, Brecon, and Radnor, as bore the name of that saint, together with several manors, lands, and villages, according to the following schedule ;[†] extracted *literatim* from " Godwin's Bishops."

IN CANTREF MAUR.[‡]

1 Lantelia maur cum suis duob. territorijs.
2 Lanteliau nant seru.
3 Lanteliau garth teuir.
4 Lanteliau maur brumur.
5 Lanteliau bechan in diffrin teiui.

---

[*] Welsh Chronicles in the Myv. Archaiology.

[†] Its heading, according to the first edition of Godwin, is :—De omnibus subscriptis vestita fuit ecclesia Landauensis, simul et episcopus Joseph, pace quietâ et tranquillâ tempore regnantis Ritherich per totam Gualiam, et admonitione Ælnod Archiepiscopi Cantuarensis simul cum literis commendatitiis Cnut regnantis Angliam.

[‡] The Hundreds of Caio and Catheiniog, in Carmarthenshire, between the rivers Towy and Tivy. The names of some of the places in this docu-

IN CANTREF GUARTAN.*

6 Lanteliau landibr guir mainaur.
7 Lantelian treficerniu.
8 Lantoulidauc icair.
9 Lanteliau aper coguin.
10 Lanteliau penn tiuinn.
11 Lanteliau luin guaidan, villa
tantum, in euilfre.
12 Lanrath.
13 Lanconguern cum trib. territorijs. Finis illarum Ofruit
Gurcant Lutglanrath.
14 Tref carn, Villa tantum, sine
ecclesia.
15 Laythty teliau, villa tantum super ripam ritec iuxta penalun.

16 Menechi arglann ritec iuxta
penalun.
17 Pull arda iuxta mainaur pir,
villa tantum.
18 Luin teliau, villa tantum.
19 Eccluis Gunniau, vbi natus est
S. Teliaus.
20 Porth medgen, villa tantum
21 Porth manacli mainaur mam-
ithiel.
22 Din guenhalf inlonian, villa
tantum.
23 Lantelian litgarth in findou-
cledif hache mei mainaur.
24 Lantelia cil retin in emm-
lim.

IN ROS.†

25 Lan issan mainaur.
26 Bronu lann.

27 Langurfrit.
28 Telich elouuan.

ment are disguised by its orthography, and others have been changed by
lapse of time; those that can be recognised, are as follow, according to
their numbers. 1, Llandeilo Fawr; 2 & 3, one of these probably represents the church of Brechfa. 4 Llandeilo Rwnnws, an extinct chapel in
the parish of Llanegwad; it is called "Llanteilan Brunus" in a charter of
the Abbey of Talley.

* The western part of Carmarthenshire with a large portion of Pembrokeshire. 6, Llanddowror. 7, The relative position of this church
agrees with the locality of Trelêch. 9, Llandeilo Abercywyn. 11, Llwyn-
Gwaddan near Llanddewi Felffre; the name indicates that a church once
stood there, which appears to have been in ruins at the time of the grant.
14, Trefgarn, now the name of a church and parish. 15 & 16, Penalun
may be recognised in Penaly near Tenby. 17, Mainaur pir,—Maenor Bŷr,
vulgo Manorbeer. 18, Written—"Lwyn Teilau"—in the second edition
of Godwin. 22, Lanion, near Pembroke. 23, Lege Llandeilo Lwydgarth,
in fin Daugleddyf a Chemmaes maenor; intended for Llandeilo, near Maenclochog, on the borders of the Hundreds of Dungleddy and Cemmaes. 24,
Cilrhedin in Emlyn.

† The Hundred of Rhos, Pembrokeshire.

IN PEMBRO.*

9 Ciltutuc.   30 Penclecir

IN PEPITIAUE.†

31 Mainaur mathru.   32 Cenarth maur.

IN BRECUA.‡

33 Languruaet mainaur.

IN CANTREF SELIM.§

34 Lancoit.

IN CANTREF TALACARN.||

35 Langors.   37 Lan idoudec seith.
36 Laumihacgel meuion gratlann.

IN CLIUAIL.*

38 Lan meilic bah gueir.   39 Lanteliau iciliou idiffrin mach-
                                 agui.

* Part of the Hundred of Castle Martin, Pembrokeshire.
† Pebidiog or Dewsland, Pembrokeshire. 31, Mathry.
‡ Qu. Brycheiniog, Brecknockshire, as the place now called Brechfa was included in Cantref Mawr. 33, This manor, probably has reference to Llandeilo'r Fân, the only existing church of Teilo, in the diocese of St. David's, which is not mentioned in this list.
§ Cantref Selyf, Brecknockshire. 34, Llangoed, in the parish of Llyswen.
|| The Hundred of Talgarth, Brecknockshire. 35, Llangors. 36, Probably Llanfihangel Cwm Du.
* The rural deanery of Elfael, Radnorshire. 38, Llowes, dedicated to St. Meilig. 39, Lege Llandeilo y ciliau yn nyffryn Machawy,—intended for Llandeilo Graban.

If this grant ever took effect, it was only for the short reign
of Rhydderch ab Iestin; for the Dimetian princes, considering him to be an usurper, took up arms against him, and a
battle ensued in which he was slain, leaving his principality
to be divided between the conquerors.* Subsequent events
prove that they did not confirm his benefactions; and his
reason for bestowing these possessions upon the see of Llandaff, if grounded upon the supposition that they once belonged
to Teilo, must have rested upon a false foundation, for that
prelate was also the acknowledged archbishop of Menevia.
That the grant was reckoned invalid, is evident from the circumstance that, about a century after the period in question,
Urban, bishop of Llandaff and a zealous assertor of its privileges, claimed to his diocese only so much of Carmarthenshire
as lay to the south of the river Towy, together with the southern part of Brecknockshire, and that portion of the county of
Hereford which lay on the western side of the Wye. He rested
his claim, mainly, upon the right of former occupation, contending that his predecessor had exercised authority and instituted
several persons to benefices in the disputed country. Upon
his appealing to the Pope, an inhibition was issued to the
bishops of St. David's and Hereford, commanding them to
with-hold the exercise of their authority in the districts then
called Gŵyr, Cydwely, Cantref Bychan, Ystrad Yw, and Erging; which were committed to the care of the bishop of
Llandaff, until the other bishops should prove their title.†
The remainder of the history of this controversy is lost; but

* Welsh Chronicles in the Myv. Archaiology. Their compilers, though
agreeing generally as to facts, sometimes betray the bias of their respective
provinces; Brut Ieuan Brechfa, written by a Dimetian, asserts that Rhydderch was an usurper; while Brut y Tywysogion, written by Caradog,
a Silurian, contends that he was entitled to the sovereignty of South
Wales by inheritance.

† Wharton's Anglia Sacra, Vol. II. and Godwin's Bishops.

its issue may be inferred from the fact, that the earliest notice[*]
of these districts subsequently, exhibits them included in the
diocese of St. David's and Hereford, in the state they are
found at present.

The grant contains the names of one or two chapels, which
must have been erected after the institution of parishes, and
therefore at a later period than the era of Teilo. But as the
bishops of St. David's were not likely to consecrate such
edifices to the memory of a saint whose name implied subjection to the rival see; it may be gathered that the bishops
of Llandaff had, upon some occasion, obtained a transient
ascendancy before the time of Rhydderch. This appears to
have been the case about the end of the eighth century, when
Maredudd was king of Dyfed or Dimetia ;[†] for it is recorded
that he gave six churches to Llandaff in the time of Guodloiu,
its eleventh bishop.[‡]

Teilo lived to an advanced age, and most of the churches
which perpetuate his name must have been founded by him
after he succeeded to the honours of Cynog ; but the account,
which asserts that he was living at the time St. Augustin
visited Britain, can hardly be admitted.[§] It is said that he
died at Llandeilo Fawr, and the following legend is related
respecting his body. Three places put in their claims for the
honour of his interment ; Llandaff, where he had been bishop;
Llandeilo Fawr, where he died ; and Penalun,[||] where his
ancestors had been buried. The dispute was not likely to be
settled, when, by a miracle, three bodies appeared in the room
of one, so like that the real one could not be distinguished !
It was therefore agreed to bury one body at each of the three

* The Taxation of Pope Nicholas.
† Obiit A. D. 796. Welsh Chronicles.
‡ Godwin; who says that Maredudd was a son of Rein, king of West
Wales.
§ Usher, p. 1155.
|| Penaly near Tenby.

places, trusting to the chance which of them might be the identical corpse of the saint !!* He was commemorated on the ninth of February, and has been recorded in the Triads as one of the three canonized saints of Britain; the two others were Dewi and Cattwg.

Mabon, the brother of Teilo, called also Mabon Wyn and Mabon Hên, was a saint; and Llanfabon, a chapel subject to Eglwys Ilan near Llandaff, is dedicated to him. It is worthy of remark that in the parish of Llandeilo Fawr, there are two manors, the one called Maenor Deilo, and the other Maenor Fabon; affording an example of the mode in which names of places frequently bear reference to historical associations.

It would appear that Teilo encouraged the poetic genius of his countrymen. Gwrhir, one of his bards, was a saint and the founder of Llysfaen, Glamorganshire.

Ystyffan, another of the bards of Teilo, was the son of Mawan ab Cyngen ab Cadell.† He was the founder of Llanstyffan, Carmarthenshire, and Llanstyffan, in the county of Radnor; both of which churches have others attributed to Teilo in the parishes adjoining.‡ A collection of stanzas, composed by him, is inserted in the third volume of the Myvyrian Archaiology.

According to the " Life of St. Oudoceus,"§ Budic, a native of Cornugallia in Armorica, and related to its chieftains, was forced to leave his country; and putting to sea with a fleet, he

* "Howbeit by diuers miracles done at the place of his buriall at Llandaffe, it appeareth that there the true body lyeth."—Godwin, from the Liber Landavensis.

† Page 207.

‡ Llandeilo Abercywyn, Carmarthenshire, and Llandeilo Graban, Radnorshire; which would imply that their association is due to the friendship of their founders.

§ Quoted by Usher p. 561, from the Regestum Landavense. The names "Budic" and "Anaumed" are here given in their Latin orthography, as they have not been seen in any Welsh writer.

landed in Dyfed, or Pembrokeshire, which was at that time
under the government of a prince, named Aercol Lawhir.
He was hospitably received, and making his abode in Dyfed,
he married Anaumed, the daughter of Ensic or Enlleu, by
whom he had two sons, Ismael already mentioned, and Tyfei.
Both the children were devoted to the service of religion by
their mother, who was the sister of St. Teilo; and in course of
time Ismael received from his uncle the appointment of suffragan bishop of Menevia.   He was the founder of St. Ishmael's
near Kidwelly, Carmarthenshire, and of Camros, Usmaston,
Rosemarket, St. Ishmael's, and East Haroldston, Pembrokeshire.

Tyfei, the brother of Ismael, was accidentally slain, when a
child, by a person named Tyrtuc,* and has therefore been styled
a martyr, though it is difficult to understand how a case of man-
slaughter could be construed into a death in testimony of the
faith of the sufferer.   He was buried at Penaly, Pembrokeshire; and is the patron saint of Llamphey† in that county.
A church near Llandeilo Fawr is called Llandyfeisant; and
the relationship of Teilo, who died in the adjoining parish,
would justify the suggestion that the name means—"the
church of St. Tyfei," and not "the church of St. Dewi" as
commonly supposed.

While Budic continued to reside in Dyfed, ambassadors
came from Cornugallia, announcing to him the death of their
king, and that the people, wishing to elect a successor of the
same family, had made choice of him, and were desirous that
he should undertake the government.   The proposal was accepted.   Budic, taking with him his wife and family, returned
to his native country, and had the good fortune to establish
his dominion over the whole of Armorica.   Soon after his

---

* Godwin's Bishops.

† Written "Lantefei" by Giraldus Cambrensis, and by Browne Willis
"Llantiffi."

arrival he had another son, named Oudoceus, who, in compliance with a promise previously made to Teilo, was, like his brothers, destined for the profession of religion. From his childhood, Oudoceus excelled in learning and eloquence, as well as in the purity and holiness of his life; and when Teilo visited Armorica, his virtues were shining as a burning light.[*] He attracted the especial notice of his uncle, whom he accompanied on his return to Wales; but the time when he succeeded him as bishop or archbishop of Llandaff, belongs to the next generation.[†]

Among the companions of St. Teilo, after his return from Armorica, are named Lunapeius, Gurmaet, Cynmur, Toulidauc, Luhil, and Fidelis.[‡] The orthography of their names is corrupt, and only three of them can be recognized. Toulidauc was the saint of a church, once called Llandeulydog, in the southern part of Pembrokeshire,[§] which was bestowed by Rhydderch ab Iestin on the bishoprick of Llandaff, probably on account of the connexion subsisting between Teilo and its founder. Gurmaet was the saint of a church called, in the grant of Rhydderch, " Languruaet," which was also given to the bishoprick of Llandaff, apparently for the same reason; its situation corresponds with that of Llandeilo'r Fân, Brecknockshire. Luhil was the saint of Llywel, a parish adjoining Llandeilo'r Fân, and which had three saints; the two others being David and Teilo.

Samson was the son of Amwn Ddu ab Emyr Llydaw by Anna, daughter of Meurig ab Tewdrig. As he was born in Glamorganshire,[||] his birth may be dated after the general emigration of the Armorican saints under Cadfan; and as

---

* " Ut candela supra candelabrum," is the Latin illustration.
† Vita S. Oudocei a Regesto Landavensi.
‡ Regestum Landavense.
§ Godwin's Bishops, and Myv. Archaiology, Vol. III. p. 350.
|| Regestum Landavense.

none of the before-mentioned children of Amwn Ddu* are described to have been children of Anna, it may be concluded that
Anna was a second wife of Amwn Ddu, married to him after his
arrival in Britain. The Life of this saint, in the Regestum
Landavense, contains several inconsistencies; but it may be
learned from Achau y Saint that he was a member of the
college of Illtyd, and that upon the death of Peirio he succeeded to the presidency of that society : he afterwards went
over to Armorica, where he was appointed bishop of Dole.
This last circumstance, as already shown,† has been attributed
to two other persons of the same name; and the confusion
thence arising has thrown an appearance of doubt upon the
history of the son of Amwn Ddu, for whom some writers have
claimed the rank of archbishop. The existence, however, of
Samson a bishop, whose age corresponds with the present, is
maintained upon authentic testimony; since it is shown by
Usher, from the Concilia Galliæ, that a prelate of that name
subscribed the decrees of the Council of Paris in the year 557.
That this was the person who held the see of Dole is generally
acknowledged, and the traditions of that place agree with the
Welsh authorities as to his family and connexions. But he was
only a bishop, as appears by his signature, though it is probable that he was appointed without the consent of his metropolitan; for the church of Tours, which claimed a superior
jurisdiction over Armorica, was in the country of the Franks,
and the Armoricans were at this time struggling for political
independence. Such was the view of the question given by
the clergy of Tours to the Pope, at the time Giraldus demanded the restitution of the pall to Menevia ;‡ and the explanation

* Page 218.
† Page 229.
‡ The statement made by the clergy of Tours was as follows:—
"Cum olim tota Britannia (Minor) fuisset Turonensi ecclssiæ tanquam
metropoli suæ subjecta ; Britannis tandem conspirantibus contra regem
Francorum. et proprium sibi constituentibus regem, occasione Beati Sam-

is supported by the authenticated fact that a council was held
at Tours A. D. 567, in which the archbishop of Tours was
acknowledged to be the metropolitan, and it was decreed that
no one should presume to ordain either a Briton or a Roman
to the office of a bishop in Armorica, without the consent and
permission of the metropolitan or the other bishops of the province.* The independence of Armorica seems to have been
asserted by Budic, who was the friend of Samson; but there
appears also to have been another chieftain, named Iudual or
Juthael, who was deprived of his dominions by an usurper
named Commorus, and sent a prisoner to Childebert, king of
the Franks, when the intercession of the bishop procured his
release, and he was restored to his possessions.† The Welsh
accounts proceed to say, though the reason is not explained,
that Samson returned from Armorica to the college of Illtyd,
where he died; and in the church-yard of Lantwit Major,
two large stone crosses still remain, one of them having three
several inscriptions, the first purporting that it was the cross
of Iltutus and Samson, the second that Samson erected the
cross for his soul, and the third that one Samuel was the
carver; the other cross has but one inscription, which, however, is longer and more legible than those on its neighbour,

sonis quondam Eboracensis archiepiscopi, qui dum in partibus Britanniæ
pateretur exilium, in Dolensi ecclesiâ cum archiepiscopalibus insignibus
ministrârat, Dolensis ecclesia contra Turonensem supercilium elationis
assumpsit: Britannis volentibus sibi novum archiepiscopum, sicut novum
regem creaverant, suscitare."—Usher, from the Register of Pope Innocent
III. A. D. 1199. The only error in this explanation seems to have been,
that Samson was an archbishop of York.

* In Turonensis II. hisce temporibus (anno videlicet DLXVII.) habiti
Canone IX. *Metropolitani* nomine non alium quam Turonensem archiepiscopum designatum constet; ubi cautum est, *nequis Britannum aut Ro-
manum in Armorico, sine metropolitani aut comprovincialium voluntate
aut literis, episcopum ordinare præsumat.* Usher, page 1011.

† Usher, pp. 1013, 1141.

and state that it was prepared by Samson for his soul, and for the souls of Juthael the king, and Arthmael.[*]

Tathan, in Latin Tathæus, another son of Amwn Ddu and Anna, was a member of the college of Illtyd, after which he settled at a place in Glamorganshire where he founded a church, since called Llandathan or St. Athan's. From hence he was called away to be the first president of a college or monastery at Caer-Went in Monmouthshire, under the patronage of Ynyr Gwent, to whom he became confessor. In his old age he returned to the church which he had founded, and was buried there. From the "Life of St. Tathæus" by John of Teignmouth it appears that he was patronized, not by Ynyr Gwent, but by Caradog, the son of Ynyr, which is more consistent with the chronological arrangement here adopted.

Armorica, from whence a large number of saints had emigrated in the past generation, seems now to have received a supply from Wales. The successor of Samson in the bishoprick of Dole was St. Maglorius, whose parents were Umbrafel a brother of Amwn Ddu, and Afrella a sister of Anna; he was therefore doubly related to his predecessor, whom he accompanied to that country, after having been brought up together with him in the school of Iltutus. In like manner, Machutus or Maclovius, a son of Caradog ab Ynyr Gwent by Derwela a sister of Amwn Ddu, is recorded to have passed over, and become bishop of Aletha, now St. Malo's. To the number may be added, Paulus and Leonorius, members of the college of Iltutus, the former of whom was appointed bishop of Leon. Their lives have been written by the biographers of the Gallican saints, a reference to whose works may be of service in authenticating Welsh traditions.[†]

* A facsimile of the last inscription, with an interesting account of the manner in which the cross was discovered by the late Mr. Edward Williams, may be seen in Turner's Vindication of the Ancient British Poems.

† The names of the four saints in this paragraph are in their Latin orthography.

Isan, a saint of the college of Illtyd; his genealogy is not given, but as he was a contemporary of Samson, his date may be assigned to this period. He was the founder of Llanishen, Glamorganshire, and Llanishen, Monmouthshire.

Cennydd, a son of Gildas ab Caw, was at first a member of the college of Cattwg, and afterwards the founder of a religious society, called Côr Cennydd, at a place in Gower, Glamorganshire, where the church of Llangennydd is now situated. It is said that he founded a church above Cardiff, which gave name to the district of Seinghennydd,* but it has not been identified with any of the churches at present existing in that neighbourhood.

Madog ab Gildas was a saint of the college of Cennydd, and the founder of Llanfadog, a church in the vicinity of Llangennydd.	.

Dolgan ab Gildas, a saint of the college of Cattwg.

Nwython, or Noethon ab Gildas, a member of the society of Cattwg. It is said that there were formerly chapels dedicated to him and his brother, Gwynnog, under Llangwm Dinmael, Denbighshire.†

Gwynno, or Gwynnog ab Gildas, a member of the society of Cattwg, and the patron saint of Y Faenor, Brecknockshire. Under the name of Gwynno, he is considered to have been one of the three founders of Llantrisaint, Glamorganshire; and Llanwynno, a chapel under Llantrisaint, is dedicated to him. Llanwnog in the county of Montgomery claims him for its founder under the name of Gwynnog; and in the chancel window of this church he is delineated in painted glass in episcopal habits, with a mitre on his head, and a crosier in his hand; underneath is an inscription in old English characters, "Sanctus Gwinocus, cujus animæ propitietur Deus. Amen."‡

* Cambrian Biography.
† Myvyrian Archaiology, Vol. II.
‡ Cambrian Quarterly Magazine, Vol. I.

His festival is Oct. 26; and he is not to be confounded with
Gwenog, a virgin, the saint of Llanwenog, Cardiganshire.

Tydecho ab *Gildas* appears in one catalogue of saints, probably by mistake for Tydecho, the son of Amwn Ddu.

Dolgar, a daughter of Gildas ab Caw.

Garci, the son of Cewydd ab Caw; a saint to whom it is
said there was a church dedicated in Glamorganshire.*

Tudwg, the son of Tyfodwg, was a member of the institution of Cennydd. Llandudwg, or Tythegston, subject to
Newcastle, Glamorganshire, is dedicated to him.

Daniel, who has been mentioned as being present at the
Synod of Brefi,† was no other than Deiniol Wyn, the son of
Dunawd Fyr by Dwywe, a daughter of Gwallog ab Llenog.
He assisted his father in the establishment of the monastery of
Bangor Iscoed; and it is said that in 516 he founded another
monastery in Carnarvonshire, called Bangor Deiniol and Bangor Fawr, of which he was abbot. Soon afterwards this place
was raised by Maelgwn Gwynedd to the rank of a bishop's
see, of which Deiniol was the first bishop; and as it is stated
that he received episcopal consecration from Dubricius, the
event must have occurred before the end of the year 522.
According to Geoffrey of Monmouth he died in 544.—Such is
the chronology of his life as arranged by Usher, but it depends
on the authority of writers comparatively late, and is sur-
rounded with difficulties which are fatal to its reception. It
appears from the authentic testimony of Bede that Dunawd,
the father of Deiniol, was living at the time of the conference
with St. Augustin about the year 600, a circumstance incom-
patible with the supposition that the son could have flourished
so early as 516. The poems of Llywarch Hên, a contemporary, prove that Dunawd was engaged in battle with the
sons of Urien Rheged, whose age is determined by the cir-

* Cambrian Biography.
† Page 192.

cumstance that their father was living so late as the year 560.*
Dunawd, therefore, was not a saint till near the close of the
past generation, about which time he might have founded the
monastery of Bangor Iscoed. The monastery of Bangor'
Deiniol was founded afterwards; and the situation of Deiniol
in his own pedigree assigns him to the present generation,
which agrees also with the time when Maelgwn Gwynedd, his
acknowledged patron, was at the height of his power. Stress
is laid upon this point, as it involves the date of the foundation
of the present bishoprick of Bangor; but the churches attributed to Deiniol are few, and not disposed in such a way as to
afford a criterion for ascertaining the extent of his diocese.
He was consecrated, probably, by St. David, as there is reason
to assert that he and his relatives lived for some time under
the protection of that saint at Llanddewi Brefi,† where
churches still retain their names; but the synod of Brefi and
the death of Dubricius were events which must have happened when he was a child. Few particulars of his life can be
collected, for tradition and the legendary writers have been all
but silent respecting him. It is said that he was a bard,
though none of his poems remain. He was buried in the Isle

---

* He survived Ida, the king of the Angles, whose death is placed in
559.—Compare Nennius with the Saxon Chronicle.
† Gwynfardd, enumerating the privileges of St. David at Brefi, says,
that he had the happiness—

> To have around him, about his plains,
> Men liberal and kindly disposed, and fair towns;
> He ensured protection to a quiet people,
> The tribe of Daniel, highly exalted, their equal
> Exists not, for lineage and morality and courtesy.

> A bod o'i gylchyn, cylch ei faesydd,
> Haelon, a thirion, a theg drefydd;
> A gorfod gwared lliwed llonydd,
> Llwyth Daniel oruchel, eu hefelydd
> Nid oes, yn cadw oes, a moes, a mynudydd.

of Bardsey, and his memory has been celebrated on the tenth of December. The churches founded by him were, Llandddeiniol in Cardiganshire, which is perhaps due to his connexion with St. David at Llanddewi Brefi; Llanddeiniol, or Itton, Monmouthshire; Hawarden, Flintshire; and Llanuwchlyn, Merionethshire: and the chapels under his tutelage are, Worthenbury, Flintshire, formerly subject to Bangor Iscoed, but now a separate benefice;* and St. Daniel's, subject to Monktown, Pembrokeshire.

Cynwyl, a brother of Deiniol, appears also to have lived under the protection of St. David, and has been deemed the founder of Cynwyl Gaio, the church of a parish adjoining that of Llanddewi Brefi. Another trace of this family may be found in the name of Llansawel, a chapel subordinate to Cynwyl Gaio,† which is dedicated to Sawyl,‡ the uncle of Deiniol. The churches of Cynwyl Elfed, Carmarthenshire, and Aberporth, Cardiganshire, have likewise been attributed to Cynwyl, and according to Ecton he is the patron saint of Penrhos, a chapel under Abererch, Carnarvonshire. He assisted at the establishment of the monastery of Bangor Iscoed; and his wake or saint's day is April 30.

Gwarthan, another brother of Deiniol, assisted at the establishment of the monastery of Bangor Iscoed, but nothing further is known respecting him.

Cynfelyn, a son of Bleiddyd ab Meirion of the line of Cunedda, was the founder of Llangynfelyn, Cardiganshire; and of a church at Welsh Pool, Montgomeryshire, which was probably connected with the religious society established there by his brother, Llewelyn ab Bleiddyd.

---

* Separated by Act of Parliament in the second year of William and Mary.—B. Willis.

† The Ordnance map notices an upright stone in this neighbourhood, which it calls "Crossgonwell," i. e. Croes Gynwyl, or St. Cynwyl's Cross.

‡ Page 207, *antea*.

Llewelyn ab Bleiddyd ab Tegonwy ab Teon, by mistake for Llewelyn ab Bleiddyd ab Meirion ab Tibion, is said to have founded a religious house at Trallwng, now called Welsh Pool. He ended his days in the monastery of Bardsey.

Mabon, a brother of Llewelyn, is presumed to have been the founder of Rhiwfabon, Denbighshire.

Cynudyn ab Bleiddyd ab Meirion, was a dean of the college of Padarn at Llanbadarn Fawr. Lewis Morris suggests that a stone in the churchyard of Llanwnws, Cardiganshire, with the inscription "Canotinn" was a monument to the memory of this person.*

Gwynlleu, the son of Cyngar ab Arthog of the line of Cunedda, was probably the founder of Nantgwnlle, Cardiganshire.

Eurgain, daughter of Maelgwn Gwynedd and wife of Elidyr Mwynfawr, was the foundress of Llaneurgain, or Northop, Flintshire.

Cyndeyrn or St. Kentigern, according to Bonedd y Saint was the son of Owain ab Urien Rheged and Dwynwen† the daughter of Llewddyn Lueddog of Dinas Eiddyn‡ in the north. According to John of Teignmouth he was born in North Britain, where he was placed under the instruction of Servanus, an Irish saint; and it is said that he earned the esteem of his instructor to such a degree that he was styled by him Mwyngu or "amiable," which later writers have rendered into St. Mungo, a name by which he is frequently known. When he grew up he founded the bishoprick of Glasgow, or, as the Welsh writers term the place, Penryn Rhionydd; but after a time the dissensions of his countrymen forced him to retire to Wales, where he was kindly received by St. David.

* Myv. Archaiology, Vol. II.—This stone is not noticed in Meyrick's Cardiganshire.

† John of Teignmouth calls her "Tanen."

‡ Dinas Eiddyn is almost a literal translation of Edenburgh.

While he remained in Wales he founded another bishoprick at Llanelwy* in Flintshire about A. D. 550; and though in its establishment he experienced some opposition from Maelgwn Gwynedd, that chieftain was eventually reconciled and became one of his patrons. After a few years he was recalled to his native country by " Rederech" or Rhydderch Hael, chief of the Strath Clyde Britons; and resigning the see of Llanelwy to Asaf, one of his disciples, he resumed the bishoprick of Glasgow, at which place he died at an advanced age.† He has been a great favourite with the legendary writers, who, in order to enlist his name in behalf of the prerogatives of Rome, have asserted that, being dissatisfied with the mode of his consecration, he applied to the Pope intreating his Holiness to rectify its irregularities. The following is Cressy's elucidation of the subject:—

" When he was come to an age wherein he might dispose his own actions, the man of God, Kentigern, went from his Master (Servanus) to a place called Glashu,† where he lived alone in great abstinence, untill the King and Clergy of that Region, calld then Cumbria (now Galloway) together with other Christians, who were but few, chose him for their Pastour and Bishop, notwithstanding the utmost resistance he could make. And sending for one single Bishop out of Ireland they caused him to be consecrated after the then usuall custome among the Brittains and Scotts. For at that time a practise had gott footing to use no other Ceremonies in the Consecration of a Bishop, but onely the infusion of Sacred Chrism on their heads with invocation of the Holy Spirit, benediction, and imposition of hands. For those Islanders,

---

* St. Asaph.

† There are several churches dedicated to St. Kentigern in Cumberland, which remain as monuments of the occupation of that country by the Britons.

‡ Qu. Glasgow ?

removed as it were from the World, by meanes of their continuall infestations by Pagans, were become ignorant in the
Ecclesiasticall Canons. For which reason the Law of the
Church condescended to them, and admitted an excuse in this
regard, so that Ecclesiasticall censures did not touch them.
* * * But a more authentic proof of the respect and depend-
ance which the British Churches had of the Roman cannot be
imagined, then the behaviour of S. Kentigern himself. For
being afterwards afflicted in his mind for the foresaid defects
in his Ordination, he did not seek for Counsel or remedy from
any Metropolitans in Brittany, Ireland, or France, but onely
from Rome and the Supreme Bishop thereof, to whom the
Custody of Ecclesiasticall Canons was by the Church committed, and who had authority to enjoyn the observation of
them, to punish the transgression, and to supply or dispence
with the defects either by negligence or necessity occurring
in the execution of them. This is expressly declared by John
of Tinmouth in his prosecution of the Life of S. Kentigern:
where he tells us, ' That the Man of God went seaven severall
times to Rome, where he simply and particularly layd open
his whole life, his Election, Consecration, and all the accidents
which had befalln him to S. Gregory the speciall Apostle of
the English. Upon which the Holy Pope perceiving that he
was a sincere man of God and full of the Grace of God's holy
Spirit, confirm'd his Consecration, knowing that it came from
God. Moreover at his often and earnest request, yet with
great unwillingnes, he condescended to supply those small
defects which were wanting in his Consecration, and having
done this he dismissed him to the work of the Ministry which
was enjoyned him by the Holy Ghost.'—Hence appears that
in the Ordination of S. Kentigern nothing was omitted that
was of any necessity, since it was only upon his importunity
and for satisfaction of his Scrupulosity that S. Gregory supplied the omission of certain Rites required by the Canons.
The greatest fault that the Holy Bishop could impute to him-

self, was his being consecrated by one onely Irish Bishop, against the Expresse Canon of a General Council.* But considering the unquietnes and danger of the times, and the want of Bishops, though there was a transgression of the words of the Canon, yet there was none of the mind of it, which certainly does not oblige to impossibilities."

The only authority for the narrative part of this dissertation is that of John of Teignmouth, who lived in the twelfth century; but granting that his assertions, so far as they related to St. Kentigern, were correct, it would still remain, that the mode of consecrating bishops in the British and Scottish churches was different from that practised in the Church of Rome, and that the opinions of St. Kentigern as an individual were at variance with those of his brethren. No change could have been effected by his example, for in the next century the Britons are found resolutely adhering to their peculiar customs, and refusing to hold intercourse with the Romish clergy. But it is not necessary to make so large a concession. The silence of St. Gregory and the writers of the following age, upon so important a subject, affords a strong presumption that no communication passed between him and St. Kentigern; and evidence of this kind, though negative, is of greater value than the assertions of a legend written six hundred years after the events which it pretends to describe. As for the statement upon which Cressy, presuming upon the truth of his author, lays so much stress, that the saint was consecrated by one bishop instead of three; the number would not have been so much the ground of objection as the fact that the Britons and Scots were out of the pale of the Church of Rome, that the consecrations of their bishops, and consequently the

---

* "The first Canon of the Apostles, confirmed by many Councils, enjoyn'd that every Bishop should be ordained by at least two or three Bishops: Whereas S. Kentigern was consecrated by one single Bishop, and him a stranger of a forrain Nation."—Cressy.

titles of their inferior clergy, were not considered valid by the
Catholics. Between the years 664 and 669, St. Chad, a bishop
of the Anglo-Saxons, was consecrated by a Romish, or as it
was then termed, a canonical bishop, assisted by two British
bishops; and the reason for this expedient was the circumstance that there was at that time but one Catholic bishop in
all Britain.* It was afterwards determined, that in consequence of the British bishops assisting, the ceremony was
invalid; and St. Chad was prepared to resign his office, when
in consideration of his humility and submission, Theodore,
who had then been appointed archbishop of Canterbury, con-
sented to grant him a fresh consecration.† In the same interval, Wilfrid, archbishop of York, undertook a journey to
Gaul, "rather than be consecrated by prelates not in communion with Rome as the Britons and Scots, or by those who
agreed with schismatics."‡

Asaf was the son of Sawyl Benuchel and Gwenaseth daughter of Rhufon Rhufoniog. He was the disciple of Cyndeyrn,

---

* "Diverterunt ad provinciam Occidentalium Saxonum, ubi erat Vini
Episcopus; et ab illo est vir præfatus (Ceadda) consecratus Antistes,
adsumptis in societatem ordinationis duobus de Brittonum gente Episcopis,
qui Dominicum Paschæ diem, ut sæpius dictum est, secus morem canoni-
cum a quartâ decimâ usque ad vicesimam Lunam celebrant. Non enim
erat tunc ullus, excepto illo Vine, in totâ Britanniâ canonicè ordinatus
Episcopus."—Bede, Lib. III. Cap. 28.

† "Itaque Theodorus perlustrans universa, ordinabat locis opportunis
Episcopos, et ea quæ minus perfecta reperit, his quoque juvantibus corri-
gebat. In quibus et Ceadda Episcopum cum argueret non fuisse ritè con-
secratum, respondens ipse voce humillimâ: 'Si me, inquit, nôsti Episcopatum non ritè suscepisse, libenter ab officio discedo: quippe qui neque
me unquam hoc esse dignum arbitrabar; sed obedientiæ causâ jussus
subire hoc, quamvis indignus consensi.' At ille audiens humilitatem res-
ponsionis ejus, dixit, non eum Episcopatum dimittere debere; sed ipse
ordinationem ejus denuo Catholicâ ratione consummavit."—Bede, Lib. IV.
Cap. 2.

‡ Eddius, Vita Wilfridi, apud Gale.

2 I

whom he succeeded about A. D. 560 in the bishoprick of
Llanelwy, which from this circumstance has ever since been
known in English by the name of St. Asaph, though in Welsh
it retains its original appellation. Asaf is also known as the
founder of the church of Llanasa in Flintshire.

Pedrog, according to Bonedd y Saint, was the son of Clement prince of Cornwall; but Cressy insists that he was born
of princely parentage in Wales. Usher makes it appear that
he was contemporary with St. Kentigern. He was the founder
of the churches of Llanbedrog, Carnarvonshire, St. Petrox,
Pembrokeshire, and of several others in Cornwall and Devon,
of which counties he may be considered the tutelar saint. He
was buried at Bodmin, where, according to some authorities,
he had established a bishoprick.

Cybi was the son of Selyf ab Geraint ab Erbin, and as his
mother was Gwen, daughter of Gynyr of Caer-gawch, he must
have been a cousin and contemporary of St. David, though apparently some years younger. If the verses, said to have been
written by Aneurin or Cattwg Ddoeth, upon the departure of
the saints for Bardsey, can be trusted, Cybi was present at the
Synod of Brefi;* and it may be said that the memory of his
presence is preserved in the name of the church of Llangybi
in the immediate neighbourhood of Llanddewi Brefi. He was
also the founder of Llangybi near Caerleon, which confirms
the probability that he was acquainted with St. David. But
he is more especially distinguished as the founder of a religious
society at Caergybi or Holyhead in Anglesey, near to the spot
where Caswallon Lawhir had slain Serigi, over whose grave a
chapel was afterwards erected. As Cybi was the president of
his society, he was, according to the usual practice of the
times, styled a bishop, though he never held jurisdiction over
a diocese. The anachronism which places him in the fourth

* See Myv. Archaiology, Vol I. p. 181, and Vol. III. p. 3. but the verses
are too modern for the authors assigned.

century and makes him acquainted with St. Hilary, Bishop of
Poictiers, may be attributed to the circumstance that one of
his contemporary saints in that island was called *Elian*, a name
which the Welsh give also to St. Hilary. Besides the churches
already mentioned, Cybi was the founder of Llangybi in Carnarvonshire. Festival, Nov. 6.

According to tradition Cybi and Elian used to meet at a
place called Llandyfrydog, between Llanelian and Holyhead,
to confer upon subjects of religion. A similar story is told of
Cybi and Seiriol of Penmon, who used to hold weekly meet-
ings at Clorach near Llannerch y Medd. "From the circumstance of Seiriol travelling westward in the morning and east-
ward in the evening, and Cybi on the contrary always facing
the sun, they were denominated ' Seiriol Wyn a Chybi Felyn,
—Seiriol the Fair, and Cybi the Tawny." These stories,
though obviously fabulous, are chronologically consistent, as
the three saints, according to their genealogy, were living at
the same time.

Elian Geimiad was the son of Gallgu Rieddog ab Carcludwys of the line of Cadrod Calchfynydd, and his mother was
Canna, a daughter of Tewdwr Mawr o Lydaw and widow of
Sadwrn. The epithet Ceimiad (pilgrim) has by one writer[*]
been changed into Cannaid (bright) to correspond with the
Latin Hilarius; but the conjecture was unnecessary, as the
sound of the name Elian, which the Welsh have thought convertible with Hilary,[†] is sufficient to account for the confusion.
Elian is celebrated in the superstitions of the Principality;
miraculous cures were lately supposed to be performed at his
shrine at Llanelian, Anglesey;[‡] and near to the church of
Llanelian, Denbighshire, is a well called Ffynnon Elian,
which is thought by the peasantry of the neighbourhood to

---

[*] The author of a "History of Anglesey."
[†] In the Welsh Calendar, St. Hilary is called Elian Esgob.
[‡] History of Anglesey, 1775.

be endued with miraculous powers even at present. His wake is held in the month of August, while the festival of St. Hilary occurs on the thirteenth of January.

Beuno was the son of Hywgi or Bugi ab Gwynllyw Filwr and Perfferen daughter of Llewddyn Luyddog of Dinas Eiddyn in the North. He was, therefore, nearly related to Cattwg and Kentigern, with the latter of whom he was contemporary. Few particulars of his life are known, though it must have extended into the following century, as it is recorded that he founded a religious society at Clynnog Fawr in Carnarvonshire in 616. The land, upon which the college or monastery of Clynnog was built, was granted by Cadfan, the reigning prince of North Wales, to whom St. Beuno gave a small golden sceptre as an acknowledgement for the donation. He was in his old age one of the instructors of Gwenfrewi or St. Winefred; his festival is April 21; and the churches and chapels dedicated to him are the following :—

Berriew, alias Aber-rhiw, V. Montgomeryshire.
Bettws, V. Mont.
Llanycil, R. Merionethshire.
Gwyddelwern,* R. Merioneth.
Clynnog Fawr, R. Carnarvonshire.
Carngiwch, a chapel to Edeyrn (St. Edeyrn,) Carn.
Pistyll, a chapel to Edeyrn (St. Edeyrn,) Carn.
Penmorfa, R.—1 chapel, Dolbenmaen (St. Mary,) Carn.
Aberffraw, R.—1 chapel, *Capel Mair* (St. Mary,) Anglesey.
Trefdraeth, R.—1 chapel, Llaugwyfen (St. Cwyfen,) Anglesey.
Llanfeuno, a chapel to Clodock (St. Clydog,) Herefordshire.

Cannen, the son of Gwyddlew ab Gwynllyw Filwr, is presumed to have been the founder of Llanganten, near Builth, Brecknockshire.

Gwodloew, the son of Glywys Cerniw ab Gwynllyw Filwr, is said to have been at first a teacher in the college of Cattwg, and afterwards bishop of Llandaff; but the last assertion is

* Built by St. Beuno on land granted to him by Cynan ab Brochwel Ysgythrog, prince of Powys.—Cambrian Register, Vol. I.

incorrect, as " Guodloiu" in the catalogue of bishops of Llan-daff* must have lived at an age too late for the son of Glywys Cerniw.

Meugan or Meigant, a son of Gwyndaf Hên ab Emyr Llydaw and Gwenonwy the daughter of Meurig prince of Glamorgan, was originally a member of the college of Iltutus, from whence he removed to the college of Dubricius at Caer-leon, of which society his father was the president. In his old age he retired to Bardsey, where he died. He may be deemed the founder of Llanfeugan, Brecknockshire ; and the chapels consecrated to his memory are St. Moughan's under Llangattwg Feibion Afel, Monmouthshire ; and Capel Meu-gan, formerly subject to Llandegfan, Anglesey. Two poems, composed by Meugan, who is thought to have been the same person as the saint, are inserted in the Myvyrian Archai-ology.

Melangell, the daughter of Tudwal Tudglyd of the line of Macsen Wledig, was the foundress of Pennant Melangell,† Montgomeryshire. She was a sister of Rhydderch Hael of Strath Clyde ; and her mother was Ethni, surnamed Wydd-eles or the Irish-woman. Festival, May 27.

Dingad, the son of Nudd Hael of the line of Macsen Wledig, is called a saint, but no churches are ascribed to him. His wife was Tonwy or Trefrïan, a daughter of Llewddyn Luyddog of Dinas Eiddyn.‡

Llidnerth ab Nudd, a brother of Dingad, and a saint.

---

* He is the eleventh bishop in Godwin's list, and is mentioned as con-temporary with Maredudd, king of Dyfed, about A. D. 790.

† " It is distinguished from other Pen Nants by the addition of *Melangell*, i. e. *Monacella*, the patron saint, whose Latin Legend is still extant; her history is also rudely sculptured on the gallery of the church; and several of her relics are still (1811) shown to the credulous, who happen to visit this sequestered spot. The cell of *Diva Monacella* is in a rock near the church."—Carlisle's Topography.

‡ Page 261, *antea.*

Clydno Eiddyn, Cynan, Cynfelyn Drwsgl, and Cadrod, sons of Cynwyd Cynwydion of the line of Coel Godebog, were chieftains of North Britain, who are said to have embraced a religious life.*

Cawrdaf, the son of Caradog Fraichfras of the line of Coel, succeeded his father as sovereign of Brecknockshire, and is distinguished in the Triads for his extensive influence, for whenever he went to battle the whole population of the country attended at his summons.† He is said to have embraced a religious life in the college of Illtyd; and Llangoed, a chapel subordinate to Llaniestin, Anglesey, is dedicated to him in conjunction with his brother Tangwn. It has been suggested that the name of Llanwrda, Carmarthenshire, is derived from Cawrdaf,‡ though the more obvious meaning of the word is "the church of the holy man," without intending to describe any particular saint. The festival of St. Cawrdaf is Dec. 5; while the wake of Llanwrda depends upon Nov. 12, or All Saints' Day, Old Style.

Cadfarch, a brother of Cawrdaf, was the founder of Penegos, Montgomeryshire, and Abererch, Carnarvonshire. Festival, Oct. 24.

Tangwn, brother of Cawrdaf, was one of the saints to whom Llangoed, Anglesey, is dedicated.

Maethlu or Amaethlu, brother of Cawrdaf, the founder of Llanfaethlu, Anglesey, and possibly of Llandyfalle, Brecknockshire. The syllable dy is introduced into the last name upon the same principle as Llandyfaelog is formed from Maelog; both the names so formed occur in Brecknockshire, while the corresponding appellations in Anglesey omit it.§ Festival, Dec. 26.

---

* Cambrian Biography, voce Cynwyd Cynwydion.
† Triad 41, Third Series.
‡ Jones's Brecknockshire, Vol. I. p. 70.
§ Page 231, antea.

Tewdwr Brycheiniog, the son of Nefydd ab Nefydd Ail ab Rhun ab Brychan, a saint of whom nothing more is known than his pedigree.

Ciwg, the son of Aron ab Cynfarch of the line of Coel, was the founder of Llangiwg, commonly called Llanguke, in Glamorganshire.

Elaeth, sometimes styled Elaeth Frenhin or "the king," was the son of Meurig ab Idno of the tribe of Coel, and Onen Grêg, a daughter of Gwallog ab Llenog. In the former part of his life he was a chieftain in the North, from whence he was driven by a reverse of fortune to spend the remainder of his days in the college of Seiriol in Anglesey, and he is also considered to have been the founder of the church of Amlwch in that county. He was a bard, and a few religious stanzas attributed to him are preserved in the Myvyrian Archaiology. Festival, Nov. 10.

Saeran, a saint, is said to have been the son of Geraint, surnamed Saer, or "the artisan," of Ireland. He was buried at Llanynys, Denbighshire, from which circumstance that church has been thought to have been dedicated to him; but its original founder, according to Llywarch Hên, was Mor ab Ceneu ab Coel. According to Usher, *Kieranus filius artificis* was an eminent saint who founded the bishoprick of Cloyne in Ireland between the years 520 and 550; and the similarity of the names suggests the idea that he was the same person as Geraint Saer, the father of Saeran, in which case the Welsh appellation ought to have been written Geraint *ab y* Saer.

The period just passed over includes the principal part of the lives of Aneurin, Taliesin, Llywarch Hên, and Myrddin, four bards, of whose compositions a very considerable portion has remained to posterity; and rude and obscure as these poems may seem to a modern reader, they should be received with the indulgence due to their antiquity, for they are perhaps the earliest specimen of a vernacular literature possessed

by any of the existing nations of Europe.   They are, however,
not destitute of the spirit of poetry, and their violation of the
rules of criticism is amply compensated by their value as historical records ; for they abound in allusions to passing events,
and when their scattered notices are collected together and
embodied, an interesting dissertation may be written upon the
history and manners of the times. The names of several other
bards of this date are preserved, whose works are entirely lost.
But the question more deeply interesting to the ecclesiastical
historian, as well as to the best feelings of the Christian, is—
Did the Welsh at this early age possess, in their own language,
a version of any part of the sacred Scriptures?   Without an-
swering this question absolutely in the negative, it may be
said that no traces of such a version have yet been discovered,
and it is to be feared that in this respect the British Church
was not so highly favoured as the Anglo-Saxon.*   But the
disadvantages of the former will appear much lessened when it
is remembered that the Latin language must have been known in
Wales to a considerable extent; for the Britons had formed a part
of the Roman empire, from which they had not been separated a
full century before the establishment of the monastic institutions
so often noticed ; and if the system of instruction adopted in
those communities was conducted in Latin, as was the case in
similar institutions on the continent, it must have had a
powerful tendency to preserve the knowledge of a language,
in which the government of the people had so lately been
administered.

---

* About the year 706, Aldhelm, the first bishop of Sherborne, translated
the Psalter into Saxon: and at his earnest persuasion, Egbert or Eadfrid,
bishop of Lindisfarne, or Holy Island, soon afterwards executed a Saxon
version of the four Gospels. Not many years after this, the learned and venerable Bede, who died A. D. 735, translated the entire Bible into that language.

SECTION XII.

The Welsh Saints from the Death of Maelgwn Gwynedd A. D. 566 to the close of the Sixth Century.

THE princes of North Wales in this interval were successively Rhun ab Maelgwn, Beli ab Rhun, and Iago ab Beli;* but according to Geoffrey of Monmouth the sovereignty of the Britons was assumed by Ceredig, a man of turbulent disposition, who was perpetually engaged in feuds with other chieftains, by which the nation was so much weakened that it could oppose but a feeble resistance to the Saxons, from whose ravages it suffered to a degree unprecedented; and though the bards and genealogists mention nothing of Ceredig, sufficient evidence may be gathered from their testimony to show that their countrymen were at this time harassed with intestine warfare. The Saxons also, as may be learned from their own accounts, had pushed their conquests so far as the Severn, and founded the kingdom of Mercia, the last and most extensive of the states of the Heptarchy. Under these circumstances it cannot be surprising that the saints of this period are few, and the information to be gleaned respecting them, though at all times meagre, is henceforward exceedingly scanty. Tradition loves to dwell on the events of prosperity, and nations, like individuals, are not fond of recounting their ill-successes.

* Maelgwn Gwynedd must have lived to a great age, for his generation properly belongs to the commencement of the century. Rhun, Beli, and Iago, (who are respectively his son, grandson, and great-grandson,) followed in rapid succession, and it is agreed that Cadfan, his descendant in the fourth degree, commenced his reign soon after the year 600.

2 K

The bishop who presided over the see of Llandaff was
Oudoceus, of whom it was asserted in the middle ages, that he
made an acknowledgement of submission to St. Augustin,
archbishop of Canterbury, and received consecration at his
hands ;* but the legend, for it deserves no better name, is so
contrary to authentic history and inconsistent with the state of
the Welsh Church for two centuries after the time of Oudoceus, that it does not require a serious refutation.   Had the
early Catholic writers of this island† been able to prove that a
Welsh bishop had submitted to Canterbury, they might have
gained a political purpose and terminated an important ecclesiastical controversy ; but they invariably describe the British
Christians as holding no communion with the Anglo-Saxons,
and celebrating the passover without fellowship with the
Church of Christ.‡   The memory of Oudoceus has been held
in great reverence at Llandaff, where he has had the honour of
ranking with Dubricius and Teilo as one of the patron saints
of the cathedral.   His commemoration is July 2.

Ceneu, the bishop of Menevia contemporary with Oudoceus,
was the founder of Llangeneu, a church which once existed in
Pembrokeshire, but the settlement of the Flemings in that
county has obliterated all traces of its situation.§

Lleuddad, called also Llawddog, the son of Dingad ab Nudd
Hael and Tefrian or Tonwy a daughter of Llewddyn Luyddog ; he ended his days in the Isle of Bardsey, and is sometimes

* Liber Landavensis.

† Aldhelm, Eddius, and Bede.

‡ The first instance of submission to Canterbury, that can be authenticated, happened between the years 871 and 889, when Lwmbert or Hubert
Sais, bishop of St. David's, and Cimeliauc or Cyfelach, bishop of Llandaff, were consecrated by Ethelred, its eighteenth archbishop. The
second instance of submission on the part of the bishops of St. David's did
not occur before the eleventh century.—Compare the Welsh Chronicles
with the notes to the Latin edition of Godwin's Bishops.

§ It is noticed in the Laws of Hywel Dda. Myv. Archaiology, Vol. III.

confounded with Lleuddad, the companion of Cadfan, who was at least half a century older. The chapel of Llanllawddog under Abergwyli, Carmarthenshire, is dedicated to the son of Dingad, who was also the founder of Cenarth, and Penboir, Carmarthenshire, and Cilgerran, Pembrokeshire. Festival Jan. 15.

Baglan, a son of Dingad, was the saint to whom Llanfaglan under Llanwnda, Carnarvonshire, and Baglan under Aberafon, Glamorganshire, are dedicated.

Gwytherin ab Dingad, the founder of a church called Gwytherin in the county of Denbigh, at which place Gwenfrewi or St. Winefred was afterwards buried.

Tygwy ab Dingad, a saint to whom Llandygwy or Llandygwydd, Cardiganshire, is ascribed.

Tyfriog, otherwise Tyfrydog, ab Dingad, the founder of Llandyfriog in the county of Cardigan, which has also been called Llandyfrydog.

Eleri, daughter of Dingad, a saint who lived at Pennant in the parish of Gwytherin, Denbighshire.

Aelhaiarn, a son of Hygarfael ab Cyndrwyn of Llystinwennan in Caereinion, Montgomeryshire. He was the founder of Llanaelhaiarn, Merionethshire, and Cegidfa or Guilsfield in the county of Montgomery. Festival, Nov. 1.

Llwchaiarn, another son of Hygarfael; the patron saint of Llanllwchaiarn and Llanmerewig, Montgomeryshire, and of Llanychaiarn, and Llanllwchaiarn, Cardiganshire.* Festival, Jan. 11.

Cynhaiarn, brother of Llwchaiarn, a saint to whom Ynys Cynhaiarn, a chapel under Cruccaith, Carnarvonshire, is dedicated.

---

* Llanmerewig was formerly a chapel to Llanllwchaiarn, its neighbour; and Llanychaiarn, Cardiganshire, was subject to Llanbadarn Fawr in the same county.

Tyfrydog, the son of Arwystli Gloff ab Seithenin and Ty-
wynwedd daughter of Amlawdd Wledig; he was the founder
of Llandyfrydog, Anglesea.   Festival, Jan. 1.

Twrnog or Teyrnog, brother of Tyfrydog; Llandyrnog,
Denbighshire, is attributed to him.

Tudur, brother of Tyfrydog, a saint to whom Darowain,
Montgomeryshire, is attributed.   Mynyddyslwyn, Monmouthshire, is ascribed by Ecton to St. Tudur, but it is doubtful
whether the same person is intended.   Festival, Oct. 15.*

Dier or Diheufyr, a brother of Tyfrydog, and founder of
Bodfari in Flintshire.   He is called Deiferus in the legend of
St. Winefred.

Marchell, a sister of Tyfrydog, the foundress of Ystrad
Marchell in Montgomeryshire, where an abbey was afterwards
built, called Strata Marcella.   Capel Marchell under Llanrwst
is called after her name.

Ufelwyn, or as he is styled in Latin, Ubilwynus, the son of
Cennydd ab Aneurin y Coed Aur, was the founder of a church
in Glamorganshire called Llanufelwyn; the situation of which
seems to correspond with St. George's near Cardiff, as in the
division of the county upon the settlement of the Normans,
the lordship of St. George, which was granted by Robert
Fitzhammon to John Fleming, is sometimes called the lordship
of Llanufelwyn.†   Ufelwyn succeeded St. Oudoceus as bishop
of Llandaff.‡

Ffili, the son of Cennydd ab Gildas§ y Coed Aur; a saint

---

* The wake at Darowain is held eleven days afterwards. See page 240.
† Myv. Archaiology, Vol. II. p. 526.
‡ It is not known who was the successor of Ufelwyn, as, according to
the Chronicle of Caradog, Aidan, the next bishop in Godwin's list, was
slain by the Saxons in the year 720, a full century after the age of Ufelwyn; but the lists of bishops of Llandaff and St. David's are very corrupt
between the sixth and ninth centuries.
§ "Gildas"—the same person as Aneurin in the notice of the preceding
saint.—See page 225.

to whom it is said the church of Rhos Ffili in Gower, now
known by the name of Rhos Sili, is dedicated.*

Tyssilio, the son of Brochwel Ysgythrog ab Cyngen ab
Cadell and Arddun daughter of Pabo Post Prydain, is said to
have been bishop of St. Asaph ; and according to the situation
which he occupies in his pedigree he must have been the immediate successor of Asaf, to whom he was cousin in the first
degree. His father, Brochwel, was the reigning prince of
Powys ; and Cynddelw, a bard of the twelfth century, adverts
with pride to the circumstance that the saint was "nobly descended of high ancestry."† The life of Brochwel, which
extends beyond the usual period, was protracted to the next
generation, but the military affairs of the province were already administered by Cynan Garwyn, one of his sons, who
shared largely in the feuds of the times, and a poem of Tal-
iesin‡ describes his victorious career along the banks of the
Wye, in the Isle of Anglesey, on the hills of Dimetia, and in
the region of Brychan ; chieftains trembled and fled at his
approach, and he slaughtered his enemies with the gory blade.
On the other hand, the pursuits of Tyssilio, independently of
his profession, were of a peaceable nature. He was a bard,
and is reported to have written an ecclesiastical history of
Britain, which is now lost, though it is alleged to have been
preserved in manuscript so late as the year 1600.§ It has
been said that the fabulous Chronicle of the Kings of Britain,
edited by Walter de Mapes and afterwards amplified by Geoffrey of Monmouth, was originally compiled by Tyssilio; but it
is now generally agreed that the statement is unfounded, and
the Chronicle contains a heap of extravagant fables respecting

* Cambrian Biography. Qu. From whom does Caerffili derive its
name?

† " Mat ganet o genedyl voned."—Myv. Archaiology, Vol. I. p. 244.

‡ Trawsganu Cynan Garwyn. Myv. Archaiology, Vol. I. p. 168.

§ Correspondence of the late Rev. Evan Evans (Prydydd Hir,) published
in the Cambrian Quarterly, Vol. I. p. 396.

Arthur which no historian would have ventured to publish as
belonging to an age immediately preceding his own, when
existing facts and the memory of persons living might have
contradicted him.   According to Browne Willis, the churches
and chapels, which own Tyssilio for their patron saint, are :—

Meifod, V. Montgomeryshire.
Llandyssilio, a chapel to Llandrinio (St. Trinio,) Mont.
Llandyssilio, C. Denbighshire.
Bryn Eglwys, C. Denb.
Llandyssilio, a chapel to Llanfair Pwll Gwyngyll (St. Mary,)
Anglesey.
Llandyssilio yn Nyfed, V. Carmarthenshire.
Llandyssilio Gogof, V.—1 chapel, Capel Cynon (St. Cynon,) Car-
diganshire.
Sellack, V. (in the Diocese of Hereford.)—3 chapels, King's Cha-
pel (St. John the Baptist,) Marstow (St. Martin,) and Pencoed (St.
Dennis,) Herefordshire.

To these should be added Llansilio near Longtown in the
county of Hereford, as shown by the obvious signification of
the name, though it is commonly said to be dedicated to St.
Peter; but this is one of the numerous instances in which
British saints have given way to others approved of by the
Saxons and Normans.   The bard Cynddelw, enumerating the
churches founded by Tyssilio, says—

A church* he raised with his fostering hand,
Llanllugyrn, with a chancel for the offertory ;
A church beyond the floods, by the glassy streams ;
A church filled to overflowing, by the palace of Dinorben ;
A church in Armorica, through the influence of his liberality ;
The church of Pengwern, the best upon the earth ;
A Church of Powys, the paradise of bliss ;
The church of Cammarch (he raised) with a hand of respect for
its owner.

---

* Llan a wnaeth a'i lawfaeth lofien,   Llan Llydaw gan llydwedd wohen ;
Llanllugyrn, llogawd offeren ;   Llan Bengwern, bennaf daearen ;
Llan tra llyr, tra lliant wydrlen ;   Llan Bywys, Baradwys burwen ;
Llan drallanw, dra llys Dinorben ;   Llangammarch, llaw barch el berchen.
                                         Myv. Archaiology, Vol. I. p. 245.

The bard then proceeds to celebrate the praises of Meifod, about which he is more diffuse but equally obscure.* Llan-llugyrn, literally—the church of war-horns, is probably Llan-llugan in Montgomeryshire: of the church in Armorica† nothing is known: Pengwern is the ancient name of Shrews-bury, where Brochwel is said to have resided, and which town was long afterwards considered the capital of Powys: the church of Cammarch is Llangammarch in Brecknockshire, of which Tyssilio may have been the second or assistant founder, as it is acknowledged that Cammarch was already its owner: and the other churches, which are vaguely described without their names, may be some of those included in the list from Browne Willis. Tyssilio seems to have founded religious edifices beyond the limits of his diocese, taking advantage probably of his brother's conquests; and there is an unusual proportion of saints from Powys in this generation, which in-dicates the ascendancy of that province; its prosperity, how-ever, was reduced upon the defeat of the Britons by Ethelfrith at the battle of Bangor Iscoed. The memory of St. Tyssilio has been celebrated on the eighth of November.

Gwrnerth, the son of Llewelyn ab Bleiddyd of Trallwng or Welsh Pool, is said to have been a saint; and a religious dialogue in verse between him and his father, Llewelyn, is inserted in the Myvyrian Archaiology, the composition of which is attributed to St. Tyssilio.

---

* One of the designations, which he applies to Meifod, is—"the abode of the three saints" (trefred y triseint;) and it is singular that its church-yard once contained three churches, all standing at the same time, the oldest was named after St. Gwyddfarch, the next after St. Tyssilio, and the third, which was consecrated in the year 1155, was dedicated to St. Mary.—See also Cambrian Quarterly Magazine, Vol. I. p. 321.

† The expression—"Llydaw" in the original, here translated Armorica, may perhaps be an appellative, meaning *maritime*, as explained in Dr. Pughe's Dictionary; and if so, the description is applicable to Llandyssilio Gogo in Cardiganshire.

Mygnach, the son of Mydno of Caer Seont or Carnarvon, was for some time the registrar of the college of St. Cybi at Holyhead, and afterwards became the principal of that society.* A dialogue in verse between him and Taliesin is published in the Myvyrian Archaiology.

Cedwyn, the son of Gwgon Gwron ab Peredur of the line of Coel; he has been accounted the patron saint of Llangedwyn, a chapel under Llanrhaiadr, Montgomeryshire.

Gwrfyw, the son of Pasgen ab Urien Rheged; a saint, to whom it is said there was a church dedicated in Anglesey; there was also a chapel called after his name at Bangor Uwch Conwy in Carnarvonshire.†

Mor, another son of Pasgen ab Urien; a saint, who was buried in the Isle of Bardsey.

Mydan ab Pasgen ab Urien, a member of the congregation of Cattwg.

Lleminod Angel ab Pasgen ab Urien, a saint.

Mechydd, a saint, was the son of Sandde Bryd Angel ab Llywarch Hên.

Buan, the son of Ysgwn ab Llywarch Hên, was the founder of Bodfuan, Carnarvonshire, and his festival has been held on the fourth of August.

Cathan or Cathen, the son of Cawrdaf ab Caradog Fraichfras, was the founder of Llangathen, Carmarthenshire. The Hundred of Catheiniog in the same county is supposed to derive its name from him. Festival, May 17.

Medrod and Iddew brothers of the preceding, have been ranked among the saints; the resemblance of the names induced the compilers of the Triads to confound them with Medrod and Iddog Corn Prydain, the leaders of the conspiracy which proved fatal to Arthur.

Elgud, a saint, the son of Cadfarch ab Caradog Fraichfras.

---

* Cambrian Biography.
† Myv. Archaiology, Vol. II. and Cambrian Biography.

Cynddilig, a son of Cennydd ab Gildas; his memory has been celebrated in the parish of Llanrhystud, Cardiganshire, on the first of November.

The last holy person, whose life may be assigned to this generation, is Deiniolen, or Deiniol ab Deiniol Ail, called also Deiniol Fab. He was a son of Deiniol, the first bishop of Bangor in Carnarvonshire; and a grandson of Dunawd, the founder of the monastery of Bangor Iscoed in Flintshire. It is recorded that he was a member of the society of Bangor Iscoed under the presidency of his grandfather, and after the destruction of that institution he retired to Bangor in Carnarvonshire, where he became the president of a similar society which had been established by his father, and of which his father had been the first abbot;*—the younger Deiniol, therefore, succeeded to the monastic honours of the elder, but whether he succeeded also to his father's bishoprick is left unexplained. It is stated that he founded the church of Llanddeiniolen in the county of Carnarvon in the year 616.† His festival has been celebrated on the twenty third of November; and Llanddeiniol Fab, a chapel under Llannidan, Anglesey, has been called after his name.

If the Welsh Church, in the period just concluded, was depressed by adverse circumstances, it is a gratification to learn that the Churches of the Scots were flourishing. St. Columba had already founded the monastery of Iona,‡ and his disciples were now engaged in diffusing the blessings of Christianity to the dark corners of the Highlands and Western Isles. The light of the Gospel had also dawned upon the Saxons. St. Augustin had landed in Kent,§ and laid the foundation of a mission, one of the most successful that have appeared since the age of the Apostles; for in less than a century after its commencement, the whole nation of

---

* Page 258, *antea*.   † Cambrian Biography.
    ‡ A. D. 565.   § A. D. 597.

2 L

the Saxons and Angles became, at least nominally, Christian. The instruments, however, in effecting the principal part of this conversion were the monks of Iona,* the conflict between whom and the clergy of Rome is an irrefragable proof of the independence of the primitive Churches of Britain; and it is not unreasonable to suppose that from this source the Anglo-Saxons derived their notions of religious liberty, for they never acknowledged an entire submission to the Pope before the Norman Conquest, and even afterwards their allegiance was badly sustained.†

* Bede, Lib. III. 3, 4.
† Soames's Anglo-Saxon Church,—and Southey's Book of the Church.

SECTION XIII.

The Welsh Saints from A. D. 600 to the Death of Cadwallon A. D. 634.

IAGO ab Beli, the last prince of North Wales mentioned in the preceding period, was killed in the year 603, when he was succeeded by his son, Cadfan ab Iago, who, upon the departure or expulsion of Ethelfrith from Powys, became the Pendragon or chief sovereign of the Britons, but the duration of his reign and the year of his death are uncertain. His honours were continued to his son, Cadwallon* ab Cadfan; who, soon after the assumption of his power, was defeated by Edwin, king of Northumbria, driven from his dominions, and forced to seek an asylum in Ireland, where he remained seven years. Upon his return, be formed an alliance with Penda, king of Mercia; and joining their forces, they marched to Northumbria, where Edwin was totally routed, himself slain, and most of his army destroyed. Cadwallon continued his victorious course; several of the princes of the Angles fell into his hands, and were put to death;† such indeed were his successes, that it was believed

---

* This name has been variously written; Bede spells it *Caedualla*; Nennius, *Catgublaun*; the Saxon Chronicle, *Ceadwalla*; and the Welsh writers, *Cadwallon* and *Katwallawn*: and though the identity of the person may be clearly proved, it is necessary to observe these particulars to distinguish him from Cadwaladr, and from another Caedualla or Ceadwalla, a king of the West Saxons; all of whom, inasmuch as they lived within a short time of each other, have been frequently confounded together.

† That Cadwallon struck terror into the nation of the Angles is evident from the manner in which Bede describes the havock which he committed, as if he ravaged the country, slaughtering its inhabitants without regard

the time had arrived when the Britons should expel the Saxons
and Angles, and be restored to the entire possession of the
island. Their good fortune, however, received a sudden check.
Cadwallon was defeated by Oswald the Bernician, and killed
in battle.* The return of the Britons to their ancient possessions never became probable again.

St. Augustin had gained a firm footing in Kent, and was
extending his mission to other parts of the island, when he
undertook the design of bringing the Britons to a conformity
with the Church of Rome, and reducing them under his own
jurisdiction. The following is the narrative of his attempt, as
extracted from the works of Bede:†—

" In the mean time, Augustin, availing himself of the assistance of king Ethelbert (Ædilberct,) summoned to a conference
the bishops or doctors of the nearest province of the Britons,
at a place which is still called in the language of the Angles
Augustinaes ac, or the Oak of Augustin,‡ on the confines of the
Huiccii and West Saxons: and he began to advise them with
brotherly admonition, that they should enter into a Catholic
peace with himself, and undertake for their Lord the common
labour of preaching the Gospel to the heathen. For they were
not accustomed to celebrate the feast of the Passover of our
Lord at its proper time, but from the fourteenth to the twentieth day of the moon, a computation which is comprised in a

---

to age or sex, putting women and children to a cruel death with the feroci-
ty of a brute: Penda, that author says, had not embraced Christianity; but
Caedwalla, though a Christian, was a barbarian more savage than a
pagan.—Lib. II. 20, and III. 1.

* Bede, Nennius, and the Triads.—Caradog of Llancarvan, and the followers of Geoffrey of Monmouth, whose account of Cadwallon is as
fabulous as any part of his history, place the death of that prince in 660,
while Bede, who was almost a contemporary, fixes it in the year 634—
See also Turner's Anglo-Saxons, Book III. Chap. VII.

† Hist. Eccl. Lib. II. Cap. II.

‡ Situated apparently, within the modern county of Worcester.

cycle of eighty four years; and they were wont to perform
many other things also contrary to the unity of the Church.
Who, after holding a long dispute, were not willing to give
assent to the entreaties, the exhortations, and the rebukes of
Augustin and his friends, but preferred their own traditions
rather than those of all the churches which throughout the
world agree in Christ. The holy father, Augustin, therefore
put an an end to this laborious and long debate, by saying :—
'We pray God, who hath made men to be of one mind in the
house of their father, that he vouchsafe to signify to us by
signs from heaven, which traditions must be followed, by what
way we must hasten to the entrance of his kingdom. Let
some sick person be brought; and by whosesoever's prayers
he shall be healed, let the faith and service of that man be
acknowledged as devoted to God and be followed by all.'—
To which proposal, when the adversaries, though unwillingly,
had agreed, a certain person of the nation of the Angles, deprived of the sight of his eyes, was produced; who, when
presented to the priests of the Britons, obtained no cure or
recovery by their ministry, until Augustin, forced by the
necessity of the case, bent his knees to the father of our Lord
Jesus Christ, praying that he would restore to the blind that
sight which he had lost, and by the bodily illumination of one
man would kindle the grace of spiritual light in the hearts of
many believers. Without delay the blind receives his sight,
and Augustin is proclaimed by all to be the true herald of
light from heaven. Then indeed the Britons confessed that
the true way of righteousness was that which Augustin
preached, but they could not renounce their ancient customs
without the consent and permission of their countrymen.
Whence they demanded that a second Synod should be held,
at which a greater number of persons should meet."

"Which being appointed, there came, as they relate, seven
bishops of the Britons, and many very learned men, principally from their most famous monastery, called in the

language of the Angles *Bancornaburg*,* over which Dinoot,†
the Abbot, is said to have presided at that time; who, being
about to attend the Council just mentioned, came first to a
certain holy and prudent man, who was wont to lead the life
of an anchorite in that country, to consult him whether they
should forsake their traditions at the preaching of Augustin.
He answered, 'If he be a man of God, follow him.' They
said, 'Whence shall we prove this?' He replied, 'The Lord
hath said, Take my yoke upon you and learn of me, for I am
meek and lowly in heart. If therefore Augustin is meek and
lowly in heart, it is to be expected that, because he bears himself the yoke of Christ, he will offer it to be borne by you;
but if he is not meek but proud, it is clear that he is not of
God, his speech is not to be regarded by us.' They said
again, 'And whence shall we discover this also?' He said,
'Contrive that he come first, with his friends to the place of
the Synod; and if he shall rise when you approach, hearken
to him obediently, knowing that he is the servant of Christ;
but if he shall despise you, and be not willing to rise in your
presence when you are more in number, then let him be despised by you.'—They did as he had said, and it was brought
to pass, that when they came, Augustin continued to sit in his
chair. Seeing which, they were soon moved to anger, and
charging him with pride strove to contradict every thing
which he said. But he told them, 'Since in many things ye
act contrary to our custom, and even to that of the universal
Church, yet if ye will obey me in these three points; that ye
celebrate the Passover at its proper time; that ye perform the
service of Baptism, by which we are born again to God, after
the manner of the holy Roman and Apostolic Church; and
that ye preach with us the word of God to the nation of the
Angles; as for the other things which ye do, although con-

---

* Bangor Iscoed.
+ Dunawd. See page 206.

trary to our customs, we will bear them all with patience.'
But they answered that they would perform none of these,
neither would they have him for an archbishop; considering
among themselves, that if he would not rise up to them at
that time, how much more would he despise them if they
became subject to him."

"To whom, Augustin, the man of God, is said to have foretold in a threatening tone, that because they would not have
peace with brothers, they should have war with enemies; and
if they were unwilling to preach to the nation of the Angles
the way of life, by their hands they should suffer the vengeance
of death. Which, by the agency of divine judgment, was so
performed in all respects as he had foretold."

"Since after this, Ethelfrith *(Aedilfrid,)* the most powerful
king of the Angles, having collected a large army, made a
very great slaughter of that perfidious race, at the city of
Legions, which is called by the people of the Angles *Legacaes-
tir,** but by the Britons more properly *Carlegion.* And when,
being about to give battle, he saw, standing by themselves in
a place of greater safety, their priests who had come to pray
to God for the soldiers engaged in the war, he enquired who
were those, and for what purpose they had come thither?
But most of them were from the monastery of *Bancor,* in which
the number of monks is said to have been so great, that when
the monastery was divided into seven classes, with superintendents set over them, none of those classes contained less
than three hundred men, all of whom were accustomed to live
by the labour of their own hands. Most of these therefore,
having performed a fast of three days, had come together, with
others, to the before-mentioned field for the sake of prayer,
having a defender, by name *Brocmail,*† to protect them while
intent upon their prayers from the swords of the barbarians.

---

* The present town of Chester, which the Welsh still call Caerlleon.
† Brochwel Ysgythrog. Seè page 208.

When king Ethelfrith understood the cause of their arrival,
he said, ' Then if they cry to their God against us, surely even
they, although they do not bear arms, fight against us when
they oppose us with their hostile prayers.' He then ordered
his arms to be turned against them first, and afterwards destroyed the other forces of that impious war, not without great
loss in his own army. They relate that there were killed in
that battle about twelve hundred men of those who had come
to pray, and that only fifty escaped by flight. Brocmail and
his troops, upon the first approach of the enemy, turned their
backs, and left those, whom he ought to have defended, unarmed and naked to men who fought with swords. And thus
was accomplished the prediction of the holy pontiff Augustin,
although he had long before been raised to a heavenly kingdom ; so that by the vengeance of a temporal death the perfidious people might perceive, that they had despised the
counsels of everlasting salvation, which had been offered to
them."—

Such is Bede's description of this memorable controversy,
the several clauses of which have been variously interpreted
according to the bias of different commentators ; some Protestants, in their zeal against Popery, contending that the
Britons differed from the Romish Church in doctrine, as well
as in discipline and ecclesiastical government; while certain
Roman Catholic writers insist, that not only was there no
difference in matters of faith, but that the apparent refusal of
submission to the Pope extended merely to their rejection of
Augustin for their archbishop, as if they were unwilling to be
subject to Rome through *him* as an intermediate prelate.* The
question may however be fairly balanced.† The points in
dispute regarded only discipline, rituals, and ecclesiastical
government ; for no difference in doctrine is mentioned, and

* Butler's Book of the Roman Catholic Church, Letter IV.
† Soames's Anglo-Saxon Church ; and Europe in the Middle Ages, by
S. A. Dunham, Vol. III.

if any had existed to a material degree, Augustin would not
have desired them to join him in preaching to the Saxons.*
Bede is not explicit as to the reason why the Britons refused
to accept Augustin for their archbishop, nor does it appear
how this point was introduced to their consideration; but the
differences in discipline and ritual are the proof that they did
not acknowledge the jurisdiction of the Pope. No fact is
more clearly asserted than that the Britons were not in communion with the Catholic Church, for it is repeated throughout the Ecclesiastical History of Bede, who was himself a
Catholic. The Catholics treated the British people as schismatics and heretics, and maintained that the consecration of
their bishops was invalid; while the Britons on the other
hand regarded the Romish clergy as unclean, and refused to
eat or hold intercourse with them until they had first under-
gone a purification;† and it is a singular argument in confirmation of British independence, that whenever terms of
reconciliation were offered, the Britons refused them, proving
that their separation was the effect of choice, and not an in-
voluntary exclusion.

It is to be regretted that the Welsh have not preserved any
authentic detailed account of these Councils, by which the
question of the archbishoprick, which Bede has not sufficiently
explained, might be placed beyond dispute. The chronicles
of Walter de Mapes and Geoffrey of Monmouth have endeavoured to supply the deficiency; and a speech, alleged to
have been taken from an ancient manuscript, has been repeat-
edly printed, purporting to be the reply of Dunawd, the
Abbot, to Augustin; in which the supremacy of the Pope is

* Milner, in his Church History, treats the case of the Britons most un-
fairly; and in his eagerness to shew that the doctrine of Gregory and
Augustin was orthodox, he insinuates that the former retained some of the
leaven of Pelagianism. Their opponents, and Bede amongst the rest,
would not have been slow to advance the charge if it were true.

† Aldhelm's Letter to Geruntius.

2 M

positively denied, and it is declared that the Britons acknowledged no spiritual ruler under heaven superior to the bishop
of Caerleon. Unfortunately the language and style of this
speech,* as well as the manner in which its subject is treated,
are too modern to allow its genuineness; and the preservation,
during many centuries of Catholic ascendancy, of a document,
in which the claims of the Pope are so openly impugned,
presents a difficulty not easily overcome. Walter and Geoffrey
state that Dunawd was the leader of the opposition to Augustin, and, without alluding to the Pope, assert that the
ground of the refusal of the Britons to submit to the jurisdiction of Canterbury, was the circumstance that they had an
archbishop of their own at Caerleon. These authors, however,
whose testimony is always of little value, wrote when the papal
power was at its height; and the only authority, upon which
any arguments relative to the subject can be founded, is that
of Bede, who lived while the separation alluded to still con-

* It is thus printed in Spelman's Concilia, from the MS. of Peter Mos-
tyn, Gent.—"Bid yspys a diogel i chwi, yn bod ni holl un ac arall yn
uvydd ac ynn ostyngedig i Eglwys Duw ac i'r Paab o Ruvain, ac i boob
kyur grissdion dwyuol, i garu pawb yn i radd mewn kariad perffaith, ac i
helpio pawb o honaunt a gair a gweithred i fod ynn blant i Dduw: Ac am-
genach ufudddod no hwn nid adwen i vod ir neb ir yddych chwi yn henwi
yn Baab ne yn Daad o daade, yw gleimio ac yw ovunn: Ar uvydddod
hwn ir yddym ni yn barod yw roddi ac yw dalu iddo ef, ac i bob Krisdion
yn dragwyddol. Hevyd ir ydym in dan lywodraeth Esgob Kaerllion ar
wysg yr hwn ysydd yn olygwr dan Dduw arnom ni y wneuthud i ni gadwyr
ffordd ysbrydol."—*Translation.* Be it known and certain to you, that
we are, all and singular, obedient and subject to the Church of God, and
to the Pope of Rome, and to every true and pious Christian, to love every
one in his degree with perfect charity, and to help every one of them by
word and deed to become the sons of God: and other obedience than this
I do not know that he whom you name the Pope, or the father of fathers,
can claim and require: but this obedience we are ready to pay to him and
to every Christian for ever. Moreover we are under the government of the
bishop of Caerleon upon Usk, who is superintendent under God over us to
make us keep the spiritual way.

tinued, and who could not in his time foresee the
effect which his admissions might have upon the question of
the supremacy of Rome as maintained at a later age.   He says
nothing of an archbishoprick of the Britons; the claims of
Augustin are rejected without noticing the rights of a rival
metropolitan; and the inferences presented by the Welsh
records would show that the dignity once assumed by the
prelates of Caerleon and Menevia had become extinct, if indeed
it had ever been firmly established.* Its continuance at the
time of the Council must have produced a collision with the
pretensions of Augustin, which it would have been disingenu-
ous in Bede to pass unobserved, and its extinction is the most
obvious mode of explaining the incidental manner in which
the subject is introduced. The plea, upon which submission
was refused, is therefore incorrectly stated by Walter and
Geoffrey. It was not a dispute respecting the rights of two
intermediate prelates, but the rejection of an archbishop sent
by the Pope.

That St. Gregory designed that the jurisdiction of Augustin
should extend over the bishops of Wales is indisputable, for in
answer to one of the questions of his missionary he says:—
" We commit to thee, our brother, all the bishops of the provinces of Britain, that the unlearned be instructed, the weak
be strengthened by persuasion, the perverse be corrected by
authority."†—Here is no recognition of the rights of a British
metropolitan. It was the intention of that Pontiff that there
should be two archbishopricks in the island, London and York,
the archbishops of which places should take precedence of
each other by priority of consecration; but in reference to
Augustin, with whom this ecclesiastical polity should com-

---

* See page 174.

† " Britanniarum vero omnes Episcopos tuæ fraternitati committimus, ut
indocti doceantur, infirmi persuasione roborentur, perversi auctoritate cor-
rigantur."—Bede, Lib. I. Cap. 27.

mence, he says, as his words may be literally rendered;—
" And thou, our brother, shalt have in subjection, not only
those bishops whom thou shalt ordain, nor those only who shall
have been ordained by the archbishop of York, but also all
the clergy of Britain, by the authority of our Lord Jesus
Christ."*—These were the commissions to which the bishops
and clergy of Wales refused to submit, and the same independence was maintained by the Christians of Cornwall and
Scotland.   Augustin had asked whether his jurisdiction extended to Gaul, a concession which St. Gregory declined to
grant, because the Popes, his predecessors, had from ancient
times sent a pall to the archbishops of Arles, who by virtue of
its possession were the metropolitans of that country ;† but as
there was no similar reason for abridging the authority of that
prelate in Britain, the inference remains, that none of the
British Christians had received that emblem of dignity ; the
prerogative of their Churches had never been sanctioned at
Rome; and now, when it was intended they should merge into
the Church of the Angles, they maintained their separate existence in spite of a papal decree.

The names and titles of the seven bishops who attended the
second Council are not specified, and later writers,‡ who differ
considerably with each other, have endeavoured to point out
the seven dioceses to which they belonged.   The bishopricks
regularly established in Wales were five, Menevia or St. Da-

* "Tua vero fraternitas non solum eos Episcopos quos ordinaverit, neque hos tantummodo qui per Eburacæ Episcopum fuerint ordinati, sed
etiam omnes Britanniæ Sacerdotes habeat, Deo Domino nostro Jesu Christo
auctore, subjectos."—Bede, Lib. I. Cap. 29.

† " In Galliarum Episcopis nullam tibi auctoritatem tribuimus: quia ab
antiquis prædecessorum meorum temporibus Pallium Arelatensis Episcopus accepit, quem nos privare auctoritate perceptâ minimè debemus."—
Bede, Lib. I. Cap. 27.

‡ Roger Hoveden, Bale, and the Archives of Menevia.—They are compared with each other in Spelman's Concilia, and Usher, Chap. V.

vid's, Llandaff, Llanbadarn, Bangor, and St. Asaph.   To these
may be added Gloucester, where according to the Welsh genealogies a British bishop resided about this time.   The seventh
must be left to conjecture; but as the Cornish or Western
Britons must have had several native prelates in this age, and
it has been asserted that there was a British bishop in Somerset so late as the reign of king Ina,* the distance of their
country from the place of meeting is not too great to suppose
that some one of them was present.   The most probable date
of the two Councils, for both are believed to have been held in
the same year, is 603.   Augustin died in 605; and the battle
of Chester, or as the Welsh have named it "the battle of the
Orchard of Bangor," appears to have been fought in 607.
Several modern commentators have charged Augustin with
instigating the inhuman slaughter of the monks which ensued
upon the last occasion, and to minds impressed with this idea
it would seem as if the assertion of Bede, that he was dead
long before,† arose from a solicitude to clear the archbishop
from a suspicion which that author knew was attached to him.
But the text warrants no such uncharitable inferences.   The
solicitude of Bede, who does not regard the slaughter of the
monks as a crime, but rather applauds it as the just judgment
of heaven, was merely to establish the credit of Augustin as a
prophet, by proving that he was not a party to the fulfilment
of his own predictions.   The threat of the archbishop was
only the ebullition of disappointment; the invasion of Wales

* A. D. 688 to 725.—The authority for this statement is a Chronicle of
Glastonbury quoted by Usher, who says it was written in 1259.—Brit.
Eccl. Primordia, Cap. V.

† "Ipso jam multo ante tempore ad celestia regna sublato."—As there
is nothing answerable to these words in King Alfred's Anglo-Saxon translation it has been conjectured by some that they are an interpolation; but
Dr. Smith, the editor of Bede, observes they are to be found in all the
Latin MSS. extant, and that the work of Alfred, being a paraphrase, has
other similar omissions.

by Ethelfrith was one of the casual operations of war; and the massacre of the monks was owing to the accident of their appearance on a neighbouring hill; for had the invasion been made for the purpose of exterminating them, would Ethelfrith have inquired ignorantly who they were, and what were they doing? He then puts them to the sword, because they were praying to their God for his defeat. Ethelfrith was a pagan, and therefore could feel no interest in a religious controversy between Christians; he was a Northumbrian, and came from a province of the Anglo-Saxons the most remote from the influence of Augustin; in short, he was the chief of the only province in the nation which refused to acknowledge the sovereignty of Ethelbert,* the patron of the archbishop.

The destruction of the monastery of Bangor Iscoed followed the massacre of its members, and the calamity must have caused a great diminution in the number of the Welsh Saints; but the national Church soon afterwards underwent a more general depression owing to the conquests of Edwin, who for a short time reduced the whole of the Britons under his sway;† and Wales, which had so often afforded an asylum to the religious of other parts, was in turn exposed to the ravages of the Saxons. From these the re-appearance of Cadwallon procured a short respite, but the interval was spent in retaliation, and little attention appears to have been paid to the duties of religion and peace. The few holy persons of this generation, whose names have reached posterity, must now be noticed.

Grwst, the son of Gwaith Hengaer ab Elffin ab Urien Rheged, and Euronwy the daughter of Clydno Eiddin; he is the

---

* This fact, which Bede (Lib. II. Cap. V.) discloses without reference to the disputed question, overthrows the assertions of Walter and Geoffrey that Ethelbert was the person who influenced Ethelfrith to invade and murder the British ecclesiastics.

† Bede, Lib. II. Cap. V. & IX.

reputed founder of Llanrwst, Denbighshire, and his festival
has been held on the first of December.

Nidan, the son of Gwrfyw ab Pasgen ab Urien, was an
officer in the college of Penmon, Anglesey; and the church of
Llannidan in the same county was named after him.[*] Festival,
Sept. 30.

Cadell, the son of Urien Foeddog ab Rhun Rhion ab Llywarch Hên; a saint to whom Llangadell, a church formerly in
Glamorganshire, was dedicated.

Dyfnog, the son of Medrod ab Cawrdaf ab Caradog, was
probably the second saint of Dyfynog, Brecknockshire,
which was originally founded by Cynog ab Brychan. Festival, Feb. 13.

Cynhafal, the son of Elgud ab Cadfarch ab Caradog Fraichfras and Tubrawst daughter of Tuthlwyniaid;[†] he was the
founder of Llangynhafal, Denbighshire, and has been commemorated on the fifth of October.

Gwenfrewi, or St. Winefred, owes her celebrity more to the
well that is called after her name than to any thing that is said
of her in Bonedd y Saint; for even her parentage is not mentioned in the Welsh accounts, and the time in which she lived
is ascertained only from the names of her contemporaries
which occur in her legendary Life. The Legend says that
" Theuith," a powerful man, the son of " Eluith," gave Beuno
a spot of ground for the erection of a church, and appointed
him to be the religious instructor of his only daughter, Winefred. Caradog, the son of Alan, a neighbouring chieftain,
endeavoured to force the chastity of Winefred, upon which she
fled towards the church of Beuno. In her flight, however,
she was overtaken, when—" the young man mad with lust and
rage presently strook of her head :[‡] and immediatly in the
place where it fell to the earth a most pure and plentifull

* Cambrian Biography.   † Bonedd y Saint.
        ‡ *Literatim* from Cressy.

Spring gushed forth, which flowes to this day, and by the
Holy Virgins merits gives health to a world of diseased persons. It being in the steep descent of a hill where the Virgins
head was cutt of, it lightly rouling down to the bottom, slidd
into the Church: whereas the body remaind in the place
where it first fell. The whole congregation there attending
to Divine Mysteries were wonderfully astonished to see the
Head tumbling among their feet, detesting the crime of the
murderer, and imprecating divine vengeance on him. But
the parents of the Virgin broke forth into tears and sad com-
plaints. They all went out, and found the murderer near the
liveles body, wiping his sword on the grasse."—Beuno takes
the head of the Virgin in his hands and pronounces a curse
upon the young man, who immediately gives up the ghost and
his corpse vanishes out of sight.—" But the man of God often
kissing the head which he held in his hands could not refrain
to weep bitterly. Afterwards ioyning it to the body, and
covering it with his mantle, he returned to the Altar, where
he celebrated Masse."—He then preaches a sermon over the
body, and intreats the congregation to unite with him in
prayer for the restoration of the Virgin.—" This Prayer being
ended, to which all the people cryed aloud, Amen: the Virgin presently rose up, as if from sleep, cleansing her face from
the dust and sweat, and filled the Congregation with wonder
and ioy. Now in the place where the head was reioyned to
the body there appeared a white Circle compassing the neck,
small as a white thread, which continued so all her life, shew-
ing the place where the Section had been made. And the
report in that countrey is that from that white circle she had
the name of Winefrid given her, whereas at first she had been
called Breuna: For in the British language Win signifies
White. And moreover the Tradition is, that after her death
whensoever she appeared to any, that White mark was always
visible. The place where her blood was first shed was not
much distant from a Monastery in North Wales calld Basing-

werk: The name of it formerly was, The dry vale, but after her death to this day it is called Saint Winefrids Well. The Stones likewise, both where the spring gushes forth, and beneath in the Current, having been sprinkled with her blood, retain the rednes to these times: which colour neither the length of so many ages, nor the continuall sliding of the water over them, have been able to wash away, and moreover a certain Mosse which sticks to the said stones, renders a fragrant odour, like Incense."*—The Legend proceeds to relate her interviews with Diheufyr, Sadwrn, and Eleri; and to say that she became abbess of a convent at " Witheriacus" (Gwytherin in the county of Denbigh,) where she died and was buried near the graves of the saints Cybi and Sannan. The eldest authority for this nonsensical fable is Robert, Prior of Shrewsbury, who says that the body of " Wenefreda" was translated from Gwytherin to the church of St. Ægidius at Shrewsbury in the reign of King Stephen.† But it is remarkable that in the survey of Domesday Book, which includes the county of Flint, neither church, chapel, nor well of St. Winefred are mentioned, affording a presumption that the story and celebrity of the saint are of a later date than the Norman Conquest.‡ Festival, Nov. 3.

Enghenel, grandson of Brochwel Ysgythrog; a saint to whom Llanenghenel under Llanfachraith, Anglesey, is dedicated.

Usteg, the son of Geraint ab Carannog, of the line of Cadell Deyrnllug, is said to have " officiated as dean of the college of Garmon.."§

* Cressy.   † Leland, Vol. IV. Appendix.

‡ This argument, the want of ancient testimony, did not shake the faith of Cressy, who says—" It ought not to be esteemd a prejudice or ground of suspicion of the Truth of these Gests of Saint Winefride, that Saint Beda and some other of our ancient Saxon Historians have not mentioned her among the other Saints of this age ;"—for no intercourse passed between the Britons and Saxons who were continually at war.

§ Cambrian Biography.

Eldad, a brother of Usteg, was a saint of the society of Illtyd, and afterwards bishop of Gloucester, where he was slain by the Saxons.

Another Eldad, the son of Arth ab Arthog Frych, and a descendant of Cynan Meiriadog, was a member of the college of Illtyd about the same time.

Egwad, a son of Cynddilig ab Cennydd ab Gildas; he was the founder of Llanegwad and Llanfynydd, Carmarthen-shire.

Edeyrn, the son of Nudd ab Beli ab Rhun ab Maelgwn Gwynedd, was a bard, who embraced a life of sanctity, and the chapel of Bodedeyrn under Holyhead is dedicated to him. Some pedigrees say that the father of Edeyrn was Beli, omitting Nudd. Festival, Jan. 6.

Padrig, the son of Alfryd ab Goronwy ab Gwdion ab Don; a saint of the monastery of Cybi at Holyhead, and the founder of Llanbadrig in Anglesey.

Idloes, the son of Gwyddnabi ab Llawfrodedd Farfog Coch; the founder of Llanidloes, Montgomeryshire.

Sadwrn, who is mentioned in the Legend of St. Winefred, is considered to be the patron saint of Henllan in the county of Denbigh, but his genealogy is not known.

Helig Foel, the son of Glanog ab Gwgan Gleddyf Rhudd ab Caradog Fraichfras, was the chieftain of a tract of low land on the coast of Carnarvonshire, called Tyno Helig; where a calamity similar to the reported submersion of Can-tref y Gwaelod* is said to have happened, and the lands overflowed form the present Lafan Sands in Beaumaris Bay. After the loss of his property Helig embraced a religious life, and has in consequence been classed among the saints, but no churches are dedicated to him.   His grandfather was engaged in the in the battle of Bangor Iscoed, A. D. 607.

* Page 234.

SECTION XIV.

The Welsh Saints from the Death of Cadwallon A. D. 634 to the Death of Cadwaladr A. D. 664.

CADWALADR, whose reign is commensurate with this interval, was the son of Cadwallon, and was the last of the Welsh nation who assumed the title of chief sovereign of Britain.* His power, however, was narrowly circumscribed, and in the early part of his reign he must have held the situation of a dependent prince; for Oswald the Bernician, upon the conquest and death of Cadwallon, is said to have extended his government over all the Britons as well as the Saxons.† After a few years Penda the Mercian revolted, and Oswald was slain in battle; upon which occasion it would appear the Welsh recovered their independence, as it is not recorded that Oswy, who succeeded Oswald as Bretwalda or chief sovereign of the Saxons, exercised the same authority over the Britons. It is generally agreed that Cadwaladr was of a peaceable diposition; his life passed without any remarkable events; and the venerable historian of the Anglo-Saxons, who lived in the next generation, does not mention his name. In the year 664 a plague broke out, which spread desolation over Britain and Ireland, and in the latter country, where it lasted three years, is swept away two thirds of the inhabitants.‡ In Britain its continuance was much shorter, but great numbers perished,‖ and Cadwaladr was one of its victims.§

* " A Phrydein dan un paladyr
    Goreu mab Kymro Katwalatyr."
          Kyvoesi Myrdin: Myv. Arch. Vol. I. page 140.
† Bede II. 5, and III. 6.   ‡ Annals of Ulster.   ‖ Bede, III. 27.
                § Nennius apud Gale.

The chronicles of Walter and Geoffrey terminate with the
death of this prince and the appointment of his successor, but
they terminate in a way worthy of their previous character;
for having begun and continued a course of fable, which has
too long usurped the place of history, they end in a blunder.
According to them the plague lasted eleven years, and mis-
placing the age of Cadwaladr they assert that to avoid its
ravages he retired to the court of Alan, the king of Armorica.
He was hospitably received, and after a while was preparing
to return, when an angel appeared, commanding him to re-
linquish his purpose and undertake a pilgrimage to Rome.
Resigning his kingdom, therefore, in favour of Ifor, his son,
he proceeded to Rome, where having been admitted among
the saints by Pope Sergius, he died on the twelfth of May,
688.*—Persons acquainted with the history of the Anglo-
Saxons will immediately perceive that Walter and Geoffrey
have confounded their hero with Ceadwalla the king of Wessex,
who resigned his kingdom, and making a pilgrimage to Rome
was baptized there by Pope Sergius, where he died on the
twelfth of the calends of May, 688.†—The story is true as
regards Ceadwalla, for it is related by Bede, who was his contemporary and who could not have mistaken a circumstance
affecting the government of one of the most powerful of the
Saxon states. Walter and Geoffrey were deceived by the
sound of the name; and three other chroniclers in the Myvyrian Archaiology‡ have followed in the wake of the error, by
assigning the true history of Ina, the king of Wessex and
successor of Ceadwalla, to Ifor, the supposed successor of Cadwaladr. A notion prevailed in the beginning of the twelfth

---

* Myv. Archaiology, Vol. II. page 388.

† So in the Saxon Chronicle. Bede is more precise, and though he admits
that Ceadwalla resigned his kingdom in 688, he says he did not reach
Rome till the year following, when, after receiving baptism, he died on the
day of the month above stated.

‡ Vol. II. p. 470.

century, and is embodied in certain fictitious prophecies of Myrddin,* that Cadwaladr should re-appear and expel the Saxons from the island, restoring the Cymry to their ancient possessions; but nothing is said of his visit to Rome or even to Armorica, and if the words of Nennius,† the oldest authority by whom he is noticed, be rightly interpreted, he must have died of the plague in his own country. He has had the credit of sanctity, an honour apparently of modern growth, and the epithet of " Bendigaid" or " Blessed" is frequently attached to his name. In the Triads he is called one of the three canonized kings of Britain. According to tradition he rebuilt the church of Eglwys Ael in Anglesey, where his grandfather, Cadfan, had been buried, and which after its restoration obtained the name of Llangadwaladr. He is deemed the patron saint of Llangadwaladr alias Bishopston, Monmouthshire, and of Llangadwaladr under Llanrhaiadr in Mochnant, Denbighshire, and his festival occurs on the ninth of October.‡

The inundation which formed the Lafan Sands, already alluded to,‖ appears to have occurred in this generation, while Helig was still living; his sons, upon the loss of their patrimony, embraced a monastic life in the colleges of Bangor Deiniol§ and Bangor Enlli;* their names were:—

* Myvyrian Archaiology, Vol. I. p. 145.

† " Verba ejus hæc sunt :—'Osquid *(Oswy)* filius Eldfrid *(Ethelfrith)* regnavit XXVIII annis et VI mensibus; dum ipse regnabat, venit mortalitas hominum, Catgualat (*al.* Catgualiter) regnante apud Britones post patrem suum, et in eâ periit.'—Si autem hæc verba—' in eâ periit,'—ad Cadwaladrum referenda sunt, omnia plana erunt. Oswius enim vixit annius V (*rectius* VI) post A. D. DCLXV (*rectius* DCLXIV) in quo mortalitas illa accidit."—Æræ Cambrobritannicæ, accurante Mose Gulielmo, published at the end of Humphrey Llwyd's Britannicæ Descriptionis Commentariolum. London, 1731.

‡ Alphabetical Calendar in Sir H. Nicolas's Chronology of History.

‖ Page 298.

§ Bangor in Carnarvonshire. * The Monastery of Bardsey.

Aelgyfarch, and Boda, saints.

Brothen, the founder of Llanfrothen, Merionethshire. Festival, Oct. 15.

Bodfan, the patron saint of Aber, or Abergwyngregyn, Carnarvonshire. Festival, June 2.

Bedwas, possibly the person from whom a church so called in Monmouthshire has derived its name.

Celynin, the founder of Llangelynin, Merionethshire. Festival, Nov. 20.

Brenda, Euryn, and Gwyar; sons of Helig, and saints.

Gwynnin, the patron saint of Llandygwynnin, Carnarvonshire; commemorated Dec. 31.

Peris, described as "a saint and cardinal of Rome;"—the description is probably a mistake, but it is the only instance admitted in Bonedd y Saint of connexion with the papal see. He was the founder of Llanberis, Carnarvonshire; and Llangian, a chapel under Llanbedrog in the same county is dedicated to him in conjunction with Cian, who was his servant. The memory of Peris has been celebrated on the twenty sixth of July, and that of Cian on the eleventh of December.*

Rhychwyn ab Helig, the patron saint of Llanrhychwyn, a chapel under Trefriw, Carnarvonshire. Festival, June, 10.

Other holy persons, who flourished about this time, were:—

Dona, the son of Selyf ab Cynan Garwyn ab Brochwel; the founder of Llanddona, Anglesey. His wake is November 1.

Collen, the son of Gwynog of the line of Caradog Fraichfras; or, according to some, the son of Petrwn ab Coleddog ab Rhydderch Hael. He was the founder of Llangollen, Denbighshire, and has been commemorated on the twentieth of May.

---

* Cambrian Register, Vol. III.

Edwen, a female saint of Saxon descent, who has been allowed a place among the saints of Wales. She is said to have been a daughter or niece of Edwin, king of Northumbria; and the statement derives probability from the circumstance admitted by the English historians, that Edwin was brought up in the court of Cadfan, king of North Wales, at Caerseiont or Carnarvon.* Llanedwen in Anglesey is dedicated to her, and her festival has been kept on the sixth of November.

* Bonedd y Saint.　Myv. Archaiology.

SECTION XV.

The Welsh Saints from the Death of Cadwaladr A. D. 664 to the End of the Seventh Century, including those of uncertain date.

LITTLE is known of the history of this time, and it forms almost a blank in Welsh tradition. The nominal sovereigns of Wales were successively a son of Cadwaladr, named Idwal Iwrch, and Hywel ab Cadwal,* the latter of whom was succeeded by Rhodri Molwynog in 720.

The saints who may be assigned to this generation are :—

Egryn, the son of Gwrydr Drwm ab Gwedrog of the line of Cadell Deyrnllug. He was the founder of Llanegryn, Merionethshire.

Cwyfen, the son of Brwyno Hên ab Dyfnog ; a descendant of Caradog Fraichfras, and the founder of Llangwyfen, Denbighshire. Tudweiliog, Carnarvonshire, and Llangwyfen a chapel under Trefdraeth, Anglesey, are dedicated to him. His mother was Camell of Bodangharad in Coleion, Denbighshire. Festival, June 3.

"Baruck," a saint who is not mentioned in the Welsh accounts, but according to Cressy he was—"a Hermite, whose memory is celebrated in the Province of the Silures and region of Glamorgan. He lyes buried in the Isle of Barry, which took its name from him."—"In our Martyrologe," adds that author, "This Holy Hermit Baruck is said to have sprung from the Noble Blood of the Brittains, and entring into a solitary strict course of life, he at this time (A. D. 700) attained to a life immortall." Festival, Nov. 29.

* Kyvoesi Myrdin. Myv. Archaiology, Vol. I. p. 140.

Degeman, in Latin Decumanus, a holy person, of whom Cressy says that he was " born of Noble parents in the South-Western parts of Wales, and forsaking his countrey the more freely to give himself to Mortification and devotion, he passed the river Severn upon a hurdle of rodds, and retired himself into a mountainous vast solitude covered with shrubbs and briars, where he spent his life in the repose of Contemplation, till in the end he was slain by a murderer."—According to Camden, he was murdered at a place called St. Decombe's in Somersetshire, where a church was afterwards raised to his memory. He is the patron saint of Rosecrowther in the county of Pembroke; and of Llandegeman, an extinct chapel in the parish of Llanfihangel Cwm Dû, Brecknockshire. He died A. D. 706, and has been commemorated on the twenty seventh of August.

The Primitive Church of Wales continued to maintain its existence, but the above are its last saints of whom any account has been preserved. In the latter part of the next century the Welsh were forced to adopt the Catholic computation of Easter, and thereby to join in communion with the church of Rome. Since that time, only five Welshmen have obtained the honours of sanctity, including Elfod or Elbodius, the prelate through whose exertions the change alluded to was effected.* The other four were:—Sadyrnin, bishop of St. David's, who died A. D. 832; his name is borne by the church of Llansadyrnin in Carmarthenshire:—Cyfelach, bishop of Llandaff from about the year 880 to 927; he probably gave his name to the church of Llangyfelach, Glamorganshire, the original founder of which was St. David:—Caradog, a hermit of Haroldston East, Pembrokeshire, and patron saint of Law-renny in that county; he was canonized by the Pope at the solicitation of Giraldus Cambrensis:†—Gwryd, a friar, who

* See page 66 of this Essay.
† Wharton's Anglia Sacra, Vol. II.

lived about the end of the twelfth century and has been commemorated on the first of November.* There are, however,
several saints whose genealogy is lost or imperfect, and therefore
their era cannot be determined ; but it may be presumed that
they belonged to the Primitive rather than the Catholic Church,
as the names of only two Welshmen, who can be proved to
have lived after the conversion of their country to Catholicism,
have been given to religious edifices on the score of saintship ;
Lawrenny does not appear to have borne the name of St. Caradog, though dedicated to him, and no churches have been
called after Elbodius and Gwryd. The following is an alphabetical list of the saints of uncertain date, with their churches
and festivals.†—

Aelrhiw ; Rhiw, Carnarvonshire ; Sept. 9.

Amo or Anno ; Llananno, Radnorshire ; and Newborough,
anciently Llananno, Anglesey.‡

Bach ab Carwed, a chieftain ; reported to have been the •
founder Eglwys Fach,§ Denbighshire.

Caron, a bishop ; Tregaron, Cardiganshire, March 5.

Cedol ; Pentir chapel, alias Llangedol, subject to Bangor,
Carnarvonshire, Nov. 1.

Celer, a martyr ; Llangeler, Carmarthenshire.

Cennych ; Llangennych, Carmarthenshire.

---

* Cambrian Register, Vol. III. p. 221; where it is said that he relieved
Einion ab Gwalchmai of some oppression, probably mental, which had
afflicted him for seven years. Einion ab Gwalchmai was a bard who
flourished between A. D. 1170 and 1290.

† Some of the names in the Myvyrian Archaiology, which are not supported by a reference to MSS. but seem to be conjectured from the names
of churches, are omitted in this list. Some of the names in the Cambrian
Biography are also omitted, which appear to be various readings of MSS.
through the carelessness of transcribers.

‡ Myv. Archaiology, Vol. II. p. 28.

§ The compiler of Bonedd y Saint in the Myvyrian Archaiology adds—
" If the story be true" (os gwir y chwedl;) the obvious signification of
Eglwys Fach is " the small church."

Ciwa; Llangiwa, Monmouthshire.

Cloffan; Llangloffan, Pembrokeshire.

Cofen; Llangofen, Monmouthshire; and St. Goven's chapel, Pembrokeshire.

Curig Lwyd, a bishop, probably of Llanbadarn Fawr; he was the founder of Llangurig, Montgomeryshire, and his crosier was preserved in the neighbouring church of St. Harmon's in the time of Giraldus Cambrensis. There was another Curig or Cyrique, a saint of Tarsus in Cilicia, who was martyred while an infant at the same time with his mother, Juliet or Julitta. Llanilid a Churig,* Glamorganshire, and "Capel Curig a'i fam Iulita,"† Carnarvonshire, are dedicated to Juliet and Cyrique together. Juliet is also the saint of Llanulid under Dyfynog, Brecknockshire. It is uncertain to which of the persons named Curig, the churches of Porth Curig, Glamorganshire, and Eglwys Fair a Churig, Carmarthenshire, are dedicated. The festival of Juliet and Cyrique is June 16.

Cwyfyn, the son of Arthalun of the vale of Achlach in Ireland.

Cwynrau.

Cynfab; Capel Cynfab formerly in the parish of Llanfair ar y Bryn, Carmarthenshire. Nov. 15.

Cynfarwy; the son of Awy ab Llênog, a prince of Cornwall; Llechgynfarwy, Anglesey. Nov. 7.

Dwyfael, the son of Pryderi ab Dolor of Deira and Bernicia.

Elenog.

Enddwyn; Llanenddwyn, Merionethshire.

Eurfyl; Llaneurfyl, Montgomeryshire. July 6.

Gartheli; Capel Gartheli, Cardiganshire.

Gwenllwyfo; Llanwenllwyfo, Anglesey.

Gwenog, a virgin; Llanwenog, Cardiganshire. Jan. 3.

---

* Myv. Archaiology, Vol. II. p. 625.

† Ibid. p. 36.

Gwrthwl; Llanwrthwl, Brecknockshire; and Maesllan-wrthwl in Caio, Carmarthenshire. March 2.

Gwyddelan; Llanwyddelan, Montgomeryshire; and Dol-wyddelan, Carnarvonshire. August 22.

Gwyddfarch; the son of Amalarus, prince of Pwyl. He was one of the saints of Meifod, Montgomeryshire.

Gwynen. Qu. Llanwnen, Cardiganshire.

Gwynio; Llanwynio, Carmarthenshire. March or May 2.*

Gwyrfarn;—Trinity Sunday.

Illog; Hîrnant, Montgomeryshire. August 8.

"Issui or Ishaw,"† a martyr; Partricio or Partrishaw, a chapel under Llanbedr, Brecknockshire. October 30.

Llawdden.

Llibio; Llanllibio, Anglesey. February 28.

Llwni; Llanllwni, Carmarthenshire. August 11.

Llwydian; Heneglwys, Anglesey. November 19.

Llyr, a virgin; Llanllyr, Cardiganshire; and Llanllyr yn Rhos, now written Llanyre, Radnorshire. October 21.

Machraith; Llanfachraith, Anglesey; and Llanfachraith, Merionethshire. January 1.

Mechell or Mechyll, the son of Echwydd ab Gwyn Go-hoyw. He was the founder of Llanfechell, Anglesey; and was buried in the church-yard of Penrhos Llugwy in the same county, where there was lately a stone with the following inscription, HIC IACIT MACCVQ ECCETI.‡

Mordeyrn; Nantglyn, and Mordeyrn's chapel formerly in the parish of Nantglyn, Denbighshire. July 25.

Morfael.

Morhaiarn; Trewalchmai, Anglesey. November 1.

Mwrog; Llanfwrog, Anglesey. Jan. 6, or Jan. 15.

Myllin; Llanfyllin, Montgomeryshire. June 17.

---

* Sir H. Nicolas's Chronology of History.
† The correct orthography of this name is unknown.
‡ Rowlands's Mona Antiqua.

Rhediw ; Llanllyfni, Carnarvonshire.   November 11.

Rhian ; Llanrhian, Pembrokeshire.   March 8.

Rhidian, a member of the college of Cennydd at Llangennydd in Gower ;—Llanrhidian, Glamorganshire.

Rhuddlad, a daughter of a king of Leinster in Ireland ;[*]
Llanrhuddlad, Anglesey.   September 4.

Rhwydrys ; a son of Rhwydrim or Rhodrem, king of Con-
naught.   Llanrhwydrys, Anglesey.   November 1.

Samled ; Llansamled, Glamorganshire.

Tudwen ; Llandudwen, Carnarvonshire.

Ulched ; Llechulched, Anglesey.   January 6.

The foregoing list concludes the series of Primitive Christians, whose names have been collected from various authorities
but principally from the records of the Welsh genealogists ;
and on a comparison of these records with each other, and
with collateral testimony wherever accessible, has been founded
the present attempt to bring order out of confusion by tracing
the history of the saints, as nearly as possible, according to
their chronological succession :—with what success, the reader
must judge for himself.   At first sight the Welsh pedigrees
present the appearance of an entangled maze, but when un-
ravelled and adjusted they form a regular tissue, the figures
interwoven in which are consistent, and by their analogies
clearly demonstrate where the threads are broken, and how
far the ravages of time may be repaired.   The clue to the
arrangement is that the web should commence about the departure of the Romans, and, this being attended to, its several
pieces will agree together.   One objection, however, to the
testimony of the genealogists, as regards the saints, must be
obviated.   From their representation it would appear that
large crowds of people, chieftains with their families and
dependents, renounced together the pursuit of arms, and becoming inmates of a monastery, devoted themselves to religion.

---

[*] Rowlands's Mona Antiqua.

This it might be urged was a practice unusual in other countries, and that the representations of the genealogists were therefore improbable; but the objection is overthrown by Bede who declares that a similar practice prevailed in Northumbria, where it had degenerated into open abuse;* for chieftains uncontrolled by ecclesiastical discipline founded monasteries, the government of which they assumed to themselves, inviting together all sorts of persons and especially their dependents, many of whom retained their wives and continued to have children.† In their lives they differed little from laymen, and Bede in his Epistle to Egbert, archbishop of York, earnestly intreats him to interfere and put an end to such irregularities. The abuse of the system is not charged against the Britons, who also differed from the Northumbrians in another particular,—they had no nunneries;‡ while those in Northumbria were numerous, and in many instances their government was irregularly committed to the wives of chieftains.§

To the churches founded according to the peculiar mode of consecration practised by the Britons,‖ succeeded in due course those of the second and third foundation, upon which it is not necessary to enlarge, as sufficient has been said already. Both these classes were Catholic, the second being founded chiefly by native princes, and the third by foreigners. But as it must be a source of gratification to Welshmen, to reflect that their churches of the first and most important

---

* " Adridente pace ac serenitate temporum, plures in gente Nordanhymbrorum, tam nobiles quam privati, se suosque liberos, depositis armis satagunt magis acceptâ tonsurâ, monasterialibus adscribere votis, quam bellicis exercere studiis. Quæ res quem sit habitura finem posterior ætas videbit."—Bedæ Hist. Eccl. A. D. 731.

† Epistola ad Ecgberctum Antistitem.

‡ Page 150.

§ Epistola ad Ecgberctum.

‖ Page 61.

class were established at a time when their ancestors did not
acknowledge the authority of Rome, it may not be improper
to adduce some positive evidence as to the degree of separation which existed between the Britons and the Catholics, and
such may be found at the period where these researches terminate. In the year 692, Aldhelm, a priest who was afterwards bishop of Sherborne, was deputed at a general synod of
the Saxons to write a treatise against the Paschal cycle and
form of Tonsure adhered to by the Britons. He accordingly
wrote an epistle to Geruntius, king of Cornwall, which is still
extant, and is important as it proves, that though the points in
dispute were in themselves of little consequence, the division
amounted to an entire separation of communion. The following extracts are given according to the translation of
Cressy.—

"But besides these enormities (the Tonsure and Paschal
cycle) there is another thing wherein they doe notoriously
swerve from the Catholick Faith and Evangelical Tradition,
which is, that the Preists of the Demetæ, or South-west
Wales, inhabiting beyond the bay of Severn, puffed up with a
conceit of their own purity, doe exceedingly abhorr communion with us, insomuch as they will neither ioyn in prayers with
us in the Church, nor enter into society with us at the Table :
yea moreover the fragments which we leave after refection
they will not touch, but cast them to be devoured by doggs
and unclean Swine. The Cupps also in which we have drunk,
they will not make use of, till they have rubbed and cleansed
them with sand or ashes. They refuse all civil salutations or
to give us the kisse of pious fraternity, contrary to the Apostles precept, 'Salute one another with a holy kisse.' They
will not afford us water and a towel for our hands, nor a vessell
to wash our feet. Whereas our Saviour having girt himself
with a towell, washed his Disciples feet, and left us a pattern
to imitate, saying ' As I have done to you, so doe you to
others.' Moreover if any of us who are Catholicks doe goe

amongst them to make an abode, they will not vouchsafe to admitt us to their fellowship till we be compelled to spend forty days in Pennance."—(Addressing Geruntius and his subjects, Aldhelm says :)—" Since therefore the truth of these things cannot be denied, we doe with earnest humble prayers and bended knees beseech and adjure you, as you hope to attain to the fellowship of Angels in Gods heavenly kingdom, that you will no longer with pride and stubbornes abhorr the doctrines and Decrees of the Blessed Apostle S. Peter, nor pertinaciously and arrogantly despise the Tradition of the Roman Church, preferring before it the Decrees and ancient Rites of your Predecessours. For it was S. Peter, who having devoutly confessed the Son of God, was honoured by him with these Words, ' Thou art Peter, and upon this Rock will I build my Church, and the gates of hell shall not prevayle against it: And to thee will I give the keyes of the kingdom of heaven, and whatsoever thou shalt bind on earth shall be bound in heaven, and whatsoever thou shalt loose on earth shall be loosed in heaven.' If therefore the Keyes of the kingdom of heaven were given to S. Peter, who is he, who, having despised the principall Statuts and ordinances of his Church, can presumingly expect to enter with ioy, through the gate of the heavenly Paradise ? And if he by a peculiar Priviledge and happines received the power of binding and the Monarchy of loosing in heaven and earth, who is he, who, having reiected the Rule of the Paschall Solemnity, and the Rite of the Roman Tonsure, will not rather apprehend to be indissolubly bound than mercifully absolved from his sins."*

Than the above, no greater proof of separation can be required, the arguments for the supremacy of the Pope being precisely the same as a modern Catholic would employ against a Protestant; and in the following observation, Aldhelm seems to allude to the Welsh saints :—" What proffit can any

* Cressy, Book XIX, Chap. 17.

one receive from good works done out of the Catholick Church, although a man would be never so strict in Regular Observances, or retire himself into a desart to practise an Anachoreticall life of Contemplation."—The priests of the Demetæ, or Diocese of St. David's, are noticed, probably because they were those with whom the writer was best ac-quainted,* for no other author has observed a distinction between them and the rest of the clergy of Wales; and the charge brought against them may, therefore, be extended to their brethren generally.   According to Bede, the exertions of Aldhelm were able to reduce to conformity, only so many of the Britons as were subject to the kingdom of Wessex;† from which it may fairly be presumed that they owed their con-version to the influence of their conquerors: those who main-tained their independence as a nation, continued to adhere to the religion of their fathers.‡   The manner, in which Catholi-cism was afterwards introduced, has been already explained.§

The evidence that the Britons, at this time, rejected with indignation the spiritual authority of Rome is the best that can be desired, for it rests upon the testimony of contemporary writers, who themselves were Catholics, and who were not Britons but Saxons.|| These researches, therefore, close, leaving the Welsh in the possession of a National Church and in the enjoyment of religious liberty.   Why they were per-mitted to lose these valuable privileges is best known to the Ruler of events, who disposes all things for good.   Posterity, however, cannot fail to observe a species of historical justice. To the descendants of the ancient Britons the Reformation was not only a restitution of blessings, which He who gave had

* The explanation—" inhabiting beyond the bay of Severn," added after Demetæ, applies equally to the Diocese of Llandaff; and South Wales taken as a whole, was the portion of Wales nearest to Wessex where Aldhelm resided.

† Hist. Eccl. V. 18.   ‡ Ibid. II. 20; et V. 23.
§ Pages 65, 66, and 305. || Aldhelm, Eddius, and Bede.

every right to take away, but it brought an overwhelming recompense in a translation of the Scriptures, which until that time the Welsh do not appear to have possessed ; and while it may be argued on the credit of history, that the Pope has no prescriptive claim to the supremacy of the Church in this island, for the religious liberty of the Britons may be asserted upon an older title, yet the Bible is the great charter of Protestants. Upon this record must they ground their reasons for refusing to join in communion with Romanists, and so long as an unrestricted perusal of the Sacred volume is permitted to the people in their own language, a safeguard against error is established, which had the Britons possessed, they might have resisted the aggressions of Popery with better success. May their descendants, therefore, appreciate the gift; and so long as they adhere faithfully to doctrines derived immediately from Scripture, they are assured their privileges shall never be taken away. The word of God remaineth for ever. Distant ages may look upon Catholicism as a short episode in the annals of the past, but the Bible, rendered into the vernacular tongue, unfolds to the illiterate a prospect far beyond the merits and the duration of contending Churches, displaying, as it does, to the weakest understandings, the sure hope of salvation and the glories of a happy immortality.

APPENDIX, No. I.

1. JOSEPH of Arimathea; apostle of the Britons and founder of a church at Glastonbury. Commemorated March 17. Died at Glastonbury July 27, A. D. 82.

2. Mansuetus, a Caledonian Briton; disciple of St. Peter at Rome, and afterwards bishop of Toul in Lorrain. Comm. Sept. 3. Died A. D. 89.

3. Aristobulus, a disciple of St. Peter or St. Paul; sent as an apostle to the Britons and was the first bishop in Britain. Comm. March 15. Died at Glastonbury A. D. 99.

4. Claudia, supposed to have been a daughter of Caractacus, and the wife of Pudens. Comm. Aug. 7. Died at Sabinum, a city of Umbria in Italy A. D. 110.

5. Beatus, converted in Britain, afterwards a disciple of St. Peter at Rome. His first name was Suetonius. He became the apostle of the Helvetians. Comm. May 9. Died A. D. 110, at Underseven in Helvetia.

6. Phagan; successor to Joseph in his Prefecture at Glastonbury.

7. Marcellus, a Briton; bishop of Tongres and Triers; the first British martyr, but he suffered out of the island. Comm. Sept. 4. Martyred A. D. 166.

8. Timotheus, a son of Pudens and Claudia, and born at Rome; apostle to the Britons. Martyred at Rome A. D. 166, and commemorated March 24.

9. Theanus, the first bishop of London, about the year 185.

10. Elvanus, successor to St. Theanus. Cressy mentions his companion Medwinus, but does not call him a saint.

11. Lucius, king of Britain, "the first among kings which received the faith of Christ." Converted in his old age A. D. 182, and his baptism is commemorated by the Romish Church May 26. After having established Christianity over the whole of his dominions he became the apostle of Bavaria, Rhætia, and Vindelicia. He was slain near Curia in Germany A. D. 201. His martyrdom is comm. Dec. 3.

12. Emerita; sister of Lucius, and his companion in Germany; martyred at Trimas near Curia, A. D. 193. Comm. Dec. 4.

13. Fugatius or Phaganus;—and

14. Damianus or Diruvianus;—Legates sent from Rome by Pope Eleutherius to baptize King Lucius. They both died in the year 191, and are commemorated together May 24.

15. Mello, Mallo, Melanius, or Meloninus, a Briton; bishop of Rouen in France. Comm. Oct. 22. Died A. D. 280.

16. Albanus of Verolam, the first martyr in Britain. His memory is celebrated in the English Martyrology on the twenty second of July, and in the Gallican on the twenty second of June. Martyred A. D. 287.

17. Amphibalus, a native of Caerleon, and the instructor of St. Alban. Martyred at Rudburn A. D. 287. His translation is comm. June 25.

18. Julius;—and

19. Aaron;—natives of Caerleon, at which place they were martyred together, soon after the martyrdom of St. Amphibalus. Comm. together July 1.

20. Stephanus;—and

21. Socrates;—"two noble British Christians" and disciples of St. Amphibalus, martyred in the persecution of Dioclesian.

22. Nicholas, a bishop of North Britain, for his piety styled Culdæus. Mart. A. D. 296.

23. Stephanus, the seventh bishop of London, is called a martyr, though he died a natural death, A. D. 300.

24. Augulus, eighth bishop of London. Died in the year 305, and comm. Feb. 7.

25. Helena, wife of Constantius emperor of Rome, and the mother of Constantine. Died A. D. 326; comm. Aug. 18.

26. Constantine, emperor of Rome. Died A. D. 337; comm. May 21.

27. Gudwal, a bishop of Britain. In the latter part of his life he lived in Flanders, where he died June 6, A. D. 403, on which day he is also commemorated. The feast of the translation of his body to the monastery of Ghent is celebrated on the third day before the Nones of December.

28. Kebius, a son of Solomon duke of Cornwall, and disciple of St. Hilary bishop of Poictiers, He was consecrated a bishop by St. Hilary, and he placed his see in the Isle of Anglesey, where he died A. D. 370.

29. Moses, apostle of the Saracens ; said to have been a Briton. Comm. Feb. 7.

30. Regulus, a native of Greece ; missionary to the Picts. Comm. August 28.

31. Melorus, son of Melianus duke of Cornwall. Martyred A. D. 411. Festival August 28.

32. Palladius, a Roman; apostle to the Scots. Died in 431. Comm. January 27: He had two distinguished disciples, Servanus, bishop of the Orkneys, and Tervanus, successor to St. Ninian or Ninianus.

33. Carantac or Cernac, son of Keredic prince of Cardigan ; a disciple and attendant of St. Patrick. Died at Chernach in Ireland on the seventeenth of the Calends of June.

34. Luman, a British saint and companion of St. Patrick. Founder of the church of Trim in Ireland.

35. Winwaloc, a famous British saint, who settled in Armorica. His death A. D. 432 is commemorated March 3, and his translation to the Blandin monastery at Ghent is celebrated August 1.

36. Ninianus, a Cumbrian Briton; the first bishop of the Southern Picts. He died A. D. 432.

37. Germanus, bishop of Auxerre ;—and

38. Lupus, bishop of Troyes ;—deputed by Pope Celestine to reform the British Church in 429. St. Germanus visited Britain a second time A. D. 435, accompanied by Severus, bishop of Triers.

39. Briocus, a Briton of the province of Corticia ; a disciple of St. Germanus, and bishop of Brieu in Armorica. Comm. April 30.

40. Bachiarius,—" by Nation a Brittain and Disciple of Saint Patrick ; he addicted himself to the study of litterature at Caer-leon." Obiit A. D. 460.

41. Ursula, daughter of Dionatus prince of Cornwall. Martyred with the eleven thousand virgins, A. D. 453. Comm. Oct. 21.

42. Cordula, one of the eleven thousand virgins; Oct. 22.

43. Voadinus, archbishop of London; martyred by the Saxons A. D. 457, Comm. July 3.

44. Patrick, the apostle of Ireland. Born A. D. 361 in a valley of the country of the Demetæ, called " Rossina," where the cathedral of St. David's was afterwards built. Died at Glastonbury A. D. 472, aged 111.

45. Brigit, an Irish saint and disciple of St. Patrick; she visited Britain in 488. Died at Down in Ireland A. D. 502. Commemorated Feb. 1.

46. Sophias, the son of Guilleicus prince of the Ordovices. " He was by another name called Cadocus." Consecrated bishop of Beneventum in Italy. Died A. D. 490; comm. January 24. (Cressy says this person ought not to be confounded with another St. Cadocus, who was an abbot.)

47. Keina, "daughter of Braganus prince of Brecknock." She died on the eighth day before the Ides of October, A. D. 490.

48. Almedha, a martyr; sister to St. Keina. Commemorated August 1.

49. Canoc, eldest son of Braganus. Comm. February 11. Floruit circa 492.

50. Clitanc or Clintanc, " King of Brecknock and Martyr. A. D. 482. Comm. August 19.

51. Richard, born in Britain A. D. 455. Consecrated bishop of Andria. The first converted Saxon. Comm. April 9.

52. Gunleus, "Prince of the Southern Brittains." Comm. March 29.

53. Cadoc, abbot of Llancarvan; son of St. Gunleus. Died about A. D. 500. Comm. February 24.

54. Tathai, a British saint; president of a college at Caerwent, and tutor to St. Cadoc the abbot.

55. Dogmael or Tegwel. "A famous Abbey in Pembrokeshire took its name from him." He died about the year 500. Commemorated June 14.

56. Bernach, an abbot: commemorated on the seventh of the Ides of April.

57. Petrock, born of princely parentage in Wales. He lived some time in Ireland and afterwards settled in Cornwall, where he died A. D. 564.

58. Meven, patron of a monastery in Armorica. He was born in Britain, but the time when he lived is not mentioned. "Judicael, Prince of the Armorici or Lesser Brittany, who descended from our Brittany, built the said Monastery."

59. Gildas Albanius, son of Can the king of Albania. Died on the fourth day before the Calends of February A. D. 512. Commemorated January 29. Not to be confounded with St. Gildas, abbot of Bangor, who is styled Sapiens, Historicus, and Badonicus.

60. Daniel, the first bishop of Bangor. Died A. D. 544, and is commemorated December 10.

61. Justinian, a native of Armorica, who suffered martyrdom from the hands of his own servants in the island of Ramsey. Commemorated August 23.

62. Paternus, a native of Armorica; he visited Wales in 516, and was the first bishop of Llanbadarn Fawr in Cardiganshire. Comm. May 15.

63. Darerca, born in Britain; sister of St. Patrick. Died A. D. 518.

64. Mel, a son of St. Darerca.

65. Rioch, a son of St. Darerca:—"by Nation a Brittain, near kinsman to Patrick, by whom he was ordained a Bishop in Ireland."

66. Menni, a son of St. Darerca.

67. Sechnallus or Secundinus, a son of St. Darerca.

68. Auxilius, a son of St. Darerca; consecrated bishop of Leinster by St. Patrick.

69. Dubricius; consecrated bishop of Llandaff by St. Germanus in 436, and raised to the archbishoprick of Caerleon in 492. Died in the Isle of Bardsey A. D. 522. His remains were translated to Llandaff on the Nones of May, 1120, and buried there on the fourth day before the Calends of June by Bp. Urban.

70. Theliau. He succeeded St. Dubricius as bishop of Llandaff— "and if the authority of the English Martyrologe fayle not, he dyed not untill the coming of S. Augustin the Monk into Brittany." He died on the fifth day before the Ides of February, but is commemorated as a martyr November 26.

71. Paulens or Paulinus, a disciple of St. Germanus, and instructor of St. David and St. Theliau.

72. Nennion, a bishop of North Britain, successor to St. Ninianus. Floruit circa 520.

73. Kined, an anchorite of Western Gower; probably the same as St. Keneth. He was contemporary with St. David.

74. Ædan, a disciple of St. David and the first bishop of Ferns. He is called by the Irish St. Maidoc or Moedhog.

75. David, the first archbishop of Menevia. Died March 1. A. D. 544, aged 82.

76. John, a British saint in France. Obiit 537; comm. June 27.

77. Móchta or Mochæus, a British saint in Ireland; consecrated bishop of Lowth by St. Patrick. Died in 537; commemorated on the thirteenth day before the Calends of September.

78. Iltutus, a saint in Glamorganshire, contemporary with St. Cadocus. The year in which died is uncertain. Comm. November 7.

79. Sampson, a disciple of St. Iltutus, and afterwards archbishop of Menevia and of Dole in Brittany. Obiit A. D. 599; comm. July 28.

80. Piro, an abbot of a monastery not from far that of St. Iltutus, with whom he was contemporary.

81. Conaid, called by the French St. Mein or Mevennius. (Qu. the same as No. 58.) He accompanied St. Samson to Bretagne, where he died in 590; comm. June 15.

82. Malo, Maclovius, or Machutus, a native of Glamorganshire; he was a kinsman of St. Sampson, and went with him to Bretagne, where he was appointed bishop of Aleth. He died in France A. D. 564; commemorated November 15.

83. Doc, "a Holy British Abbot," who flourished about the year 540.

84. Kentigern, a North Briton; bishop of St. Asaph in Wales and of Glasgow in Scotland. Obiit A. D. 601, ætatis suæ 85; comm. Jan. 13.

85. Theodoric, prince of Glamorganshire. He died at Merthyr Teudric, now called Merthirn.

86. Oudoceus, successor of St. Theliau in the see of Llandaff; commemorated on the sixth day before the Nones of July.

87. Gildas Badonicus; the historian, and second apostle of Ireland. Obiit A. D. 583; comm. Jan. 28.

88. Columba, a native of Ireland, and missionary to the Picts. Died A. D. 597.

89. Beuno, a monk of North Wales, and instructor of St. Winefride. Died A. D. 660; comm. Jan. 14.

90. Senan, another instructor of St. Winefride. Obiit 660; comm. April 29.

91. Winefride, a holy virgin of North Wales; comm. Nov. 3.

92. Deifer, the successor of St. Beuno in the tuition of St. Winefride. Died A. D. 664; comm. March 7.

93. Elerius, abbot of a monastery in the Vale of Clwyd. He flourished about the year 650.

94. Winoc, a son of Judicael king of the Britons: he and three of his brothers, Kadanoc, Ingenoc, and Madoc, were monks of the monastery of St. Sithiu under St. Bertin. Obiit 717; comm. Nov. 6. This saint founded the monastery of St. Winoc on the confines of France and Flanders.

95. Judoc, another brother of St. Winoc; he flourished about 650.

96. Baruck, a hermit. Buried in the Isle of Barry, Glamorganshire, about the year 700.

97. Decumanus, a hermit, born of noble parents in the South-western parts of Wales. Murdered A. D. 706; comm. Aug. 27.

98. Juthwara, a devout British virgin, martyred in some part of South Wales, A. D. 740; comm. Dec. 23.

99. Eadwara,—

100. Wilgitha,—and

101. Sidwella; sisters of St. Juthwara.

APPENDIX, No. II.

___

ANGLO-SAXON SAINTS, TO WHOM CHURCHES HAVE BEEN DEDICATED IN WALES.

Oswald, king of Northumbria; he died A. D. 642. Jeffreyston, Pembrokeshire; and Oswestry, in the county of Salop but in the diocese of St. Asaph.

Ina, king of Wessex; he died at Rome in the year 727, and is commemorated on the seventh of February. Llanina, Cardiganshire.

Tecla, a female saint, born in England; abbess of the monastery of Kirzengen at Ochnafort in Germany. Obiit A. D. 750; comm. Oct. 15. Llandegla, Denbighshire; and Llandegle, Radnorshire.

Tetta, abbess of Winburn in Wessex about A. D. 750. Llanddetty, Brecknockshire.

Milburg, a virgin; abbess of Wenlock in Shropshire about the middle of the seventh century. Comm. February 23. Llanfilo, Brecknockshire.

Kenelm, king of Mercia and martyr. Obiit A. D. 819. Rockfield, Monmouthshire.

Edmund, king of the East Angles, murdered by the Danes A. D. 870; commemorated November 20. Crickhowel, Brecknockshire.

Edith or Editha; Five Saxon saints of this name. Llanedy, Carmarthenshire.

Edward, king and martyr, A. D. 979. Comm. February 18, March 18, and June 20.—Do. king and confessor; Obiit A. D. 1066. Commemorated Jan. 5, and Oct. 13. Knighton, Radnorshire.

APPENDIX, No. III.

A LIST OF CHURCHES AND CHAPELS IN WALES,

Including the County of Monmouth and part of the County of Hereford,
arranged with reference to their subordination.

N. B. The names at the head of each group are those of parent
churches, or such as are not known to have been chapels; and wherever
the names are printed in Italic, the church or chapel is extinct or in ruins.
The name of the patron saint is placed after that of the edifice.

ANGLESEY.*

ABERFFRAW, Beuno. *Eglwys y Baili. Capel Mair*, St Mary.
Amlwch, Elaeth. Llanwenllwyfo, Gwenllwyfo. *Llangadog, Cadog.*
Llanlleianau.
Heneglwys, Llwydian. Trefwalchmai, Morhaiarn.
Holyhead alias Caergybi, Cybi. *Llanygwyddyl. Capel y Llochwyd.*
Capel y Gorlas. Capel Sanffraid, Ffraid. Capel Gwyn-
geneu, Gwyngeneu. Bodedeyrn, Edeyrn. Bod-Twrog, Twrog.
Llandrygarn. Gwndy.
Llanbadrig, Padrig.
Llanbeulan, Peulan. Llechulched, Ulched. Llanfaelog, Maelog.
Tal-y-llyn, St. Mary. Llannerch-y-Medd, St. Mary. Ceirchiog
or Bettws-y-Grôg, Holy Rood.

* This county contains more chapels dedicated to Welsh saints than any
other; but it was, at an early age, considered to be the most populous
and fertile part of Wales; and according to Bede, it contained, in the
eighth century, nine hundred and sixty families, or about three times the
population of the Isle of Man.

Llanddeusant, Sts. Marcellus and Marcellinus. Llanbabo, Pabo.
Llanfair Ynghornwy, St. Mary.

Llanddona, Dona.

Llanddwyn or *Llanddwynwen, Dwynwen*, a parish church in ruins.

Llanddyfnan, Dyfnan. Llanbedr Goch, St. Peter. Llanfair ym
Mathafarn Eithaf, St. Mary. Pentraeth or Llanfair Bettws
Geraint, St. Mary.

Llandegfan, Tegfan. *Capel Meugan, Meugan. Capel Tydecho,
Tydecho.* Llanfaes, St. Catherine. Beaumaris, St. Mary. *A
Chapel in the Castle of Beaumaris.*

Llandyfrydog, Tyfrydog. Llanfihangel Tre'r Beirdd, St. Michael.

Llaneigrad, Eigrad. Llanallgo, Gallgo. *Llugwy, St. Michael.*

Llanelian, Elian. Coed Ane, Anc. Rhos Peirio, Peirio. Bodewryd.

Llanfachraith, Machraith. Llanenghenel, Enghenel. *Llanfigel,
St. Vigilius.*

Llanfaethlu, Maethlu. Llanfwrog, Mwrog.

Llanfair Pwll Gwyngyll, St. Mary. ·Llandyssilio, Tyssilio.

Llanfechell, Mechell. *Llanddogfael, Dogfael.*

Llanfihangel Ysgeifiog, St. Michael. Llanffinan, Ffinan.

Llangadwaladr or Eglwys Ael, Cadwaladr. *Llanfeirion, Meirion.*

Llangefni, Cyngar. Tregaian, Caian.

Llangeinwen, Ceinwen. Llangaffo, Caffo.

Llangristiolus, Cristiolus. Cerrig Ceinwen, Ceinwen.

Llangwyllog, Cwyllog.

Llaniestin, Iestin. Llangoed, Cawrdaf and Tangwn. Llanfihangel
Tinsylwy, St. Michael.

Llannidan, Nidan. Llanddeiniol Fab, Deiniolen. *Capel Cadwaladr, Cadwaladr.* Llanedwen, Edwen. Llanfair yn y Cwmmwd, St. Mary.

Llanrhuddlad, Rhuddlad. Llanfflewin, Fflewin. Llanrhwydrys,
Rhwydrys.

Llansadwrn, Sadwrn.

Llantrisaint, Sannan, Afran, and Ieuan. *Llanllibio, Llibio.* Llechgynfarwy, Cynfarwy. Rhodwydd Geidio, Ceidio. Gwaredog,
St. Mary. Bettws Bwchwdw.

Newborough anciently Llananno,* Amo or Anno, and St. Peter.

Penmon, Seiriol. *A Chapel in Priestholm Island.*
Penmynydd, Gredifael.
Penrhos-Llugwy, St. Michael.
Rhôs Colyn, Gwenfaen. Llanfihangel yn Nhywyn, St. Michael.
    Llanfair yn Neubwll, St. Mary.
Tref-draeth, Beuno. Llangwyfen, Cwyfen.

BRECKNOCKSHIRE.

Aberysgyr, Cynidr and St. Mary.
Brecon, St. John the Evangelist. Do. St. Mary. Battle, Cynog.
    Slwch Chapel, Elined or St. Almedha. Llanywern or Monkton,
    St. Mary. *A Hospitium, St. Catherine.*
Brynllys or Brwynllys, St. Mary.
Cantref, St. Mary. Capel Nant Du.
Cathedin, St. Michael.
Crickhowel, St. Edmund. *Llanfair Chapel, St. Mary.*
Devynock or Dyfynog, Cynog and Dyfnog. Llanilltyd, Illtyd. Capel
    Callwen, Callwen. Llanulid or Crai Chapel, St. Julitta. Ystrad
    Fellte, St. Mary.
Y Faenor, Gwynno or Gwynnog.
Garthbrengi, Dewi or St. David. Llanddew or Llandduw, Holy
    Trinity.* Llanfaes, St. David. Christ's College, Holy Trinity,
    formerly a church of St. Nicholas.
Glasbury, Cynidr and St. Peter. *Aberllyfni or Pipton. Velindre
    Chapel.*
Gwenddwr.
Hay, *St. John.* Do. St. Mary, now the parish church. *A Chapel
    in the suburbs.*

---

* Jones in his History of Brecknockshire supposes Llanddew to be an
abbreviation of Llanddewi; but as the parish wake is held upon Trinity
Sunday, the true etymology appears to be *Llanddur* "the Church of
God," which was once the name of Llandrindod, or the Church of the
Holy Trinity, in Radnorshire; there is also a church in Glamorganshire,
dedicated to the Trinity, the name of which is generally written "Llandow."

Llanafan Fawr, Afan. Llanfechan, Afan. Llanfihangel Bryn Pabuan,
    St. Michael. Llanfihangel Abergwesin, St. Michael. Capel
    Alltmawr. *Llysdinam. Gelli Talgarth or Rhos y Capel.*
Llanbedr Ystrad Yw, St. Peter. Partrishow, Issui or Ishow.
Llanddetty, St. Tetta. Taf-fechan Chapel.
Llanddulas or Tir yr Abad.
Llandeilo'r Fân, Teilo. *Capel Maes y Bwlch.*
Llandyfaelog Fach, Maelog. Llanfihangel Fechan, St. Michael.
Llandyfalle, Maethlu. Crug-cadarn, St. Mary.
Llaneigion or Llaneingion, Eigion or Eingion. *Cilonw Chapel.*
    Capel y Ffin.
Llanelyw, Ellyw.
Llanfeugan, Meugan. Capel Glyn Collwyn. *A Free Chapel in the*
    Castle of Pencelli, St. Leonard.
Llanfihangel Cwm-dû, St. Michael. *Llandegeman, Degeman or St.*
    Decumanus. Tretŵr Chapel, St. John.
Llanfihangel Tal-y-llyn, St. Michael.
Llanfilo, St. Milburg. Llandyfaelog Tref y Graig, Maelog.
Llanfrynach, Brynach Wyddel.
Llangammarch, Cammarch. Llanwrtyd, St. David. Llanddewi
    Abergwesin, St. David. *Llanddewi at Llwyn y Fynwent,*
    St. David. Llansanffraid Cwmmwd Deuddwr, Ffraid. *Llan-*
    fadog, Madog. Nantgwyllt Chapel. (The last three are in the
    county of Radnor.)
Llanganten, Cannen. Llangynog, Cynog.
Llangasty Tal-y-Llyn, Gastayn.
Llangattwg Crug-hywel, Cattwg. Llangeneu, Ceneu. Llanelly,
    Ellyw. *Oratory of St. Keyna, Ceneu.*
Llangors, Pawl Hên or St. Paulinus.
Llangynidr, Cynidr and Mary. *Eglwys Vesey.*
Llanhamlech or Llanamwlch, Illtyd and St. Peter. *Llechfaen*
    Chapel.
Llansanffraid, Ffraid or St. Bride.
Llanspyddyd, Cadog. Capel y Bettws or Penpont Chapel.
Llanwrthwl, Gwrthwl. Llanlleonfel.
Llyswen.
Llywel, David, Teilo, and Llywel. Trallwng, St. David. Rhydy-
    briw Chapel. *Dolhywel, St. David.*

Macsmynys, St. David. Llanynys, St. David. Llanddewi'r Cwm,
    St. David. Llanfair in Builth, St. Mary
Merthyr Cynog, Cynog. Llanfihangel Nant Bran, St. Michael.
    Capel Dyffryn Honddu.
Penderin, Cynog.
Talachddu, St. Mary.
Talgarth, Gwen.
Ystrad Gynlais, Cynog. Capel Coelbren.

CARDIGANSHIRE.

Aberporth, Cynwyl. *Llanannerch.*
Bangor, St. David. Henllan, St. David.
Bettws Bledrws.
Blaenporth, St. David.
Cardigan, St. Mary. Tremaen, St. Michael.
Caron or Tregaron, Caron. Ystrad Fflur or Strata Florida, St.
    Mary.
Cellan, All Saints.
Ciliau Aeron, St. Michael.
Dihewyd or Llanwydalus, St. Vitalis.
Henfynyw, St. David. Llanddewi Aberarth, St. David.
Llanafan, Afan. Llanwnws, Gwynws. Ysbytty Ystwyth, St. John
    the Baptist. Ystrad Meurig, St. John the Baptist.
Llanarth, St. David. Llanina, St. Ina. *Capel Crist, Holy Cross.*
Llanbadarn Fawr, Padarn. Llanychaiarn, Llwchaiarn. *Llanger-*
    waen. Yspytty Cenfaen, St. John the Baptist. Aberystwyth,
    St. Michael.
Llanbadarn Odin, Padarn.
Llanbadarn Trefeglwys, Padarn. Cilcennin, Holy Trinity.
Llanbedr Pont Stephan or Lampeter, St. Peter. *St. Thomas's*
    Chapel. Capel Ffynnon Fair, St. Mary.
Llanddeiniol or Carrog, Deiniol.
Llanddewi Brefi, St. David. Blaenpennal, St. David. Capel Bettws
    Leuci, St. Lucia. Capel Gartheli, Gartheli. *Capel Gwenfyl,*
    Gwenfyl.
Llandyfriog, Tyfriog or Tyfrydog. *Llanfair Tref Helygen,*
    St. Mary.

Llandygwy or Llandygwydd, Tygwy. *Parc y Capel. A Chapel near Cenarth Bridge.*

Llandyssilio Gogo, Tyssilio. Capel Cynon, Cynon.

Llandyssul, Tyssul. *Llandyssulfed, St. Sylvester. Llanfair, St. Mary. Faerdre. Capel Dewi, St. David. Capel Ffraid, St. Bride. Capel Borthin, St. Martin.*

Llanfair y Clywedogau, St. Mary.

Llanfair Orllwyn, St. Mary.

Llanfihangel y Creuddin, St. Michael. *Llantrisaint.* Eglwys Newydd.

Llanfihangel Genau'r Glyn or Llanfihangel Castell Gwallter, St. Michael. Eglwys Fach or Llanfihangel Capel Edwin, St. Michael.

Llanfihangel Lledroed, St. Michael.

Llanfihangel Ystrad, St. Michael. *Llanllyr, Llyr Forwyn. Capel Sant Silin, Silin.*

Llangeitho, Çeitho.

Llangoedmor, Cynllo. Llechryd, Holy Cross. Mount, Holy Cross.

Llangrannog, Carannog.

Llangybi, Cybi.

Llangynfelyn, Cynfelyn.

Llangynllo, Cynllo.

Llanilar, Ilar.

Llanllwchaiarn, Llwchaiarn.

Llannerch Aeron or Llan Uwch Aeron, Non mam Dewi.

Llanrhystud, Rhystud. *Capel Cynddilig, Cynddilig.*

Llansanffraid, Ffraid or St. Bride. *Llannon, Non.*

Llanwenog, Gwenog. *Capel Whŷl. Capel Santesau. Llanfechan. Capel Bryneglwys.*

Llanygweryddon, St. Ursula and the Eleven Thousand Virgins.

Nantgwnlle, Gwynlleu.

Penbryn or Llanfihangel Penbryn, St. Michael. Bettws Ifan, St. John. Bryngwyn, St. Mary. *Capel Gwnda, Gwyndaf.*

Rhosdeiau, St. Michael.

Silian or Llansilian, Sulien. Llanwnen, St. Lucia.

Trefilan, St. Hilary.

Troed yr Aur, St. Michael. *Capel Twr Gwyn.*

Verwick, Pedrog.

CARMARTHENSHIRE.

Abergwyli, St. David. Llanpumsant, Celynin, Ceitho, Gwyn, Gwynno, and Gwynnoro. Llanllawddog, Llawddog. Llanfihangel Uwch Gwyli, St. Michael. *Bettws Ystum Gwyli. Henllan. Capel Bach. Capel Llanddu.*

Abernant, St. Lucia. Cynwyl Elfed, Cynwyl. *Capel Troed y Rhiw.*

Bettws, St. David. *Pentre'r Eglwys.*

Brechfa, Teilo.

Carmarthen, St. Peter. *Do.* St. Mary. Llangain, Cain. Llanllwch. Newchurch or Llannewydd. *Capel y Groesfeini. The Rood-church, a Free Chapel in the Castle of Carmarthen, Holy Cross.*

Cenarth, Llawddog. Newcastle in Emlyn Chapel.

Cilrhedin, Teilo, in Pembrokeshire. *Capel Ifan, St. John,* in Carmarthenshire.

Cil-y-Cwm, St. Michael.

Cilymaenllwyd, St. Philip and St. James. Castell Dwyran.

Cynwyl Gaio, Cynwyl. Llansawyl, Sawyl. Llansadwrn, Sadwrn. Llanwrda. *Pumsant, Celynin, Ceitho, Gwyn, Gwynno, and Gwynnoro. Maesllanworthwl, Gwrthwl. Henllan or Bryneglwys. Cwrt y Cadno. Aberbranddu.*

Egermond, St. Michael.

Eglwys Cymmun, St. Margaret Marlos.

Henllan Amgoed, St. David. Eglwys Fair a Churig, St. Mary and Curig.

Kidwelly, St. Mary. *Llangadog, Cadog. Llanfihangel, St. Michael. Capel Teilo, Teilo. Capel Coker.* * St. *Thomas's Chapel.*

Laugharne, St. Martin. Cyffyg. Marros, St. Laurence. *Craseland.*

Llanarthne, St. David. Llanlleian Chapel. *Capel Dewi, St. David.*

Llanboidy or Llanbeudy, St. Brynach. Eglwys Fair Lan Tâf, St. Mary.

Llandawg, St. Margaret Marlos. Pendŷn.

Llanddarog. *An old Chapel, St. Bernard. Capel Bach.*

* Named after Galfridus de Coker, Prior of Kidwelly in 1301.

2 R

Llanddowror, Teilo.

Llandeilo Abercywyn, Teilo.

Llandeilo Fawr or Llandilo, Teilo.   Taliaris Chapel, Holy Trinity.
  *Llandyfaen.   Capel yr Ywen.   A Chapel in Carreg Cennen
  Castle.*

Llandingad, Tingad or Dingad.   Llanfair ar y Bryn, St. Mary.
  Capel Peulin, St. Paulinus or Pawl Hen.   *Capel Cynfab, Cynfab.   Eglwys Newydd.*

Llandybie, Tybie.   *Capel yr Hendre.   Glyn yr Henllan.*

Llandyfaelog, Maelog.   *Llangynheiddon, Cynheiddon.*   Llangyndeyrn,
  Cyndeyrn.   *Capel Ifan, St. John.   Capel Dyddgen.   Bettws.*

Llandyfeisant, Tyfei.   *A Chapel in Dinefwr Castle, St. David.*

Llandyssilio yn Nyfed, Tyssilio.

Llanedy, St. Edith.

Llanegwad, Egwad.   *Llandeilo Rwnnws, Teilo.   Llanhirnin.   Capel
  Gwilym Foethus.   Dolwyrdd Chapel.*

Llanelly, Ellyw.   Llangennych, Cennych.   *Capel Dewi, St. David.
  Capel Ifan, St. John,   Berwick Chapel.*

Llanfallteg.

Llanfihangel Aberbythych, St. Michael.

Llanfihangel ar Arth, St. Michael.   *Pencadair Chapel.*

Llanfihangel Cilfargen, St. Michael.

Llanfynydd, Egwad.

Llangadog Fawr or Llangadock, Cadog and St. David.   Llanddeusant, St. Simon and St. Jude.   Capel Gwynfai.   *Capel Tydyst.*

Llangan, Canna.

Llangathen, Cathan.   *Capel Penarw.*

Llangeler, Celer.   *Capel Mair, St. Mary.*

Llanglydwyn, Clydwyn.

Llangynnor.

Llanllwni, Llwni.   Llanfihangel Rhos y Corn, St. Michael.   *Capel
  Maesmonni.   Ffynnon y Capel.*

Llansadyrnin, Sadyrnin.

Llanstephan, Ystyffan.   Llangynog, Cynog.   *Llanybri, St. Mary.*

Llanwynio, Gwynio.

Llanybyddair, St. Peter.   Abergorlech.   *Capel Iago, St. James.
  Capel Mair, St. Mary.*

Llanycrwys, St. David.

Meidrym, St. David.   Llanfihangel Abercywyn, St. Michael.
Merthyr, Enfail.
Myddfai or Mothvey, St. Michael.
Penboir, Llawddog.   Trinity Chapel, Holy Trinity.
Penbre, Illtyd.   Llan-non, Non.   Llandurry.
Pencarreg.
St. Clare's.   Llangynin, Cynin.
St. Ishmael's or Llanishmael, Ismael.   Llansaint, All Saints.   Ferry
    Side, St. Thomas,
Talley or Tal-y-Llychau, St. Michael.   *Llanfihangel, St. Michael.
    Capel Mair, St. Mary.   Capel Crist, Holy Trinity.   Capel
    Cynhwm.   Capel Teilo, Teilo.*
Trelech a'r Bettws, Teilo.   Capel Bettws.

CARNARVONSHIRE.

Aber or Abergwyngregyn, Bodfan.
Aberdaron, Hywyn.   Llanfaelrys, Maelrys.   *Eglwys Fair, St. Mary.*
Abererch, Cawrdaf.   Penrhos or Llangynwyl, Cynwyl.
Bangor Fawr, Deiniol.   Pentir or Llangedol, Cedol,   *Capel Gwrfyw,
    Gwrfyw.   King Edgar's Chapel, St. Mary.*
Bardsey or Ynys Enlli, Cadfan and Lleuddad ; now Extra-parochial.
Beddgelert, St. Mary.   *Nant Hwynen Chapel.*
Bodfuan, Buan.
Caer-rhun, St. Mary.
Ceidio or Llangeidio, Ceidio.
Clynnog Fawr, Beuno.
Conway or Aberconway, St. Mary.
Cruccaith, St. Catherine.   Ynys Cynhaiarn, Cynhaiarn.   Treflys,
    St. Michael.
Cyffin, St. Benedict.
Dolwyddelan, Gwyddelan.
Dwygyfylchi, Gwynnin.
Edeyrn, Edeyrn,   Carngiwch, Beuno.   Pistyll, Beuno.
Eglwys Rhos, St. Hilary.   *Penrhyn, a Free Chapel, St. Mary.*
Llanaelhaiarn, Aelhaiarn.
Llanbeblig, Peblig.   Carnarvon, St. Mary.   *Do. St. Helen.*
Llanbedr y Cennin, St. Peter,

Llanbedrog, Pedrog. Llangian, Cian and Peris. *Cir Ferthyr*. Llanfihangel Bachellaeth, St. Michael.

Llanberis, Peris.

Llanddeiniolen, Deiniolen. *Dinas Orweg Chapel*.

Llandegai, Tegai. Capel Curig, Curig, or Cyrique and Julitta.

Llandudno, Tudno.

Llandwrog, Twrog.

Llanengan or Llaneingion Frenhin, Einion. *Ynys Tudwal, Tudwal*.

Llanfair Fechan, St. Mary.

Llanfair Isgaer, St. Mary. Bettws Garmon, St. Germanus.

Llanfihangel y Pennant, St. Michael.

Llanfor, Mor. Pwllheli or Eglwys Dyneio, Tyneio.

Llangelynin, Celynin.

Llangwynodl, Gwynodl. Tudweiliog, Cwyfen. Bryn Croes, Holy Cross.

Llangybi, Cybi. Llanarmon, St. Germanus.

Llaniestin, Iestin. Llandygwynnin, Gwynnin. Bodferin, Merin or Merini. Penllech, St. Mary. St. Julian's Chapel.

Llanllechid, Llechid.

Llanllyfni, Rhedyw.

Llanrhug, St. Michael.

Llanwnda, Gwyndaf Hên. Llanfaglan, Baglan.

Llanystyndwy, St. John the Baptist.

Melldeyrn, St. Peter ad vincula. Bod-twnog, Beuno.

Nantgyndanyll, Deiniol.

Nefyn, St. Mary.

Penmachno, Tyddud.

Penmorfa, Beuno. Dolbenmaen, St. Mary.

Rhiw, Aelrhiw. Llandudwen, Tudwen.

Trefriw, St. Mary. Llanrhychwyn, Rhychwyn. Bettws y Coed, St. Michael.*

* For Llangystennyn and Llysfaen, see Abergele and Llandrillo, Denbighshire.

DENBIGHSHIRE.

Abergele, St. Michael. *A Chapel in the Church-Yard of Ditto, St. Michael*, Bettws Abergele, St. Michael. Llangystennyn in the County of Carnarvon, St. Constantine. *Llanwddin, Gwddin.*

Bryn Eglwys, Tyssilio. Llandyssilio, Tyssilio.

Cegidog or Llansansiôr, St. George.

Cerrig y Drudion or Llanfair Fadlen, St. Mary Magdalen.

Chirk or Eglwys y Waun, St. Mary.

Clog-caenog, Caenog.

Denbigh, St. Marcellus. Do. St. Hilary. *A Free Chapel in the Castle.*

Derwen yn Iâl, St. Mary.

Efenechtyd, St. Michael.

Eglwys Fach, St. Martin.

Erbistock, St. Hilary.

Gresford, All Saints. *A Chapel at Rosset Green.* Holt, St. Chad. Iscoed Chapel.

Gwytherin, Gwytherin.

Henllan, Sadwrn. *The Abbey Chapel.*

Llanarmon Dyffryn Ceiriog, St. Germanus.

Llanarmon yn Iâl, St. Germanus.

Llanbedr, St. Peter.

Llanddoged, Doged.

Llanddulas, Cynbryd.

Llandegla, St. Tecla.

Llandrillo in Rhos* or Dinerth, Trillo. Llanelian, Elian. Llansanffraid Glyn Conwy or Diserth, Ffraid. *Capel Sanffraid, Ffraid.* Llysfaen in the County of Carnarvon, Cynfran.

Llandyrnog, Tyrnog.

Llanelidan.

Llanfair Dyffryn Clwyd, Cynfarch and St. Mary.

Llanfair Talhaiarn, Talhaiarn and St. Mary.

Llanferras.

---

* "Llanelian, Llansanffraid. and Llysfaen are supposed to have been Chapels of Ease to this parish, because the Rector and Vicar have a share of the tithes in each."—Edwards's Cathedral of St. Asaph.

Llanfihangel Glyn y Myfyr, St. Michael.

Llanfwrog, Mwrog.

Llangerniw, Digain.   Marchaled or Capel Foelas.

Llangollen, Collen.   Trefor Isaf Chapel.

Llangwm Dinmael, St. Jerome.

Llangwyfen, Cwyfen.

Llangynhafal, Cynhafal.

Llanhychan, Hychan.

Llannefydd, Nefydd.

Llanrhaiadr, Dyfnog.

Llanrhaiadr in Mochnant, Dogfan. Llanwddin in the County of
    Montgomery, Gwddin. Llanarmon Mynydd Mawr, St. Ger-
    manus. Llangedwyn, Cedwyn. Llangadwaladr, Cadwaladr.

Llanrhydd, Meugan.   Rhuthin, St. Peter.

Llanrwst, Grwst. Capel Garmon, St. Germanus. *Capel Marchell,*
    Marchell. Capel Rhyddyn. Gwydir Chapel.

Llansanffraid Glyn Ceiriog, Ffraid.

Llansannan, Sannan or St. Senanus.

Llansilin, Silin or Sulien.

Llanynys, Mor and Saeran. Cyffylliog, St. Mary.

Nantglyn, Mordeyrn.   *Mordeyrn's Chapel, Mordeyrn.*

Rhiw Fabon, Mabon.

Wrexham, Silin or Sulien. *Capel Silin, Silin.* Minera Chapel.
    Berse Drelincourt Chapel.

Ysbytty Ifan, St. John the Baptist.*

FLINTSHIRE.

Bangor Iscoed or Bangor in Maelor, Dunawd. Worthenbury,
    Deiniol. Overton or Orton Madoc, St. Mary. Marchwiail in
    the County of Denbigh, Deiniol.

Bodfari, St. Stephen. *Hwlkin's Chapel.*

Caerwys, St. Michael. *St Michael's Chapel near the Well.*

Cilcain or Kilken, St. Mary.

Cwm, Mael and Sulien.

---

* For Marchwiail, see Bangor Iscoed, Flintshire.

Diserth, Ffraid or St. Bridget. Rhywlyfnwyd.
Dymeirchion, Holy Trinity.
Estyn or Hope formerly Llangynfarch, Cynfarch. *Plâs y Bwl Chapel.*
Gwaunesgor, St. Mary.
Halkin or Helygen, St. Mary.
Hanmer, St. Chad.
Hawarden, Deiniol.
Holywell, Gwenfrewi or St. Winefred. *A Chapel over the Well.*
Iscoed, a Chapel to Malpas (St. Oswald) in the County of Chester.
Llanasa, Asaf. *Capel Beuno Yngwespyr, Beuno.*
Meliden.
Mold, St. Mary. Nerquis, St. Mary. Treuddin, St. Mary. *Capel y Spon.*
Nannerch, St. Mary.
Newmarket.
Northop or Llaneurgain, Eurgain afterwards St. Peter. Flint, St. Mary.
Penley in Maelor, St; Mary, a Chapel to Ellesmere (St. Mary) in the County of Salop.
Rhuddlan, St. Mary. *A Chapel at Cefn Du.*
St. Asaph, Cyndeyrn or St. Kentigern and Asaf.
Whitford, St. Mary. *Capel y Gelli. Tre'r Abad Chapel.*
Ysgeifiog, St. Mary.

GLAMORGANSHIRE.

Aberafon, St. Mary. Baglan, Baglan.
Barry, St. Nicholas. *A Chapel in Barry Island, St. Baruck or* •*Barrog. Another in Do.*
Bishopston or Llandeilo Ferwallt, Teilo. *Caswell Chapel.*
Bonvilston, St. Mary.
Britton Ferry, St. Mary.
Cadoxton juxta Barry, Cattwg.
Cadoxton juxta Neath or Llangattwg Glyn Nedd, Cattwg. Creinant, St. Margaret. Aberpergwm.
Caerau, St. Mary.

Cardiff,* St. John the Baptist. *Do. St. Mary. St. Perine's Chapel. A Chapel near Miskin Gate.*

Cheriton.

Cilybebyll, St. John the Evangelist.

Coetty, St. Mary. Nolton Chapel, St. Mary.

Cogan, St. Peter.

Colwinston, St. Michael.

Coychurch or Llangrallo, Crallo. Peterston super Montem or Llanbedr ar Fynydd, St. Peter.

Eglwys Brewys, St. Brise.

Eglwys Ilan or Eglwys Elian, Elian. Llanfabon, Mabon. Caerffili, St. Martin.

Ewenny, St. Michael.

Flemingston, St. Michael.

Gelligaer, Cattwg. Brithdir Chapel. *Capel Gwladus, Gwladus.*

Gileston, St. Giles.

Glyncorwg, St. John the Baptist. Capel Blaengwrach.

Ilston or Llanilltyd, Illtyd. *Llannon, Non.*

Kenfig, St. Mary Magdalen. Pyle, St. James.

Lantwit Major or Llanilltyd Fawr, Illtyd. *The Lady's Chapel, St. Mary.*

Lantwit juxta Neath, Illtyd. Neath, St. Thomas.† Resolven. *Ynys Fach Chapel.*

Leckwith, St. James.

Llanbleiddian, Bleiddian or St. Lupus, afterwards St. John the Baptist. Llanddunwyd or Welsh St. Donat's, Dunwyd. Cowbridge, St. Mary.

Llancarfan, Cattwg. *Llanfeithin. Llangadell, Cadell. Liege Castle.*

Llandaff or Llandâf, Dyfrig, Teilo, and Oudoceus, afterwards St. Peter. Whitchurch, St. Mary.

---

* "Ther be 2 Paroche Chirches in the Towne, wherof the principale lying sumwhat by Est is one, the other of our Lady is by Southe on the Water side. There is a Chapelle beside in Shoemaker streat of S. Perine, and a nother hard within Meskin Gate side."—Leland.

† Neath, now a Rectory, is called a Chapel in the Grant of Richard de Grainville to the Abbey of Savigny.—Dugdale's Monasticon.

Llanddewi in Gower, St. David. *Knelston, St. Maurice.*
Llandeilo Talybont, Teilo.
Llandough or Llandocha near Cardiff, Dochdwy.
Llandough or Llandocha near Cowbridge, Dochdwy.
Llandow or Llandduw, Holy Trinity.
Llandyfodwg, Tyfodwg.
Llandymor, an extinct church in Gower.
Llanedeyrn, Edeyrn.
Llanfedwy, Medwy or Medwinus. Llanfihangel or Michaelston
    Fedwy in the County of Monmouth, St. Michael.
Llanfihangel y Bont Faen, St. Michael.
Llanfrynach, Brynach Wyddel. Penllin.
Llanganna or Llangan, Canna.
Llangeinwyr, Ceneu or Ceinwyry'.
Llangennydd, Cennydd.
Llangiwg, Ciwg.
Llangyfelach, St. David afterwards Cyfelach. Llansamled, Samled.
    An old Chapel, St. Mary. Morriston.
Llangynwyd Fawr, Cynwyd.
Llanhary, Illtyd.   [Sts. Julius and Aaron.
Llanilid, Ilid a Churig or Sts. Julitta and Cyrique. Llanharan,
Llanisan, Isan.
Llanmadog, Madog.
Llanmaes, Cattwg.
Llanrhidian, Rhidian. Llanrhidian Chapel. *Llanelen, St. Helen.*
Llansannwr. *Brigam Chapel.*
Llantrisaint, Illtyd, Tyfodwg, and Gwynno. Llanilltyd or Lantwit
    Faerdre, Illtyd. Ystrad Dyfodwg, Tyfodwg. Llanwynno,
    Gwynno. Aberdâr, St. John the Baptist. St. John's Chapel,
    St. John the Baptist. *Talygarn.*
Llantryddid, Illtyd.
Llavernock, (Qu. Llanfyrnach?) St. Laurence.
Llysfaen, Gwrhir'afterwards St. Dennis.
Llyswerni, Tydfyl. *Nash.*
Loughor or Castell Llychwr, St. Michael.
Marcross, Holy Trinity.
Margam, St. Mary. *Eglwys Nunyd. Hafod y Porth. Trisaint.*
    Craig y Capel.

Merthyr Dyfan, Dyfan and Teilo.

Merthyr Mawr, Teilo. *St. Roque's Chapel.*

Merthyr Tydfyl. Tydfyl.

Michaelston upon Afon, St. Michael.

Michaelston upon Elai, St. Michael.

Michaelston le Pitt or Llanfihangel yn y Gwaelod, St. Michael.

Monk Nash, St. Mary.

Newcastle, Illtyd. *Llangewydd, Cewydd.* Bettws, St. David.
   Laleston, St. David. Tithegston, Tudwg.

Newton Nottage, St. John the Baptist.

Nicholaston, St. Nicholas.

Oxwich, Illtyd.

Oystermouth, All Saints.

Penard or Penarth in Gower, St. Mary.

Penarth near Cardiff, St. Augustine.

Pendeulwyn, Cattwg.

Penmaen, St. John the Baptist.

Penmark, St. Mary. *East Aberddaw. Rhos Chapel.*

Penrice or Penrhys, St. Mary.

Pentyrch, Cattwg.

Peterston upon Elai or Llanbedr ar Fro, St. Peter.

Porthcurig, Curig.

Portheinion, Cattwg.

Radyr, St. John the Baptist.

Reynoldston, St. George.

Rhosili, St. Mary.

Roath, St. Margaret.   [Andrew the Apostle.

St. Andrew's Major or Llanandras, Andras ab Rhun, afterwards St.

St. Andrew's Minor, St. Andrew the Apostle.

St. Bride's upon Elai, Ffraid, St. Bridget, or Bride.

St. Bride's Major, Ffraid. *Ogmore Chapel. Llamphey, St. Faith.
   Wick, St. James.*

St. Bride's Minor, Ffraid.

ι····· St. Donat's, Dunwyd.

St. Fagan's, (in ruins,) Ffagan. St. Fagan's, (the present Church,)
   St. Mary.* Llanelldeyrn, Elldeyrn. *Llanfair, St. Mary.*

* " The Paroch Chirch of S. Fagan is now of our Lady ; but ther is yet by
the Village a Chapelle of S. Fagan sumtime the Paroch Chirch."—Leland.

St. George's or Llanufelwyn, Ufelwyn or Ubilwynus, afterwards
St. George.

St. Hilary. *Beaupre Chapel, St. Mary.*

St. Lythian's or Llanfleiddian Fach, Bleiddian or St. Lupus.

St. Mary Church or Eglwys Fair, St. Mary.

St. Mary on the Hill or Eglwys Fair y Mynydd, St. Mary.

St. Nicholas.

St. Tathan's, Tathan,

Sully, St. John the Baptist.

Swansea, St. Mary. *Do. St. Thomas.* Do. St. John.

Wenvo, St. Mary.

Ystrad Owain.*

HEREFORDSHIRE,
SOUTH-WEST OF THE RIVER WYE.

Abbey-Dore, Holy Trinity and St. Mary.

Acornbury, St. John the Baptist,

Allensmore, St. Andrew.

Arcop or Orcop, St. Mary.

Bacton, St. Faith.

Birch Magna or Much Birch, St. Mary and St. Thomas à Becket.

Birch Parva or Little Birch, St. Mary.

Blackmere, St. Leonard.

Bredwardine, St. Andrew.

Bridstow, St. Bride or Bridget. *A Chapel in Wilton Castle.*

Bullingham, a Chapel to All Saints in the City of Hereford.

Clehonger, All Saints.

Clifford, St. Mary.

Clodock, Clydog. Llanveyno or Llanfeuno, Beuno afterwards St.
Peter. *Llanwynnog, Gwynnog.* Longtown, St. Peter. Cresswell, St. Mary.

Cusop, St. Mary. *Pen Henllan.*

Dewchurch Magna or Much Dewchurch, St. David. Little Dewchurch, St. David. Kilpeck, St. David afterwards St. Mary.
Dewshall, St. David. Callow, St. Michael.

* For Rhydri, see Bedwas, Monmouthshire.

Llanddowror, Teilo.

Llandeilo Abercywyn, Teilo.

Llandeilo Fawr or Llandilo, Teilo. Taliaris Chapel, Holy Trinity.
    *Llandyfaen. Capel yr Ywen. A Chapel in Carreg Cennen
    Castle.*

Llandingad, Tingad or Dingad. Llanfair ar y Bryn, St. Mary.
    Capel Peulin, St. Paulinus or Pawl Hen. *Capel Cynfab, Cyn-
    fab. Eglwys Newydd.*

Llandybie, Tybie. *Capel yr Hendre. Glyn yr Henllan.*

Llandyfaelog, Maelog. *Llangynheiddon, Cynheiddon.* Llangyndeyrn,
    Cyndeyrn. *Capel Ifan, St. John. Capel Dyddgen. Bettws.*

Llandyfeisant, Tyfei. *A Chapel in Dinefwr Castle, St. David.*

Llandyssilio yn Nyfed, Tyssilio.

Llanedy, St. Edith.

Llanegwad, Egwad. *Llandeilo Rwnnws, Teilo. Llanhirnin. Capel
    Gwilym Foethus. Dolwyrdd Chapel.*

Llanelly, Ellyw. Llangennych, Cennych. *Capel Dewi, St. David.
    Capel Ifan, St. John, Berwick Chapel.*

Llanfallteg.

Llanfihangel Aberbythych, St. Michael.

Llanfihangel ar Arth, St. Michael. *Pencadair Chapel.*

Llanfihangel Cilfargen, St. Michael.

Llanfynydd, Egwad.

Llangadog Fawr or Llangadock, Cadog and St. David. Llanddeu-
    sant, St. Simon and St. Jude. Capel Gwynfai. *Capel Tydyst.*

Llangan, Canna.

Llangathen, Cathan. *Capel Penarw.*

Llangeler, Celer. *Capel Mair, St. Mary.*

Llanglydwyn, Clydwyn.

Llangynnor.

Llanllwni, Llwni. Llanfihangel Rhos y Corn, St. Michael. *Capel
    Maesnonni. Ffynnon y Capel.*

Llansadyrnin, Sadyrnin.

Llanstephan, Ystyffan. Llangynog, Cynog. *Llanybri, St. Mary.*

Llanwynio, Gwynio.

Llanybyddair, St. Peter. Abergorlech. *Capel Iago, St. James.
    Capel Mair, St. Mary.*

Llanycrwys, St. David.

Meidrym, St. David. Llanfihangel Abercywyn, St. Michael.
Merthyr, Enfail.
Myddfai or Mothvey, St. Michael.
Penboir, Llawddog. Trinity Chapel, Holy Trinity.
Penbre, Illtyd. Llan-non, Non. Llandurry.
Pencarreg.
St. Clare's. Llangynin, Cynin.
St. Ishmael's or Llanishmael, Ismael. Llansaint, All Saints. Ferry
    Side, St. Thomas,
Talley or Tal-y-Llychau, St. Michael. *Llanfihangel, St. Michael.*
    Capel Mair, St. Mary. Capel Crist, Holy Trinity. Capel
    Cynhwm. Capel Teilo, Teilo.
Trelech a'r Bettws, Teilo. Capel Bettws.

CARNARVONSHIRE.

Aber or Abergwyngregyn, Bodfan.
Aberdaron, Hywyn. Llanfaelrys, Maelrys. *Eglwys Fair, St. Mary.*
Abererch, Cawrdaf. Penrhos or Llangynwyl, Cynwyl.
Bangor Fawr, Deiniol. Pentir or Llangedol, Cedol, *Capel Gwrfyw,*
    Gwrfyw. King Edgar's Chapel, St. Mary.
Bardsey or Ynys Enlli, Cadfan and Lleuddad; now Extra-parochial.
Beddgelert, St. Mary. *Nant Hwynen Chapel.*
Bodfuan, Buan.
Caer-rhun, St. Mary.
Ceidio or Llangeidio, Ceidio.
Clynnog Fawr, Beuno.
Conway or Aberconway, St. Mary.
Cruccaith, St. Catherine. Ynys Cynhaiarn, Cynhaiarn. Treflys,
    St. Michael.
Cyffin, St. Benedict.
Dolwyddelan, Gwyddelan.
Dwygyfylchi, Gwynnin.
Edeyrn, Edeyrn, Carngiwch, Beuno. Pistyll, Beuno.
Eglwys Rhos, St. Hilary. *Penrhyn, a Free Chapel, St. Mary.*
Llanaelhaiarn, Aelhaiarn.
Llanbeblig, Peblig. Carnarvon, St. Mary. *Do. St. Helen.*
Llanbedr y Cennin, St. Peter,

Trawsfynydd, Madrun and Anhun.

Tywyn Merioneth, Cadfan. Llanfihangel y Pennant, St. Michael. Pennal, St. Peter ad vincula. Tal y Llyn, St. Mary.

MONMOUTHSHIRE.

Abergavenny, St. Mary. St. John the Baptist's Chapel.

Basaleg. *Llandderfel, Derfel Gadarn.* Henllys, St. Peter. Risca, St. Peter.

Bedwas, Barrog or St. Baruck. Rhydri in the County of Glamorgan, St. James.

Bedwellty, Sannan.

Bicknor Wallica or Welsh Bicknor, St. Margaret.

Bryngwyn, St. Peter.

Caerleon, Cattwg. *St. Julius's Chapel. St. Aaron's Do.*

Caerwent, St. Stephen.

Caldicot.

Chapel Hill or Tinteyrn Magna.

Chepstow, St. Mary.

Christ-Church or Eglwys y Drindod, Holy Trinity.

Cilgwrwg.

Coedcerniw, All Saints.

Cwm Yoy or Cwm Iau, St. Martin.

Dingatstow or Llaningad, Dingad afterwards St. Mary. Tregaer, St. Mary.

Dixton, St. Peter.

Goldcliff* or Gallteurin, The Blessed Saviour, St. Mary Magdalen, and St. Mary the Virgin. Nash, St. Mary the Virgin.

Goytre or Coed-tre, St. Peter.

Grosmond, St. Nicholas.

Gwernesey, St. Michael.

Ifton.

Kemmys or Cemmaes, St. Michael.

Kemmys Commander, All Saints.

Langston.

Llanarth, Teilo. Bettws Newydd. Clitha Chapel.

---

* Founded by Robert de Candos A. D. 1113.

Llanbadog.

Llanddewi Fach, St. David.

Llanddewi Ysgyryd, St. David, Llanddewi Rhydderch, St. David.

Llandefâd. Llanbedr, St. Peter.

Llandegfedd or Llandegwedd, Tegwedd.

Llandeilo Bertholeu or Llandeilo Porth-halawg, Teilo.

Llandeilo Cressenny or Llandeilo Groes Ynyr, Teilo, Penrhos, Cattwg.

Llandenny or Llandenfi.

Llandogo,

Llanelen, St. Helen.

Llanfabli, Mabli.

Llanfaches, Maches.

Llanfair Cilgydyn, St. Mary.

Llanfair Disgoed, St. Mary.   *Dinam Chapel.*

Llanferin or Llanfetherin, Merin.

Llanfihangel Crug-corneu, St. Michael.

Llanfihangel in Nether Went, St. Michael.

Llanfihangel Lantarnam or Llanfihangel Tan y Groes, St. Michael.

Llanfihangel Pont y Moel, St. Michael.

Llanfihangel Tor y Mynydd, St. Michael.

Llanfihangel juxta Usk, St. Michael.

Llanfihangel Ystern Llewern, St. Michael.

Llanfoist, St. Faith.

Llanfrechfa.

Llangadwaladr or Bishopston, Cadwaladr.

Llangattock or Llangattwg Feibion Afel, Cattwg. St. Moughan's Chapel, Meugan.

Llangattwg Lenig, Cattwg.

Llangattwg Lingoed, Cattwg.

Llangattwg Dyffryn Wysg or Llangattock juxta Usk, Cattwg.

Llangiwa, Ciwa.

Llangofen, Cofen.   Penclawdd, St. Martin.

Llangwm Ucha.   Llangwm Isa.

Llangybi, Cybi.

Llangyfyw or Llangynyw, Cyfyw or Cynyw.

Llangynog, Cynog ab Brychan.*

* There is a place near the site of this Church called "Cwrt Brychan."

Llanhenog or Llanhynog, St. John the Baptist.

Llanhileth or Llanhyledd, Illtyd.

Llanisan or Llanishen, Isan.

Llanllywel, Llywel.

Llanmartin, St. Martin.

Llanofer, St. Bartholomew. Mamhilad. Trefethin, Cattwg.

Llansanffraid or St. Bride's near Abergavenny. Ffraid or St. Bride.

Llansanffraid or St. Bride's in Nether Went, Ffraid.

Llansanffraid or St. Bride's Wentloog, Ffraid.

Llansoy.

Llantoni or Llanddewi Nant Honddu, St. David afterwards St. John
    the Baptist.

Llantrisaint, St. Peter, St. Paul, and St. John. Bertholeu Chapel,
    St. Bartholomew.

Llanwenarth, St. Peter. Aberystruth or Blaenau Gwent, St. Peter.

Llanwern, St. Mary.

Machen or Mechain, St. Michael.

Magor or Magwyr, St. Mary. Redwick, St. Thomas.

Malpas, St. Mary.

Marshfield.

Mathern or Mertheyrn, Tewdrig. *Crick. Runston.*

Merthyr Geryn, Geryn.

Monkswood.

Monmouth, St. Mary. Do. St. Thomas.

Mounton.

Mynyddyslwyn, Tudur ab Hywel.

Newchurch or Eglwys Newydd ar y Cefn.

Newport alias St. Woolos, Gwynllyw Filwr. Bettws, St. David.

Oldcastle, St. John the Baptist.

Pant-teg, St. Mary.

Penhow, St. John the Baptist.

Penterry.

Peterston Wentloog or Llanbedr Gwynllwg, St. Peter.

Portskewet or Porthysgewydd, St. Mary. *Sudbrook or Southbrook,
    Holy Trinity.*

Ragland, St. David. Trostrey or Trawsdre, St. David.

Rogiet.

Rockfield, St. Kenelm.

Rumney or Rhymni, St. Augustine.

Shire-Newton or Trenewydd Gellifarch, St. Thomas a Becket.

Skenfreth or Ysgynfraith, Ffraid or St. Bride.

St. Arvan's. *Porthcaseg.*

St. Kinemark's, Cynfarch.

St. Melan's.

St. Pierre's, St. Peter.

Tintern Parva, St. Michael.

Tredonock or Trefrhedynog, St. Andrew.

Treleck or Tryleg, St. Nicholas. Penallt. Treleck's Grange.

Troy, Michel Troy, or Llanfihangel Troddi, St. Michael. Cwm-carfan Chapel.

Undy or Gwndi.

Usk, St. Mary.

Wilcrick or y Foelgrug.

Witston.

Wolves-Newton, St. Thomas a Becket.

Wonstow or Llanwarwg, Gwynno.

Ytton or Llanddeiniol, Deiniol.*

MONTGOMERYSHIRE.

Aberhafesb, Gwynno or Gwynnog.

Berriew or Aber-rhyw, Beuno. Bettws, Beuno.

Carno, St. John the Baptist.

Castell Caer-Einion, Garmon or St. Germanus.

Cemmaes, Tydecho.

Chirbury in the County of Salop,† St. Michael. Church Stoke, St. Nicholas. Forden. Hissington. Montgomery, St. Nicholas. Snead.

---

* For Michaelston Fedwy, see Llanfedwy, Glamorganshire. The Compiler is unable to determine the situation of the following, from a list in the Myvyrian Archaiology:—Llaniau, Llanirwydd, Llanwnell, Hywig Fach, Carn, Tredelerch, Llanrhyddol, Meiryn, and Llanleirwg. He suspects there were Churches formerly at Dewstow near Caldicot, and at Llanwyny, Llanfair, and Llanardil near Llangofen.

† Its Chapels are in the County of Montgomery.

Crugèon, a Chapel to Alberbury (St. Michael) in the County of Salop.

Darowain, Tudur.   Llanbrynmair, St. Mary.   *Talerddig Chapel.*

Guilsfield or Cegidfa, Aelhaiarn.   Llanfechan.

Hirnant, Illog.

Kerry or Ceri, St. Michael.   *Gwernygo Chapel.*

Llanddinam, Llonio.   Benhaglog Chapel.

Llandrinio, Trinio.   Llandyssilio, Tyssilio.   Melverley. . New Chapel, Holy Trinity.

Llandyssul, Tyssul.

Llaneurfyl, Eurfyl.

Llanfair Caer-Einion, St. Mary.   *Cilyrġch Chapel.*

Llanfechain, Garmon or St. Germanus.

Llanfihangel y Gwynt, St. Michael.

Llanfyllin, Myllin.

Llangadfan, Cadfan.

Llangurig, Curig.

Llangynog, Cynog.

Llangynyw, Cynyw.

Llanidloes, Idloes.

Llanllwchaiarn, Llwchaiarn.   Llanymerewig, Llwchaiarn.

Llanlugan or Llanllugyrn, Tyssilio afterwards St. Mary.

Llansanffraid in Mechain, Ffraid.

Llanwnog, Gwynno or Gwynnog.

Llanwrin, Ust and Dyfnig.   Penegos or Penegwest.   Cadfarch. Machynllaith, St. Peter.

Llanwyddelan, Gwyddelan.

Manafon, St. Michael.   *Dolgynfelyn Chapel.*

Meifod, Gwyddfarch.   Do. Tyssilio.   Do. St. Mary.

Moughtre or Mochdref, All Saints.

Newtown, St. Mary.

Pennant Melangell, Melangell.

Penystrywad, Gwrhai.

Trefeglwys, St. Michael.

Tregynon, Cynon.

Welshpool, Cynfelyn afterwards St. Mary.   Buttington in the County of Salop, All Saints.*

* For Llanwddin, see Llanrhaiadr in Mochnant, Denbighshire; and for Mallwyd and Garthbeibio, see Llan ym Mawddwy, Merionethshire.

PEMBROKESHIRE.

Ambleston or Tref Amlod, St. Mary.

Amroth, Elidyr.

Angle or Nangle, St. Mary.

Bayvil, St. Andrew.

Begelly or Bugeli.   Williamston.   Reynoldston.

Bosheston or Stackpool Boscher, St. Michael.   *St. Goven's Chapel, Gofen.*

Boulston.

Burton.

Camros, Ismael.

Carew, St. John the Baptist.   Redbert.

Castle Beith, St. Michael.

Castle Martin, St. Michael.   Flimston.

Cilgerran, Llawddog.   *Capel Bach in the Castle.*

Clarbeston, St. Martin.

Clydai, Clydai.

Cosheston, St. Michael.

Crinow.

Cronwear, Elidyr.

Dale, St. James.

Dinas, Brynach.

Eglwys Erw, Cristiolus.   *Pencelli Chapel.*

Freystrop.

Grandston, St. Catherine.

Gumfreston.

Haroldston East, Ismael.

Haroldston West, Madog.

Hasguard, St. Peter.

Haverford West, St. Mary.   Do. St: Thomas.   Do. St. Martin.

Hays Castle or Castell yr Haidd, St. Mary.   Forde Chapel.

Henry's Moat or Castell Harri, St. Bernard.

Herbrandston, St. Mary.

Hodgeston.

Hubberston, St. David.

Jeffreyston, St. Oswald.

Johnston.

Jordanston or Tref Iwerddon.

Lambston or Lammerston.

Lampeter Velfrey or Llanbedr Felffre, St. Peter.

Lamphey or Llandyfei, Tyfei.

Lawrenny, Caradog.

Letterston or Treletert, St. Giles,   Llanfair Nant y Gôf, St. Mary.

Little Newcastle, St. Peter.

Llanddewi Felffre, St. David. *Llandeilo Llwyngwaddan, Teilo. Henllan.*

Llandeilo, Teilo.

Llandeloi or Llandylwyf.

Llanfihangel Penbedw, St. Michael. Capel Colman, St. Colman.

Llanfyrnach, Brynach. *A Chapel in ruins.*

Llangolman, St. Colman.

Llangwm.

Llanhywel.

Llanrheithion.

Llanrhian, Rhian.

Llanstadwel, Tudwal.

Llanstinan, Stinan or St. Justinian.

Llantwyd or Lantwood, Illtyd.

Llanuchllwydog, St. David. Llanychaer, St. David. Llanllawern.

Llanûst, Ust. Llanfartin, St. Martin. Capel Llanfihangel, St. Michael; all included in the modern parish of Fishguard, St. Mary.*

Llanwnda, Gwyndaf.

Llan y Cefn.

Llawhaden, Llanhuadain, or Llansaeddan, Aeddan. Bletherston. *St. Mary's Chapel.*

Llys y Fran, Meilyr.

Loveston.

Ludchurch or Eglwys Lwyd, Elidyr.

Maenclochog, St. Mary,

Maenor Bŷr or Manorbeer, St. James.

Maenor Deifi, St. David. Bridell, St. David. *Cilfywyr Chapel.*

Maenor Owain or Maenor Ieuan, St. Mary.

* Carlisle's Topography, *voce* Fishguard.

Marloes, St. Peter.

Martletwy, St. Marcellus. Coed Canlas, St. Mary.

Mathri or Merthyri, The Holy Martyrs.

Melinau, Dogfael.

Minwear.

Monington or Eglwys Wythwr, St. Nicholas.

Morfil, St. John the Baptist.

Moylgrove or Trewyddel.

Mynachlog Ddu, Dogfael.

Narberth, St. Andrew. Robeston Wathan. Mounton or Monkton. *Templeton.*

Nash. Upton.

Nefern, Brynach. Cilgwyn, St. Mary.

New Moat, St. Nicholas.

Newport, St. Mary.

Newton.

Nolton or Knowelton, Madog. *Druidston Chapel.*

Pembroke, St. Nicholas, alias Monkton. Do. St. Mary. Do. St. Michael. St. Daniel's Chapel, Deiniol. *St. Anne's Chapel. St. Mary Magdalen's Do.*

Penaly. *A Chapel in Caldey Island or Ynys Pŷr.*

Penrhydd, Cristiolus. Castellan.

Pontfaen, St. Bernard.

Prendergast, St. David.

Puncheston or Castell Mâl, St. Mary.

Pwllcrochan, St. Mary.

Robeston or Robertston West.

Roch, St. Mary. *Two Chapels in ruins.*

Rosecrowther or Rhôs Gylyddwr, Degeman or St. Decumanus.

Rosemarket, Ismael.

Rudbaxton, St. Michael. *St. Catherine's Chapel. St. Leonard's Do.*

Slebech, St. John the Baptist.

Spittal, St. Mary.

Stackpool Elidyr or Cheriton, Elidyr and St. James.

Stainton, St. Cewyll afterwards St. Peter. *A Chapel near Pille.* Milford, St. Catherine.

St. Bride's, Ffraid or St. Bride. " *The Chapel.*"

St. David's Cathedral, St. David and St. Andrew. Whitchurch, St. David. Brawdy, St. David. *Capel y Gwrhyd, St. David. Capel Non, Non. Capel Padrig, St. Patrick. Capel y Pistyll. Capel Stinan, St. Justinian.* St. Mary's Chapel adjoining the Cathedral.

St. Dogmael's or Llandudoch, Dogfael afterwards St. Thomas.

St. Dogwel's, Dogfael.

St. Edren's or Llanedeyrn, Edeyrn.

St. Elveis or Llanailfyw, Ailfyw.

St. Florence.

St. Ishmael's, Ismael.

St. Issel's or Llanussyllt.

St. Laurence.

St. Nicholas.

St. Petrox or Llanbedrog, Pedrog.

St. Twinel's.

Talbenny, St. Mary.

Tenby, St. Mary. *A Free Chapel, St. John the Baptist.*

Trefgarn.

Uzmaston or Osmundeston, Ismael.

Walton East, St. Mary.

Walton West.

Walwyn's Castle. St. James.

Warren, St. Mary.

Whitchurch or Eglwys Wen, St. Michael. Llanfair Nantgwyn, St. Mary.

Wiston, or Castell Gwys, St. Mary.

Yerbeston, St. Laurence.*

RADNORSHIRE.

Aberedw, Cewydd. Llanfaredd, St. Mary.

Bleddfa, St. Mary.

Boughrood or Bochrwd, Cynog. Llanbedr Painscastle, St. Peter.

Bryngwyn, St. Michael.

Bugeildy, St. Michael. *Velindre Chapel.*

---

* For Cilrhedin, see Carmarthenshire.

Casgob, St. Michael.

Cefn Llys, St. Michael.

Clyro, St. Michael. Bettws Clyro.

Cregruna or Craig Furuna, St. David. Llanbadarn y Garreg, Padarn. *Llannon, Non.*

Diserth, Cewydd. Bettws Diserth, St. Mary.

Gladestry or Llanfair Llethonw, St. David.

Glascwm, St. David. Colfa, St. David. Rhiwlen, St. David.

Knighton, St. Edward, a Chapel to Stow (St. Michael) in the County
of Salop.

Llanbadarn Fawr, Padarn.

Llanbister, Cynllo. Llanbadarn Fynydd, Padarn. Llananno, Amo
or Anno. Llanddewi Ystrad Enui, St. David. Llanfihangel
Rhydeithon, St. Michael. *Caerfaelog, Maelog. Llanfair
Trellwydion, St. Mary.* Abbey Cwm Hir, St. Mary.

Llandegle, St. Tecla. *Llanifan, St. John.*

Llandeilo Graban, Teilo.

Llandrindod anciently Llandduw, The Holy Trinity. *Llanfaelog,
Maelog.*

Llanelwedd.

Llanfihangel Nant Melan, St. Michael.

Llangynllo, Cynllo. Pilleth, St. Mary. *Llanbrynhir.* And probably Heyop, St. David. Whitton, St. David.

Llansanffraid in Elfael, Ffraid or St. Bridget.

Llanstephan or Llanstyffan, Ystyffan.

Llowes, Maelog or Meilig. Llanddewi Fach, St. David.

Michael-church upon Arrow or Llanfihangel y Dyffryn, St. Michael,
a Chapel to Kington (St. Mary) in the County of Hereford.

Nantmel, Cynllo. Llanfihangel Helygen, St. Michael. Llanyre or
Llanllyr yn Rhos, Llyr Forwyn. Rhayader Gwy, St. Clement.
Pant yr Eglwys near Rhayader.

Newchurch, St. Mary.

New Radnor,* *The Old Church.* Do. The present Church, St.
Mary.

---

* "There is an olde Churche stondynge now as a Chapell by the
Castle. Not very farre thens is the new Paroche Churche buildyd by
one William Bachefield and Flory his Wyfe."—Leland.

Old Radnor, St. Stephen. Kinnerton, St. Mary. Ednal. *Llaniago,
St. James.*

Presteign or Llanandreas, St. Andrew. Norton, St. Andrew. Discoed, St. Michael. Lingen in the County of Hereford, St. Michael. Kinsham Ford in Do. Byton in Do. St. Mary.

St. Harmon's, Garmon or St. Germanus. *Drysgol Chapel.* *

* For Glasebury and Llansanffraid Cwmmwd Deuddwr, see Glasebury and Llangammarch, Brecknockshire.

INDEX TO THE NAMES OF SAINTS.

Aaron	. .	96
Aeddan Foeddog	.	227
Aelgyfarch	. .	302
Aelhaiarn	. .	275
Aelrhiw	. .	306
Aerdeyrn	. .	186
Afan Buallt	. .	208
Ailfyw	. .	163
Alan	. .	221
Alban	. .	96
Amaethlu or Maethlu	.	270
Amo or Anno	. .	306
Amphibalus	. .	96
Amwn Ddu	. .	218
Andras ab Rhun	.	146
Ane ab Caw	.	225
Aneurin or Gildas	.	225
Anhun	. .	164
Anna, daughter of Meurig	.	218
Anno or Amo	. .	306
Arddun	. .	207
Arianwen	. .	146
Arthen	. .	141
Arwystli Gloff	.	236
Arwystli Hên	.	75, 81
Asaf or St. Asaph	262, 265
Bach ab Carwed	.	306
Baglan ab Dingad	.	275
Baglan ab Ithel Hael	.	223
"Baruck"	. .	304
Bedwas	. .	302
Bedwini	. .	238
Beuno	. .	268

Bleiddian or St. Lupus	119, 126, 160
Boda	. . .	302
Bodfan	. ,	302
Bran ab Llyr	. ,	76
Brenda	. .	302
Bride, Bridget, or Ffraid	.	189
Brynach Wyddel	.	156
Buan	. . .	280
Bugi or Hywgi	.	233
Cadell	. .	295
Cadfan	. .	213
Cadfarch	.	270
Cadfrawd	.	92, 100
Cadgyfarch	.	102
Cado or Cataw	.	232
Cadog	.	142
Cadrod	.	270
Cadwaladr	.	299, 301
Caffo	. .	227
Caian	. .	146
Cain	. .	228
Callwen	. .	153
Cammab	.	233
Cammarch	.	233
Canna	.	222
Caradog	.	305
Carannog	.	209
Caron	. .	306
Carwyd	.	207
Cattwg Ddoeth	155, 176, 233
Cathan or Cathen	.	280
Cawrdaf	.	270
Cedol	.	306

2 v

Cedwyn	.	280
Ceidio ab Caw	.	227
Ceidio ab Ynyr Gwent	.	234
Ceindrych	.	150
Ceinwen	.	151
Ceitho	.	213
Celer	.	306
Celynin ab Cynyr	.	213
Celynin ab Helig	.	302
Cenedlon	.	150
Ceneu, a bishop	245, 274
Ceneu ab Coel	102, 104
Ceneu or St. Keyna	.	153
Cennych	.	306
Cennydd	.	257
Cewydd	.	230
Cian	.	302
Ciwa	.	307
Ciwg	.	271
Cloffan	.	307
Clydai	.	151
Clydno Eiddyn	.	270
Clydog	.	145
Clydwyn	.	140
Cof	.	208
Cofen	.	307
Collen	.	302
Colman	.	190
Constantine the Great	.	97
Crallo	.	222
Cristiolus	.	220
Curig Lwyd	.	307
Curig or Cyrique	82, 307
Cwyfen	.	304
Cwyfyn	.	307
Cwyllog	.	228
Cwynrau	.	307
Cybi	162, 266
Cyfelach	. 50, 274, 305
Cyflefyr	.	141
Cyflewyr	.	233
Cyfyw	.	233
Cyllin	.	82
Cymorth	.	150

Cynan	.	270
Cynbryd	.	144
Cyndaf	76, 81
Cynddilig	.	281
Cyndeyrn ab Arthog	.	211
Cyndeyrn or St. Kentigern	.	261
Cynfab	.	307
Cynfarch	.	168
Cynfarwy	.	307
Cynfelyn ab Bleiddyd	.	260
Cynfelyn Drwsgl	.	270
Cynfran	.	144
Cynfyw or Cynyw	.	233
Cyngar ab Arthog	.	211
Cyngar or Docwinus	.	183
Cyngar ab Geraint	.	232
Cyngen ab Cadell	161, 207
Cynhafal	.	295
Cynhaiarn	.	275
Cynheiddion	.	152
Cynheiddion ab Ynyr Gwent	.	234
Cynidr	.	148
Cynin	.	144
Cynllo	12, 133
Cynmur	.	253
Cynog ab Brychan	.	138
Cynog of Llanbadarn	241, 244
Cynon	.	215
Cynndyn	.	261
Cynwyd	208, 270
Cynwyl	206, 260
Cynyw or Cynfyw	.	233
DANIEL or Deiniol	192, 206, 258
David or Dewi	43, 162, 191, 193
Dedyn or Neubedd	.	146
Degeman	.	305
Deiniol or Daniel	192, 206, 258
Deiniolen or Deiniol Fab	.	281
Derfel Gadarn	.	221
Dewi or St. David	43, 162, 191, 193
Dier or Diheufyr	.	276
Digain	.	134
Diheufyr or Dier	.	276
Dingad ab Brychan	.	140

Dingad ab Nudd Hael .	269
Dirdan . .	162
Dirynig . .	228
Dochdwy . .	183, 219
Docwinus or Cyngar . .	183
Doged . .	209
Dogfael . .	211
Dogfan . .	145
Dolgan . .	257
Dolgar . .	258
Dona . .	302
Dubricius or Dyfrig 144,170,176, 191	
Dunawd Fyr . .	206
Durdan . .	224
Dwyfael . .	307
Dwynwen . .	151
Dwywau . .	221
Dwywe . .	207
Dyfan . .	82, 84
Dyfnan . .	142
Dyfnig . .	224
Dyfnog . .	295
Dyfrig or St. Dubricius 144, 170, 176,	
	191
Edeyrn ab Gwrtheyrn .	186
Edeyrn ab Nudd .	298
Edı ʃfed . .	115
Edwen . .	303
Egryn . .	304
Egwad . .	298
Eigen . .	81
Eigrad . .	228
Eigron . .	230
Einion Frenhin .	212
Eithras . .	224
Elaeth . .	271
Elbodius or Elfod .	66, 305
Eldad ab Arth .	298
Eldad ab Geraint .	298
Elenog . .	307
Eleri, daughter of Brychan .	147
Eleri, daughter of Dingad .	275
Elfan . . .	83, 87
Elffin . . .	236

Elfod or Elbodius .	66, 305
Elgud . . .	280
Elian . . .	267
Elined . .	149
Elldeyrn . .	186
Ellyw . .	156
Emyr Llydaw .	165
Enddwyn . .	307
Enfail . .	152
Enghenel . .	297
Erbin . .	134
Eurfyl . .	307
Eurgain . .	261
Euryn . .	302
Ffagan . .	83, 84
Ffili . .	276
Ffinan . .	240
Ffinian . .	239
Fflewyn . .	222
Ffraid or St. Bride .	189
" Fidelis" . .	253
Gallgo . .	230
Garci . .	258
Garmon or St.Germanus 119,129, 159	
Gartheli . .	307
Gasty or Gastayn .	157
Geraint ab Erbin .	169
Germanus or Garmon 119, 129, 159	
Gerwyn . .	142
Gildas or Aneurin .	225
Gistlianus . .	162
Glywys Cerniw .	233
Goleuddydd . .	149
Gredifael . .	222
Grwst . .	294
"Gurmaet" . .	253
Gwarthan . .	260
Gwawr . .	147
Gwen . .	150
Gwenafwy . .	230
Gwenaseth . .	166
Gwenddolau . .	208
Gwenddydd . .	149
Gwenfaen . .	237

Gwenfrewi or St. Winefred	.	295
Gwenfyl	.	. 153
Gwenlliw	.	. 142
Gwenllwyfo	.	. 307
Gwennan	.	. 142
Gwenog	.	258, 307
Gwenteirbron	.	. 215
Gwerydd	.	. 102
Gwladus	.	. 146
Gwodloew	.	. 268
Gwrddelw	.	. 231
Gwrfyw	.	. 280
Gwrgon	.	. 147
Gwrhai	.	. 231
Gwrhir	.	. 251
Gwrmael	.	. 102
Gwrnerth	.	. 279
Gwrthefyr or Vortimer	.	134
Gwrthwl	.	. 308
Gwryd	.	. 305
Gwyddelan	.	. 308
Gwyddfarch	.	. 308
Gwyddlew	.	. 233
Gwyn	.	. 213
Gwynau	.	. 153
Gwyndaf Hên	.	. 219
Gwynen	.	. 308
Gwyngeneu	.	. 237
Gwynio	.	. 308
Gwynlleu	.	. 261
Gwynllyw Filwr	.	. 170
Gwynnin	.	. 302
Gwynno ab Cynyr	.	. 213
Gwynno or Gwynnog	.	. 257
Gwynnoro	.	. 213
Gwynodl	.	. 236
Gwynws	.	. 153
Gwyrfarn	.	. 308
Gwytherin	.	. 275
Gynyr of Caer Gawch	.	. 162
HAWYSTL	.	. 152
Helen	.	. 97
Helig Foel	.	. 298
Huail	.	. 232
Hychan	.	. 144
Hywgi or Bugi	.	. 233
Hywyn	.	. 219
IDDEW	.	. 280
Iddon	.	. 233
Idloes	.	. 298
Iestyn ab Cadfan	.	. 102
Iestyn ab Geraint	.	. 232
Ifor ab Tudwal	.	. 148
Ilar	.	. 224
Ilid	.	76, 81
Ilid or Julitta	.	82, 307
Illog	.	. 308
Illtyd or St. Iltutus	.	125, 178
Isan	.	. 257
Ismael	.	244, 252
"Issui or Ishaw"	.	. 308
JULITTA or Ilid	.	82, 307
Julius	.	. 96
Justinian or Stinan	.	. 238
KENTIGERN or Cyndeyrn	.	261
"Keurbreit"	.	. 152
Keyna or Ceneu	.	. 153
LEONORIUS	.	. 256
Llawdden	.	. 308
Llawddog or Lleuddad	.	. 274
Llecheu	.	. 144
Llechid	.	. 223
Lleian	.	. 147
Lleminod Angel	.	. 280
Lles ab Coel or Lucius	.	. 83
Lleuddad ab Alan	.	. 221
Lleuddad or Llawddog	.	. 274
Lleurwg or Lucius	.	. 82
Llewelyn	.	. 261
Llibio	.	. 308
Llidnerth	.	. 269
Llonio Lawhir	.	. 221
Llwchaiarn	.	. 275
Llwni	.	. 308
Llwydian	.	. 308
Llynab	.	. 221
Llyr Forwyn	.	161, 308
Llyr Merini	.	. 169
Llywan	.	. 224
Llywel	.	. 253

Lucius, Lles, or Lleurwg . 83
"Lunapeius" . . 253
Lupus or Bleiddian 119, 126, 160

MABON ab Bleiddyd . 261
Mabon ab Enlleu . 251
Maches . 233
Machraith . 308
Machutus or Maclovius . 256
Madog ab Gildas . 257
Madog Morfryn . 169
Madog ab Owain . 133
Madrun . 164
Mael . . 220
Maelog . 230
Maelrys . 222
Maethlu or Amaethlu . 270
Maglorius . 256
Marchell . 276
Mathaiarn . 143
Mawan 76, 81
Mawan ab Cyngen . 207
Mechell, daughter of Brychan 147
Mechell ab Echwydd . 308
Mechydd . 280
Medrod ab Cawrdaf . 280
Medwy 83, 84
Meigyr . 166
Meilig . 231
Meilyr ab Gwron . 166
Meilyr ab Gwyddno . 222
Meirion . 212
Melangell . 269
Merin or Merini . 236
Meugan or Meigant . 269
Meurig ab Tewdrig . 184
Mor ab Ceneu . 117
Mor ab Pasgen . 280
Mordeyrn . 308
Morfael . 308
Morhaiarn . 308
Mwrog . 308
Mwynen . 142
Mydan . 280
Mygnach . 280
Myllin . 308

Neffai . . 143
Nefydd, daughter of Brychan 148
Nefydd ab Nefydd Ail . 238
Nefydd ab Rhun . 146
Nefyn . . 147
Neubedd or Dedyn . 146
Nidan . . 295
Non . . 163
Nudd . . 208
Nwython . 257
Oudoceus 253, 274
Owain ab Macsen . 109
Pabiali or Papai . 144
Pabo Post Prydain . 167
Padarn 197, 215
Padrig ab Alfryd . 298
Padrig or St. Patrick . 128
Papai or Pabiali . 144
Pasgen . 143
Paul de Leon . 256
Pawl Hên or Paulinus 187, 191
Peblig . . 115
Pedita . 146
Pedr . . 211
Pedrog . 266
Pedrwn . 211
Peillan . 230
Peirio . 230
Peithien . 230
Peris . 302
Peulan . 237
Rhain Dremrudd . 141
Rhawin . 145
Rhediw . 309
Rhian . 309
Rhidian . 309
Rhiengar . 148
Rhuddlad . 309
Rhun . 145
Rhwydrys . 309
Rhystud . 220
Sadwrn Farchog . 222
Sadwrn of Henllan . 298
Sadyrnin . 305

Saeran .	118, 271
Samled . .	. 309
Samson ab Amwn Ddu	228, 253
Samson ab Caw .	. 228
Sandde . .	. 166
Sannan . .	. 240
Sawyl . .	. 207
Seiriol . .	. 211
Selyf . .	. 232
Senefyr or Senewyr	. 236
Silin or Sulien .	. 220
Stinan or St. Justinian	. 238
Sulien or Silin .	. 220
Tanglwst .	. 147
Tangwn ab Caradog	. 270
Tangwn ab Talhaiarn	. 208
Tanwg . .	. 222
Tathan . .	. 256
Tecwyn . .	. 223
Tegai . .	. 223
Tegfan . .	. 238
Tegfedd . .	. 218
Tegiwg . .	. 234
Tegonwy . .	. 236
Tegwedd . .	. 167
Teilo . .	195, 197, 241
Teon . .	. 238
Teulydog .	. 256
Tewdrig ab Teithfallt	. 188
Tewdwr Brycheiniog	. 271
Teyrnog or Twrnog	. 276
Teyrnog or Tyrnog	. 211
Trillo . .	. 233
Trinio . .	. 219
Tudglyd . .	. 236
Tudno . .	. 236
Tudur . .	. 276
Tudwal Befr .	. 133
Tudwen . .	. 309
Tudwg . .	. 258
Twrnog or Teyrnog	. 276
Twrog . .	. 223
Tybie . .	. 152
Tydecho ab Amwn Ddu	. 218
Tydecho ab Gildas	. 258
Tydfyl . .	. 151
Tydie . .	. 149
Tyfei . .	. 252
Tyfodwg . .	. 223
Tyfriog or Tyfrydog	. 275
Tyfrydog ab Arwystli Gloff .	. 276
Tyfrydog or Tyfriog	. 275
Tygwy . .	. 275
Tyneio . .	. 236
Tyrnog or Teyrnog	. 211
Tyssilio . .	. 277
Tyssul . .	. 209
Ulched .	. 309
Umbrafel .	. 219
Urien Rheged .	. 203
Ust . .	. 224
Usteg . .	. 297
Vortimer or Gwrthefyr	. 134
Winefred or Gwenfrewi	. 295
Ynyr Gwent .	. 164
Ysgin ab Erbin .	. 170
Ystyffan . .	. 251

WILLIAM REES, PRINTER, LLANDOVERY.

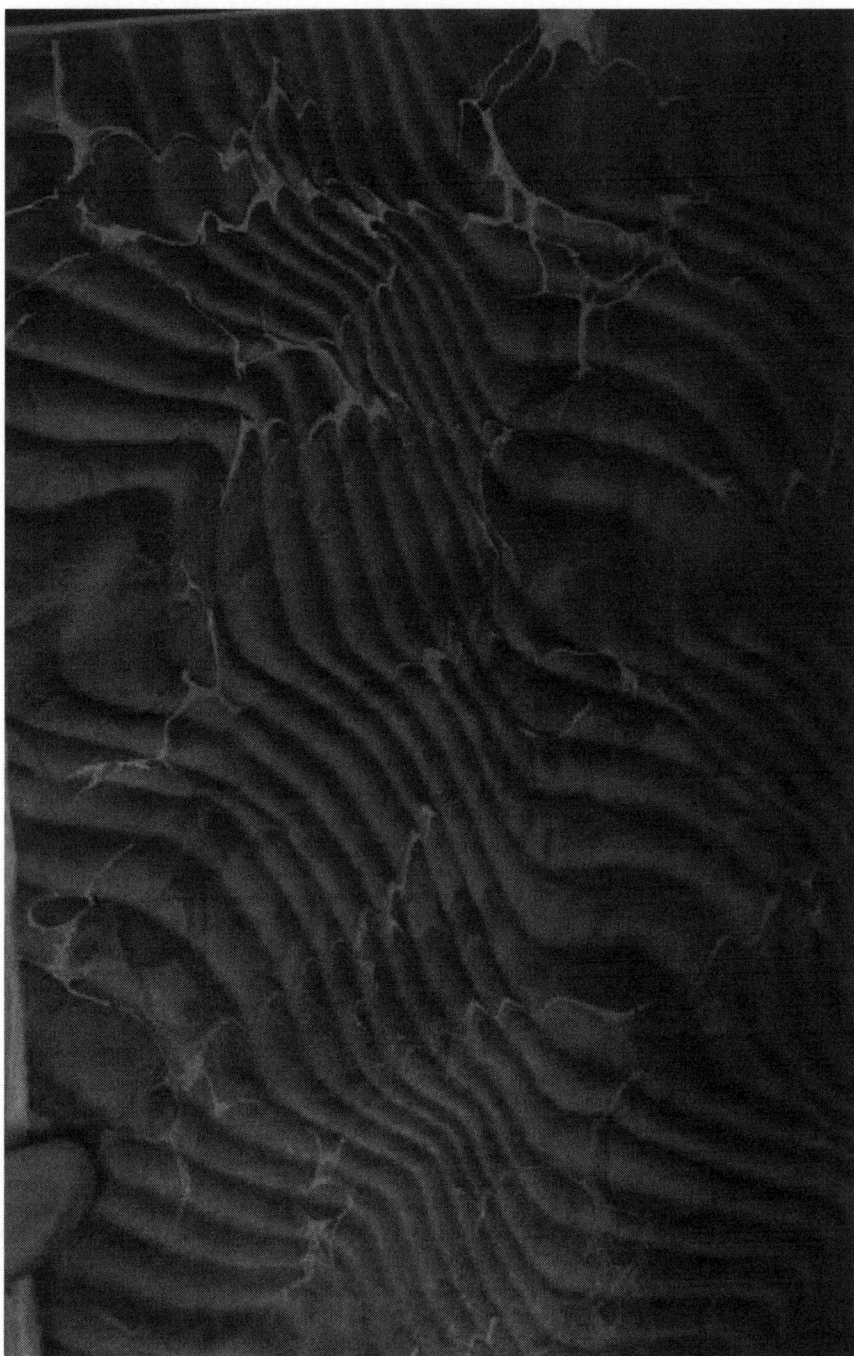

Milton Keynes UK
Ingram Content Group UK Ltd.
UKHW050202130124
435898UK00021B/139

9 781016 696050